D0206311

FEDERAL
LEGISLATIVE
HISTORIES

FEDERAL LEGISLATIVE HISTORIES

An Annotated Bibliography and Index to Officially Published Sources

Compiled by
Bernard D. Reams, Jr.

Bibliographies and Indexes in Law and Political Science,
Number 21

GREENWOOD PRESS
Westport, Connecticut • London

Library of Congress Cataloging-in-Publication Data

Federal legislative histories : an annotated bibliography and index to
  officially published sources / compiled by Bernard D. Reams, Jr.
      p. cm. – (Bibliographies and indexes in law and political
  science, ISSN 0742-6909 ; 21)
    Includes bibliographical references and index.
    ISBN 0-313-23092-7 (alk. paper)
    1. Legislative histories – United States – Bibliography. I. Reams,
  Bernard D. II. Series: Bibliographies and indexes in law and
  political science ; no. 21.
  KF42.2 1994
  016.32873 – dc20   93-38809

British Library Cataloguing in Publication Data is available.

Library of Congress Catalog Card Number: 93-38809
ISBN: 0-313-23092-7
ISSN: 0742-6909

First published in 1994

Greenwood Press, 88 Post Road West, Westport, CT 06881
An imprint of Greenwood Publishing Group, Inc.

Printed in the United States of America

The paper used in this book complies with the
Permanent Paper Standard issued by the National
Information Standards Organization (Z39.48-1984).

10 9 8 7 6 5 4 3 2

In memory of my father
Major Bernard D. Reams
1913-1993

"... the most universal and effectual way of discovering the true meaning of a law, when the words are dubious, is by considering the reason and spirit of it; or the cause which moved the legislator to enact it. For when this reason ceases, the law itself ought likewise to cease with it."

1 WILLIAM BLACKSTONE
COMMENTARIES 61
(Philadelphia, Robert Bell 1771).

Contents

Introduction: The Use of Legislative History In Statutory Interpretation

"When I use a word," Humpty Dumpty said, in a rather scornful tone, "it means just what I choose it to mean -- neither more nor less."[1]

"But words are inexact tools at best and for that reason there is wisely no rule of law forbidding resort to explanatory legislative history..."[2]

I.   Overview of the Problem

Whether a court should use a statute's legislative history as an aid to interpreting that statute is an issue which seems to have prickled both judges and commentators for as long as there has been legislative history upon which to draw. Finding, construing, and using statutory language are fundamental legal skills, but their exercise can be difficult when statutory language is unclear or subject to multiple meanings. The English language can be imprecise in ordinary usage, and frequently becomes even more so when subjected to the "delicate dance of the legislative process."[3]   It is simply a truism that many statutes are

---

1   Lewis Carroll, *Through the Looking Glass* 94 (Random House ed. 1946).
2   *Harrison v. Northern Trust Co.*, 317 U.S. 476, 479 (1943).
3   Orrin Hatch, *Legislative History: Tool of Construction or Destruction*, 11 HARV. J.L. & PUB. POL'Y 43, 47 (1988).

ambiguous, whether because of imprecise drafting or legislative compromise,[4] yet judges must deal with a statute as it is written, warts and all.

Courts have long sought tools to help them interpret ambiguous statutes. The most venerable aids have been maxims of construction, which are general rules designed to permit reasonable interpretation.[5] Courts also have sought to use, and argued over the propriety of using, a statute's legislative history as an aid to construction.[6] The debate over whether and when to use legislative history has escalated recently, in part because of Justice Scalia's focus on the issue since joining the Supreme Court.[7]

While the proper point for recourse to legislative history and the proper scope of the use of legislative history will probably provide fodder for debate for some time to come, one fact that is readily acknowledged is that courts turn regularly to legislative history for interpretive assistance. The United States Supreme Court turns often to legislative history in its statutory analysis, demonstrating the importance of that resource as an interpretive aid.[8] A large number of cases turn on statutory issues which means that finding, using, and construing a legislative history is not only relevant but critical to the lawyer's presentation and the court's determination.[9]

A necessary prerequisite in debating the use of legislative history is to first define how legislative history will apply to the clarification of a questioned term. "Legislative history," as used in the context of statutory interpretation, refers to the background and events leading up to the enactment of a law. This includes bills in all iterations, reports, hearings, and debates.[10] Legislative history is thus different from other kinds of history relevant to the legal practitioner, such as a statutory text's general

---

4   Warren E. Burger, Forward, *Conference on Statutory Interpretation: The Role of Legislative History in Judicial Interpretation*, 1987 DUKE L.J. 361 [hereinafter cited as "*Conference on Interpretation*"].

5   *See, e.g.*, Fortunatus W. Dwarris, *A General Treatise on Statutes* 562-63 (2d ed. 1848): "The rules by which the sages of the law have ever been guided in searching for the intention of the Legislature, are maxims of sound interpretation, which have been accumulated by the experience, and ratified by the approbation of ages." For explanation of specific canons of construction, *see generally* Reed Dickerson, *The Interpretation and Application of Statutes* 233-35 (1975).

6   *See, e.g.*, Sanford Levinson, *On Dworkin, Kennedy, and Ely: Decoding the Legal Past*, 51 PARTISAN REV. 248, 254-64 (1984) (describing evolution in literary and legal domains of the philosophical debate over interpretation).

7   Marshall J. Breger, *Conference on Interpretation*, *supra* note 4, at 367. *See also* Bruce Fein, *Scalia's Way*, 76 A.B.A. J. 38 (Feb. 1990).

8   *See, e.g.*, *Blum v. Stenson*, 465 U.S. 886 (1984); *Rostker v. Goldberg*, 453 U.S. 57 (1981); *Steelworkers v. Weber*, 442 U.S. 193 (1979).

9   As one federal judge has said, "Statutes are the federal courts' daily bread. The way in which courts go about reading those statutes in the federal system is therefore of particular importance to our jurisprudence." Kenneth W. Starr, *Observations About the Use of Legislative History*, 1987 DUKE L. J. 371.

10   J. Myron Jacobstein and Roy M. Mersky, *Fundamentals of Legal Research* 180-182 (5th ed. 1990); Morris L. Cohen, Robert C. Berring, and Kent C. Olson, *How to Find the Law* 219-241 (9th ed., 1989).

social history as developed over the course of repeated enactments, and the general legal history denoting the state of the law at a specific point in time.[11] It is the collection of the background information in a legislative history which is applicable to the sources supplied in this bibliography.

A fundamental reason for reviewing legislative history is to ascertain the intent of the legislature for the statute in question. Legislative history can be considered the raw intent of Congress.[12]   To determine the legislative intent of an ambiguous statute, courts can turn for help to the statute's legislative history.[13]   In fact, even when statutory language does not appear ambiguous on its face, courts can look to legislative history for a clearly expressed legislative intent,[14] and insight into the general policy of the questioned statute.[15] Therefore, legislative history is inextricably bound with the search for legislative intent. The issue generating controversy today appears not to be *whether* legislative history can be used to help ascertain legislative intent and the meaning of a statute, but *when* to use legislative history.[16]

The judicial role must balance two extreme concepts in exercising its responsibilities: to read the statute in its proper context to determine whether and how its meaning relates to the controversy at hand; and, where the meaning of the statute as ascertained does not resolve the controversy, to apply, adjust, or create a judicial rule to resolve the problem.[17] Statutory construction has been defined as drawing conclusions with respect to subjects that are beyond the direct expression of the text, while interpretation is viewed as the process of discovering the true meaning of the language used. When a court goes beyond the language of the statute and seeks the assistance of extrinsic aids in order to determine if a case falls under the statute's purview, it resorts to construction.[18] The goal is to strike a balance between conservative literalism and judicial legislation.[19]

II.   Historical Background

The proper point to use legislative history as an interpretive aid has long been a point of historical controversy. The controversy divides itself generally into three periods: the first covering the fourteenth century (Henry IV and Edward I) during which time the early common law courts

---

[11]   Gwendolyn B. Folsom, *Legislative History: Research for the Interpretation of Laws* 1 (1972).
[12]   Frank H. Easterbrook, *The Role of Original Intent in Statutory Construction*, 11 HARV. J.L. & PUB. POL'Y 59, 60 (1988).
[13]   *See, e.g. , Maniz v. Hoffman,* 422 U.S. 454, 468-470 (1975).
[14]   *See INS v. Cardoza-Fonseca,* 480 U.S. 421, 428-430 (1987).
[15]   *See Wirtz v. Local 153 Glass Bottle Blowers Ass'n.,* 389 U.S. 463 (1968).
[16]   *See* Peter C. Schanck, *The Uses and Values of Legislative Histories: A Reply,* 82 L. LIBR. J. 303 (1990).
[17]   Dickerson, *supra* note 5, at 18.
[18]   Earl T. Crawford, *The Construction of Statutes* 241 (1940).
[19]   Archibald Cox, *Judge Learned Hand and the Interpretation of Statutes* 60 HARV. L. REV. 370, 376 (1947).

in England initially reserved statutory interpretation to the king and his justices with later flexibility recognized by appealing directly to the legislator when faced with interpretation problems.[20] This approach was eminently logical because at this time the rulers of society -- the clergy, barons, earls and judges -- met with the King's court to discuss and draft laws.[21] The era following was dominated by judicial interpretation of statutes as the judiciary took over drafting legislation. The early Parliament period was too fragmented to be involved in interpretation.[22] The increased lawmaking role of Parliament which emerged in the final era created a different situation from the previous two. The mechanization of legislative actions in printed form fostered the demise of judicial discretion in statutory interpretation.

The English courts since the early eighteenth century have steadfastly declined to use legislative history in statutory construction. Recall that in medieval England the courts looked for the intent of the legislators in construing a statute.[23] The judges themselves had the largest share in making the statute,[24] and so they knew as well as anyone the intent behind the laws, and consequently disdained suggestions for statutory construction. As one early English judge advised a barrister before him, "[d]o not gloss the statute, for we know better than you; we made it."[25]

When Parliament emerged as a more independent legislative body, English judges were separated from the law-making function. The judiciary began to "treat legislation as the product of an alien body, of which they knew nothing save from the words of the statute itself."[26] In the middle of the eighteenth century English judges began following the plain meaning rule: "[t]he sense and meaning of an act of parliament must be collected from what it says when passed into a law, and not from the history of changes it underwent in the house where it took rise. That history is not known to the other house, or to the sovereign."[27] By the mid-nineteenth century, it was black letter English law that, while legislative intention was important to statutory construction, "it must be an intention that the Legislature have used fit words to describe."[28] This rule of statutory construction prohibiting the use of extrinsic aids, such as legislative history, is still followed in England, and is known as the English rule on legislative history.

The American courts took their cue from their English counterparts, i.e., early decisions of the United States Supreme Court followed the

---

20   Theodore F. Plucknett, *A Concise History of Common Law* 329, (5th ed. 1956).

21   Fleta, Vol. II, Book II, Chap. 2 (H. G. Richardson and G. O. Sayles, eds., Seldon Society, 1955).

22   Plucknett, *supra* note 20, at 331.

23   U.S. Department of Justice, *Report to the Attorney General* 58 (Jan. 5, 1989) [hereinafter cited as *Justice Report*].

24   Plucknett, *supra* note 20, at 331.

25   *Id.* (quoting Y.B. 33 & 35 Edward I (Rolls Series) 82).

26   Plunknett, *supra* note 20, at 335.

27   *Miller v. Taylor*, 4 Barr. 2303, 2332 (1769), quoted in Plunknett, *supra* note 20, at 335.

28   Dwarris, *supra* note 5, at 561.

English rule.[29] As in England, the Supreme Court looked for legislative intention, but believed "intention is to be searched for in words which the legislature has employed to convey it."[30] The Supreme Court thus embraced the Plain Meaning Rule, "that the legislative history of the passage of a statute furnishes no rule for its exposition,"[31] and American courts followed this rule through most of the nineteenth century.[32]

In addition to its reliance on established English legal principles, the American judiciary's adoption of the Plain Meaning Rule was arguably attributable, at least in part, to the lack of reliable legislative history documentation. The Senate did not permit stenographic recording of debates until 1802,[33] and the accuracy of the public press daily accounts of House debates is questionable.[34] While some committee reports were published in the mid-1800's,[35] not until 1873 did recordation and publication of debates become an official congressional function, fulfilled by the *Congressional Record*.[36]

By the end of the nineteenth century, references to legislative history documents began appearing in the United States Supreme Court's opinions.[37] These cases reflected an increasing trend away from the strictly literal approval of the Plain Meaning Rule, and toward the use of extrinsic aids to glean legislative intention.[38] By the 1940's, the Supreme Court relied on legislative history frequently in its construction of statutes,

---

[29]   *See* Felix Frankfurter, *Some Reflections on the Reading of Statutes*, 47 COLUM. L. REV., 527, 542-543 (1947).
[30]   *Schooner Paulina's Cargo v. United States*, 11 U.S. (7 Cranch) 52, 60 (1812).
[31]   *Proprietors of the Charles River Bridge v. Proprietors of the Warren Bridge*, 36 U.S. 420, 469 (1837).
[32]   *See*, *e.g.*, *Aldridge v. Williams*, 44 U.S. (3 How.) 9, 24 (1845) ("the only mode in which [the legislators'] will is spoken is in the act itself . . ."); *Mitchell v. Great Works Milling & Mfg. Co.*, 17 F. Cas. 496, 499 (C.C.D. Me. 1843) (No. 9,662) ("[w]e must take it to be true, that the legislature intend precisely what they say . . ."); *see also* Theodore Sedgwick, *A Treatise on the Rules Which Govern the Interpretation and Application of Statutory and Constitutional Law* 383 (1857) (the "only safe rule" to determine legislative intent is "as expressed by the words which the legislature has used.").
[33]   Roy Swanstrom, *The United States Senate* (1787-1801): *A Dissertation of the First Fourteen Years of the Upper Legislative Body*, S. Doc. No. 19, 99th Cong., 1st Sess. 251 (1985).
[34]   *Id.* at 239, 250.
[35]   The *Annals of Congress*, printed in 1834, contains House and Senate debates through 1824. *See* Robert Percy Williams, *The First Congress, March 4, 1789-March 3, 1791: A Compilation of Significant Debates* 19 (1970). The *Congressional Debates*, containing debates and some committee reports, were published between 1833 and 1873. *See* Swanstrom, *supra* note 33, at 250.
[36]   Swanstrom, *supra* note 33, at 250.
[37]   *See*, *e.g.*, *United States v. Trans-Missouri Freight Ass'n*, 166 U.S. 290, 316-19 (1897) (analyzing congressional debate but then holding them inadmissible); *Church of the Holy Trinity v. United States*, 143 U.S. 457, 464-65 (1892) (considering contents of committee report); *American Net and Twine Co. v. Worthington*, 141 U.S. 468, 473-74 (1891) (refusing to use statute's sponsors' statements as interpretive aid, but permitting use as method of determining reasons for enactment).
[38]   *See* Harry W. Jones, *The Plain Meaning Rule and Extrinsic Aids in the Interpretation of Federal Statutes*, 25 WASH. U. L.Q. 2, 20 (1939).

holding such history a decisive factor in over one hundred-thirty cases in that decade.[39]

III.   Current Authority of Legislative History Materials

Today, federal courts turn regularly to legislative history. Few judges, lawyers or legal scholars question the legitimacy of reliance on such history as an aid to construction.[40] By the 1970's the Supreme Court was referring to legislative history between three hundred and four hundred times each term.[41] The current trend among American judges is toward using legislation as a source of guidance.[42]

Despite the increasing entrenchment of the use of legislative history in statutory construction, some calls have recently been made for a return to the Plain Meaning Rule. Supreme Court Justice Antonin Scalia's consistent attempts to sway the Court back to the Plain Meaning Rule have been highly publicized. Justice Scalia espouses the view that judges should "interpret laws rather than reconstruct legislators' intentions. When the language of those laws is clear, we are not free to replace it with an enacted legislative intent."[43]

Adding fuel to the return of the literalist movement is the U.S. Department of Justice issuance of a policy statement and report to the U.S. Attorney General addressing the appropriate role of legislative history as an interpretive aid.[44] The Report criticizes the presently prevalent use of legislative history as "seriously flawed,"[45] and advocates instead a return to the Plain Meaning Rule, with recourse to legislative history permissible only when the most plausible meaning of the statutory language cannot be clearly ascertained solely from the context of the statute.[46] While an exhaustive discussion of the arguments for and against using legislative history in statutory construction is beyond the scope of this commentary,[47] it is useful to consider both sides of the issue.

---

39   *See Commissioner v. Estate of Church*, 335 U.S. 632, 687 (1949) (J. Frankfurter, dissenting) (listing cases in which legislative history was a determinative interpretive factor).

40   *Justice Report, supra* note 23, at 1. *See also* Jorge L. Carro & Andrew R. Brann, *The U.S. Supreme Court and the Use of Legislative Histories: A Statistical Analysis*, 22 JURIMETRICS J. 294 (1982).

41   Carro & Brann, *supra* note 40, at 298.

42   2A Jalez G. Sutherland, *Statutes and Statutory Construction* §47.01 (4th ed. 1984). *See, e.g., INS v. Cardoza-Fonseca*, 480 U.S. 421, 430-432 (1987) (although Court observed that the plain language of the statute in question settled the issue at bar, Court reviewed legislative history for evidence of contrary legislative intent). *See* Starr, *supra* note 9 at 374.

43   *INS v. Cardoza-Fonseca* 480 U.S. 421 (1987) (Scalia, J., concurring). For a discussion of Justice Scalia's methodology of statutory interpretation, *see* Fein, *supra* note 7; Breger, *supra* note 7, at 367-69.

44   *Justice Report, supra* note 23.

45   *Id.* at 2.

46   *Id.* at 119.

47   For detailed discussion of the role of legislative history in statutory interpretation, *see* Folsom, *supra* note 11; Easterbrook, *supra* note 12; Hatch, *supra* note 3; Symposium: 1987 DUKE L.J. 361; Patricia M. Wald, *Some Observations on the Use of Legislative*

Proponents of using legislative history believe that the documents of the law process are a tool which Congress uses to explain what it is doing and should be, therefore, used by courts when necessary.[48] Legislative history, it is said, can provide indicia of the legislative intention behind the statute.[49] While not everything that constitutes legislative history is legitimate for use in statutory construction, it is not difficult to determine the weight a particular source of legislative history should carry in the hierarchy of documentation.[50] Use of such history, it is also argued, is a realistic approach to a real problem. The court has to solve the issues before it,[51] notwithstanding the ambiguity common in statutes (whether because of poor draftsmanship or political compromise[52]), and the documentary sources of legislative history have proved, over time, to be a useful aid in interpreting such language.[53]

Opponents of reliance on legislative history also make cogent arguments, based on both the reality of the political process and the constitutional requirement demanding the separation of the legislative and judicial branches. One concern is the vulnerability of legislative history to manipulation, as members of Congress seek to please their constituents or influence a future judicial decision by insertions into the legislative history.[54] Some aspects which constitute part of a statute's legislative history are written by congressional staff members, or may be the work of someone who could not achieve majority support for their policy position or proposed statutory language.[55] Basing statutory construction on a legislative history is also seen as potentially dangerous to the democratic process for introducing the views of the courts into the process of legislation.[56] This constitutional concern is heightened by the fact that the President cannot veto the language of a report or other segment of legislative history.[57] Under the Constitution he can only sign into law the language of a bill or veto that same language. Finally, using legislative history for statutory construction has been characterized as a process which creates an answer in a place where the Congress gives no answer.[58]

History in the 1981 Supreme Court Term, 68 IOWA L. REV. 195 (1983); *Justice Report, supra* note 23.

48   Abner J. Mikva, *A Reply to Judge Starr's Observations,* 1987 DUKE L.J. 380, 386.

49   *See, e.g., INS v. Cardoza-Fonseca, supra* note 38, at 432, n. 12 (Court looked to legislative history for legislative intention); *Consumer Product Safety Comm'n v. GTE Sylvania, Inc.,* 447 U.S. 102, 108 (1980) (Court must consider "clearly expressed legislative intention" in interpreting statute).

50   Hatch, *supra* note 3, at 43.

51   Mikva, *supra* note 49, at 382 ("We [judges] cannot just tell Congress that they could have said it more plainly, and that until they do, we are not going to enforce it. We can't just say, 'We pass.'" *Id.*).

52   Breger, *supra* note 7, at 361.

53   Mikva, *supra* note 48, at 385.

54   Starr, *supra* note 9, at 375-377.

55   *See Herschy v. FERC,* 777 F. 2d 1, 6-8 (D.C. Cir. 1985) (J. Scalia).

56   Starr, *supra* note 9, at 376.

57   *Herschy v. FERC, supra* note 55.

58   Folsom, *supra* note 11, at 12.

   While the   propriety of using legislative history in statutory construction is an issue engendering great controversy, and on which some of this country's greatest jurists are divided, it is incontrovertible that the Supreme Court does, in fact, find such history useful in the interpretation of statutes, and uses it as a basis for case resolution.[59] While the use of a legislative history prompts fascinating consideration on the derivation of legislative intent, the meaning and usage of language, the process of interpretation, and the distinction between the judicial and legislative branches, all must agree that the legislative history is important in today's courts, and cannot be ignored by lawyer or judge.[60] The bibliography which follows is submitted in the hope that it will assist in the day-to-day effort of legal professionals in finding, understanding, and presenting the law.

---

[59]   *See* Paul M. Barrett, *David Souter Emerges As Reflective Moderate on the Supreme Court*, WALL STREET J. 1A (February 2, 1993). *See, e.g.,* J. Myron Jacobstein and Roy M. Mersky, *Congressional Intent and Legislative Histories: Analysis and Psychoanalysis?*, 82 L. LIBR. J. 297 (1990).

[60]   In *United States v. Thompson/Center Arms Co.*, 112 S. Ct. 2102, 2109 n.8 (1992), Justice Souter stated: [t]he shrine [of legislative history] . . . is well peopled (though it has room for one more). . . . " This stance was attacked by Justice Scalia in his concurring opinion. *See also Lee v. Weisman*, 112 S. Ct. 2649 (1992) (Souter, J., concurring; Scalia, J., dissenting).

Acknowledgments

The author expresses his gratitude for the contributions of many professionals since the inception of this research project in 1981, including Margaret A. Goldblatt, M.S., Mark J. Ricciardi, J.D., Lisa McNulty, J.D., and Carolyn R. Moore, M.S.W. This final draft reached closure with the expert drafting and editing of the following individuals:

Faye L. Couture, M.A., J.D.,
Kimberly A. Martin, M.L.S.,
and
Dora R. Bertram, M.S.

The many drafts of the final manuscript were expertly handled by Ann M. Schweninger and Kim A. DeHart. They dutifully kept the author on track and suffered the author's whims and fancies. The success of this research text rests in the contributions of all those noted. Its shortcomings are solely those of the author. In the final analysis, it is the author's hope that this reference book will prove a useful guide and starting point to the vast information contained in federal agency and legislative documents.

Bernard D. Reams, Jr., J.D., Ph.D.
Saint Louis, Missouri
September, 1993

Explanatory Guide and Table

The work is comprised of an annotated bibliography and five indices which provide access to it. The entries in the Bibliography describe approximately 255 legislative histories compiled during the 37th Congress in 1862 through the 101st Congress, second session, in 1990. The actual public laws covered by these documents begin with the 4th Congress, first session (1796). The documents that have been included appear as Congressional committee prints, insertions in Congressional hearings, or Congressional Research Service studies or issue briefs. They have been compiled by:

(1) the staff of Congressional committees;
(2) the Congressional Research Service (CRS) for Congressional committees;
(3) executive agencies of the federal government (e.g. the Environmental Protection Agency).

The indices provide access by author of the document, popular name of the public law, Congressional session law numbers before 1901, public law numbers after 1900, and bill number. Each entry in the indices directs the user to the record number used to identify the legislative history in the Bibliography.

This guide will detail the contents of each section of this work.

BIBLIOGRAPHY

Each entry consists of bibliographic information for a legislative history, location information, and an annotation covering the scope of the material contained in that history. Entries are arranged by public law number. Information for each entry has been taken from the following sources:

(1)	the title page of the legislative history;
(2)	<u>Monthly Catalog</u>;
(3)	Congressional Information Service's (CIS) <u>CIS Index to Publications of the United States Congress</u> or <u>CIS US Congressional Committee Prints Index</u>;
(4)	University Publications of America's (UPA) <u>Major Studies and Issue Briefs of the Congressional Research Service</u>;
(5)	OCLC Online Union Catalog.

Where information for some fields in an entry is not available or not applicable, the designation "N/A" has been listed for that field.

Record No:

A unique number has been assigned to each legislative history in order to identify it for the purposes of this work. All indices refer to this number.

Public Law No.:

When a public law is enacted, it is assigned a number. This number is indexed in the Public Law Number Index. Public law numbers have been assigned since 1901, although public laws enacted between 1901 and 1957 are cited by chapter number. For those entries concerning public laws enacted before 1901, no public law number is given. Congress, chapter and session numbers for these entries are included in the Congressional Session Index.

Bill No.:

Congress assigns a number to the bill that is being considered for passage as public law. This number is indexed in the Bill Number Index. The Congress which considered the bill appears in parentheses after the bill number.

Statutes at Large Citation:

The page in <u>Statutes at Large</u> is where the text of the public law may be found. For those entries concerning public laws enacted before 1901, this citation will also include the chapter number.

Title of Act:

Popular name is that given to the public law most extensively covered by the legislative history. It is indexed in the Popular Name Index.

Title:

It is the title of the legislative history as it appears on the title page of the document.

Publication Date:

The year the legislative history was published is given for each entry.

Author:

The person or body responsible for compiling the legislative history is considered the author. It is indexed in the Author Index.

Pages:

The number of pages in the document is given for each entry. When numbering is not continuous or there are several volumes to a work, the Pages will described as "various".

L/C Card Number:

The Library of Congress assigns a number to the bibliographic record for the document.

OCLC No.:

The bibliographic record for the document on the OCLC Online Union Catalog has been assigned a number to expedite retrieval on that database. This may prove particularly useful for interlibrary loan requests.

SuDoc No.:

A number is assigned to the document according to the Superintendent of Documents classification scheme. This number facilitates location of those legislative histories that are produced by the United States government.

CIS No.:

A number is assigned to the document by the Congressional Information Service to locate the document on microfiche in the CIS Microfiche Library and the CIS Committee Prints Microfiche Collection.

UPA Citation:

University Publications of America assigns a number to the document on microfilm in the Major Studies and Issue Briefs of the Congressional Research Service Set. These numbers consist of symbols for the main manuscript (MS) or manuscript supplements by the years (MS yr.-yr. Suppl.), microfilm reel number and frame number.

Relevant Bills:

Bills which received significant coverage in the legislative history are listed here. They are indexed in the Bill Number Index. Some documents covered more bills than what could reasonably be listed in this section. All bill numbers covered by the document, however, are included in the Bill

Number Index, although they may not be listed specifically in the bibliographic treatment, i.e., the Bill Number Index is more extensive than the bibliographic annotation.

Annotation

The annotation for each legislative history entry in the bibliography:

(1)   summarizes the organization and content of the work;
(2)   indicates what public laws are covered;
(3)   describes the depth and order of coverage;
(4)   explains the type of documentation included in the work;
(5)   notes whether the legislative history includes full citations and pagination of the original documents;
(6)   explains what indexes are included in the work.

AUTHOR INDEX

All authors of a document are included in the Author Index.

Entries in this index are rotated so that there are entries for each part of the author's name. For example, an individual associated with the Congressional Research Service is entered under the individual's name and also under the Congressional Research Service. A Congressional subcommittee is entered under the subcommittee and also under the committee.

POPULAR NAME INDEX

Popular names entered in this index were taken from:

(1)   the popular name tables of West's United States Code Annotated (USCA);
(2)   Lawyers Co-Operative's United States Code Service (USCS);
(3)   Shepard's Acts and Cases by Popular Names;
(4)   the public law title if no popular name has been listed in any other source.

If a public law has more than one popular name, all of them are included in this index. In addition, the popular names of all public laws receiving coverage in a legislative history have entries in this index. The popular names of public laws that are peripheral may not appear in the annotation for that document. When a public law amends a previous act, the popular name of the act amended is given.

A popular name entered with a year designation is for the public law as originally passed. An identical entry without the year designation is for the public law as amended to a certain date. For example, "Clean Water Act of 1977" (Entries 208 and 218) refers to P.L. 95-217 originally passed in 1977, while "Clean Water Act" (Entry 254) refers to the act as amended through 1987.

The words "An Act" have been omitted from the beginning of public law title entries, and the words "and for Other Purposes" have been omitted from the end. For example, the title "An Act to Amend Section 5" would appear as "To Amend Section 5" in the Popular Name Index.

CONGRESSIONAL SESSION INDEX

Congressional session law designations for all public laws up to and including those passed during the 56th Congress, second session (ending in 1901) are included in this Index. Those public laws that are peripheral are not specifically mentioned in the annotation for that document. Such peripheral laws appear in italics in the Index.

Public laws passed before 1901, when public law numbers were first assigned, are listed by their Congress, session and chapter.

PUBLIC LAW NUMBER INDEX

Public law numbers for all public laws after 1900 given coverage in a legislative history are included in this Index. Those public laws that are peripheral are not specifically mentioned in the annotation for that document. Such peripheral public laws appear in italics in the Index.

BILL NUMBER INDEX

Bill numbers for all bills given coverage in a legislative history are included in this Index. Those bills that are peripheral are not specifically listed in the Relevant Bills portion of the annotation for that document. Such peripheral bills appear in italics in the Index.

Entries in this Index consist of the bill number, the Congress considering it, and the year when Congress actively considered the bill. The year was determined by consulting the following sources:

(1)   the legislative history itself;
(2)   "History of Bills and Resolutions" section of the Congressional Record;
(3)   "Status of Senate Bills" or "Status of House Bills" tables in Commerce Clearing House's Congressional Index;
(4)   LEXIS© and Westlaw© online versions of the Congressional Record.

STATUTES AT LARGE / RECORD NUMBER TABLE

The Table provides the Statutes at Large cite with its Record Number as the corresponding entry. It gives access when one has only the Statutes at Large cite.

EXPLANATORY TABLE

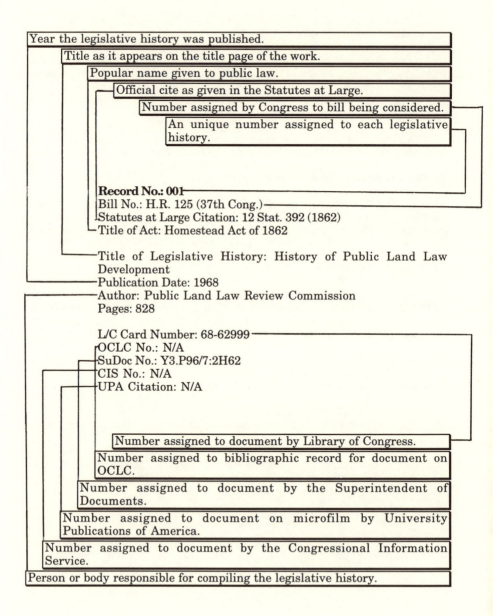

Year the legislative history was published.

Title as it appears on the title page of the work.

Popular name given to public law.

Official cite as given in the Statutes at Large.

Number assigned by Congress to bill being considered.

An unique number assigned to each legislative history.

Record No.: 001
Bill No.: H.R. 125 (37th Cong.)
Statutes at Large Citation: 12 Stat. 392 (1862)
Title of Act: Homestead Act of 1862

Title of Legislative History: History of Public Land Law Development
Publication Date: 1968
Author: Public Land Law Review Commission
Pages: 828

L/C Card Number: 68-62999
OCLC No.: N/A
SuDoc No.: Y3.P96/7:2H62
CIS No.: N/A
UPA Citation: N/A

Number assigned to document by Library of Congress.

Number assigned to bibliographic record for document on OCLC.

Number assigned to document by the Superintendent of Documents.

Number assigned to document on microfilm by University Publications of America.

Number assigned to document by the Congressional Information Service.

Person or body responsible for compiling the legislative history.

Bibliography

Record No.: 001
Bill No.: H.R. 125 (37th Cong.)
Statutes at Large Citation: 12 Stat. 392 (1862)
Title of Act: Homestead Act of 1862

Title of Legislative History: History of Public Land Law Development
Publication Date: 1968
Author: Public Land Law Review Commission
Pages: 828

L/C Card Number: 68-62999
OCLC No.: N/A
SuDoc No.: Y3.P96/7:2H62
CIS No.: N/A
UPA Citation: N/A
Relevant Bills: H.R. 125 (37th Cong.), H.R. 85 (39th Cong.), H.R. 365 (39th Cong.), S. 257 (39th Cong.), H.R. 562 (41st Cong.), H.R. 1016 (42nd Cong.), S. 680 (42nd Cong.), H.R. 4261 (44th Cong.), S. 20 (45th Cong.), S. 926 (45th Cong.), S. 54 (49th Cong.), H.R. 16 (55th Cong.), S. 3057 (57th Cong.), H.R. 14826 (58th Cong.), H.R. 17576 (59th Cong.), S. 6155 (60th Cong.), H.R. 11798 (61st Cong.), H.R. 24070 (61st Cong.), S. 2775 (66th Cong.), H.R. 4830 (68th Cong.), H.R. 6462 (73rd Cong.), S. 3344 (83rd Cong.).

This is the legislative history of the public land system as it affected those seeking land ownership, as settlers rather than speculators. It includes thirty public laws. Each of these public laws provides legislative history information. The text discusses and quotes the public laws, the Congressional debates, and Congressional hearings which preceded them. The footnotes give access to primary and secondary source materials: presidential proclamations, Land Office reports, dissertations, theses, journal articles, and related monographs. The public laws discussed are: Homestead Act of 1862, H. 125 (37th Cong.), 37th Cong., 2nd Sess., Ch. 75; Mines and Mining Act of 1872, H. 1016 (42nd Cong.), 42nd Cong., 2nd Sess., Ch. 152; Desert Land Act of 1877, H. 4261 (44th Cong.), 44th Cong., 2nd Sess., Ch. 107; Forest Lieu Lands Act, H. 16 (55th Cong.), 55th Cong., 1st Sess., Ch 2; Weeks Act (Protection of Watersheds), H. 11798 (61st Cong.), P.L. 61-435; Mineral Lands Leasing Act of 1920, S 2775 (66th Cong.), P.L. 66-146; Clarke-McNary Act (Reforestation), H. 4830 (68th Cong.), P.L. 68-270; Taylor Grazing Act, H. 6462 (73rd Cong.), P.L. 73-482.

Record No.: 002
Bill No.: H.R. 2934 (42nd Cong.)
Statutes at Large Citation: 17 Stat. 424 (1873)
Title of Act: Coinage Act of 1873

Title of Legislative History: History of the Coinage Act of 1873, Being A
                                Complete Record of All Documents Issued and
                                the Legislative Proceedings Concerning the Act,
                                56th Cong., 1st Sess. (Comm. Print 1900)
Publication Date: 1900
Author: House Committee on Coinage, Weights, and Measures
Pages: 323

L/C Card Number: N/A
OCLC No.: 13735159
SuDoc No.: Y4.C66:C66
CIS No.: Committee-Print: H3792
UPA Citation: N/A
Relevant Bills: S. 859 (41st Cong.), H.R. 5 (42nd Cong.), H.R. 1427 (42nd Cong.), H.R. 2934 (42nd Cong.)

The legislative history of the Coinage Act of 1873, H.R. 2934 (42d Cong.) Ch. 131, 3d Sess., reveals the revision of the laws relating to mint and coinage. The stated intent of the law was to improve the economy and efficiency of the mint, to abolish the coinage charge, and to reduce wastage and tolerance in the manufacture of coins. The history begins with the text of the original bill as drafted by the Treasury Department. The text of the first coinage bill introduced in Congress, S. 859 (41st Cong.) is included. The documents provided include the report which was submitted to the Congress as well as the internal correspondence of the Treasury Department. The solicited comments from the officers of the mints and the assay offices are given. The Senate and House debates focus on different areas of the law. The Senate debates attempted to resolve the question of abolishing the coinage charge, S. 859 (41st Cong.). The House debates focused on approval of the reorganization of the Mint, the terms of office, and the compensation of its new officers, H.R. 5 (42d Cong.). H.R. 2934 (42d Cong.) was introduced as a substitute for H.R. 1427 (42d Cong.) and was sent to Conference. The *Congressional Record* contains the Conference Report on H.R,. 2934 (42d Cong.) and the notice of its passage in both Houses. Dates given in the *Congressional Record* are provided in the legislative history. The history concludes with the full text of the Coinage Act of 1873.

Record No.: 003
Bill No.: H.R. 2575 (44th Cong.)
Statutes at Large Citation: 19 Stat. 90 (1876)
Title of Act: To Amend Section 3893 and 3894 of the Revised Statutes Providing a Penalty for Mailing Obscene Books and Other Matters therein Contained, and Prohibiting Lottery-Circulars Passing through the Mails

Title of Legislative History: The Development of the Law of Gambling: 1776-1976
Publication Date: 1977
Author: National Institute of Law Enforcement and Criminal Justice
Pages: 934

L/C Card Number: N/A
OCLC No.: 3410042
SuDoc No.: J1.2:G14/776-976
CIS No.: N/A
UPA Citation: N/A

The legislative history provides access to the expected components of the law as well as those documents related to the common and civil law traditions. It is divided into chapters in order to separate the federal documentation from discussions of political activities associated with federal control of gambling. In addition, court cases which provided interpretation of selected laws are included. The history treats the chapter divisions as discrete elements: laws related to lotteries; political inquiries (Kefauver Investigations); federal programs against organized crime; tax laws related to gambling; and, questions of states' rights.

Record No.: 004
Bill No.: H.R. 4261 (44th Cong.)
Statutes at Large Citation: 19 Stat. 377 (1877)
Title of Act: Desert Land Act

Title of Legislative History: Federal Water Rights Legislation, Three Papers,
by T. Richard Witmer, Hatfield Chilson, Perry W.
Morton; Mar. 1, 1960, 86th Cong., 2nd Sess.
(Comm. Print 1960)
Publication Date: 1960
Author: House Committee on Interior and Insular Affairs
Pages: v, 60

L/C Card Number: 60-60899
OCLC No.: 6021935
SuDoc No.: Y4.In8/14:W29
CIS No.: Committee-Print: H0290
UPA Citation: N/A
Relevant Bills: H.R. 365 (39th Cong.), H.R. 562 (41st Cong.), H.R. 4261 (44th
Cong.), H.R. 9486 (51st Cong.), S. 3057 (57th Cong.), H.R. 3184 (66th
Cong.), H.R. 8455 (74th Cong.), S. 418 (80th Cong.), H.R. 5735 (82nd
Cong.), H.R. 5736 (82nd Cong.), H.R. 7691 (82nd Cong.), H.R. 997 (83rd
Cong.), H.R. 8624 (83rd Cong.), H.R. 741 (84th Cong.), H.R. 3404 (84th
Cong.), H.R. 6147 (84th Cong.), H.R. 8325 (84th Cong.), H.R. 8347 (84th
Cong.), H.R. 8560 (84th Cong.), H.R. 9489 (84th Cong.), H.R. 9505 (84th
Cong.), H.R. 10873 (84th Cong.), S. 863 (84th Cong.), S. 890 (84th Cong.),
H. R. 2211 (85th Cong.), H.R. 5871 (85th Cong.), H.R. 1234 (86th Cong.),
H.R. 2363 (86th Cong.), H.R. 4567 (86th Cong.), H.R. 4604 (86th Cong.),
H.R. 4607 (86th Cong.), H.R. 5555 (86th Cong.), H.R. 5587 (86th Cong.),
H.R. 5618 (86th Cong.), H.R. 5718 (86th Cong.), H.R. 5748 (86th Cong.),
H.R. 6140 (86th Cong.), S. 851 (86th Cong.)

The document is a series of collected papers which individually discuss and
explain the conflict inherent in the laws governing federal and state water
rights. The initial paper is an analysis of the Pelton Dam Case, (*Federal
Power Commission v. Oregon*, 349 U.S. 435 (1955)). Bills and statutes are
included in the discussions -- which is a departure from the usual presentation
of primary source documents in a legislative history. The inclusion of text of
two speeches is given as the footnotes provide more information than the mere
notation of the speeches. It is in these footnotes that one finds the citations to
Congresssional hearings, statutory materials, and case law. The document
concludes with the text of two speeches, one pro-state water rights, the other
pro-centralized federal water planning. Both of these addresses provide in
footnotes full citations to relevant case and statutory law and Congressional
hearings.

Record No.: 005
Bill No.: H.R. 11023 (55th Cong.)
Statutes at Large Citation: 30 Stat. 922 (1899)
Title of Act: To Regulate the Height of Buildings in the District of Columbia

Title of Legislative History: Building Height Limitations, 94th Cong., 2nd
                               Sess. (Comm. Print 1976)
Publication Date: 1976
Author: House Committee on the District of Columbia
Pages: ix, 272

L/C Card Number: 85-601621
OCLC No.: 13332091
SuDoc No.: Y4.D63/1:94-S-5
CIS No.: 76-H302-15
UPA Citation: N/A
Relevant Bills: H.R. 11023 (55th Cong.), H.R. 19070 (61st Cong.), H.R. 19962
    (61st Cong.), S. 5714 (61st Cong.), S. 9439 (61st Cong.), S. 3269 (68th
    Cong.), H.R. 11214 (68th Cong.), H.R. 9398 (69th Cong.), S. 3495 (69th
    Cong.), S. 2400 (71st Cong.), H.R. 10528 (71st Cong.), S. 686 (71st Cong.),
    H.R. 5660 (76th Cong.), H.R. 2506 (79th Cong.), S. 686 (79th Cong.), H.R.
    7670 (81st Cong.), H.R. 9009 (87th Cong.), S. 1529 (87th Cong.), H.R.J.
    Res. 934 (88th Cong.), H.R. 15083 (90th Cong.), H.R. 4830 (91st Cong.),
    H.R. 5528 (91st Cong.), H.R. 7070 (91st Cong.), H.R. 7705 (91st Cong.),
    H.R. 2499 (92nd Cong.)

The legislative history examines selected executive and legislative
actions limiting building heights in Washington, D.C. from 1791-1975.
Included are presidential proclamations by George Washington and Thomas
Jefferson. The history contains information on two early building height acts:
the Building Height Act of 1899 and the Building Height Limitation Act of
1910. The history examines the laws which granted authority to the United
States Commisssion of Fine Arts to advise on the height of certain buildings in
Washington, D.C. The Fine Arts Commission Act and other relevant
newspaper articles are noted.

Record No.: 006
Public Law No.: 60-320 (Sess. II)
Bill No.: H.R. 28192 (60th Cong.)
Statutes at Large Citation: 35 Stat. 1075 (1909)
Title of Act: Copyright Act of 1909

Title of Legislative History: Copyright Law Revision, Studies, Prepared for
                               Subcommittee on Patents, Trademarks, and
                               Copyrights, 86th Congress, 1st Session, Pursuant
                               to S. Res. 53; Studies 1-4, 86th Cong., 1st Sess.
                               (Comm. Print 1959)

Publication Date: 1960
Author: Subcommittee on Patents, Trademarks, and Copyrights, Senate
Committee on the Judiciary
Pages: xi, 142

L/C Card Number: 60-60692
OCLC No.: 1968087
SuDoc No.: Y4.J89/2:C79/no.1-4
CIS No.: Committee-Print: S0440
UPA Citation: N/A
Relevant Bills: H.R. 19853 (59th Cong.), H.R. 25133 (59th Cong.), S.
    6330 (59th Cong.), S. 8190 (59th Cong.), H.R. 243 (60th Cong.), H.R.
    11794 (60th Cong.), H.R. 21592 (60th Cong.), H.R. 21984 (60th Cong.),
    H.R. 22071 (60th Cong.), H.R. 22183 (60th Cong.), H.R. 24782 (60th
    Cong.), H.R. 27310 (60th Cong.), H.R. 28192 (60th Cong.), S. 2499 (60th
    Cong.), S. 2900 (60th Cong.), S. 9440 (60th Cong.), H.R. 8177 (68th
    Cong.), H.R. 9137 (68th Cong.), H.R. 11258 (68th Cong.), H.R. 5841
    (69th Cong.), H.R. 10434 (69th Cong.), H.R. 8912 (70th Cong.), H.R. 6990
    (71st Cong.), H.R. 12549 (71st Cong.), H.R. 139 (72nd Cong.), H.R. 10364
    (72nd Cong.), H.R. 10740 (72nd Cong.), H.R. 10976 (72nd Cong.), H.R.
    11948 (72nd Cong.), H.R. 12094 (72nd Cong.), H.R. 12425 (72nd Cong.), S.
    176 (72nd Cong.), H.R. 5853 (73rd Cong.), S. 1928 (73rd Cong.), H.R. 8557
    (74th Cong.), H.R. 10632 (74th Cong.), H.R. 11420 (74th Cong.), S. 2465
    (74th Cong.), S. 3047 (74th Cong.), H.R. 2695 (75th Cong.), H.R. 3004
    (75th Cong.), H.R. 5275 (75th Cong.), S. 7 (75th Cong.), S. 2240 (75th
    Cong.), H.R. 926 (76th Cong.), H.R. 4871 (76th Cong.), H.R. 6160 (76th
    Cong.), H.R. 9703 (76th Cong.), H.R. 6616 (83rd Cong.), H.R. 6670 (83rd
    Cong.), S. 2559 (83rd Cong.)

The Senate Subcommittee on Patents, Trademarks, and Copyrights of the
Senate Committee on the Judiciary commissioned a series of studies to be
prepared under the supervision of the Copyright Office of the Library of
Congress. The Subcommittee published the series. The studies were divided
into groups and numbered consecutively. There are thirty-four studies and a
subject index in the seriex. One of the most notable things about the series in
general is that the individual topics are signed pieces of analytical writing as
well as the historical presentation. In addition, the Subcommittee disclaimed
any acceptance or approval of the statements made in the analyses. Studies 1-
4 cover: no. 1. The History of the U.S.A. Copyright Law Revision from 1901 to
1954 (A. Goldman); No.2. Size of the Copyright Industries (W. Blaisdell); No. 3.
The Meaning of "Writings" in the Copyright Clause of the Constitution (W.
Derenberg and the Staff of the New York University Law Review); No. 4. The
Moral Right of the Author (W. Strauss). Each study contains a discussion of
the legislative documents and activities associated with the revisions of the
Copyright Act. One of the most valuable aspects of any one of the studies, in a
historical sense, is the inclusion and analysis of the applicable case law.

Record No.: 007
Public Law No.: 60-320 (Sess. II)
Bill No.: H.R. 28192 (60th Cong.)
Statutes at Large Citation: 35 Stat. 1075 (1909)
Title of Act: Copyright Act of 1909

Title of Legislative History: Copyright Law Revision, Studies, Prepared for
                                 Subcommittee on Patents, Trademarks, and
                                 Copyrights, 86th Congress, 1st Session, Pursuant
                                 to S. Res. 53; Studies 1-4, 86th Cong., 1st Sess.
                                 (Comm. Print 1959)
Publication Date: 1960
Author: Subcommittee on Patents, Trademarks, and Copyrights, Senate
Committee on the Judiciary
Pages: xi, 142

L/C Card Number: 60-60692
OCLC No.: 1968087
SuDoc No.: Y4.J89/2:C79/no.1-4
CIS No.: Committee-Print: S0440
UPA Citation: N/A
Relevant Bills: H.R. 28192 (60th Cong.), H.R. 24224 (62nd Cong.), H.R. 6990
    (71st Cong.), H.R. 12549 (71st Cong.), H.R. 10364 (72nd Cong.), H.R.
    10740 (72nd Cong.), H.R. 10976 (72nd Cong.), H.R. 11948 (72nd Cong.),
    H.R. 10632 (74th Cong.), H.R. 11420 (74th Cong.), S. 3047 (74th Cong.),
    H.R. 1270 (80th Cong.)

This is one of thirty-four copyright law revision studies which appeared in 11
committee prints published in 1960 and 1961 by the Senate Subcommittee
on Patents, Trademarks, and Copyrights. The Subcommittee also published
a subject index to these studies. "Study No. 3: The Meaning of 'Writings'
in the Copyright Clause of the Constitution" examines the definitions
of "writings" and "authors" in copyright law, both in statutes and case law.
The study examines how the Copyright Act of 1909, H.R. 28192 (60th
Cong.), P.L. 60-349 added a "catch-all" phrase to the list of enumerated
works qualifying for copyright protection. The study also examines how the
1912 Amendment to the Copyright Act, H.R. 24224 (62nd Cong.), P.L. 62-303
expanded the list of enumerated works qualifying for copyright to include
motion pictures. The study examines in detail a series of bills in the 71st -
80th Congresses (1929-1947) which attempted to expand copyright protection
to bring it into harmony with modern media.   The narrative study
summarizes, compares, and quotes the bills, as well as describing the
Congressional action on them.   Footnotes provide complete citations to
Congressional reports and Congressional debate, as well as journal articles.

Record No.: 008
Public Law No.: 60-349 (Sess. II)
Bill No.: H.R. 28192 (60th Cong.)
Statutes at Large Citation: 35 Stat. 1075 (1909)
Title of Act: Copyright Act of 1909

Title of Legislative History: Copyright Law Revision, Studies, Prepared for
                                 Subcommittee on Patents, Trademarks, and
                                 Copyrights, 86th Congress, 1st Session,
                                 Pursuant to S. Res. 53; Studies 5-6, 86th Cong.,
                                 1st Sess. (Comm. Print 1959)
Publication Date: 1960
Author: Subcommittee on Patents, Trademarks, and Copyrights, Senate
Committee on the Judiciary
Pages: xi, 125

L/C Card Number: 60-60692
OCLC No.: 1968087
SuDoc No.: Y4.J89/2:C79/no.5,6
CIS No.: Committee-Print: S0441
UPA Citation: N/A
Relevant Bills: H.R. 19853 (59th Cong.), H.R. 25133 (59th Cong.), S. 6330
       (59th Cong.), S. 8190 (59th Cong.), H.R. 243 (60th Cong.), H.R. 11794
       (60th Cong.), H.R. 20388 (60th Cong.), H.R. 21592 (60th Cong.), H.R.
       21984 (60th Cong.), H.R. 22071 (60th Cong.), H.R. 22183 (60th Cong.),
       H.R. 24782 (60th Cong.), H.R. 25162 (60th Cong.), H.R. 27310 (60th
       Cong.), H.R. 28192 (60th Cong.), S. 2499 (60th Cong.), S. 2900 (60th
       Cong.), H.R. 11258 (68th Cong.), S. 4355 (68th Cong.), H.R. 5841 (69th
       Cong.), H.R. 10353 (69th Cong.), H.R. 10434 (69th Cong.), H.R. 10987
       (69th Cong.), H.R. 17276 (69th Cong.), S. 2328 (69th Cong.), H.R. 8912
       (70th Cong.), H.R. 10655 (70th Cong.), H.R. 13452 (70th Cong.), S. 3160
       (70th Cong.), H.R. 6989 (71st Cong.), H.R. 9639 (71st Cong.), H.R. 12549
       (71st Cong.), H.R. 139 (72nd Cong.), S. 176 (72nd Cong.), S. 2465 (74th
       Cong.), S. 3047 (74th Cong.), H.R. 2695 (75th Cong.), H.R. 3004 (75th
       Cong.), H.R. 5275 (75th Cong.), H.R. 10633 (75th Cong.), S. 7 (75th
       Cong.), S. 2240 (75th Cong.), H.R. 926 (76th Cong.), H.R. 4871 (76th
       Cong.), H.R. 6160 (76th Cong.), H.R. 6243 (76th Cong.), H.R. 9703 (76th
       Cong.), S. 3043 (76th Cong.), H.R. 3456 (77th Cong.), H.R. 3997 (77th
       Cong.), H.R. 7173 (77th Cong.), H.R. 1571 (78th Cong.), H.R. 3190 (79th
       Cong.), S. 1206 (79th Cong.), H.R. 1270 (80th Cong.), H.R. 2083 (80th
       Cong.)

The second publication in the Copyright Series covers Studies 5 - 6. The
prefatory remarks point out that the first grouping was designed to cover the
general background and analysis of the Act with substantive issues explicated
by the ensuing publications. The studies are: No. 5. The Compulsory License
Provisions of the U.S. Copyright Law (H. Henn) and No. 6. The Economic
Aspects of the Compulsor License (W. Blaisdell). This grouping contains the
letters of comment which were submitted to the Copyright Office in regard to
the published analyses.

Record No.: 009
Public Law No.: 60-320 (Sess. II)
Bill No.: H.R. 28192 (60th Cong.)
Statutes at Large Citation: 35 Stat. 1075 (1909)
Title of Act: Copyright Act of 1909

Title of Legislative History: Copyright Law Revision, Studies, Prepared for
Subcommittee on Patents, Trademarks, and
Copyrights, 86th Congress, 2nd Session,
Pursuant to S. Res. 240; Studies 7-10, 86th
Cong., 2nd Sess. (Comm. Print 1960)
Publication Date: 1960
Author: Subcommittee on Patents, Trademarks, and Copyrights, Senate
Committee on the Judiciary
Pages: vii, 125

L/C Card Number: 60-60692
OCLC No.: 1968087
SuDoc No.: Y4.J89/2:C79/no.7-10
CIS No.: Committee-Print: S0442
UPA Citation: N/A
Relevant Bills: H.R. 19853 (59th Cong.), H.R. 28192 (60th Cong.), H.R.
9137 (68th Cong.), H.R. 11258 (68th Cong.), H.R. 10434 (69th Cong.),
H.R. 8912 (70th Cong.), H.R. 15086 (70th Cong.), H.R. 6990 (71st
Cong.), H.R. 12549 (71st Cong.), H.R. 10364 (72nd Cong.), H.R. 10740
(72nd Cong.), H.R. 10976 (72nd Cong.), H.R. 11948 (72nd Cong.), H.R.
12094 (72nd Cong.), H.R. 12425 (72nd Cong.), S. 3985 (72nd Cong.),
H.R. 5853 (73rd Cong.), S. 342 (73rd Cong.), S. 1928 (73rd Cong.), H.R.
10632 (74th Cong.), H.R. 11420 (74th Cong.), S. 2465 (74th Cong.),
S. 3047 (74th Cong.), H.R. 5275 (75th Cong.), S. 2240 (75th Cong.),
H.R. 926 (76th Cong.), H.R. 4871 (76th Cong.), H.R. 6160 (76th Cong.),
H.R. 9703 (76th Cong.), S. 3043 (76th Cong.), H.R. 3997 (77th Cong.),
H.R. 6608 (83rd Cong.), H.R. 782 (84th Cong.), H.R. 287 (85th Cong.)

Studies 7 - 10 continued the series commissioned by the Subcommittee. It
contains: No. 7. Notice of Copyright (V. Doyle, G. Cary, M. McCannon, and B.
Ringer); No. 8. Commercial Use of the Copyright Notice (W. Blaisdell); No. 9.
Use of the Copyright Notice by Libraries (J. Rogers); No. 10. False Use of
Copyright Notice (C. Berger). Study No. 7 contains the legislative history of
the Copyright Act before 1909. The citations are exhaustive. Study No. 8 is
followed by an Appendix which sets out the questionnaire used by the Office of
the Register of Copyrights relating to notice. Study No. 9 was written to
provide the framework for a survey conducted to determine the uses actually
made of the copyright notice by libraries. Study No. 10 provides the legislative
history beginning in 1802, the judicial decisions, legislative proposals since
1909, Federal statutes penalizing false marking, other (foreign) countries
penalties, an indepth analysis of § 105, and a restatement of the issues -- in
1959. Again, the footnotes are exhaustive.

Record No.: 010
Public Law No.: 60-320 (Sess. II)
Bill No.: H.R. 28192 (60th Cong.)
Statutes at Large Citation: 35 Stat. 1075 (1909)
Title of Act: Copyright Act of 1909

Title of Legislative History: Copyright Law Revision, Studies, Prepared for
                                 Subcommittee on Patents, Trademarks, and
                                 Copyrights, 86th Congress, 2nd Session,
                                 Pursuant to S. Res. 240; Studies 11-13, 86th
                                 Cong., 2nd Sess. (Comm. Print 1960)
Publication Date: 1960
Author: Subcommittee on Patents, Trademarks, and Copyrights, Senate
Committee on the Judiciary
Pages: xi, 155

L/C Card Number: 60-60692
OCLC No.: 1968087
SuDoc No.: Y4.J89/2:C79/no.11-13
CIS No.: Committee-Print: S0443
UPA Citation: N/A
Relevant Bills: H.R. 19853 (59th Cong.), S. 6330 (59th Cong.), S. 8190
    (59th Cong.), H.R. 11794 (60th Cong.), H.R. 21592 (60th Cong.), H.R.
    24782 (60th Cong.), H.R. 27310 (60th Cong.), H.R. 28192 (60th Cong.),
    S. 2900 (60th Cong.), S. 9440 (60th Cong.), H.R. 8177 (68th Cong.), H.R.
    9137 (68th Cong.), H.R. 11258 (68th Cong.), S. 4355 (68th Cong.), H.R.
    5841 (69th Cong.), H.R. 10434 (69th Cong.), H.R. 16808 (69th Cong.),
    H.R. 8912 (70th Cong.), H.R. 8913 (70th Cong.), H.R. 6900 (71st
    Cong.), H.R. 6987 (71st Cong.), H.R. 12549 (71st Cong.), H.R.
    139 (72nd Cong.), H.R. 10364 (72nd Cong.), H.R. 10740 (72nd Cong.),
    H.R. 10976 (72nd Cong.), H.R. 11948 (72nd Cong.), H.R. 12094 (72nd
    Cong.), H.R. 12425 (72nd Cong.), S. 176 (72nd Cong.), S. 3985 (72nd
    Cong.), S. 342 (73rd Cong.), H.R. 8557 (74th Cong.), H.R. 10632 (74th
    Cong.), H.R. 11420 (74th Cong.), S. 2465 (74th Cong.), S. 3047 (74th
    Cong.), H.R. 2695 (75th Cong.), H.R. 3004 (75th Cong.), H.R. 5275 (75th
    Cong.), S. 7 (75th Cong.), S. 3043 (76th Cong.)

The fourth publication of the series contains Studies 11-13. These were
written to explore the issues related to ownership of the copyright. The
contents are: No. 11. Divisibility of Copyrights (A. Kaminstein, L. Margolis,
and A. Bogsch); No. 12. Joint Ownership of Copyrights (G. Cary); No. 13.
Works Made for Hire and on Commission (B. Varmer). There are several
items of note in No. 11, to wit: an historical survey; a legislative history;
and, an explication of the theory, needs, and issues associated with
divisibility. In addition, there are Appendices and Supplements which deal
with the related political battle, the tax ramifications, and the laws of
foreign countries. Study No. 12 gives the judicial treatment and analysis.
Study No. 13 gives the legislative history and then explores the court
decisions, the legislative proposals since 1909, and the foreign laws related

to works for hire or commission. Each Study is followed by a section containing the comments received from the industry and scholarly communities.

Record No.: 011
Public Law No.: 60-320 (Sess. II)
Bill No.: H.R. 28192 (60th Cong.)
Statutes at Large Citation: 35 Stat. 1075 (1909)
Title of Act: Copyright Act of 1909

Title of Legislative History: Copyright Law Revision, Studies, Prepared for Subcommittee on Patents, Trademarks, and Copyrights, 86th Congress, 2nd Session, Pursuant to S. Res. 240; Studies 11-13, 86th Cong., 2nd Sess. (Comm. Print 1960)
Publication Date: 1960
Author: Subcommittee on Patents, Trademarks, and Copyrights, Senate Committee on the Judiciary
Pages: xi, 155

L/C Card Number: 60-60692
OCLC No.: 1968087
SuDoc No.: Y4.J89/2:C79/no.11-13
CIS No.: Committee-Print: S0443
UPA Citation: N/A
Relevant Bills: H.R. 8177 (68th Cong.), H.R. 9137 (68th Cong.), H.R. 11258 (68th Cong.), H.R. 10434 (69th Cong.), H.R. 12549 (71st Cong.), H.R. 10364 (72nd Cong.), H.R. 10632 (74th Cong.), H.R. 11420 (74th Cong.), S. 2465 (74th Cong.), S. 3047 (74th Cong.), S. 3043 (76th Cong.)

This is one of thirty-four copyright law revision studies which appeared in 11 committee prints published in 1960 and 1961 by the Senate Subcommittee on Patents, Trademarks, and Copyrights. The Subcommittee also published a subject index to these studies. Study No. 13: Works Made for Hire and on Commission briefly examines the wording of the sections dealing with the ownership and authorship of copyright for works made for hire and/or on commission in the Copyright Act of 1909, H.R. 28192 (60th Cong.), P.L. 60-320 (Sess. II) and in an earlier draft bill included in this act's legislative history. The study also contains a section which examines in detail the bills introduced in the 68th - 76th Congresses (1924-1940) which contained provisions on works made for hire and/or on commission which differed from the Copyright Act of 1909's provisions. The narrative study summarizes, compares, and quotes the bills, as well as describing the Congressional action on them. The study summarizes and quotes relevant Congressional hearings and Congressional reports. Footnotes provide complete citations to Congressional documents. The study examines the case law on works made for hire and on commision, as well as the law of foreign countries on these topics. The study includes an analysis of the basic issues in these topics. The study concludes with the comments and views of copyright experts on works made for hire and on commission.

Record No.: 012
Public Law No.: 60-320 (Sess. II)
Bill No.: H.R. 28192 (60th Cong.)
Statutes at Large Citation: 35 Stat. 1075 (1909)
Title of Act: Copyright Act of 1909

Title of Legislative History: Copyright Law Revision, Studies, Prepared for
                                Subcommittee on Patents, Trademarks, and
                                Copyrights, 86th Congress, 2nd Session,
                                Pursuant to S. Res. 240; Studies 14-16, 86th
                                Cong., 2nd Sess. (Comm. Print 1960)
Publication Date: 1960
Author: Subcommittee on Patents, Trademarks, and Copyrights, Senate Committee on the Judiciary
Pages: vii, 135

L/C Card Number: 60-60692
OCLC No.: 1968087
SuDoc No.: Y4.J89/2:C79/no.14-16
CIS No.: Committee-Print: S0444
UPA Citation: N/A
Relevant Bills: H.R. 8177 (68th Cong.), H.R. 9137 (68th Cong.), H.R.
        139 (72nd Cong.), H.R. 10364 (72nd Cong.), H.R. 10740 (72nd Cong.),
        H.R. 10976 (72nd Cong.), H.R. 11948 (72nd Cong.), H.R. 12094 (72nd
        Cong.), H.R. 12425 (72nd Cong.), S. 176 (72nd Cong.), S. 3985 (72nd
        Cong.), H.R. 11420 (74th Cong.), S. 2465 (74th Cong.), S. 3047 (74th
        Cong.), S. 3043 (76th Cong.)

Studies 14 - 16 address three separate issues: No. 14 Fair Use of Copyrighted Works (A. Latman); No. 15 Photoduplication of Copyrighted Material by Libraries (B. Varmer); and, No. 16. Limitations on Performing Rights (B. Varmer). Study No. 14 does not contain a legislative history as it was intended to show the development of the Act through case law interpretation and scholarly law articles. Study No. 15 has as its focus the present law and practice; the legislative proposals, specifically the Thomas Shotwell Bill of 1940 and the Lucas Bill of 1944; and, foreign laws of selected countries, Austria, France, the German Federal Republic, Mexico, the United Kingdom, and the Scandinavian countries. It concludes with a summary and analysis of the problem and a proposed solution. Study No. 16 gives the legislative history associated with performing rights in literary and musical works. It provides the case law interpretation that was available at the time. The Study places the analyses of these two topics into the "for profit" context as a limiting factor. Exhibition rights in motion pictures are treated separately. The inclusion of comments and views submitted to the Copyright Office in relation to the Studies are worthy of note, in particular, Melville B. Nimmer's comments are given.

Record No.: 013
Public Law No.: 60-320 (Sess. II)
Bill No.: H.R. 28192 (60th Cong.)
Statutes at Large Citation: 35 Stat. 1075 (1909)
Title of Act: Copyright Act of 1909

Title of Legislative History: Copyright Law Revision, Studies, Prepared for
Subcommittee on Patents, Trademarks, and
Copyrights, 86th Congress, 2nd Session,
Pursuant to S. Res 240; Studies 14-16, 86th
Comg., 2nd Sess. (Comm. Print 1960)
Publication Date: 1960
Author: Subcommitee on Patents, Trademarks, and Copyrights, Senate Committee on the Judiciary
Pages: vii, 135

L/C Card Number: 60-60692
OCLC No.: 1968087
SuDoc No.: Y4.J89/2:C79/no.14-16
CIS No.: Committee-Print: S0444
UPA Citation: N/A
Relevant Bills: H.R. 28192 (60th Cong.), S. 3043 (76th Cong.), S. 2039 (78th
Cong.)

This is one of thirty-four copyright law revision studies which appeared in 11 committee prints published in 1960 and 1961 by the Senate Subcommittee on Patents, Trademarks, and Copyrights. The Subcommittee also published a subject index to these studies. "Study No. 15: Photo-duplication of Copyrighted Material by Libraries" first notes that the judicial doctrine of fair use has a role to play in regulating the photocopying of copyrighted material, although in 1959 at the time of the study there had been no court cases specifically dealing with photocopying. The study summarizes, quotes, and comments upon the "Gentlemen's Agreement" on photocopying reached in 1937 by the American Council of Learned Societies, the Social Science Research Council, and the National Association of Book Publishers. The study similarly treats the American Library Association's Reproduction of Materials Code of 1941. The study summarizes, quotes, and comments upon the two bills S. 3043 (76th Cong.) and S. 2039 (78th Cong.) which at the study's publication had specifically dealt with the photocopying of copyrighted material by libraries.

The study also examines the photocopying laws of foreign countries. The study concludes with the comments and views of copyright experts on the photoduplication of copyrighted material by libraries.

Record No.: 014
Public Law No.: 60-320 (Sess. II)
Bill No.: H.R. 28192 (60th Cong.)
Statutes at Large Citation: 35 Stat. 1075 (1909)
Title of Act: Copyright Act of 1909

Title of Legislative History: Copyright Law Revision, Studies, Prepared for
                                Subcommittee on Patents, Trademarks, and
                                Copyrights, 86th Congress, 2nd Session,
                                Pursuant to S. Res. 240; Studies 14-16, 86th
                                Cong., 2nd Sess. (Comm. Print 1960)
Publication Date: 1960
Author: Subcommittee on Patents, Trademarks, and Copyrights, Senate
Committee on the Judiciary
Pages: vii, 135

L/C Card Number: 60-60692
OCLC No.: 1968087
SuDoc No.: Y4.J89/2:C79/no.14-16
CIS No.: Committee-Print: S0444
UPA Citation: N/A
Relevant Bills: H.R. 19853 (59th Cong.), S. 6330 (59th Cong.), H.R.
     28192 (60th Cong.), H.R. 11258 (68th Cong.), S. 4355 (68th
     Cong.), H.R. 10434 (69th Cong.), H.R. 8912 (70th Cong.), H.R.
     6990 (71st Cong.), H.R. 12549 (71st Cong.), H.R. 139 (72nd
     Cong.), H.R. 10364 (72nd Cong.), H.R. 10740 (72nd Cong.), H.R.
     10976 (72nd Cong.), H.R. 11948 (72nd Cong.), H.R. 12094
     (72nd Cong.), H.R. 12425 (72nd Cong.), S. 176 (72nd Cong.), S.
     3985 (72nd Cong.), H.R. 10632 (74th Cong.), H.R. 11420 (74th Cong.),
     S. 3047 (74th Cong.), S. 3043 (76th Cong.), H.R. 3589 (82nd Cong.), H.R.
     673 (85th Cong.), H.R. 4572 (85th Cong.)

This is one of thirty-four copyright law revision studies which appeared in 11 committee prints published in 1960 and 1961 by the Senate Subcommittee on Patents, Trademarks, and Copyrights.The Subcommittee also published a subject index to these studies. Study No. 16: Limitations on Performing Rights separately treats first the performing rights in literary and musical works, then the exhibition rights in motion pictures. The study briefly examines the legislative history of the statutory law in each of these areas. The study examines in detail the bills introduced in the 68th - 85th Congresses (1924-1957) which contained provisions to change the law in these areas. One of these bills, H.R. 3589 (82nd Cong.), P.L. 82-575 became law. This public law extended the author's public performing rights to nondramatic literary works. The study summarizes, compares, and quotes the bills in each of these areas, as well as describing the Congressional action on them. The study also summarizes and quotes relevant Congressional hearings and Congressional reports. Footnotes provide complete citations to Congressional documents. For each area, the study examines the case law, as well as the law in foreign countries and international conventions. The study concludes with the comments and views of copyright experts on the limitations on performing rights.

Record No.: 015
Public Law No.: 60-320 (Sess. II)
Bill No.: H.R. 28192 (60th Cong.)
Statutes at Large Citation: 35 Stat. 1075 (1909)
Title of Act: Copyright Act of 1909

Title of Legislative History: Copyright Law Revision, Studies, Prepared for
                                 Subcommittee on Patents, Trademarks, and
                                 Copyrights, 86th Congress, 2nd Session,
                                 Pursuant to S. Res. 240; Studies 17-19, 86th
                                 Cong., 2nd Sess. (Comm. Print 1960)
Publication Date: 1960
Author: Subcommittee on Patents, Trademarks, and Copyrights, Senate Committee on the Judiciary
Pages: xi, 135

L/C Card Number: 60-60692
OCLC No.: 1968087
SuDoc No.: Y4.J89/2:C79/no.17-19
CIS No.: Committee-Print: S0445
UPA Citation: N/A
Relevant Bills: H.R. 19853 (59th Cong.), H.R. 25133 (59th Cong.), S. 6330 (59th Cong.), S. 8190 (59th Cong.), H.R. 28192 (60th Cong.), H.R. 9137 (68th Cong.), H.R. 11258 (68th Cong.), H.R. 12549 (71st Cong.), H.R. 12094 (72nd Cong.), H.R. 10632 (74th Cong.), S. 3047 (74th Cong.), H.R. 4433 (76th Cong.), H.R. 5319 (76th Cong.), S. 3043 (76th Cong.), H.R. 8873 (85th Cong.)

The sixth in the Series presents Studies 17-19. The Studies include: No. 17. The Registration of Copyright (B. Kaplan); No. 18 Authority of the Register of Copyrights to Reject Applications for Registration (C. Berger); and, No. 19. The Recordation of Copyright Assignments and Licenses (A. Latman, L. Margolis, and M. Kaplan). Each study has the comments and views submitted documents at the end. Study No. 17 is an exhaustive presentation of the issues beginning with English version in the Statute of Anne (1710), with case interpretation, and continuing through the American experience. The

Canadian experience is set out to give an example of current practice. It concludes with a restatement of the issues and summary remarks. Study No. 18 works its way through the statutory provisions, court decisions (including administrative), Attorney General opinions, and the legislative proposals of revision. The penultimate section is an explanation of the powers and political actions of the various Registers of the Copyright. Study No. 19 analyzes the issue of recordation -- the scope, the requirements, and the effects. It differs somewhat from the other studies in that it uses treatises and other scholarly writings as source cites. Particular attention is given to the problem of assignation of the rights. The piece concludes with a restatement of issues.

Record No.: 016
Public Law No.: 60-320 (Sess. II)
Bill No.: H.R. 28192 (60th Cong.)
Statutes at Large Citation: 35 Stat. 1075 (1909)
Title of Act: Copyright Act of 1909

Title of Legislative History: Copyright Law Revision, Studies, Prepared for
                                 Subcommittee on Patents, Trademarks, and
                                 Copyrights, 86th Congress, 2nd Session,
                                 Pursuant to S. Res. 240; Studies 17-19, 86th
                                 Cong., 2nd Sess. (Comm. Print 1960)
Publication Date: 1960
Author: Subcommittee on Patents, Trademarks, and Copyrights, Senate Committee on the Judiciary
Pages: xi, 135

L/C Card Number: 60-60692
OCLC No.: 1968087
SuDoc No.: Y4.J89/2:C79/no.17-19
CIS No.: Committee-Print: S0445
UPA Citation: N/A
Relevant Bills: H.R. 28192 (60th Cong.), H.R. 8177 (68th Cong.), H.R. 11258 (68th Cong.), H.R. 10434 (69th Cong.), H.R. 8912 (70th Cong.), H.R. 6990 (71st Cong.), H.R. 12549 (71st Cong.), S. 3043 (76th Cong.)

This is one of thirty-four copyright law revision studies which appeared in 11 committee prints published in 1960 and 1961 by the Senate Subcommittee on Patents, Trademarks, and Copyrights. The Subcommittee also published a subject index to these studies. Study No. 18: Authority of the Register of Copyrights to Reject Applications for Registration briefly examines the legislative history of the provisions in the Copyright Act of 1909, H.R. 28192 (60th Cong.), P.L. 60-349 which imply that the Register of Copyrights has the administrative discretion to refuse to register claims which do not meet the requirements for copyright. The study also briefly examines the general revision bills in the 68th - 76th Congresses (1924-1940). Most of these bills seemed to imply the same right to refuse registration as the Copyright Act of 1909. Some of them, however, explicitly denied the Register the right to refuse registration. The study summarizes, compares, and briefly quotes these bills, as well as describing the Congressional action on them. The study also briefly quotes and provides the citation to a relevant Congressional hearing. In addition, the study examines court cases and attorney general opinions which deal with the authority of the Register to reject applications. The study concludes with the comments and views of copyright experts on the authority of the Register to reject applications.

Record No.: 017
Public Law No.: 60-320 (Sess. II)
Bill No.: H.R. 28192 (60th Cong.)
Statutes at Large Citation: 35 Stat. 1075 (1909)
Title of Act: Copyright Act of 1909

Title of Legislative History: Copyright Law Revision, Studies, Prepared for Subcommittee on Patents, Trademarks, and Copyrights, 86th Congress, 2nd Session, Pursuant to S. Res. 240; Studies 20-21, 86th Cong., 2nd Sess. (Comm. Print 1960)
Publication Date: 1960
Author: Subcommittee on Patents, Trademarks, and Copyrights, Senate Committee on the Judiciary
Pages: xi, 81

L/C Card Number: 60-60692
OCLC No.: 1968087
SuDoc No.: Y4.J89/2:C79/no.20,21
CIS No.: Committee-Print: S0446
UPA Citation: N/A
Relevant Bills: H.R. 19853 (59th Cong.), S. 6330 (59th Cong.), H.R. 28192 (60th Cong.), H.R. 9137 (68th Cong.), H.R. 11258 (68th Cong.), H.R. 12549 (71st Cong.), H.R. 12425 (72nd Cong.), H.R. 11420 (74th Cong.), S. 3047 (74th Cong.), H.R. 3699 (75th Cong.), H.R. 5275 (75th Cong.), S. 1510 (75th Cong.), H.R. 1644 (76th Cong.), H.R. 4433 (76th Cong.), H.R. 5319 (76th Cong.), S. 3043 (76th Cong.), H.R. 4486 (77th Cong.)

Studies 20 and 21 are narrowly focused on the deposit and the catalog of entries of copyrighted works. The comments and views submitted sections follow the analysis of each study. The presentation is: No. 20 Deposit of Copyrights Works (E. Dunne) and No. 21. The Catalog of Copyright Entries (E. Dunne and J. Rogers). Study No. 20 discusses library deposit systems in general and includes countries whose systems are varied and disparate: the

United Kingdom, France, Italy, Switzerland, and the Soviet Union. The system used in the United States is presented through a legislative history and the law revision attempts of 1924 - 1940. The operation of the deposit system since 1909 is discussed in detail. Of particular note is the inclusion of a chart which gives the receipt and disposition of copies of works for copyright registration, 1901 - 57. Study No. 21 speaks to the relationship between the development of the law and the registration process to implement the law. The Study states its primary purpose as the decision making document to determine the form, the content, and the publication of the Catalog. It traces the development of the first copyright law and the early experiments in publishing a record of the registered copyright notices. The issues involved with the distribution and use of the Catalog are given. The Study concludes with a restatement of issues and a comments section.

Record No.: 018
Public Law No.: 60-320 (Sess. II)
Bill No.: H.R. 28192 (60th Cong.)
Statutes at Large Citation: 35 Stat. 1075 (1909)
Title of Act: Copyright Act of 1909

Title of Legislative History: Copyright Law Revision, Studies, Prepared for Subcommittee on Patents, Trademarks, and Copyrights, 86th Congress, 2nd session, Pursuant to S. Res. 240; Studies no. 22-25, 86th Cong., 2nd Sess. (Comm. Print 1960)
Publication Date: 1960
Author: Subcommittee on Patents, Trademarks, and Copyrights, Senate Committee on the Judiciary
Pages: xi, 169

L/C Card Number: 60-60692
OCLC No.: 1968087
SuDoc No.: Y4.J89/2:C79/no.22-25
CIS No.: Committee-Print: S0447
UPA Citation: N/A
Relevant Bills: H.R. 28192 (60th Cong.), H.R. 24224 (62nd Cong.), H.R. 10434 (69th Cong.), H.R. 6990 (71st Cong.), H.R. 12549 (71st Cong.), H.R. 10632 (74th Cong.), H.R. 11420 (74th Cong.), S. 3047 (74th Cong.), S. 3043 (76th Cong.), H.R. 3589 (82nd Cong.)

Studies 22-25 represent the sixth publication in the Series from the Subcommittee. The initial remarks from the Chair of the Subcommittee contain the expected admonition that is given with each Series publication. And, again, each Study concludes with a section of comments and views solicited and received. The grouping contains: Study No. 22: The Damage Provisions of the Copyright Law (W. Strauss); No. 23: The Operation of the

Damage Provisions of the Copyright Law: An Exploratory Study (R. Brown, W. O'Brien, and H. Turkington); No. 24: Remedies other than Damages for Copyright Infringement (W. Strauss); No. 25: Liability of Innocent Infringers of Copyrights (A. Latman and W. Tager). Study No. 22 covers the damages issue thoroughly beginning with the history of damage provisions, continuing through the current practice and ending with previous revisions and proposals to revise the law. The section on costs and attorneys' fees is set out separately. It concludes with a recapitulation of the major issues. Study No. 23 was written to explain and analyze the use of case law, questionnaires, interviews, and correspondence. The interviews were conducted with the copyright practicing Bar. The questionnaire that was used with the Bar is reproduced as part of the Study. Study No. 24 divides the discussion between civil remedies and criminal penalties with foreign law treatments added to each discussion. The issues presented section analyzes the various relief theories: injunction, impounding and destruction, and criminal penalties. It concludes with a summary. Study No. 25 consists of the historical evaluation; the present law practice; legislative proposals since 1909; laws of foreign countries; and, a review of underlying problems. The historical evaluation is worthy of particular note as it covers the Colonial statutes, 1783-86.

Record No.: 019
Public Law No.: 60-320 (Sess. II)
Bill No.: H.R. 28192 (60th Cong.)
Statutes at Large Citation: 35 Stat. 1075 (1909)
Title of Act: Copyright Act of 1909

Title of Legislative History: Copyright Law Revision, Studies, Prepared for Subcommittee on Patents, Trademarks, and Copyrights, 86th Congress, 2nd Session, Pursuant to S. Res. 240; Studies 22-25, 86th Cong., 2nd Sess. (Comm. Print 1960)
Publication Date: 1960
Author: Subcommittee on Patents, Trademarks, and Copyrights, Senate Committee on the Judiciary
Pages: xi, 169

L/C Card Number: 60-60692
OCLC No.: 1968087
SuDoc No.: Y4.J89/2:C79/no.22-25
CIS No.: Committee-Print: S0447
UPA Citation: N/A

Relevant Bills: H.R. 28192 (60th Cong.), H.R. 9137 (68th Cong.), H.R. 10434 (69th Cong.), H.R. 9639 (71st Cong.), H.R. 12549 (71st Cong.), S. 5687 (71st Cong.), H.R. 10364 (72nd Cong.), H.R. 10740 (72nd Cong.), H.R. 10976 (72nd Cong.), H.R. 11948 (72nd Cong.), H.R. 12094 (72nd Cong.), H.R. 12425 (72nd Cong.), S. 176 (72nd Cong.), S. 3985 (72nd Cong.), S. 342 (73rd Cong.), H.R. 10632 (74th Cong.), H.R. 11420 (74th Cong.), S. 3047 (74th Cong.), S. 3043 (76th Cong.)

This is one of thirty-four copyright law revision studies which appeared in 11 committee prints published in 1960 and 1961 by the Senate Subcommittee on Patents, Trademarks, and Copyrights. The Subcommittee also published a subject index to these studies. "Study No. 24: Remedies Other Than Damages for Copyright Infringement" briefly examines the legislative history of the injunction, impounding and destruction, and criminal penalty provisions of the Copyright Act of 1909. The study then examines in detail the provisions dealing with these areas in the general copyright revision bills introduced in the 68th - 76th Congresses (1924-1940). Some of these bills tried to limit these non-money damages. Others altogether omitted such provisions. The study summarizes, compares, and very briefly quotes the bills, as well as describing the Congressional action on them. The study also examines the case law interpreting these provisions in the 1909 act. In addition, the study briefly examines similar remedies in the laws of foreign countries. The study concludes with the comments and views of copyright experts on non-money damages.

Record No.: 020
Public Law No.: 60-320 (Sess. II)
Bill No.: H.R. 28192 (60th Cong.)
Statutes at Large Citation: 35 Stat. 1075 (1909)
Title of Act: Copyright Act of 1909

Title of Legislative History: Copyright Law Revision, Studies, Prepared
                                 for Subcommittee on Patents, Trademarks,
                                 and Copyrights, 86th Congress, 2nd
                                 Session, Pursuant to S. Res. 240; Studies 22-25,
                                 86th Cong., 2nd Sess. (Comm. Print 1960)
Publication Date: 1960
Author: Subcommittee on Patents, Trademarks, and Copyrights, Senate Committee on the Judiciary
Pages: xi, 169

L/C Card Number: 60-60692
OCLC No.: 1968087
SuDoc No.: Y4.J89/2:C79/no.22-25
CIS No.: Committee-Print: S0447
UPA Citation: N/A

Relevant Bills: H.R. 19853 (59th Cong.), S. 6330 (59th Cong.), H.R. 28192 (60th Cong.), H.R. 24224 (62nd Cong.), H.R. 8177 (68th Cong.), H.R. 9137 (68th Cong.), H.R. 11258 (68th Cong.), S. 4355 (68th Cong.), H.R. 5841 (69th Cong.), H.R. 10434 (69th Cong.), H.R. 6990 (71st Cong.), H.R. 12549 (71st Cong.), H.R. 10364 (72nd Cong.), H.R. 10740 (72nd Cong.), H.R. 10976 (72nd Cong.), H.R. 11948 (72nd Cong.), H.R. 12094 (72nd Cong.), H.R. 12425 (72nd Cong.), S. 3985 (72nd Cong.), S. 342 (73rd Cong.), H.R. 10632 (74th Cong.), H.R. 11420 (74th Cong.), S. 2465 (74th Cong.), S. 3047 (74th Cong.), S. 3043 (76th Cong.), H.R. 3589 (82nd Cong.)

This is one of thirty-four copyright law revision studies which appeared in 11 committee prints published in 1960 and 1961 by the Senate Subcommittee on Patents, Trademarks, and Copyrights. The Subcommittee also published a subject index to these studies. Study No. 25: Liability of Innocent Infringers of Copyrights very briefly examines the legislative history of the innocent infringement provisions of the Copyright Act of 1909, H.R. 28192 (60th Cong.), P.L. 60-320 (Sess. II). The study then examines in detail the innocent infringement provisions in the general copyright revision bills introduced in the 68th - 76th Congresses (1924-1940). Some of these bills contained comprehensive provisions mitigating the effects of innocent infringment. Other bills contained no provisions modifying the 1909 act's treatment of innocent infringers. The study summarizes, compares, and quotes these bills, as well as describing the Congressional action on them. The study summarizes and quotes the relevant Congressional reports and summarizes the relevant Congressional hearings. In addition, the study examines the interpretation of the 1909 act in the courts. The study examines how the laws of foreign countries treat infringers. The study also examines the Amendments of 1912, H.R. 24224 (62nd Cong.), P.L. 62-303 and H.R. 3589 (82nd Cong.), P.L. 82-575. These bills provided for low maximum damages for innocent infringement by the mass media. The study concludes with the comments and views of copyright experts on the liability of innocent infringers of copyrights.

Record No.: 021
Public Law No.: 60-320 (Sess. II)
Bill No.: H.R. 28192 (60th Cong.)
Statutes at Large Citation: 35 Stat. 1075 (1909)
Title of Act: Copyright Act of 1909

Title of Legislative History: Copyright Law Revision, Studies, Prepared
for Subcommittee on Patents, Trademarks,
and Copyrights, 86th Congress, 2nd
Session, Pursuant to S. Res. 240; Studies 26-28,
86th Cong., 2nd Sess. (Comm. Print 1960)

Publication Date: 1961
Author: Subcommittee on Patents, Trademarks, and Copyrights, Senate Committee on the Judiciary
Pages: xi, 116

L/C Card Number: 60-60692
OCLC No.: 1968087
SuDoc No.: Y4.J89/2:C79/no.26-28
CIS No.: Committee-Print: S0499
UPA Citation: N/A
Relevant Bills: H.R. 19853 (59th Cong.), S. 6330 (59th Cong.), S. 8190 (59th Cong.), H.R. 243 (60th Cong.), H.R. 11794 (60th Cong.), H.R. 21592 (60th Cong.), H.R. 21984 (60th Cong.), H.R. 22071 (60th Cong.), H.R. 22183 (60th Cong.), H.R. 24782 (60th Cong.), H.R. 25162 (60th Cong.), H.R. 27310 (60th Cong.), H.R. 28192 (60th Cong.), S. 2499 (60th Cong.), S. 2900 (60th Cong.), S. 9440 (60th Cong.), H.R. 21776 (62nd Cong.), H.R. 11258 (68th Cong.), S. 4355 (68th Cong.), H.R. 5841 (69th Cong.), H.R. 10434 (69th Cong.), H.R. 8912 (70th Cong.), H.R. 10655 (70th Cong.), H.R. 13452 (70th Cong.), H.R. 6990 (71st Cong.), H.R. 9639 (71st Cong.), H.R. 12549 (71st Cong.), H.R. 10364 (72nd Cong.), H.R. 10740 (72nd Cong.), H.R. 10976 (72nd Cong.), H.R. 11948 (72nd Cong.), H.R. 12094 (72nd Cong.), H.R. 12425 (72nd Cong.), S. 342 (73rd Cong.), H.R. 10632 (74th Cong.), H.R. 11374 (74th Cong.), H.R. 11420 (74th Cong.), S. 3047 (74th Cong.), H.R. 5275 (75th Cong.), S. 2240 (75th Cong.), H.R. 926 (76th Cong.), H.R. 4871 (76th Cong.), H.R. 5791 (76th Cong.), H.R. 6160 (76th Cong.), H.R. 6695 (76th Cong.), H.R. 9703 (76th Cong.), S. 3043 (76th Cong.), H.R. 7173 (77th Cong.), H.R. 1570 (78th Cong.), H.R. 3190 (79th Cong.), S. 1206 (79th Cong.), H.R. 1270 (80th Cong.), H.R. 2464 (82nd Cong.)

The seventh publication in the Series contains 26-28. The areas of law are: No. 26: The Unauthorized Duplication of Sound Recordings (B. Ringer); No., 27: Copyright in Architectural Works (W. Strausss); No. 28: Copyright in Choreographic Works (B. Varner). The Studies begin with the admonition and end with the comments and views section. However, notice is given that the writers are members of the Copyright Office Staff. Study No. 26 groups the analytical discussion around the present law of the United States -- both historical and proposed since 1909 -- as well as the laws of foreign countries. In addition, there is a section on international treaties and conventions. It concludes with a review of the problems and a summary of the issues. Study No. 27 encompasses the present law in the United States, proposed bills of revision, and international conventions and foreign laws. It ends with an analysis and summary of issues. The comments and views has a comment letter from Melville B. Nimmer. Study No. 28 presents the analysis of the present law (common and statutory), international conventions and foreign laws, and bills to revise the United States statutes. It adds an analysis and summary of issues.

Record No.: 022
Public Law No.: 60-320 (Sess. II)
Bill No.: H.R. 28192 (60th Cong.)
Statutes at Large Citation: 35 Stat. 1075 (1909)
Title of Act: Copyright Act of 1909

Title of Legislative History: Copyright Law Revision, Studies, Prepared
                                 for Subcommittee on Patents, Trademarks,
                                 and Copyrights, 86th Congress, 2nd
                                 Session, Pursuant to S. Res. 240; Studies 26-28,
                                 86th Cong., 2nd Sess. (Comm. Print 1960)
Publication Date: 1961
Author: Subcommittee on Patents, Trademarks, and Copyrights, Senate
Committee on the Judiciary
Pages: xi, 116

L/C Card Number: 60-60692
OCLC No.: 1968087
SuDoc No.: Y4.J89/2:C79/no.26-28
CIS No.: Committee-Print: S0499
UPA Citation: N/A
Relevant Bills: H.R. 28192 (60th Cong.), H.R. 9137 (68th Cong.), H.R.
    11258 (68th Cong.), H.R. 12549 (71st Cong.), H.R. 10976 (72nd Cong.),
    S. 3047 (74th Cong.), S. 3043 (76th Cong.), H.R. 8873 (85th Cong.), S.
    2075 (86th Cong.)

This is one of thirty-four copyright law revision studies which appeared in 11
committee prints published in 1960 and 1961 by the Senate Subcommittee
on Patents, Trademarks, and Copyrights. The Subcommittee also published
a subject index to these studies. "Study No. 27: Copyright in Architectural
Works" examines the protection afforded architectural plans and architectural
works under the common law and the Copyright Act of 1909, H.R. 28192
(60th Cong.), P.L. 60-349. Although the 1909 act clearly protected
architectural drawings against unauthorized copying, the courts interpreted it
to not protect against the use of copyrighted plans in building a structure.
An architectural structure was not protected unless it was a "work of art,"
in practice, a monument. The study then examines the provisions
concerning architectural works in the general copyright revision bills
introduced in the 68th - 76th Congresses (1924-1940). Most of these bills
extended protection to structures to the extent of their artistic character. The
study summarizes and compares these bills. In addition, the study examines
the protection afforded architectural plans and structures under the common
law. The study also examines the copyright protection afforded architectural
plans and structures in international treaties and under the laws of
foreign countries. The study concludes with the comments and views of
copyright experts on copyright in architectural works.

Record No.: 023
Public Law No.: 60-320 (Sess. II)
Bill No.: H.R. 28192 (60th Cong.)
Statutes at Large Citation: 35 Stat. 1075 (1909)
Title of Act: Copyright Act of 1909

Title of Legislative History: Copyright Law Revision, Studies, Prepared
                              for Subcommittee on Patents, Trademarks,
                              and Copyrights, 86th Congress, 2nd Session,
                              Pursuant to S. Res. 240; Studies 26-28, 86th
                              Cong., 2nd Sess. (Comm. Print 1960)
Publication Date: 1961
Author: Subcommittee on Patents, Trademarks, and Copyrights, Senate
Committee on the Judiciary
Pages: xi, 116

L/C Card Number: 60-60692
OCLC No.: 1968087
SuDoc No.: Y4.J89/2:C79/no.26-28
CIS No.: Committee-Print: S0499
UPA Citation: N/A
Relevant Bills: H.R. 28192 (60th Cong.), H.R. 9137 (68th Cong.), H.R.
    11258 (68th Cong.), H.R. 12549 (71st Cong.), H.R. 10976 (72nd Cong.),
    H.R. 11420 (74th Cong.), S. 3047 (74th Cong.), S. 3043 (76th Cong.)

This is one of thirty-four copyright law revision studies which appeared in 11
committee prints published in 1960 and 1961 by the Senate Subcommittee on
Patents, Trademarks, and Copyrights. The Subcommittee also published
a subject index to these studies. "Study No. 28: Copyright in Choreographic
Works" examines the protection afforded choreographic works under
the Copyright Act of 1909, H.R. 28192 (60th Cong.), P.L. 60-349. The courts
and Copyright Office interpreted the 1909 act to include choreographic works
as a kind of dramatic composition and to protect choreographic works which
told a story, portrayed a character, or conveyed an emotion. The choreography
had to be in a fixed form which could serve as directions for the performance of
a dance.   The copyright owner was protected from the copying of
the description and the public performance of the dance. The study also
examines the provisions concerning choreographic works in the general
copyright revision bills introduced in the 68th - 76th Congresses (1924-1940).
Most of these bills included choreographic works among the enumerated
categories of copyrightable works and required that they be fixed in some form
from which they could be acted. In addition, the study examines the protection
afforded choreographic plans and structures in international treaties and
under the laws of foreign countries.The study concludes with the comments
and views of copyright experts on copyright in choreographic works.

Record No.: 024
Public Law No.: 60-320 (Sess. II)
Bill No.: H.R. 28192 (60th Cong.)
Statutes at Large Citation: 35 Stat. 1075 (1909)
Title of Act: Copyright Act of 1909

Title of Legislative History: Copyright Law Revision, Studies, Prepared
for Subcommittee on Patents, Trademarks,
and Copyrights, 86th Congress, 2nd Session,
Pursuant to S. Res. 240; Studies 29-31, 86th
Cong., 2nd Sess. (Comm. Print 1960)

Publication Date: 1961
Author: Subcommittee on Patents, Trademarks, and Copyrights, Senate
Committee on the Judiciary
Pages: xi, 237

L/C Card Number: 60-60692
OCLC No.: 1968087
SuDoc No.: Y4.J89/2:C79/no.29-31
CIS No.: Committee-Print: S0500
UPA Citation: N/A
Relevant Bills: H.R. 19853 (59th Cong.), S. 6330 (59th Cong.), H.R.
21984 (60th Cong.), H.R. 22183 (60th Cong.), H.R. 24782 (60th Cong.),
H.R. 25162 (60th Cong.), H.R. 27310 (60th Cong.), H.R. 28192 (60th
Cong.), S. 9440 (60th Cong.), H.R. 9137 (68th Cong.), H.R. 11258 (68th
Cong.), H.R. 12549 (71st Cong.), H.R. 10364 (72nd Cong.), H.R. 11948
(72nd Cong.), S. 3985 (72nd Cong.), H.R. 10632 (74th Cong.), H.R.
11420 (74th Cong.), S. 3047 (74th Cong.), S. 3043 (76th Cong.)

Studies 29-31 were issued to further analyze and explain the machinations of
the revisions of the Copyright Act. The caveat toward bias is given as is the
comments submitted section. The analyses in the Committee Print are: No.
29. Protection of Unpublished Works (W. Strauss); No. 30. Duration of
Copyright (J. Guinan, Jr.); and, No. 31. Renewal of Copyright (B. Ringer and
J. Culp). Study No. 29 provides a presentation of unpublished works through
case law interpretation, statutory constraints, and an application of the
principles involved in the notable treatises of the time. The legislative
proposals are given a separate discussion. The Study ends with an analysis of
the problem using alternative protection, such as voluntary registration. The
piece provides a summary of major issues as its concluding remarks. Study
No. 30 describes and discusses the duration of copyright using the historical
practice, a summary of provisions of other countries (foreign), applicable
international conventions; and, various revising proposals. The Study has
three unique appendices which set out the classification scheme of
registrations, the percentage of original registrations which affect renewals;
and questions related alternative solutions. Study No. 31 is an explication of
the renewal of copyright problem. It begins with the legislative history of the
Renewal Provision, continues through the present law applications, and
concludes with review of the problems and a summary of the issues. Three
appendices follow the Study and provide sources to other primary materials.

The three appendices are divided as follows: legislative proposals since 1909; analogies to renewal under other legal systems; and, a statistical survey of registrations.

Record No.: 025
Public Law No.: 60-320 (Sess. II)
Bill No.: H.R. 28192 (60th Cong.)
Statutes at Large Citation: 35 Stat. 1075 (1909)
Title of Act: Copyright Act of 1909

Title of Legislative History: Copyright Law Revision, Studies, Prepared
                                  for Subcommittee on Patents, Trademarks,
                                  and Copyrights, 86th Congress, 2nd Session,
                                  Pursuant to S. Res. 240; Studies 29-31, 86th
                                  Cong., 2nd Sess. (Comm. Print 1960)
Publication Date: 1961
Author: Subcommittee on Patents, Trademarks, and Copyrights, Senate
Committee on the Judiciary
Pages: xi, 237

L/C Card Number: 60-60692
OCLC No.: 1968087
SuDoc No.: Y4.J89/2:C79/no.29-31
CIS No.: Committee-Print: S0500
UPA Citation: N/A
Relevant Bills: H.R. 28192 (60th Cong.), H.R. 11476 (76th Cong.), H.R.
    13676 (67th Cong.), H.R. 14035 (67th Cong.), S. 4101 (67th Cong.), H.R.
    573 (68th Cong.), H.R. 2663 (68th Cong.), H.R. 2704 (68th Cong.), H.R.
    8177 (68th Cong.), H.R. 9137 (68th Cong.), H.R. 11258 (68th Cong.), S.
    74 (68th Cong.), H.R. 10434 (69th Cong.), H.R. 8912 (70th Cong.), H.R.
    6990 (71st Cong.), H.R. 12549 (71st Cong.), S. 5687 (71st Cong.), H.R.
    10364 (72nd Cong.), H.R. 10740 (72nd Cong.), H.R. 10976 (72nd
    Cong.), H.R. 11948 (72nd Cong.), H.R. 12094 (72nd Cong.), H.R.
    12425 (72nd Cong.), S. 176 (72nd Cong.), S. 3985 (72nd Cong.),
    H.R. 585 (73rd Cong.), S. 1928 (73rd Cong.), H.R. 10632 (74th Cong.),
    H.R. 11420 (74th Cong.), S. 2465 (74th Cong.), S. 3043 (76th Cong.)

This is one of thirty-four copyright law revision studies which appeared in 11 committee prints published in 1960 and 1961 by the Senate Subcommittee on Patents, Trademarks, and Copyrights. The Subcommittee also published a subject index to these studies. "Study No. 30: Duration of Copyright" briefly examines the duration terms in pre-1909 copyright statutes and the Copyright Act of 1909, H.R. 28192 (60th Cong.), P.L. 60-349. The 1909 act provided for a term of 28 years, renewable for another term of 28 years. The study also examines in detail the duration provisions in the general copyright revision bills introduced in the 68th - 76th Congresses (1924-1940). These bills varied widely in all of their duration terms: beginning date of term, length of term, and single or renewable terms. The study summarizes and compares these bills, as well as describing the Congressional action on them. The study also summarizes the relevant Congressional hearings and notes the relevant Congressional reports. In addition, the study examines the duration of copyright in international treaties and in the laws of other countries. The study concludes with the comments and views of copyright experts on the best term for the duration of copyright.

Record No.: 026
Public Law No.: 60-320 (Sess. II)
Bill No.: H.R. 28192 (60th Cong.)
Statutes at Large Citation: 35 Stat. 1075 (1909)
Title of Act: Copyright Act of 1909

Title of Legislative History: Copyright Law Revision, Studies, Prepared
                                 for Subcommittee on Patents, Trademarks,
                                 and Copyrights, 86th Congress, 2nd Session,
                                 Pursuant to S. Res. 240; Studies 29-31, 86th
                                 Cong., 2nd Sess. (Comm. Print 1960)
Publication Date: 1961
Author: Subcommittee on Patents, Trademarks, and Copyrights, Senate
Committee on the Judiciary
Pages: xi, 237

L/C Card Number: 60-60692
OCLC No.: 1968087
SuDoc No.: Y4.J89/2:C79/no.29-31
CIS No.: Committee-Print: S0500
UPA Citation: N/A
Relevant Bills: H.R. 19853 (59th Cong.), H.R. 25133 (59th Cong.), S. 6330
        (59th Cong.), S. 8190 (59th Cong.), H.R. 243 (60th Cong.), H.R. 11794
        (60th Cong.), H.R. 21592 (60th Cong.), H.R. 21984 (60th Cong.), H.R.
        22071 (60th Cong.), H.R. 22183 (60th Cong.), H.R. 24782 (60th Cong.),
        H.R. 25162 (60th Cong.), H.R. 27310 (60th Cong.), H.R. 28192 (60th
        Cong.), S. 2499 (60th Cong.), S. 2900 (60th Cong.), S. 9440 (60th Cong.),
        H.R. 139 (72nd Cong.), H.R. 10364 (72nd Cong.), H.R. 10740 (72nd
        Cong.), H.R. 10976 (72nd Cong.), H.R. 11948 (72nd Cong.), H.R. 12094
        (72nd Cong.), H.R. 12425 (72nd Cong.), S. 176 (72nd Cong.), S. 3985
        (72nd Cong.), H.R. 5853 (73rd Cong.), S. 342 (73rd Cong.), S. 1928 (73rd
        Cong.), H.R. 10632 (74th Cong.), H.R. 11420 (74th Cong.), S. 2465 (74th
        Cong.), S. 3047 (74th Cong.), H.R. 2695 (75th Cong.), H.R. 3004 (75th
        Cong.), H.R. 5275 (75th Cong.), H.R. 10503 (75th Cong.), S. 7 (75th
        Cong.), S. 2240 (75th Cong.), S. 3969 (75th Cong.), H.R. 926 (76th
        Cong.), H.R. 4871 (76th Cong.), H.R. 6160 (76th Cong.), H.R. 9703 (76th
        Cong.), S. 547 (76th Cong.), S. 3043 (76th Cong.), H.R. 3997 (77th Cong.)

This is one of thirty-four copyright law revision studies which appeared in 11 committee prints published in 1960 and 1961 by the Senate Subcommittee on Patents, Trademarks, and Copyrights. The Subcommittee also published a subject index to these studies. "Study No. 31: Renewal of Copyright" briefly examines the copyright renewal provisons in the pre-1909 copyright statutes. It then examines in detail the legislative history of the renewal provisons of the Copyright Act of 1909, H.R. 28192 (60th Cong.), P.L. 60-349. The study summarizes, compares, and quotes the relevant bills, as well as describing the Congressional action on them. The study also summarizes and quotes the relevant Congressional hearings, Congressional reports, and Congressional debate. The first appendix contains a detailed examination of the renewal provisions, if any, in the general copyright revision bills introduced in the 68th - 76th Congresses (1924-1940). Some of these bills allowed for copyright renewal while others did not. The appendix summarizes, compares, and briefly quotes these bills, as well as describing the Congressional action on them. The appendix also summarizes and briefly quotes the relevant Congressional hearings, Congressional reports, and Congressional debates.

Record No.: 027
Public Law No.: 60-320 (Sess. II)
Bill No.: H.R. 28192 (60th Cong.)
Statutes at Large Citation: 35 Stat. 1075 (1909)
Title of Act: Copyright Act of 1909

Title of Legislative History: Copyright Law Revision, Studies, Prepared for
                                 Subcommittee on Patents, Trademarks, and
                                 Copyrights, 86th Congress, 2nd Session,
                                 Pursuant to S. Res. 240; Studies 32-34, 86th
                                 Cong., 2nd Sess. (Comm. Print 1960)
Publication Date: 1961
Author: Subcommittee on Patents, Trademarks, and Copyrights, Senate
Committee on the Judiciary
Pages: xi, 57

L/C Card Number: 60-60692
OCLC No.: 1968087
SuDoc No.: Y4.J89/2:C79/no.32-34
CIS No.: Committee-Print: S0501
UPA Citation: N/A
Relevant Bills: H.R. 28192 (60th Cong.), H.R. 8177 (68th Cong.), H.R. 9137 (68th Cong.), H.R. 11258 (68th Cong.), H.R. 10434 (69th Cong.), H.R. 12549 (71st Cong.), H.R. 10976 (72nd Cong.), H.R. 12425 (72nd Cong.), H.R. 10632 (74th Cong.), H.R. 11420 (74th Cong.), S. 2465 (74th Cong.), S. 3047 (74th Cong.), S. 3043 (76th Cong.)

The last of the Series of Committee Prints contains Studies 32 - 34. The warning concerning the bias of the individual writers is given as well as the concluding section with the letters of comments or views. The range of inquiry is: No. 32. Protection of Works of Foreign Origin (A. Bogsch); No. 33. Copyright in Government Publications (C. Berger); and , No. 34. Copyright in Territories and Possessions of the United States (B. Varmer). Study No. 32 gives an overview of the development of the law since 1790, the present law usage, the reform efforts since 1909, and the laws of foreign countries. Although it should be noted that the laws of foreign countries section deals equally with foreign workds protected under Conventions. The Study ends with a selection of questions to be considered during revision of the Act. Study No. 33 places its emphasis on the interpretations of the law, both judicial and statutory, as they relate to Federal government publications. The present law is discussed in historical and developmental terms. A section of comparative law is provided. Of particular note is the inclusion of the Federal government agency views. The Study concludes with an analysis of the issues concerning the Act and the territories and/or possessions. It has an explanation of the differences between unorganized territories and territories as geographical parts of the United States for purposes of the Act. Two appendices are added which deal with related problems and issues: the status of organized territories and organic acts extending the Act to organized territories.

Record No.: 028
Public Law No.: 60-320 (Sess. II)
Bill No.: H.R. 28192 (60th Cong.)
Statutes at Large Citation: 35 Stat. 1075 (1909)
Title of Act: Copyright Act of 1909

Title of Legislative History: Copyright Law Revision, Studies, Prepared for Subcommittee on Patents, Trademarks, and Copyrights, 86th Congress, 2nd Session, Pursuant to S. Res. 240; Studies 32-34, 86th Cong., 2nd Sess. (Comm. Print 1960)

Publication Date: 1961
Author: Subcommittee on Patents, Trademarks, and Copyrights, Senate Committee on the Judiciary
Pages: xi, 57

L/C Card Number: 60-60692
OCLC No.: 1968087
SuDoc No.: Y4.J89/2:C79/no.32-34
CIS No.: Committee-Print: S0501
UPA Citation: N/A

Relevant Bills: H.R. 2650 (53rd Cong.), H.R. 19853 (59th Cong.), S. 6330 (59th Cong.), H.R. 28192 (60th Cong.), H.R. 6539 (63rd Cong.), S. 1107 (64th Cong.), S. 7795 (64th Cong.), S. 3983 (65th Cong.), H.R. 8362 (66th Cong.), S. 579 (66th Cong.), S. 637 (67th Cong.), H.R. 12549 (71st Cong.), H.R. 12425 (72nd Cong.), S. 3043 (76th Cong.)

This is one of thirty-four copyright law revision studies which appeared in 11 committee prints published in 1960 and 1961 by the Senate Subcommittee on Patents, Trademarks, and Copyrights. The Subcommittee also published a subject index to these studies. "Study No. 33: Copyright in Government Publications" briefly examines the pre-1895 case law which prohibited copyright in laws and decisions. The study briefly examines the legislative history of the Printing and Binding Law of 1895, H.R. 2650 (53rd Cong.), 53rd Cong., 3rd Sess., Ch. 23. This law prohibited copyright in any "government publication." The study summarizes the relevant Congressional debate and summarizes and quotes the relevant Congressional report. The study also briefly examines several bills introduced in the 63rd - 66th Congresses (1916-1919) which attempted to revise the Printing and Binding Law of 1895 by adding a definition of "government documents." These bills would have prohibited those who reprinted government publications from using the Government Printing Office imprint or inserting advertisements into their reproductions. The study briefly quotes these bills and a relevant Congressional report. The study also briefly examines the legislative history of the provisions of the Copyright Act of 1909, H.R. 28192 (60th Cong.), P.L. 60-320 (Sess. II) which prohibited copyright in government publications. The study summarizes the relevant Congressional hearings and briefly quotes the relevant Congressional report. The study notes a series of bills introduced in the 65th - 67th Congresses (1918-1921) which attempted to permit the government to secure copyright for its works. The study notes that the general copyright revision bills introduced in the 68th - 76th Congresses (1924-1940) retained the prohibition on copyright in United States government publications. In addition, the study also briefly examines the treatment afforded government publications under the laws of foreign countries.

Record No.: 029
Public Law No.: 64-114 (Sess. II)
Bill No.: S. 703 (64th Cong.)
Statutes at Large Citation: 39 Stat. 929 (1917)
Title of Act: Vocational Education Act of 1917

Title of Legislative History: History of Federal Vocational Education
Legislation in the Twentieth Century

Publication Date: 1975
Author: Angela M. Giordano-Evans of the Congressional Research Service
Pages: 66

L/C Card Number: N/A
OCLC No.: 24593513
SuDoc No.: N/A
CIS No.: N/A
CRS No.: JK1108≠b.1735 Suppl. 1975/76 reel 5

UPA Citation: UPA Film No.: MS 75-76 Supp., Reel No. V, Frame No. 0344.
CRS No.: LC 1043 U.S., 75-126 ED
Relevant Bills: H.R. 7951 (63rd Cong.), S. 3091 (63rd Cong.), S. 703
   (64th   Cong.), H.J. Res. 277 (65th Cong.), H.R. 4121 (68th Cong.),   S.
   1731 (70th Cong.), H.R. 12901 (71st Cong.), S. 5139 (71st   Cong.), H.R.
   7059 (73rd Cong.), H.R. 8024 (74th Cong.), H.R.   12120 (74th Cong.), S.
   2883 (74th Cong.), H.R. 9611 (75th   Cong.), S. 1946 (78th Cong.), H.R.
   4384 (79th Cong.), S. 619   (79th Cong.), S. 3958 (84th Cong.), H.R.
   10433 (84th Cong.),   S. 2379 (84th Cong.), H.R. 13247 (85th Cong.), S.
   4237 (85th   Cong.), S. 1 (87th Cong.), H.R. 4955 (88th Cong.), H.R.
   18366   (90th Cong.), H.R. 514 (91st Cong.), H.R. 7248 (92nd Cong.),   S.
   659 (92nd Cong.), H.R. 69 (93rd Cong.)

The legislative history of the federal vocational education legislation enacted
from 1914-1974 is divided into four sections covering: 1900-1916, 1917-1947,
1950s, and 1960s. The history of each public law begins with a chart which
shows the progress of the public law through Congress. The chart provides
citations to the *Congressional Record* for such procedural events as
Congressional reports, Congressional debate, bill amendments, bill
substitutions, and votes. Congressional report numbers and bill numbers
are also indicated. A number of the charts have an explanatory essay. The
essay describes the historical events which led to the legislation, how funds
were provided for vocational education, the amendment process, and how the
public law amended earlier laws. The nineteen public laws treated are: Smith-
Hughes Act or Vocational Education Act of 1917, S. 703 (64th Cong.), P.L. 64-
114 (Sess. II); George-Barden Act or Vocational Education Act of 1946, S. 619
(79th Cong.), P.L. 79-586; Vocational Education Act of 1963, H.R. 4955 (88th
Cong.), P.L. 88-210; and Vocational Education Amendments of 1968, H.R.
18366 (90th Cong.), P.L. 90-576. The history concludes with an appendix and
a bibliography. The appendix includes tables summarizing data on vocational
education enrollments and federal support for vocational education from 1917
to 1973. The bibliography is a short list of books and government documents
on the history of vocational education.

Record No.: 030
Public Law No.: 65-106 (Sess. I0
Bill No.: H.R. 4960 (65th Cong.)
Statutes at Large Citation: 40 Stat. 411 (1917)
Title of Act: Trading with the Enemy Act

Title of Legislative History: Legislative History of Section 5(b) of the
Trading with the Enemy Act In Trading with
the Enemy: Legislative and Executive
Documents Concerning Regulation of
International Transactions in Time of Declared
National Emergency, 94th Cong., 2nd Sess.
(Comm. Print 1976)
Publication Date: 1976
Author: Subcommittee on International Trade and Commerce, House
Committee on International Relations
Pages: x, 684

L/C Card Number: 77-600579
OCLC No.: 2579218
SuDoc No.: Y4.In8/16:T67
CIS No.: 76-H462-47
UPA Citation: N/A
Relevant Bills: H.R. 4960 (65th Cong.), H.R. 12923 (65th Cong.), H.J.
Res. 382 (66th Cong.), H.R. 1491 (73rd Cong.), H.R. 6976
(93rd Cong.), S.J. Res. 252 (76th Cong.), H.R. 6233 (77th Cong.), S.
2129 (77th Cong.)

This volume contains the relevant documents to the legislative history of
Section 5(b) of the Trading with the Enemy Act, H.R. 4960 (65th Cong.), P.L.
65-106 (Sess. I). Section 5(b) grants the President the authority to regulate
the nation's international and domestic finance during periods of declared
national emergency. The volume contains documents for the Trading with the
Enemy Act as it was passed, as well as for four acts which amended Section
5(b) and two acts which relate to Section 5(b) without actually amending it.
The volume provides a more complete legislative history for the original act
than for the other acts. The section on the original act includes the text of
the Trading with the Enemy Act as passed, as well as the Conference, Senate,
and House reports, excerpts from Senate and House debate, and excerpts
from Senate hearings. The volume provides full citations to all documents.
This section includes materials dealing with the act as a whole, as well
as materials specifically dealing with Section 5(b). The other sections contain
materials more specifically relevant to Section 5(b). The sections on the other
acts are presented in chronological order of the acts' passage. The included
acts which amended Section 5(b) are: Second Liberty Bond Act, Amendment of
1918, H.R. 12923 (65th Cong..). P.L. 65-217; Emergency Banking Relief Act,
H.R. 1491 (73rd Cong.), P.L. 73-1; Trading with the Enemy Act, Amendment of
1940, S.J. Res. 252 (76th Cong.), Pub. Res. No. 76-69; First War Powers Act of
1941, H.R. 6233 (77th Cong.), P.L. 77-354. The included acts which related to
Section 5(b) without actually amending it are: Knox Resolution, H.J. Res. 382
(66th Cong.), Pub. Res. No. 66-64; Gold Reserve Act of 1934, H.R. 6976 (73rd

Cong.), P.L. 73-87. The sections on these acts include the text or partial text of the act and excerpts from the relevant Congressional reports and/or Congressional debate. The volume also contains the text of the Trading with the Enemy Act as amended through 1976 and codified in the *United States Code*, as well as the regulations authorized by Section 5(b) from the 1976 *Code of Federal Regulations*. In addition, the volume contains the executive orders from 1933-1976 which invoked the authority of Section 5(b).

Record No.: 031
Public Law No.: 65-106 (Sess. I)
Bill No.: H.R. 4960 (65th Cong.)
Statutes at Large Citation: 40 Stat. 411 (1917)
Title of Act: Trading with the Enemy Act

Title of Legislative History: Alien Property Custodian, Legislative
                                 Chronological History and Bibliography of
                                 Trading with Enemy Act, 50 U.S. Code App. 1-
                                 40, and Operations of Office of Alien Property
                                 Custodian, 1917-52
Publication Date: 1953
Author: Subcommittee on Trading with the Enemy Act, Senate Committee on the Judiciary
Pages: vii, 50

L/C Card Number: 53-60254
OCLC No.: 6310496
SuDoc No.: Y4.J89/2:Al4/4
CIS No.: Committee-Print: S3481
UPA Citation: N/A
Relevant Bills: H.R. 4960 (65th Cong.), H.R. 14222 (67th Cong.), S. 2780 (67th Cong.), S. 4100 (76th Cong.), S. 1226 (69th Cong.), H.R. 7201 (70th Cong.), S. 5452 (70th Cong.), H.R. 3083 (71st Cong.), S.J. Res. 109 (71st Cong.), S. 852 (73rd Cong.), S. 2901 (75th Cong.), S.J. Res. 252 (76th Cong.), H.R. 6233 (77th Cong.), H.R. 4571 (79th Cong.), H.R. 6890 (79th Cong.), S. 2345 (79th Cong.), H.R. 4044 (80th Cong.), H.R. 6116 (80th Cong.), S.J. Res. 138 (80th Cong.), H.R.J. Res. 516 (81st Cong.), S. 1292 (81st Cong.), H.R.J. Res. 289 (82nd Cong.), S. 302 (82nd Cong.)

The legislative history of the original Trading with the Enemy Act (1917) and the 1952 Amendments is presented as a chronological chart with seven columns. The columns are (in order of presentation): the acting Congress; bills, resolutions, and laws entered and acted upon; *Congressional Record* and law review articles; executive orders; summaries of court cases; declarations of war and treaties; and, pertinent *New York Times* articles.

Record No.: 032
Bill No.: S. Res. 5 (65th Cong.)
Title of Act: Senate Cloture Rule

Title of Legislative History: Legislative History of Paragraphs 2 and 3 of
                                 Rule XXII of the Standing Rules of the United
                                 States Senate (Cloture Rule) IN Senate Cloture
                                 Rule: Limitation of Debate in the Congress of
                                 the U.S. and Legislative History of Paragraphs
                                 2 and 3 of Rule XXII of the Standing Rules of
                                 the U.S. Senate (Cloture Rule), 96th Cong., 1st
                                 Sess. (Comm. Print 1979)
Publication Date: 1979
Author: Senate Committee on Rules and Administration
Pages: v, 108

L/C Card Number: 79-600865
OCLC No.: 4616489
SuDoc No.: Y4.R86/2:C62/2/979
CIS No.: 79-S682-2
UPA Citation: N/A
Relevant Bills: S. Res. 195 (64th Cong.), S. Res. 5 (65th Cong.), S. Res.
    25 (80th Cong.), S. Res. 15 (81st Cong.), S. Res. 30 (85th Cong.), S.
    Res. 5 (86th Cong.), S. Res. 4 (94th Cong.), S. Res. 268 (94th Cong.)

The legislative history is a collection of five essays on Senate Rule XXII
(Cloture Rule). Part I is entitled "Limitation of Debate in the Congress of the
United States". It lists the Senate Rules, famous filibusters, and both sides of
the arguments on filibustering. Part II is entitled "Legislative History of
Paragraphs 2 and 3 of Rule XXII of the Standing Rules of the United States
Senate (Cloture Rule):" and contains the essays. The essays provides some of
the historical motivation for a change in the Rule.

Record No.: 033
Public Law No.: 66-85 (Sess. II)
Bill No.: S. 2775 (66th Cong.)
Statutes at Large Citation: 41 Stat. 437 (1920)
Title of Act: Mineral Lands Leasing Act of 1920

Title of Legislative History: Legislative History of Section 2(c) of the
                                 Mineral Lands Leasing Act of 1920 IN Repeal
                                 of Prohibition of Railroad Ownership of Coal
                                 Leases: Hearings on S. 1542 Before the
                                 Subcommittee on Energy and Mineral
                                 Resources of the Senate Committee on Energy
                                 and Natural Resources, 97th Cong., 1st Sess.
                                 (1981)

Publication Date: 1981
Author: Subcommittee on Energy and Mineral Resources, Senate Committee on Energy and Natural Resources
Pages: iii, 508

L/C Card Number: 81-603698
OCLC No.: 8004433
SuDoc No.: Y4.En2:97-32
CIS No.: 81-S311-70
UPA Citation: N/A
Relevant Bills: H.R. 14094 (63rd Cong.), H.R. 16136 (63rd Cong.), S. 1269 (66th Cong.), S. 2775 (66th Cong.)

The legislative activities dealing with The Mineral Leasing Act of 1920 as Amended produced a legislative history which contains more than the usual four components. The record contains letters prepared by the Departments of Interior and Justice for internal use. In addition, the record provides interpretive letters which were produced to augment departmental political positions. These documents, as well as the *Congressional Record* papers, give a more expansive view to the legislative history.

Record No.: 034
Public Law No.: 67-58 (Sess. II)
Bill No.: H.R. 7077 (67th Cong.)
Statutes at Large Citation: 42 Stat. 389 (1922)
Title of Act: To Increase the Force and Salaries in the Patent Office

Title of Legislative History: Patent Office Fees, Legislative History, Study of Subcommittee on Patents, Trademarks, and Copyrights, 85th Congress, 2nd Session, Pursuant to S. Res. 236, Study No. 13, 85th Cong., 2nd Sess. (Comm. Print 1958)

Publication Date: 1958
Author: Subcommittee on Patents, Trademarks, and Copyrights, Senate Committee on the Judiciary
Pages: vii, 16

L/C Card Number: 58-61541
OCLC No.: 4873731
SuDoc No.: Y4.J89/2:P27/3/no.13
CIS No.: Committee-Print: S0304
UPA Citation: N/A

Relevant Bills: H.R. 5011 (66th Cong.), H.R. 5012 (66th Cong.), H.R. 7010
(66th Cong.), H.R. 11984 (66th Cong.), H.R. 7077 (67th Cong.), H.R.
13487 (69th Cong.), H.R. 15537 (69th Cong.), S. 4812 (69th Cong.), S.
4956 (69th Cong.), H.R. 10076 (71st Cong.), H.R. 11267 (72nd Cong.),
H.R. 2520 (80th Cong.), H.R. 3700 (80th Cong.), S. 2328 (81st Cong.), S.
2433 (81st Cong.), H.R. 9794 (83rd Cong.), S. 3738 (83rd Cong.), H.R.
4983 (84th Cong.), H.R. 7416 (84th Cong.), H.R. 7151 (85th Cong.), S.
2156 (85th Cong.)

The legislative history is contained within the overall study of the fee and fee
schedules of the U.S. Patent Office. The study provides: the legislative history
from the Congressional actions; summary of provisions of proposed fee raises;
schedule of fees; and, related matters. The study is also available in the
reprint Research Studies in Patent Law (Buffalo: Hein, 1979).

Record No.: 035
Public Law No.: 69-344 (Sess. I)
Bill No.: S. 41 (69th Cong.)
Statutes at Large Citation: 44 Stat. 568 (1926)
Title of Act: Air Commerce Act of 1926

Title of Legislative History: Civil Aeronautics, Legislative History of Air
                                 Commerce Act of 1926, Approved May 20, 1926,
                                 with Miscellaneous Legal Materials Relating to
                                 Civil Air Navigation, Revision of 1923 Edition
                                 of Law Memoranda Upon Civil Aeronautics,
                                 Corrected to Aug. 1928, 78th Cong., 1st Sess.
                                 (Comm. Print 1943)
Publication Date: 1943
Author: House Committee on Interstate and Foreign Commerce
Pages: v, 178

L/C Card Number: 43-50976
OCLC No.: N/A
SuDoc No.: Y4.In8/4:Ae8/2-2
CIS No.: Committee-Print: H2673
UPA Citation: N/A
Relevant Bills: S. 41 (69th Cong.)

Documents comprising the legislative history of the Air Commerce Act of 1926
offer more than the ordinary. The expected documents are provided. In
addition, the collection contains: a comparative sidebar to the Senate and
House Reports; a summary of differences between the Houses; an article
prepared by the legislative counsel to the Senate; reports from the American
Bar Association and the Conference of Commissioners; texts from cases
dealing with trespass and nuisance from the flight of aircraft over land;

excerpts from state legislation on aeronautics; extracts from state bar associations; the text of the Uniform State Law on Aeronautics; and two early treaties on aviation.

Record No.: 036
Public Law No.: 69-347 (Sess. I)
Bill No.: H.R. 9463 (69th Cong.)
Statutes at Large Citation: 44 Stat. 577 (1926)
Title of Act: Railway Labor Act

Title of Legislative History: Legislative History of Railway Labor Act, As
                               Amended (1926-66), 93rd Cong., 2nd Sess. (
                               Comm. Print 1974)
Publication Date: 1974
Author: Subcommittee on Labor, Senate Committee on Labor and Public Welfare
Pages: v, 1381

L/C Card Number: 74-600995
OCLC No.: 861016
SuDoc No.: Y4.L11/2:R13/18/926-66
CIS No.: 74-S542-6
UPA Citation: N/A
Relevant Bills: H.R. 9463 (69th Cong.), H.R. 9861 (73rd Cong.), S. 3266
       (73rd Cong.), S. 2496 (74th Cong.), S. 3295 (81st Cong.), H.R.
       8344 (88th Cong.), H.R. 706 (89th Cong.)

The compilation contains a chronological history of public laws pertaining to labor relations between railroads and their employees including the Railway Labor Act of 1926 and the five amendments to this act through 1966. This history includes the text of the statute, bills, reports, and debates for each of these acts: Railway Labor Act as amended (1934), as amended (1936), as amended (1951), as Amendment of 1964, H.R. 8344 (88th Cong.), P.L. 88-542; Amendment of 1966, H.R. 706 (89th Cong.), P.L. 89-456.

Record No.: 037
Public Law No.: 69-347 (Sess. I)
Bill No.: H.R. 9463 (69th Cong.)
Statutes at Large Citation: 44 Stat. 577 (1926)
Title of Act: Railway Labor Act

Title of Legislative History: Federal Legislation to End Strikes,
                                  Documentary History, 90th Cong., 1st Sess.
                                  (Comm. Print 1967)
Publication Date: 1967
Author: Subcommittee on Labor, Senate Committee on Labor and Public
Welfare
Pages: ix, 1-667; v, 669-1354

L/C Card Number: 67-61687
OCLC No.: 305486
SuDoc No.: Y4.L11/2:St8/2/pt.1,2
CIS No.: Committee-Print: S0878
UPA Citation: N/A
Relevant Bills: H.R. 17700 (64th Cong.), H.R. 10453 (66th Cong.), H.R.
    9463 (69th Cong.), H.R. 5315 (72nd Cong.), H.R. 9861 (73rd Cong.), S.
    2496 (74th Cong.), S. 796 (78th Cong.), H.R. 4908 (79th Cong.), H.R.
    5262 (79th Cong.), H.R. 2861 (80th Cong.), H.R. 3020 (80th Cong.), S.
    55 (80th Cong.), S. 1126 (80th Cong.), H.R. 2032 (81st Cong.), S. 2999
    (82nd Cong.), H.R. 6590 (84th Cong.), S. 1555 (86th Cong.), H.R. 1897
    (88th Cong.), H.R. 2004 (88th Cong.), H.R. 2331 (88th Cong.), S.J. Res.
    102 (88th Cong.), H.R. 706 (89th Cong.), S.J. Res. 181 (89th Cong.),
    S.J. Res. 186 (89th Cong.)

The history traces the efforts of Congress to draft legislation to deal
with labor-management disputes.   It includes chapters which focus on
specific labor disputes arising under both the Railway Labor Act and the
Labor Management Relations Act of 1947 or Taft-Hartley Act. The chapters
proceed chronologically. The majority of the chapters include the text of a
public law with which Congress responded to a labor dispute or ongoing labor-
management problems, commentary on the legislation and dispute, or
discussion of the issues from books and journal articles. Two charts are added
to the legislative history: one summarizing legislation authorizing seizure of
industrial property; and, one summarizing seizures of industrial plants and
facilities by the President.

Record No.: 038
Public Law No.: 69-169 (Sess. II)
Bill No.: H.R. 9971 (69th Cong.)
Statutes at Large Citation: 44 Stat. 1162 (1927)
Title of Act: Radio Act of 1927

Title of Legislative History: Legislative History of Fairness Doctrine, Staff
                                 Study, 90th Cong., 2nd Sess. (1968)

Publication Date: 1968
Author: Special Subcommittee on Investigations, House Committee on Interstate and Foreign Commerce
Pages: v, 29

L/C Card Number: 79-600565
OCLC No.: 9371
SuDoc No.: Y4.In8/4:F16
CIS No.: Committee-Print: H1124
UPA Citation: N/A
Relevant Bills: H.R. 9971 (69th Cong.), H.R. 7716 (72nd Cong.), S. 3285 (73rd Cong.), S. 658 (82nd Cong.), H.R. 7985 (86th Cong.), S. 2424 (86th Cong.)

The Federal Communications Commission (FCC) efforts to produce and enforce the fairness doctrine through legislation provides the basis for the legislative history of the Radio Act of 1927; the Communications Act of 1934; and the Communications Act Amendments of 1952 and 1959. The compiled history describes and documents all the relevant issues: equal access opportunities to candidates for public office; the forum for discussion of any public questions; access for discussion of public questions to be voted upon at an election; and the exemptions for broadcasters.

Record No.: 039
Public Law No.: 70-460 (Sess. I)
Bill No.: H.R. 6103 (70th Cong.)
Statutes at Large Citation: 45 Stat. 467 (1928)
Title of Act: To Amend An Act Entitled "An Act Making Appropriations for Sundry Civil Expenses of the Government for Fiscal Year Ending June 30, 1884"

Title of Legislative History: Government Assistance to Invention and Research, Legislative History, Study of Subcommittee on Patents, Trademarks, and Copyrights, 86th Congress, 1st Session, Pursuant to S. Res. 53, Study No. 22, 86th Cong., 1st Sess. (Comm. Print 1959)
Publication Date: 1960
Author: Subcommittee on Patents, Trademarks, and Copyrights, Senate Committee on the Judiciary
Pages: xi, 199

L/C Card Number: 60-60470
OCLC No.: 16761429
SuDoc No.: Y4.J89/2:P27/3/no.22
CIS No.: Committee-Print: S0434
UPA Citation: N/A

Relevant Bills: H.R. 5 (29th Cong.), H.R. 20975 (63rd Cong.), H.R. 6103
(70th Cong.), H.R. 10435 (70th Cong.), H.R. 4692 (81st Cong.), S. 247
(81st Cong.), H.R. 3975 (82nd Cong.), S. 1537 (82nd Cong.), H.R. 12575
(85th Cong.)

The legislative history is presented as a three part study. Each part is the
attempt to focus on a primary issue. The title given to each treatment reveals
the focus: "Inventions Made by Government Employees; Inventions Made by
Nongovernment Employees or by Government Finances Research; and Patent
Extensions" [for veterans]. The study is also available in reprint as Research
Studies in Patent Law (Buffalo: Hein, 1979).

Record No.: 040
Public Law No.: 71-863 (Sess. II)
Bill No.: H.R. 10630 (71st Cong.)
Statutes at Large Citation: 46 Stat. 1016 (1930)
Title of Act: Veterans' Administration Act

Title of Legislative History: Provision of Federal Benefits for Veterans,
                                 Historical Analysis of Major Veterans'
                                 Legislation, 1862-1954, Dec. 28, 1955, 84th
                                 Cong., 1st Sess. (Comm. Print 1955)
Publication Date: 1955
Author: House Committee on Veterans' Affairs
Pages: vii, 305

L/C Card Number: 56-60311
OCLC No.: 1462909
SuDoc No.: Y4.V64/3:B31/2
CIS No.: Committee-Print: H0213
UPA Citation: N/A
Relevant Bills: H.R. 10630 (71st Cong.)

The legislation associated with the rights of veterans and the machinations of
the Veteran's Administration spans decades and is voluminous. This is the
legislative history of the significant pieces of legislation within the time frame
of 1862 - 1954 -- roughly from the Civil War to the Korean War. The history is
divided into eight chapters: "Disability Payments; Service Pensions;
Dependents' Benefits, Medical and Hospital Care; Education and Vocational
Rehabilitations; Insurance; Domiciliary Care; and, Employment Preferences
and Other Privileges" with each chapter in chronological order. It provides a
subject index, with notes, and a table of all examined statutes.

Record No.: 041
Public Law No.: 71-117 (Sess. III)
Bill No.: S. 5776 (71st Cong.)
Statutes at Large Citation: 46 Stat. 1084 (1931)
Title of Act: Employment Stabilization Act of 1931

Title of Legislative History: History of the Employment Stabilization Act of
                                 1931.Report Relating to the Bill (S. 380) to
                                 Establish a National Policy and Program for
                                 Assuring Continuing Full Employment in a
                                 Free Competitive Economy, Through the
                                 Concerted Efforts of Industry, Agriculture,
                                 Labor, State, and Local Governments, and the
                                 Federal Government, 79th Cong., 1st Sess.
                                 (Comm. Print 1945)
Publication Date: 1945
Author: Senate Committee on Banking and Currency
Pages: vi, 25

L/C Card Number: N/A
OCLC No.: 20870443
SuDoc No.: N/A
CIS No.: Committee-Print: S1749
UPA Citation: N/A
Relevant Bills: S. 3059 (71st Cong.), S. 5776 (71st Cong.)

The historical treatment of the Employment Stabilization Act of 1931 provides
the expected documents of a legislative history.   It also includes the
transmittal letter from the Chair of the Senate Committee to the full
Committee to set the political tone.   The letter is presented as part of the
compiled history by the Committee.   The history is treated as a report with
major divisions set out: "Background..., including explanation, comparisons,
precedents, and related legislation; Legislative history..., with Senate actions,
House actions, Conference committee work, Presidential action, State actions;
Administration..., with emphasis on the Federal Employment Stabilization
Board and its activities."   Appendices are set out separately with notes, full
texts, and selected reports being designated.

Record No.: 042
Public Law No.: 71-411 (Sess. III)
Bill No.: S. 5904 (71st Cong.)
Statutes at Large Citation: 46 Stat. 1494 (1931)
Title of Act: Davis-Bacon Act

Title of Legislative History: Legislative History of Davis-Bacon Act, 87th
                                Cong., 2nd Sess. (Comm. Print 1962)
Publication Date: 1962
Author: House Committee on Education and Labor
Pages: v, 90

L/C Card Number: 64-61562
OCLC No.: 7440986
SuDoc No.: Y4.Ed8/1:D29/4
CIS No.: Committee-Print: H1923
UPA Citation: N/A
Relevant Bills: H.R. 17069 (69th Cong.), H.R. 11141 (70th Cong.), H.R.
     7995 (71st Cong.), H.R. 9232 (71st Cong.), H.R. 16619 (71st Cong.), S.
     5904 (71st Cong.), H.R.J. Res. 38 (72nd Cong.),   H.R. 12 (72nd Cong.),
     H.R. 122 (72nd Cong.), H.R. 7005 (72nd Cong.), H.R. 7254 (72nd
     Cong.), H.R. 10739 (72nd Cong.), H.R. 11865 (72nd Cong.), S. 3847
     (72nd Cong.), S. 3303 (74th Cong.), H.R. 9021 (76th Cong.), S. 3650
     (76th Cong.), H.R. 3325 (77th Cong.), H.R. 5312 (77th Cong.)

The House Committee on Education and Labor produced this document which
is a combination of legislative history and historical treatment of the process.
It is divided into four parts. Part I contains a brief narrative of the events
leading to the passage and amendment of the Davis-Bacon Act. Part II has
the bibliography of the legislative materials as originally passed in 1931 and
the 1932 Amendment which was vetoed by the President. Part III consists of
reproductions of selected laws and documents. The documents in Part III
provide the veto message as well as the memorandum on the 1932. Part IV is
a comparison of text between the present Act and the original Act.

Record No.: 043
Public Law No.: 71-411 (Sess. III)
Bill No.: S. 5904 (71st Cong.)
Statutes at Large Citation: 46 Stat. 1494 (1931)
Title of Act: Davis-Bacon Act

Title of Legislative History: Davis-Bacon Act: History, Administration, Pro
                                and Con Arguments, and Congressional
                                Proposals
Publication Date: 1978
Author: Joseph F. Fulton of the Congressional Research Service
Pages: 64

L/C Card Number: N/A
OCLC No.: 12347179
SuDoc No.: N/A
CIS No.: N/A
UPA Citation: UPA Film No.: MS 78-79 Supp., Reel No. VIII, Frame No. 0919.
CRS No.: 78-161E.
Relevant Bills: S. 5904 (71st Cong.), S. 3303 (74th Cong.), S. 3650 (76th Cong.), H.R. 3325 (77th Cong.), H.R. 5312 (77th Cong.), H.R. 11602 (86th Cong.), H.R. 6041 (88th Cong.), H.R. 6100 (95th Cong.), S. 1540 (95th Cong.)

The Congressional Research Service has produced the legislative history for the Davis-Bacon Act of 1931, as amended. The history includes the texts of the 1935 and 1964 Amendments. The 1941 and 1960 are discussed, but full text is not given. The history concludes with proposals to reduce Federal construction costs. An Appendix provides a list of statutes which are patterned after the Davis-Bacon Act in that the predetermined wage rates from the Secretary of Labor are applicable.

Record No.: 044
Public Law No.: 71-411 (Sess. III)
Bill No.: S. 5904 (71st Cong.)
Statutes at Large Citation: 46 Stat. 1494 (1931)
Title of Act: Davis-Bacon Act

Title of Legislative History: Davis-Bacon Act, as Amended, IN Legal Compilation, Statutes and Legislative History, Executive Orders, Regulations, Guidelines, and Reports: [General, with Bibliographies]
Publication Date: 1973
Author: Environmental Protection Agency
Pages: xxxvi, 1233-1867

L/C Card Number: 73-602602
OCLC No.: 800286
SuDoc No.: EP 1.5/3:G28/v.3
CIS No.: N/A
UPA Citation: N/A
Relevant Bills: H.R. 16619 (71st Cong.), S. 5904 (71st Cong.), S. 3303 (74th Cong.), H.R. 9021 (76th Cong.), S. 3650 (76th Cong.), H.R. 11602 (86th Cong.), H.R. 6041 (88th Cong.)

The Environmental Protection Agency has produced the legislative history as one of its own reports, to wit, Legal Compilation: Statutes and Legislative History, Executive Orders, Regulations, Guidelines and Reports (Washington, D.C.: Environmental Protection Agency, 1973). It is published separately. This print of the history contains the text of the original Davis-Bacon Act, plus the 1935, 1940, 1960, and 1964 Amendments. Each public law is followed by reprints of reports and excerpts from the *Congressional Record*. In addition, the Reorganization Plan No. 14 of 1950, Presidential Proclamations No. 4031 and 4040 are given.

Record No.: 045
Public Law No.: 72-271 (Sess. I)
Bill No.: S. 1525 (72nd Cong.)
Statutes at Large Citation: 47 Stat. 326 (1932)
Title of Act: Lindbergh Kidnapping Act

Title of Legislative History: Lindbergh Kidnapping Act: A Legislative History and an Analysis of H.R. 4191 and H.R. 8722 as Proposed Amendments, IN Amendments to the Federal Kidnapping Statute: Hearings Before the Subcommittee on Crime of the House Committee on the Judiciary, 93rd Congress, 2nd Session (1974)
Publication Date: 1974
Author: Subcommittee on Crime, House Committee on the Judiciary
Pages: iv, 119

L/C Card Number: 74-602300
OCLC No.: 1092376
SuDoc No.: Y4.J89/1:93-38
CIS No.: 74-H521-57
UPA Citation: N/A
Relevant Bills: S. 1525 (72nd Cong.), S. 2252 (73rd Cong.), S. 2421 (73rd Cong.), H.R. 3190 (80th Cong.), H.R. 800 (84th Cong.), H.R. 15883 (92nd Cong.), H.R. 4191 (93rd Cong.), H.R. 8722 (93rd Cong.)

The legislative history is an analysis and history associated with the legislative efforts to rewrite the Lindbergh Kidnapping Act. The text discusses the original Act and all Amendments. An analysis of bills introduced, but not passed, is provided.

Record No.: 046
Public Law No.: 73-89 (Sess. I)
Bill No.: H.R. 5661 (73rd Cong.)
Statutes at Large Citation: 48 Stat. 162 (1933)
Title of Act: Banking Act of 1933

Title of Legislative History: Legislative History of the Glass-Steagull and
Bank Holding Company Acts IN Brokerage
and Related Commercial Bank Services:
Hearings in Furtherance of the Study of the
Securities Activities of Commercial Banks
before the Subcommittee on Securities of the
Senate Committee on Banking, Housing, and
Urban Affairs, 94th Cong., 2nd Sess. (1976)

Publication Date: 1976
Author: Subcommittee on Securities, Senate Committee on Banking, Housing,
and Urban Affairs
Pages: vi, 1140

L/C Card Number: N/A
OCLC No.: 2694759
SuDoc No.: Y4.B22/3:B78/2
CIS No.: 77-S241-11
UPA Citation: N/A
Relevant Bills: H.R. 5661 (73rd Cong.), H.R. 6227 (84th Cong.), S. 2577 (84th
Cong.), H.R. 6778 (91st Cong.)

The legislative history of the Glass-Seagull and Bank Holding Company Acts
represent the desires of its authors to provide historical background as well as
the documents of a legislative history. The papers constituting historical
background are: a memorandum prepared by the Securities Industry
Association; an appendix to the memorandum; and, analytically discrete
sections dealing with the individual laws.

Record No.: 047
Public Law No.: 74-372 (Sess. I)
Bill No.: S. 1958 (74th Cong.)
Statutes at Large Citation: 49 Stat. 449 (1935)
Title of Act: National Labor Relations Act

Title of Legislative History: Legislative History of the Exclusion of
Agricultural Employees from the National
Labor Relations Act of 1935 and the Fair Labor
Standards Act of 1938

Publication Date: 1966
Author: James R. Wason of the Congressional Research Service
Pages: 32

L/C Card Number: N/A
OCLC No.: 21779450
SuDoc No.: N/A
CIS No.: N/A
UPA Citation: UPA Film No.: MS, Reel No. 1, Frame No. 0194.
CRS No.: HD 1521, E-152
Relevant Bills: S. 2926 (73rd Cong.), H.R. 7978 (74th Cong.), S. 1958 (74th
    Cong.), H.R. 7200 (75th Cong.), S. 2475 (75th Cong.)

The legislative history was produced under the aegis of the Congressional
Research Service to delineate a particular area of the National Labor
Relations Acts, namely the exclusion of agricultural employees. The first part
of the history traces the development of the exemption (exclusion) from the Act
by reviewing similar proposed laws. The second part deals specifically with
the exemption. It is in this section that the discussion of the definition of
agricultural employees was broadened to incorporate employees handling,
transporting, packing, or processing agricultural commodities. The appendices
give the names and statements of individuals who were in support of and in
opposition to the exemptions.

Record No.: 048
Public Law No.: 74-372 (Sess. I)
Bill No.: S. 1958 (74th Cong.)
Statutes at Large Citation: 49 Stat. 449 (1935)
Title of Act: National Labor Relations Act

Title of Legislative History: Statutes and Congressional Reports Pertaining
                                to National Labor Relations Board
Publication Date: 1945
Author: National Labor Relations Board
Pages: i, 141

L/C Card Number: 45-37851
OCLC No.: 6295691
SuDoc No.: LR1.5:St2/945
CIS No.: N/A
UPA Citation: N/A
Relevant Bills: H.R. 6288 (74th Cong.), H.R. 7978 (74th Cong.), S. 1958 (74th
    Cong.)

The legislative history is not confined to the materials related to the National Labor Relations Board. Included with the Board documents are related laws, specifically the National Labor Relations Act, and a progress chart of the laws considered.

Record No.: 049
Public Law No.: 74-372 (Sess. I)
Bill No.: S. 1958 (74th Cong.)
Statutes at Large Citation: 49 Stat. 449 (1935)
Title of Act: National Labor Relations Act

Title of Legislative History: Legislative History of the National Labor
                                Relations Act, 1935
Publication Date: 1949
Author: National Labor Relations Board
Pages: clxxxi, 1616; 1617-3305

L/C Card Number: 49-45500
OCLC No.: 8840947
SuDoc No.: LR1.5:L11/6/v.1,2
CIS No.: N/A
UPA Citation: N/A
Relevant Bills: H.R.J. Res. 375 (73rd Cong.), H.R. 8423 (73rd Cong.), S. 2926 (73rd Cong.), S.J. Res. 143 (73rd Cong.), H.R. 6187 (74th Cong.), H.R. 6288 (74th Cong.), H.R. 7937 (74th Cong.), H.R. 7978 (74th Cong.), S. 1958 (74th Cong.)

The legislative history which belongs to the National Labor Relations Act is a massive two volume set. The sheer quantity of the information, primary and secondary, required an internal organization as well as an external presentation. The internal organization is to set out the various subject matter areas within the individual volume. Judicious use of subject matter headings is apparent. The management of the external presentation forced the publication into two volumes with each running in excess of one thousand pages. The focal points of Volume I are: a listing of all pertinent documents reprinted and indexed; a chronological statement; a sectional index; a topical index; and, an index of cases and names. The four components that constitute a legislative history are presented in historical order. Volume II is devoted almost exclusively to giving the data of the four components. However, of special note is the inclusion of the statements of individuals and of Briefs filed on behalf of persons and professional associations.

Record No.: 050
Public Law No.: 74-814 (Sess. I)
Bill No.: H.R. 8870 (74th Cong.)
Statutes at Large Citation: 49 Stat. 977 (1935)
Title of Act: Federal Alcohol Administration Act

Title of Legislative History: Legislative History of Federal Alcohol
                                Administration Act
Publication Date: 1935
Author: Federal Alcohol Control Administration, Office of General
Counsel, Russell, W.A.
Pages: ix, 205

L/C Card Number: 35-26890
OCLC No.: 6282679
SuDoc No.: Y3.F31/10:2L52
CIS No.: N/A
UPA Citation: N/A
Relevant Bills: H.R. 8539 (74th Cong.), H.R. 8870 (74th Cong.)

The history is arranged according to sections of the Federal Alcohol
Administration Act. The text of the Federal Alcohol Administration Act is
quoted and accompanied by extensive notes. The notes refer to related
materials in hearings, committee reports, and debates. The introductory
material includes a chronological table and a table of sources/prints of the act,
committee hearings, committee reports and debates. There are six appendices
which include the texts of H.R. 8870 (74th Cong.) as passed.

Record No.: 051
Public Law No.: 74-858 (Sess. II)
Bill No.: H.R. 8555 (74th Cong.)
Statutes at Large Citation: 49 Stat. 1985 (1936)
Title of Act: Merchant Marine Act, 1936

Title of Legislative History: Index to Legislative History, Merchant Marine
                                Act, 1936 , 81st Cong., 1st Sess. (Comm. Print
                                1949)
Publication Date: 1949
Author: House Committee on Merchant Marine and Fisheries
Pages: iii, 87

L/C Card Number: N/A
OCLC No.: 17392524
SuDoc No.: N/A
CIS No.: Committee-Print: H8396
UPA Citation: N/A

Relevant Bills: H.R. 7521 (74th Cong.), H.R. 7981 (74th Cong.), H.R.
8555 (74th Cong.), S. 2582 (74th Cong.), S. 3376 (74th Cong.), S. 3500
(74th Cong.), S. 3501 (74th Cong.), S. 4110 (74th Cong.), S. 4332 (74th
Cong.)

The document is a collection of indices to the materials which constitute the
legislative history of the Merchant Marine Act of 1936. Two simple lists are
used to provide citations to bill versions and to subject headings used to
compose the indices. The indices can be separated and used as individual
access points to the Act. The first index traces the development of the
language of the Merchant Marine Act of 1936 across the legislative activities of
the entire 74th Congress. The follow-on indices cover: hearings, subject
headings; debates; sections of the Act; and, miscellaneous documents and
reports.

Record No.: 052
Public Law No.: 75-229 (Sess. I)
Bill No.: S. 595 (75th Cong.)
Statutes at Large Citation: 50 Stat. 189 (1937)
Title of Act: Communications Act of 1934, Amendment of 1937

Title of Legislative History: Communications Act of 1979: Hearings on H.R.
3333 Before the Subcommittee on
Communications of the House Committee on
Interstate and Foreign Commerce, 96th Cong.,
1st Sess. (1979)
Publication Date: 1980
Author: Subcommittee on Communications, House Committee on Interstate
and Foreign Commerce
Pages: 525

L/C Card Number: 80-602432
OCLC No.: 6667822
SuDoc No.: Y4.In8/4:96-125
CIS No.: N/A
UPA Citation: N/A
Relevant Bills: S. 3285 (73rd Cong.), S. 595 (75th Cong.), S. 2453 (83rd Cong.)

The legislative history of the Communications Act of 1934 is Appendix B in the
collection. It treats each public law separately and adds a summary. The
history includes a discussion of the Convention on Safety of Life at Sea, May
31, 1929, 50 Stat. 1121, T.S. No. 910, 136 L.N.T.S. 81 and the Convention on
Safety of Life at Sea, June 10, 1948, 3 U.S.T. 3450, T.I.A.S. No. 2495, 164
U.N.T.S. 113. The significance of the inclusion is that these conventions were

used as models for the laws enacted are not ordinarily a part of a legislative history. In addition, citations to several 1958 court cases are given which interpreted these laws.

Record No.: 053
Public Law No.: 75-382 (Sess. I)
Bill No.: H.R. 7519 (75th Cong.)
Statutes at Large Citation: 50 Stat. 307 (1937)
Title of Act: Railroad Retirement Act of 1937

Title of Legislative History: The Legislative History of the Railroad
                                Retirement and Railroad Unemployment
                                Insurance Systems
Publication Date: 1978
Author: David B. Schreiber of the Railroad Retirement Board
Pages: xv, 492

L/C Card Number: 79-600816
OCLC No.: 4121536
SuDoc No.: RR1.2:H62
CIS No.: N/A
UPA Citation: N/A
Relevant Bills: S. 3231 (73rd Cong.), H.R. 8651 (74th Cong.), H.R. 8652
     (74th Cong.), H.R. 7519 (75th Cong.), H.R. 7589 (75th Cong.),
     H.R. 10127 (75th Cong.), S. 3920 (76th Cong.), H.R. 1362
     (79th Cong.), H.R. 6766 (80th Cong.), H.R. 3669 (82nd Cong.), S. 2639
     (82nd Cong.), H.R. 356 (83rd Cong.), H.R. 7840 (83rd Cong.), H.R. 4744
     (84th Cong.), S. 3616 (84th Cong.), H.R. 5610 (86th Cong.), H.R. 5075
     (87th Cong.), S. 2395 (87th Cong.), H.R. 8100 (88th Cong.), H.R. 6675
     (89th Cong.), H.R. 10874 (89th Cong.), H.R. 14355 (89th Cong.), H.R.
     17285 (89th Cong.), H.R. 14563 (90th Cong.), H.R. 13300 (91st
     Cong.), H.R. 15733 (91st Cong.), H.R. 6444 (92nd Cong.), H.R.
     15927 (92nd Cong.), H.R. 7200 (93rd Cong.), H.R. 15301 (93rd Cong.),
     H.R. 8714 (94th Cong.)

The legislative history of the railroad retirement and unemployment insurance systems is set out in chronological fashion within the time period of 1934 - 1975. The structure is provided to trace the development of these railroad compensation systems. The broader issues of a separate railroad retirement system are discussed in addition to the ordinary documentation of a legislative history. The history concludes with a list of public laws which affected the retirement and unemployment insurance laws as well as a list of personal names of individuals who were associated with the legislative activities.

Record No.: 054
Public Law No.: 75-675 (Sess. III)
Bill No.: S. 5 (75th Cong.)
Statutes at Large Citation: 52 Stat. 1040 (1938)
Title of Act: Food, Drug, and Cosmetic Act

Title of Legislative History: A Legislative History of the Federal Food,
                               Drug, and Cosmetic Act and Its Amendments
Publication Date: 1979
Author: Department of Health, Education, and Welfare, Public Health Service,
Food and Drug Administration
Pages: various

L/C Card Number: 80-600754
OCLC No.: 5929678
SuDoc No.: HE20.4005:F73/2/v.1-24,app.A-J
CIS No.: N/A
UPA Citation: N/A
Relevant Bills: S. 5 (75th Cong.), H.R. 3298 (82nd Cong.)

The legislative history which was compiled by the HEW to cover the Federal
Food, Drug, and Cosmetic Act and its Amendments (1933 - 1974) is a thirty-
four volume set (twenty-four and ten appendices). It was intended to show the
activity across twenty Congressional periods, the 73d Congress through the
93d Congress. Each volume is set out in chronological fashion will Bill Digests
provided for each entry. Each Bill Digest has its *Congressional Record* cite.
The Bills are reproduced in full with the remaining components of a legislative
history attached. The Appendices contain additional hearings which are
grouped by subject matter. An added feature in Appendix J is the inclusion of
the letters from government officers to the appropriate heads of agencies and
committee chairs or members expressing concern related to the language of
the amendments and to the perceived conflicts of interest. These letters cut
across the three branches of the Federal government.

Record No.: 055
Public Law No.: 76-410 (Sess. I)
Bill No.: S. 1871 (76th Cong.)
Statutes at Large Citation: 53 Stat. 1147 (1939)
Title of Act: Hatch Act (Political Activity)

Title of Legislative History: Hatch Act Proscription Against Participation
                               by State and Federal Employees in Political
                               Management and Political Campaigns: A
                               Legislative History

Publication Date: 1975
Author: Patricia Fiori of the Congressional Research Service
Pages: 71

L/C Card Number: N/A
OCLC No.: 22851759
SuDoc No.: N/A
CIS No.: N/A
UPA Citation: UPA Film No.: MS, Reel No. IV, Frame No. 0983.
CRS No.: JK 516 U.S.G., 75-31A, 561/103R
Relevant Bills: S. 1871 (76th Cong.), S. 3046 (76th Cong.)

The Hatch Act of 1939 and the 1940 Amendments contain the prohibition for Federal executive agency employees from taking an active part in political management or in political campaigns. The legislative history covers this prohibition stated in §9(a) of the Act. The text of the original Hatch Act is given along with remaining documents which constitute a legislative history. Documentation ins provided for the 1940 Amendments which extended coverage to state employees who are paid from Federal funds. Additional materials are in the Appendix: the 1939 report from the Senate Special Committee to Investigate Senatorial Campaign Expenditures and [the] Use of Governmental Funds; the Presidential message on signing the Hatch Act; a summary of the rules of the Civil Service Commission; miscellaneous Federal government documents; and, a list of references from the 75th Congress through the 93d Congress.

Record No.: 056
Public Law No.: 76-720 (Sess. III)
Bill No.: S. 4164 (76th Cong.)
Statutes at Large Citation: 54 Stat. 885 (1940)
Title of Act: Selective Training and Service Act of 1940

Title of Legislative History: Selective Service Act, Its Legislative History,
                                 Amendments, Appropriations, Cognates and
                                 Prior Instruments of Security: Special
                                 Monograph No. 2
Publication Date: 1954
Author: Selective Service System
Pages: various

L/C Card Number: 55-61165
OCLC No.: 3825787
SuDoc No.: Y3.Se4:17/2/v.1-5
CIS No.: N/A
UPA Citation: N/A
Relevant Bills: H.R. 10132 (76th Cong.), S. 4164 (76th Cong.)

The legislative history of the Selective Training and Service Act of 1940 is a five volume set within a series of special monographs issued under the auspices of the Selective Service System. The five volume set is officially designated: Special Monograph No. 2. The stated purpose of the monograph is to trace the historical background to the Act -- this is in addition to the documents of the legislative history. The Monograph has its review and clearance statement signed by Lewis B. Hershey, Director. The set is an exhaustive and definitive treatment of the Act. Volumes I and II are divided into chapter segments which cover all sections of the Act. One of the most valuable aspects of the entire set is Chapter III in Volume One. It starts the historical framework with the English Cradle, suitably called 'the Anglo-Saxon Canvas, Norman Pigment' and continues through the American Colonial period and the Reformation of 1903. The Appendices which have the supporting documents of this early historical treatment plus the supporting legislative "foreground" documents are published as Volumes III (A-B), IV (B-D), and V (E-F). Volume IV contains a catalog of Amendments to Selective Service Act (no date) which is in chart format and tracks the legislative activities across the Congresses. Volume V has an extensive bibliography which covers all stated sources, United States and foreign.

Record No.: 057
Public Law No.: 77-312 (Sess. II)
Bill No.: H.R. 6293 (77th Cong.)
Statutes at Large Citation: 56 Stat. 278 (1942)
Title of Act: To Establish a Women's Army Auxiliary Corps for Service
        with the Army of the United States

Title of Legislative History: Women's Auxiliary Army Corps and Women's
        Army Corps, IN To Provide Recognition to the
        Women's Air Force Service Pilots: Hearings
        Before the Select Subcommittee to Review
        WASP Bills of the House Committee on
        Veterans' Affairs, 95th Cong., 1st Sess. (1977)
Publication Date: 1977
Author: Select Subcommittee to Review WASP Bills, House Committee on Veterans' Affairs
Pages: iv, 461

L/C Card Number: 78-602235
OCLC No.: 3901502
SuDoc No.: Y4.V64/3:W84
CIS No.: 78-H761-10
UPA Citation: N/A
Relevant Bills: H.R. 4906 (77th Cong.), H.R. 6293 (77th Cong.), H.R.
      7280 (77th Cong.), S. 2751 (77th Cong.), H.R. 1188 (78th Cong.), S.

The legislative history of the Women's Auxiliary Army Corps and the Women's Army Corps was prepared in conjunction with the hearings related to the Women's Air Force Service Pilots (WASP). The legislative history is contained within the presentation of documentation of the hearings of the 77th Congress related to these matters. The materials include an article on the history of the Women's Air Force Service Pilots.

Record No.: 058
Public Law No.: 78-120 (Sess. I)
Bill No.: H.R. 2570 (78th Cong.)
Statutes at Large Citation: 57 Stat. 126 (1943)
Title of Act: Current Tax Payment Act of 1943

Title of Legislative History: Legislative History of Current Tax Payment
                                Act of 1943, 79th Cong., 2nd Sess. (Comm. Print
                                1946)
Publication Date: 1946
Author: Department of Justice
Pages: iii, 15

L/C Card Number: N/A
OCLC No.: N/A
SuDoc No.: J12:T19/3
CIS No.: Committee-Print: S4104
UPA Citation: N/A
Relevant Bills: H.R. 2042 (78th Cong.), H.R. 2218 (78th Cong.), H.R. 2245 (78th Cong.), H.R. 2277 (78th Cong.), H.R. 2570 (78th Cong.), H.R. 2577 (78th Cong.)

The legislative history of the Current Tax Payment Act of 1943 was prepared by Carleton Fox at the Department of Justice to provide materials to the Act in addition to the expected components of a legislative history. Specifically, Fox reveals the step by step process of the development of the Act and adds the relevant secondary source material cites. The official documents are reprinted in 109 *Internal Revenue Acts of the United States, 1909-1950* (B. Reams, editor, Buffalo: Hein, 1979).

Record No.: 059
Public Law No.: 78-239 (Sess. I)
Bill No.: H.R. 1900 (78th Cong.)
Statutes at Large Citation: 57 Stat. 564 (1943)
Title of Act: Renegotiation Act (War Contracts), Amendment of 1943

Title of Legislative History: Legislative History of Public Law 149, 78th
Cong., 1st Sess., July 14, 1943
Publication Date: 1946
Author: Department of Justice
Pages: iv, 65

L/C Card Number: 46-27950
OCLC No.: N/A
SuDoc No.: J1.2:W19/6
CIS No.: N/A
UPA Citation: N/A
Relevant Bills: H.R. 3642 (77th Cong.), H.R. Res. 347 (77th Cong.), H.R. 7304
(77th Cong.), H.R. Res. 162 (77th Cong.), H.R. 1900 (78th Cong.), H.R.
2380 (78th Cong.)

The legislative history addresses only the efforts of the 77th and 78th
Congressional sessions to deal with the question of brokers' fees and Federal
government war contracts. The history summarizes portions of the public
laws passed in 1942 and 1944; but, the emphasis is with the 1943 endeavors.
The history provides the materials in excerpted format with citations to
relevant executive orders and investigations.

Record No.: 060
Public Law No.: 78-210 (Sess. II)
Bill No.: H.R. 4646 (78th Cong.)
Statutes at Large Citation: 58 Stat. 231 (1944)
Title of Act: Individual Income Tax Act of 1944

Title of Legislative History: Legislative History of the Standard Deduction
and the Zero Bracket Amount in Federal Income
Taxation IN Charitable Contribution
Deductions: Hearings on S. 219 Before the
Subcommittee on Taxation and Debt
Management Generally of the Senate
Committee on Finance, 96th Cong., 2nd Sess.
(1980)
Publication Date: 1980
Author: Subcommittee on Taxation and Debt Management Generally, Senate
Committee on Finance
Pages: vi, 572

L/C Card Number: 80-602151
OCLC No.: 6319473
SuDoc No.: Y4.F49:C76/8
CIS No.: 80-S361-33
UPA Citation: N/A
Relevant Bills: H.R. 4646 (78th Cong.)

The legislative history was prepared by the Congressional Research Service to provide an historical context to the 1980 hearings on the Individual Income Tax Act of 1944. The specific issue of the history is: whether the standard deduction options was intended to replace all itemized deductions, including the charitable deduction. The critical item which has been added to the standard legislative history documents is the extensive use of materials from the 1944 Congressional debates.

Record No.: 061
Public Law No.: 78-665 (Sess. II)
Bill No.: H.R. 4485 (78th Cong.)
Statutes at Large Citation: 58 Stat. 887 (1944)
Title of Act: Flood Control Act of 1944

Title of Legislative History: Federal Power Marketing Revolving Fund Act
                                of 1979: Hearing on S. 734 and S. 1440 Before the
                                Subcommittee on Energy Conservation and
                                Supply of the Senate Committee on Energy and
                                Natural Resources, 96th Cong., 1st Sess. (1979)
Publication Date: 1980
Author: Subcommittee on Energy Conservation and Supply, Senate Committee on Energy and Natural Resources
Pages: iii, 486

L/C Card Number: 80-600793
OCLC No.: 6075952
SuDoc No.: Y4.En2:96-57
CIS No.: 80-S311-17
UPA Citation: N/A
Relevant Bills: H.R. 3961 (78th Cong.), H.R. 4485 (78th Cong.), H.R.
        6335 (79th Cong.), H.R. 3123 (80th Cong.), H.R. 6705 (80th
        Cong.), H.R. 3838 (81st Cong.), H.R. 7786 (81st Cong.), H.R.
        3790 (82nd Cong.), H.R. 7176 (82nd Cong.)

The document is designed to present the record of the hearings on the Federal Power Marketing Revolving Fund Act of 1979. The legislative history of the Flood Control Act of 1944 is provided as an appendix to the document. The appendix also contains the legislative histories of the Appropriations Acts 1947 - 1953, Department of the Interior, as they relate to the funding of the Southwestern Power Administration.

Record No.: 062
Public Law No.: 79-251 (Sess. II)
Bill No.: S. 2 (79th Cong.)
Statutes at Large Citation: 60 Stat. 170 (1946)
Title of Act: Federal Airport Act

Title of Legislative History: Legislative History of Federal Airport Act,
                               Public Law 377, Chap. 251, 79th Cong., 2nd
                               Sess., Apr. 1948
Publication Date: 1948
Author: Department of Commerce, Civil Aeronautics Administration
Pages: iv, 659; iv, 799

L/C Card Number: 48-46423
OCLC No.: 1965739
SuDoc No.: C31.105:F31/2/v.1-2
CIS No.: N/A
UPA Citation: N/A
Relevant Bills: H.R. 4 (78th Cong.), H.R. 3170 (78th Cong.), H.R. 3615 (78th
    Cong.), S. 2 (79th Cong.), S. 34 (79th Cong.)

The legislative history is a compilation of all the printed records and
documents reflecting Congressional intent relating to the enactment of the
Federal Airport Act. This intent was the basis for the formulation of early
administrative policies of the Civil Aeronautics Administration. Volume I
contains the text of the Senate bills, hearings, reports, and debates. Volume II
presents the House bills, committee reports, and debates. The text of the final
act is included.

Record No.: 063
Public Law No.: 79-324 (Sess. II)
Bill No.: S. 7 (79th Cong.)
Statutes at Large Citation: 60 Stat. 237 (1946)
Title of Act: Administrative Procedure Act

Title of Legislative History: Administrative Procedure Act, Legislative
                               History, 79th Congress, 1944-46, S. Doc No.
                               248, 79th Cong., 2nd Sess. (1946)
Publication Date: 1946
Author: Senate Committee on the Judiciary
Pages: v, 458

L/C Card Number: 46-27794
OCLC No.: 8808801
SuDoc No.: Y1.1/2:serial 11034
CIS No.: N/A
UPA Citation: N/A

Relevant Bills: S. 7 (79th Cong.), H.R. 184 (79th Cong.), H.R. 339 (79th Cong.), H.R. 1117 (79th Cong.), H.R. 1203 (79th Cong.), H.R. 1206 (79th Cong.), H.R. 2602 (79th Cong.)

This legislative history originally published as S. Doc. No. 248, 79th Cong., 2nd Sess. (1946) is reprinted in Volume 113, *Internal Revenue Acts of the United States, 1909-1950* (B. Reams, editor, Buffalo: Hein, 1979). The full text of the act is followed by the Senate Judiciary Committee print, House Judiciary Committee hearings, and the reports of the Senate and House Judiciary Committees. Appendix B contains the proceedings in the House and Senate as taken from the *Congressional Record.* Access to all documents is gained through three detailed indexes: 1) an index to sections of the act; 2) a subject index; 3) an index of names, agencies, and organizations.

Record No.: 064
Public Law No.: 80-120 (Sess. I)
Bill No.: H.R. 3020 (80th Cong.)
Statutes at Large Citation: 61 Stat. 136 (1947)
Title of Act: Labor-Management Relations Act, 1947

Title of Legislative History: Legislative History of Labor Management
                                  Relations Act, 1947
Publication Date: 1948
Author: National Labor Relations Board
Pages: xcvi, 1680

L/C Card Number: 48-50097
OCLC No.: 2002414
SuDoc No.: LR1.5:L11/3/v.1,2
CIS No.: N/A
UPA Citation: N/A
Relevant Bills: H.R. 3020 (80th Cong.), S. 1126 (80th Cong.)

This two volume work is a compilation of the basic records constituting the legislative history of the Labor-Management Relations Act, 1947. It includes the full text of the act, the House and Senate bills -- including early drafts of bills, and all the House, Senate, and Conference reports. House and Senate proceedings, as recorded in the *Congressional Record*, are also included. A comparison of the National Labor Relations Act of 1935, P.L. 74-198, with Title I of the Labor-Management Relations Act, 1947 concludes the history. Congressional hearings and drafts of related bills are not included. All documents are photoreproductions of the originals. The work includes both a topical index and an index based on the sectional arrangement of the act. The introductory material contains a chronological statement of the legislative history and a table of cases referred to in reports and debate.

Record No.: 065
Public Law No.: 80-120 (Sess. I)
Bill No.: H.R. 3020 (80th Cong.)
Statutes at Large Citation: 61 Stat. 136 (1947)
Title of Act: Labor-Management Relations Act, 1947

Title of Legislative History: Legislative History of Labor Management
                       Relations Act, 1947, 93rd Cong., 2nd Sess.
                       (Comm. Print 1974)
Publication Date: 1974
Author: Subcommittee on Labor, Senate Committee on Labor and Public
Welfare
Pages: i, 1680

L/C Card Number: 74-601801
OCLC No.: 903720
SuDoc No.: Y4.L11/2:L11/15
CIS No.: 74-S542-8
UPA Citation: N/A
Relevant Bills: H.R. 3020 (80th Cong.), S. 1126 (80th Cong.)

This history is a reprint of the preceding entry in this bibliography.   See
Record No. 064.

Record No.: 066
Public Law No.: 81-227 (Sess. I)
Bill No.: H.R. 2663 (81st Cong.)
Statutes at Large Citation: 63 Stat. 208 (1949)
Title of Act: Central Intelligence Agency Act of 1949

Title of Legislative History: Legislative History of the Central Intelligence
                       Agency as Documented in Published
                       Congressional Sources
Publication Date: 1975
Author: Grover S. Williams of the Congressional Research Service
Pages: 307

L/C Card Number: N/A
OCLC No.: 22851700
SuDoc No.: N/A
CIS No.: N/A
UPA Citation: UPA Film No.: MS, Reel No. 4, Frame No. 0753; CRS No. : UB
250 USA, 75-5A
Relevant Bills Bills: H.R. 4214 (80th Cong.), H.R. 5871 (80th Cong.), S. 758
    (80th Cong.), S. 2668 (80th Cong.), H.R. 2663 (81st Cong.)

This document contains two legislative histories of statutes as well as other material relevant to the history of the CIA. The first history is of Section 102 of the National Security Act of 1947, S. 758 (80th Cong.), P.L. 80-253. This section established the Central Intelligence Agency (CIA). It is "Title III" of the document and appears on its pages 25-150. The second history is of the Central Intelligence Agency Act of 1949, H.R. 2663 (81st Cong.), P.L. 81-227 (Sess. I). This Act provided the basic provisions for the administration of the CIA. It is "Title IV" of the document and appears on pages 151-172. Each history begins with a narrative summary of the progress of the relevant bills through Congress. The essays briefly quote relevant portions of Congressional documents. In each history, the essay is followed by full citations to and relevant excerpts from any Senate and House Hearings -- including some insertions, the Senate and House reports, and the Senate and House debates. The appendices to the document contain the full text of several relevant Congressional documents. Those full text documents relevant to Section 102 of the National Security Act of 1947 include: the text of Section 102 of P.L. 80-253; the Senate Report on S. 758 (80th Cong.); and the House report on the related bill H.R. 4214 (80th Cong.). Those full text documents relevant to P.L. 81-227 (Sess. I) include: the text of P.L. 81-227 (Sess. I); the House report on H.R. 5871 (80th Cong.) and the Senate report on S. 2688 (80th Cong.); and, the House and Senate reports on H.R. 2663 (81st Cong.).

Record No.: 067
Public Law No.: 81-626 (Sess. I)
Bill No.: H.R. 5895 (81st Cong.)
Statutes at Large Citation: 63 Stat. 714 (1949)
Title of Act: Mutual Defense Assistance Act of 1949

Title of Legislative History: Legislative History of the Contingency Fund in the Foreign Assistance Act IN Foreign Assistance Legislation for Fiscal Year 1981 (Part 1), Hearings Before the House Committee on Foreign Affairs, 96th Cong., 2nd Sess. (1980)
Publication Date: 1980
Author: House Committee on Foreign Affairs
Pages: v, 324

L/C Card Number: 80-602504
OCLC No.: 6474046
SuDoc No.: Y4.F76/1:F76/57/981/pt.1
CIS No.: 80-H381-59
UPA Citation: N/A

Relevant Bills: H.R. 5895 (81st Cong.), H.R. 7005 (82nd Cong.), H.R. 5710 (83rd Cong.), H.R. 9678 (83rd Cong.), H.R. 11356 (84th Cong.), S. 2090 (84th Cong.), S. 2130 (85th Cong.), H.R. 7500 (86th Cong.), H.R. 11510 (86th Cong.), S. 1983 (87th Cong.), S. 2966 (87th Cong.), H.R. 7885 (88th Cong.), H.R. 7750 (89th Cong.), H.R. 12169 (89th Cong.), H.R. 15750 (89th Cong.), H.R. 15263 (90th Cong.), S. 1872 (90th Cong.), H.R. 14580 (91st Cong.), H.R. 19911 (91st Cong.), S. 2819 (92nd Cong.), S. 1443 (93rd Cong.), S. 3394 (93rd Cong.), H.R. 9005 (94th Cong.), H.R. 13680 (94th Cong.), H.R. 3173 (96th Cong.)

This legislative history appears as Appendix 5 to these 1980 hearings. It traces from 1949-1979 the development of the President's contingency fund in acts subsequent to the Mutual Defense Assistance Act of 1949, H.R. 5895 (81st Cong.), P.L. 81-626 (Sess. I). The form of the document is a narrative essay which discusses and quotes Congressional reports and Congressional debate. It provides Congressional report numbers, but not page numbers and does not provide any citations to debate. Some of the major changes to the President's contingency fund provisions occurred in these subsequent acts: Mutual Defense Assistance Act of 1949, H.R. 5895 (81st Cong.), P.L. 81-626 (Sess. I); Mutual Security Act of 1952, H.R. 7005 (82nd Cong.), P.L. 82-400; Mutual Security Act of 1957, S. 2130 (85th Cong.), P.L. 85-141; Foreign Assistance Act of 1961, S. 1983 (87th Cong.), P.L. 87-195; Foreign Assistance Act of 1969, H.R. 14580 (91st Cong.), P.L. 91-175; Foreign Assistance Act of 1973, S. 1443 (93rd Cong.), P.L. 93-189; Foreign Assistance Act of 1974, S. 3394 (93rd Cong.), P.L. 93-559; International Security Assistance Act of 1979, H.R. 3173 (96th Cong.), P.L. 96-92. For each fiscal year 1956-1979, the appendices list the authorizing and appropriations committees' recommendations for contingency fund activities, as well as the actual contingency fund expenditures.

Record No.: 068
Public Law No.: 81-932 (Sess. II)
Bill No.: H.R. 9176 (81st Cong.)
Statutes at Large Citation: 64 Stat. 798 (1950)
Title of Act: Defense Production Act of 1950

Title of Legislative History: Legislative History of Laws Extending the Termination of the Defense Production Act of 1950, as Amended IN Revitalization and the U.S. Economy: Hearings Before the Subcommittee on Economic Stabilization of the House Committee on Banking, Finance, and Urban Affairs, Part IV, 97th Cong., 1st Sess. (1981)

Publication Date: 1981
Author: Subcommittee on Economic Stabilization, House Committee on Banking, Finance, and Urban Affairs
Pages: vi, 990

L/C Card Number: 81-602814
OCLC No.: 7883524
SuDoc No.: Y4.B22/1:97-11/pt.4
CIS No.: 82-H241-10
UPA Citation: N/A
Relevant Bills: H.R. 9176 (81st Cong.), S. 3936 (81st Cong.), H.J. Res. 278 (82nd Cong.), S. 1717 (82nd Cong.), S. 2594 (82nd Cong.), S. 1081 (83rd Cong.), S.J. Res. 85 (84th Cong.), H.R. 9852 (84th Cong.), S. 2391 (84th Cong.), H.R. 10969 (85th Cong.), H.R. 12052 (86th Cong.), S. 3203 (87th Cong.), H.R. 10000 (88th Cong.), H.R. 14025 (89th Cong.), H.R. 17268 (90th Cong.), H.J. Res. 1259 (91st Cong.), H.J. Res. 1336 (91st Cong.), S. 3302 (91st Cong.), S. 3715 (92nd Cong.), H.J. Res. 1056 (93rd Cong.), S.J. Res. 228 (93rd Cong.), S. 3270 (93rd Cong.), H.J. Res. 672 (94th Cong.), S.J. Res. 94 (94th Cong.), S. 1537 (94th Cong.), S. 853 (95th Cong.), H.J. Res. 406 (96th Cong.), H.J. Res. 478 (96th Cong.), H.J. Res. 520 (96th Cong.), S. 932 (96th Cong.), S.J. Res. 175 (96th Cong.)

A legislative history of the laws extending the termination of the Defense Production Act of 1950, H.R. 9176 (81st Cong.), P.L. 81-932 (Sess. II) appears on pages 146-159 of these hearings. The history very narrowly focuses on the stated policy behind the original act and its extensions and begins with a brief section on the Defense Production Act of 1950 and quotes the policy behind the act as stated in a Congressional report. The act and its progress through Congress are briefly summarized. Coverage is given to the original Defense Production Act of 1950 and to the public laws from 1951-1980 which extended the act. Some of these public laws were two-year extensions, others were stop-gap extensions until the next two-year act could be passed. For two-year extensions, the history provides a short quote on the extension's purpose from a Congressional report. The House or Senate report numbers for these quotes are supplied. Listed at the end of the report are two-year extensions whose purposes were merely quoted from an earlier Congressional report. For the stop-gap extensions, the history summarizes or quotes any pertinent debate on the purpose of the extension from the *Congressional Record*. Full citations to this debate are supplied. Listed at the end of the history are stop-gap extensions passed without Congressional comment.

Record No.: 069
Public Law No.: 81-115 (Sess. II)
Bill No.: S. 2609 (81st Cong.)
Statutes at Large Citation: 64 Stat. 1085 (1950)
Title of Act: Federal Youth Corrections Act

Title of Legislative History: Legislative History of Observation and Study
Publication Date: 1977
Author: Robert Schwaneberg of the Federal Judicial Center
Pages: 46 leaves

L/C Card Number: 83-108892
OCLC No.: 4677240
SuDoc No.: N/A
CIS No.: N/A
UPA Citation: N/A
Relevant Bills: S. 2609 (81st Cong.), S. 1114 (81st Cong.), H.R.J. Res.
    424 (85th Cong.), H.R.J. Res. 425 (85th Cong.), H.R. 8923
    (85th Cong.), H.R.J. Res. 615 (85th Cong.)

This is a narrative legislative history which discusses aspects of two acts: the
Federal Youth Corrections Act of 1950, S. 2609 (81st Cong.), P.L. 81-115 (Sess.
II) and the federal sentencing legislation of 1958, H.R.J. Res. 424 (85th
Cong.), P.L. 85-752. Numerous footnotes are included which give citations
to hearings, reports, the *United States Code*, and earlier acts. Also
included are a chronology of the Youth Corrections Act's passage and a
chronology of the federal sentencing legislation of 1958's passage.

Record No.: 070
Bill No.: N/A
Statutes at Large Citation: N/A
Title of Act: N/A
Title of Legislative History: Recordation of Patent Agreements, A Legislative
                               History, Study of Subcommittee on Patents,
                               Trademarks, and Copyrights, 85th Congress,
                               2nd Session, Pursuant to S. Res. 236, Study No.
                               9, 85th Cong., 2nd Sess. (Comm. Print 1958)
Publication Date: 1958
Author: Subcommittee on Patents, Trademarks, and Copyrights, Senate
Committee on the Judiciary
Pages: vii, 27

L/C Card Number: 58-61066
OCLC No.: 5044837
SuDoc No.: Y4.J89/2:P27/3/no.9
CIS No.: Committee-Print: S0300
UPA Citation: N/A

Relevant Bills: H.R. 4523 (74th Cong.), H.R. 7713 (77th Cong.), S. 2438 (77th Cong.), S. 2491 (77th Cong.), S. 2730 (77th Cong.), H.R. 109 (78th Cong.), H.R. 1371 (78th Cong.), H.R. 3786 (78th Cong.), H.R. 3874 (78th Cong.), H.R. 4493 (78th Cong.), S. 10 (78th Cong.), S. 1476 (78th Cong.), H.R. 97 (79th Cong.), H.R. 2612 (79th Cong.), H.R. 2632 (79th Cong.), H.R. 3462 (79th Cong.), H.R. 3756 (79th Cong.), S. 10 (79th Cong.), S. 11 (79th Cong.), S. 10 (80th Cong.), S. 72 (80th Cong.), S. 10 (81st Cong.), S. 11 (81st Cong.)

This study is also available in the reprint *Research Studies in Patent Law* (Buffalo: Hein, 1979). Legislative proposals for the recordation of patent agreements, none of which proposals became law, are examined. The history contains a chapter for any Congress from the 74th - 81st Congresses (1935-1950) in which any bills with patent recordation provisions were introduced. Each chapter summarizes the bills which contain patent recordation provisions, then quotes relevant sections of those bills. The chapters also contain summaries of and quotes from relevant testimony from any Congressional hearings held on these bills. Also provided are summaries and quotes from additional bills on which no Congressional hearings were held. Any bills identical to the summarized bills are identified. Separate sections of the study summarize Congressional hearings which discussed patent recordation, but did not discuss specific legislation. The Appendix to the study lists the full citations to the hearings summarized and quoted in the study.

Record No.: 071
Bill No.: N/A
Statutes at Large Citation: N/A
Title of Act: N/A

Title of Legislative History: Compulsory Licensing of Patents, Legislative History, Study of Subcommittee on Patents, Trademarks, and Copyrights, 85th Congress, 2nd Session, Pursuant to S. Res. 236, Study No. 12, 85th Cong., 2nd Sess. (Comm. Print 1958)
Publication Date: 1958
Author: Subcommittee on Patents, Trademarks, and Copyrights, Senate Committee on the Judiciary
Pages: viii, 70

L/C Card Number: 58-61540
OCLC No.: 1059530
SuDoc No.: Y4.J89/2:P27/3/no.12
CIS No.: Committee-Print: S0303
UPA Citation: N/A

Relevant Bills: H.R. 23417 (62nd Cong.), H.R. 15989 (63rd Cong.), H.R.
14944 (65th Cong.), S. 5265 (65th Cong.), H.R. 9932 (66th
Cong.), H.R. 11984 (66th Cong.), S. 3223 (66th Cong.), S. 1838
(67th Cong.), S. 3325 (67th Cong.), S. 3410 (67th Cong.), H.R. 12412
(69th Cong.), H.R. 12695 (70th Cong.), H.R. 8984 (72nd Cong.), H.R.
9259 (75th Cong.), H.R. 9815 (75th Cong.), S. 2303 (77th Cong.), S.
2721 (77th Cong.), S. 702 (78th Cong.), H.R. 2630 (79th Cong.), H.R.
3757 (79th Cong.), H.R. 5940 (79th Cong.), H.R. 6448 (79th Cong.), S.
1248 (79th Cong.), S. 1297 (79th Cong.), S. 1850 (79th Cong.)

This study is also available in the reprint *Research Studies in Patent Law*
(Buffalo: Hein, 1979). It examines legislative proposals for compulsory patent
licensing. A patent license permits someone other than the patent owner to
use a patent. The study contains three chapters which examine bills from the
62nd to 81st Congresses (1911 - 1950). The first chapter examines bills which
would have required the compulsory licensing of privately owned patents. The
second chapter examines bills which would have provided for the registration
of patents voluntarily made available for licensing. The third chapter
examines bills which would have required the dedication or compulsory
licensing of government-owned patents. None of these bills ever became law.
The chapters summarize and quote relevant bills, and also list the
Congressional action taken on each bill. For some bills, summaries of and
quotes from the relevant Congressional reports and testimony at
Congressional hearings are given. Footnotes provide full citations to all
summarized and quoted Congressional documents. The study's bibliography is
divided into the same three divisions as the study itself. The bibliography
contains citations to relevant books and pamphlets, Congressional documents
and other government publications, journal articles, court cases, and consent
decrees. Because the study examines such a large number of bills, many bills
are included in the indexes to this bibliography which could not be included in
the "relevant bills" portion of this annotation.

Record No.: 072
Public Law No.: 82-578 (Sess. I)
Bill No.: H.R. 3298 (82nd Cong.)
Statutes at Large Citation: 65 Stat. 648 (1951)
Title of Act: Durham-Humphrey Act (Drug Prescriptions)

Title of Legislative History: Legislative History of the Durham-Humphrey
Amendment, 1951, Public Law 215 (H.R. 3298),
82nd Congress, to Federal Food, Drug and
Cosmetic Act: Drug Dispensing and Labeling
Publication Date: 1972
Author: Food and Drug Administration, Office of Legislative Services
Pages: 197

L/C Card Number: N/A
OCLC No.: 3955068
SuDoc No.: N/A
CIS No.: N/A
UPA Citation: N/A
Relevant Bills: H.R. 3298 (82nd Cong.)

The documents in this volume include the text of H.R. 3298 (82nd Cong.), four House reports, the debates and passage of the bill as reported in the *Congressional Record*, and the text of the public law. There is no continuous pagination and no table of contents, although a chronological outline of the legislative history serves as an introduction to the compilation. Two hearings are listed in the outline.

Record No.: 073
Public Law No.: 82-568 (Sess. II)
Bill No.: H.R. 6578 (82nd Cong.)
Statutes at Large Citation: 66 Stat. 328 (1952)
Title of Act: Saline Water Conversion Act

Title of Legislative History: Legislative History, Saline Water Conversion
                                Act
Publication Date: 1971-1972
Author: Department of Interior, Office of Saline Water
Pages: various

L/C Card Number: 72-611533
OCLC No.: 144230
SuDoc No.: I1.2:Sa3/6/v.1-11
CIS No.: N/A
UPA Citation: N/A
Relevant Bills: H.R. 6578 (82nd Cong.), S. 5 (82nd Cong.), H.R. 2126 (84th Cong.), S. 516 (84th Cong.), S.J. Res. 135 (85th Cong.), S. 3370 (85th Cong.), S. 1576 (86th Cong.), S. 2816 (86th Cong.), S. 3446 (86th Cong.), S. 3557 (86th Cong.), H.R. 7916 (87th Cong.), S. 22 (87th Cong.), S. 2156 (87th Cong.), H.R. 7092 (89th Cong.), S. 24 (89th Cong.), S. 3823 (89th Cong.), H.R. 207 (90th Cong.), H.R. 6133 (90th Cong.), S. 1101 (90th Cong.), S. 2912 (90th Cong.), H.R. 6716 (91st Cong.), H.R. 15700 (91st Cong.), S. 1011 (91st Cong.), S. 3426 (91st Cong.), H.R. 5333 (92nd Cong.), H.R. 5334 (92nd Cong.), H.R. 7366 (92nd Cong.), H.R. 9093 (92nd Cong.), H.R. 12749 (92nd Cong.), S. 716 (92nd Cong.), S. 991 (92nd Cong.)

This is a legislative history of the Saline Water Conversion Act, H.R. 6578 (82nd Cong.), P.L. 82-568 (Sess. II) and its amendments. The eleven volumes in this work cover the 82nd - 92nd Congresses. They contain legislative history materials on unpassed bills or public laws. Each volume is divided into six sections: Laws; Bills; Committee Reports; Hearings - House; Hearings - Senate; and *Congressional Record*. Sometimes there is a seventh category "Miscellaneous" which contains Congressional materials such as oversight hearings on the Saline Water Conversion program. The volumes contain the full text of the relevant public laws, bills, Congressional reports, and Congressional debate, but sometimes contain only excerpts from Congressional hearings. The public laws which are included in the indexes to this bibliography but not mentioned in this annotation were not given significant discussion in the text of the materials provided.

Record No.: 074
Public Law No.: 82-950 (Sess. II)
Bill No.: H.R. 7794 (82nd Cong.)
Statutes at Large Citation: 66 Stat. 792 (1952)
Title of Act: Patent Act of 1952

Title of Legislative History: Efforts to Establish Statutory Standard of
                                 Invention, Study of Subcommittee on Patents,
                                 Trademarks, and Copyrights, 85th Congress,
                                 1st Session, Pursuant to S. Res. 55, Study No. 7,
                                 85th Cong., 1st Sess. (Comm. Print 1957)
Publication Date: 1958
Author: Subcommittee on Patents, Trademarks, and Copyrights, Senate Committee on the Judiciary
Pages: vi, 29

L/C Card Number: 58-60368
OCLC No.: 23018499
SuDoc No.: Y4.J89/2:P27/3/No.7
CIS No.: Committee-Print: S0298
UPA Citation: N/A
Relevant Bills: H.R. 3694 (79th Cong.), H.R. 4061 (80th Cong.), H.R. 5248 (80th Cong.), H.R. 4798 (81st Cong.), H.R. 6436 (81st Cong.), H.R. 9133 (81st Cong.), S. 2518 (81st Cong.), H.R. 3760 (82nd Cong.), H.R. 7794 (82nd Cong.)

Chapter III of this document is a legislative history of Section 103 of the Patent Act of 1952, H.R. 7794 (82nd Cong.), P.L. 82-950 (Sess. II).Section 103 established the standard of patentability. A 1943 study declared that a weakness of the patent system was its lack of a definition of invention. Bills including various definitions of invention were proposed in the 79th-82nd Congresses, 1945-1952. The chapter examines these bills in roughly chronological order, supported by quotes from the bills and the hearings on them. The quotes have been selected with particular attention to the definitions of invention contained in the bills. The study is also available in the reprint *Research Studies in Patent Law* (Buffalo: Hein, 1979).

Record No.: 075
Public Law No.: 82-950 (Sess. II)
Bill No.: H.R. 7794 (82nd Cong.)
Statutes at Large Citation: 66 Stat. 792 (1952)
Title of Act: To Revise and Codify the Laws Relating to Patents and the
              Patent Office and to Enact into Law Title 35 of the United
              States Code Entitled "Patents"

Title of Legislative History: Expediting Patent Office Procedure, Legislative
                                 History, Study of Subcommittee on Patents,
                                 Trademarks, and Copyrights, 86th Congress,
                                 1st Session, Pursuant to S. Res. 240, Study No.
                                 23, 86th Cong., 2nd Sess. (Comm. Print 1960)
Publication Date: 1960
Author: Subcommittee on Patents, Trademarks, and Copyrights, Senate
Committee on the Judiciary
Pages: vii, 105

L/C Card Number: N/A
OCLC No.: 825462
SuDoc No.: Y4.J89/2:P27/3/no.23
CIS No.: Committee-Print: S0435
UPA Citation: N/A
Relevant Bills: H.R. 9815 (55th Cong.), H.R 20585 (61st Cong.), S. 4812
        (69th Cong.), H.R 6873 (76th Cong.), H.R. 6874 (76th Cong.),
        H.R. 6875 (76th Cong.),H.R. 6878 (76th Cong.), S. 2328 (81st Cong.),
        H.R. 7794 (82nd Cong.)

This study is also available in the reprint *Research Studies in Patent Law* (Buffalo: Hein, 1979). Divided into two parts, it examines legislative proposals for reforming procedures within the Patent Office. The first part quickly treats the laws and proposals regarding patent procedure between the establishment of the Patent Office in 1790 and the recodification of patent law in 1870. The study proceeds chronologically. It examines one major post-1870 public law, the 1952 recodification of the patent law, H.R. 7794 (82nd Cong.), P.L. 82-950 (Sess II), summarizing and quoting the relevant bills. For bills which received action, the study notes Congressional action and summarizes and quotes Congressional hearings and Congressional reports. Full citations to the relevant Congressional documents are provided. The Addenda includes a subject index to public laws and bills discussed in the study, as well as a bibliography of law review articles on the reform of Patent Office procedures. Because the study examines such a large number of bills, many bills are included in the indexes to this bibliography which could not be included in the "relevant bills" portion of this annotation as they did not receive significant discussion in the materials provided.

Record No.: 076
Public Law No.: 83-505 (Sess. I)
Bill No.: H.R. 1063 (83rd Cong.)
Statutes at Large Citation: 67 Stat. 588 (1953)
Title of Act: To Confer Jurisdiction on the States of California, Minnesota, Nebraska, Oregon, and Wisconsin, with Respect to Criminal Offenses and Civil Causes of Action Committed or Arising on Indian Reservations within Such States

Title of Legislative History: Background Report on Public Law 280, 94th Cong., 1st Sess. (Comm. Print 1975)
Publication Date: 1975
Author: Senate Committee on Interior and Insular Affairs
Pages: 65

L/C Card Number: 75-601449
OCLC No.: 1501726
SuDoc No.: Y4.In8/13:P96/15
CIS No.: 75-S442-11
UPA Citation: N/A
Relevant Bills: H.R. 4725 (80th Cong.), H.R. 1537 (81st Cong.), H.R. 459 (82nd Cong.), H.R. 6695 (82nd Cong.), H.R. 1063 (83rd Cong.), S. 51 (84th Cong.), S. 961 (89th Cong.), S. 962 (89th Cong.), S. 963 (89th Cong.), S. 964 (89th Cong.), S. 965 (89th Cong.), S. 966 (89th Cong.), S. 967 (89th Cong.), S. 968 (89th Cong.), S.J. Res. 40 (89th Cong.), H.R. 2516 (90th Cong.), S. 1843 (90th Cong.), S. 1844 (90th Cong.), S. 1845 (90th Cong.), S. 1846 (90th Cong.), S. 1847 (90th Cong.), S.J. Res. 87 (90th Cong.), S. Con. Res. 11 (90th Cong.)

This narrative legislative history explains the policy context of the passage of H.R. 2516 (83rd Cong.), P.L. 83-505 (Sess. I), in 1953 and its Amendment of 1968, H.R. 2516 (90th Cong.), P.L. 90-284 (Title IV), in 1968. These laws represent the federal government's adoption of and retreat from a policy of termination of special federal responsibility for Indian tribes. They concern civil and criminal jurisdiction by the states over Indian reservations. The narrative includes excerpts from related bills, Congressional debate, hearings, and reports. Footnotes provide complete citations to these documents. Litigation concerning P.L. 83-505 (Sess. I) and its amendments is also discussed. Footnotes provide citations to the case reports. The appendices include the complete text of P.L. 83-505 (Sess. I) and P.L. 90-284 (Title IV).

Record No.: 077
Public Law No.: 83-469 (Sess. II)
Bill No.: S. 2475 (83rd Cong.)
Statutes at Large Citation: 68 Stat. 454 (1954)
Title of Act: Agricultural Trade Development and Assistance Act of 1954

Title of Legislative History: Food for Peace, 1954-1978: Major Changes in
                                Legislation, 96th Cong., 1st Sess. (Comm. Print
                                1979)
Publication Date: 1979
Author: Subcommittee on Foreign Agricultural Policy, Senate Committee on
Agriculture, Nutrition, and Forestry
Pages: v, 59

L/C Card Number: 79-602489
OCLC No.: 5053237
SuDoc No.: Y4.Ag8/3:F73/6
CIS No.: 79-S162-8
UPA Citation: N/A
Relevant Bills: S. 2475 (83rd Cong.), H.R. 8609 (86th Cong.), S. 1711
     (86th Cong.), S. 2687 (88th Cong.), H.R. 14929 (89th Cong.), S. 2986
     (90th Cong.), H.R. 9005 (94th Cong.), H.R. 6714 (95th Cong.)

This is a narrative legislative history of the Agricultural Trade
Development and Assistance Act of 1954, S. 2475 (83rd Cong.), P.L. 83-469
(Sess. II) and six important amendments to this act: Amendment of 1959, H.R.
8609 (86th Cong.), P.L. 86-341; Amendment of 1964, S. 2687 (88th Cong.), P.L.
88-638; Food for Peace Act of 1966, H.R. 14929 (89th Cong.), P.L. 89-808;
Amendment of 1968, S. 2986 (90th Cong.), P.L. 90-436; International
Development and Food Assistance Act of 1975, H.R. 9005 (94th Cong.), P.L.
94-161; and International Development and Food Assistance Act of 1977, H.R.
6714 (95th Cong.), P.L. 95-88. The history traces the development from 1954-
1978 of food aid policy under the Agricultural Trade Development and
Assistance Act of 1954. For instance, the shift in policy from disposing of
surplus to meeting world food needs is noted.   Policy also increasingly
emphasized self-help programs to help recipient countries meet their own food
needs. In tracing the development of these policies through these public laws,
the work summarizes and quotes the relevant bill versions,
Congressional reports, Congressional debate in the *Congressional Record*, and
Congressional hearings. Full citations to all summarized or quoted documents
are provided. Appendix A contains several charts showing agricultural
exports, including one showing the quantities of agricultural exports for 1955-
1975 under government-financed programs. Appendix B is the text of
the Agricultural Trade Development and Assistance Act of 1954 as amended to
1978. Footnotes show how public laws created the text of the 1978
Amendments.

Record No.: 078
Public Law No.: 83-656 (Sess. II)
Bill No.: H.R. 6788 (83rd Cong.)
Statutes at Large Citation: 68 Stat. 666 (1954)
Title of Act: Watershed Protection and Flood Prevention Act

Title of Legislative History: Legislative History of the Watershed Protection
and Flood Prevention Act, Public Law 566, 83rd
Congress, REPRINTED IN Watershed Work
Plans: Hearings Before the Subcommittee on
Water Resources of the Senate Committee on
Environment and Public Works, 96th Congress,
1st Session (1979)
Publication Date: 1979
Author: Subcommittee on Water Resources, Senate Committee on the
Environment and Public Works
Pages: iii, 141

L/C Card Number: 79-603544
OCLC No.: 5847374
SuDoc No.: Y4.P96/10:96-H18
CIS No.: 79-S321-27
UPA Citation: N/A
Relevant Bills: H.R. 6788 (83rd Cong.), S. 2549 (83rd Cong.)

This legislative history of the Watershed Protection and Flood Prevention
Act of 1954, H.R. 6788 (83rd Cong.), P.L. 83-656 (Sess. II), is included as pages
58-141 of hearings before the Subcommittee on Water Resources of the Senate
Committee on Environment and Public Works. These hearings were held in
1979. The text of P.L. 83-656 (Sess. II) is followed by an arrangement of the
Act into sections. Each section is followed by quotations from relevant bills,
hearings, reports, and debate. Footnotes denote provisions which were added
or amended by the Conference committee or appeared in bills but were omitted
from the act. The history's preface includes a list of the documents from which
it was compiled.

Record No.: 079
Public Law No.: 83-736 (Sess. II)
Bill No.: H.R. 8300 (83rd Cong.)
Statutes at Large Citation: 68A Stat. 3 (1954)
Title of Act: Internal Revenue Code of 1954

Title of Legislative History: Legislative History of Tax Return
Confidentiality: Section 6103 of the Internal
Revenue Code of 1954 and Its Predecessors

Publication Date: 1974
Author: Howard M. Zaritsky of the Congressional Research Service
Pages: 235

L/C Card Number: N/A
OCLC No.: 22695492
SuDoc No.: N/A
CIS No.: N/A
UPA Citation: UPA Film No.: MS, Reel No. 4, Frame No. 0488.CRS No.:
HJ5001A; 74-211A; 557/275.
Relevant Bills Bills: H.R. 312 (37th Cong.), H.R. 4864 (53rd Cong.), H.R.
        1438 (61st Cong.), H.R. 3321 (63rd Cong.), H.R. 6715 (68th
        Cong.), H.R. 7835 (73rd Cong.), H.R. 6359 (74th Cong.), H.R.
        8300 (83rd Cong.)

This essay examines and discusses the development of tax
return confidentiality in Section 6103 of the Internal Revenue Code of 1954,
H.R. 8300 (83rd Cong.), P.L. 83-736 (Sess. II) by providing excerpts from and
citations to relevant hearings, reprints, bills, and debates. Predecessor acts
which are examined in detail include: Civil War Income Tax Act, H.R. 312
(37th Cong.), 37th Cong., 2nd Sess., Ch. 119; Income Tax Act of 1894,
H.R.4864 (53rd Cong.), 53rd Cong., 2nd Sess., Ch. 349; Tariff Act of 1909, H.R.
1438 (61st Cong.), P.L. 61-5; 1913 Income Tax Act, H.R. 3321 (63rd Cong.),
P.L. 63-16; Revenue Act of 1924, H.R. 6715 (68th Cong.), P.L. 68-176; and
"pink slip" provisions in the Revenue Act of 1934, H.R. 7835 (73rd Cong.) P.L.
73-216.

Record No.: 080
Public Law No.: 83-736 (Sess. II)
Bill No.: H.R. 8300 (83rd Cong.)
Statutes at Large Citation: 68A Stat. 3 (1954)
Title of Act: Internal Revenue Code of 1954

Title of Legislative History: Legislative History of Internal Revenue Code of
                                 1954 Covering All Changes Made in the Code
                                 from Date of Its Enactment Aug. 16, 1954 to
                                 End of 1st Session of 89th Congress 1965,
                                 Together with Effective Dates and Applicability,
                                 Pertinent Ancillary Provisions, Explanatory
                                 and Historical Notes, Tables and Appendices,
                                 and Cumulative Supplement
Publication Date: 1967
Author: Joint Committee on Internal Revenue Taxation
Pages: vi, 1374

L/C Card Number: 68-60670
OCLC No.: 65907
SuDoc No.: Y4.In8/11:In8/14
CIS No.: N/A
UPA Citation: N/A
Relevant Bills: H.R. 2762 (76th Cong.), H.R. 8300 (83rd Cong.)

This document (H.R. 8300 (83rd Cong.), P.L. 83-736 (Sess. II)), shows all changes made to the Internal Revenue Code of 1954 from its enactment through 1965. Each section of the 1954 Code is treated in numerical order. Laws which changed each section are presented chronologically. The text includes amendments, additions, revisions, repeals, and redesignations. It also includes "ancillary provisions" or laws which related to or affected the operation of certain portions of the 1954 Code without specifically amending them. For each law, the history includes the date of enactment, bill number, public law number, *Statutes at Large* citation, text as passed, and effective date. The original text of sections is often presented in footnotes. Several tables and appendices conclude the document. Two of these tables show the corresponding sections of the 1954 Code and the Internal Revenue Code of 1939, H.R. 2762 (76th Cong.), P.L. 76-1. Another table chronologically lists all of the laws which amended the 1954 Code through 1965 and for each law provides: public law number, date of approval, bill number, Congressional report numbers, title, and *Statutes at Large* citation. The appendices contain the text of several additional original sections and amending laws.

Record No.: 081
Public Law No.: 83-1073 (Sess. II)
Bill No.: H.R. 9757 (83rd Cong.)
Statutes at Large Citation: 68 Stat. 919 (1954)
Title of Act: Atomic Energy Act of 1954

Title of Legislative History: Nature and History of the Classification
Category of "Formerly Restricted Data" IN The
Government's Classification of Private Ideas:
Hearings Before a Subcommittee of the House
Committee on Government Operations, 96th
Cong., 2nd Sess. (1980)
Publication Date: 1981
Author: Subcommittee on Government Information and Individual Rights, House Committee on Government Operations
Pages: v, 842

L/C Card Number: 82-601120
OCLC No.: 8093749
SuDoc No.: Y4.G74/7:G74/5
CIS No.: 81-H401-69
UPA Citation: N/A
Relevant Bills: H.R. 8862 (83rd Cong.), H.R. 9757 (83rd Cong.), S. 3323 (83rd
    Cong.)

This 1981 hearing contains on its pages 500-527 some legislative
history materials relevant to Section 142(d) of the Atomic Energy Act of 1954,
H.R. 9757 (83rd Cong.), P.L. 83-1073 (Sess. II). The Atomic Energy Act of
1954 changed the security provisions of the Atomic Energy Act. Section 142(d)
added the new classification category of "formerly restricted data," which is
data related to the military utilization of atomic weapons and can be revealed
to allies if certain procedures are followed. The excerpted legislative materials
include 1954 hearings on S. 3323 (83rd Cong.) and H.R. 8862 (83rd Cong.).
Also included are short passages from the relevant 1954 Congressional debate
as excerpted from the *Congressional Record*. Full citations to these excerpted
materials are provided. The materials narrowly focus on the security
provisions added in 1954 and especially on the new "formerly restricted data "
category. At the Committee's request, the Assistant Secretary for Defense
Programs at the Department of Energy in 1981 gathered and submitted these
materials on the nature and history of the "formerly restricted data"
classification category. He had earlier testified at the 1981 hearings as to the
current interpretation of the "formerly restricted data" classification category.

Record No.: 082
Public Law No.: 83-1073 (Sess. II)
Bill No.: H.R. 9757 (83rd Cong.)
Statutes at Large Citation: 68 Stat. 919 (1954)
Title of Act: Atomic Energy Act of 1954

Title of Legislative History: Legislative History of Atomic Energy Act of
                                 1954 (Public Law 703; 83rd Congress)
Publication Date: 1955
Author: Madeleine S. Losee of the Atomic Energy Commission
Pages: cccv, 3394

L/C Card Number: 55-63313
OCLC No.: 507464
SuDoc No.: Y3.At7:5-2/954/v.1-3
CIS No.: N/A
UPA Citation: N/A

Relevant Bills: H.R. 9757 (83rd Cong.), H.R. 8862 (83rd Cong.), S. 3323 (83rd Cong.), S. 3690 (83rd Cong.), S.J. Res. 172 (83rd Cong.), H.R.J. Res. 555 (83rd Cong.)

This three volume legislative history traces the history of the Atomic Energy Act of 1954. Volume I contains the text of the law, House and Senate bills, amendments, reports and committee prints. The introductory material of this volume includes: a synopsis of action arranged by date of introduction with page references to this compilation; a section index which, for each section of the act, gives citations to pertinent material in these volumes; and a subject index. Volume II contains the text of hearings before the Joint Committee on Atomic Energy on S. 3323 (83rd Cong.), and H.R. 8862 (83rd Cong.), held in May and June 1954. Volume III contains excerpts from the Congressional debates.

Record No.: 083
Public Law No.: 84-859 (Sess. I)
Bill No.: H.R.J. Res. 330 (84th Cong.)
Statutes at Large Citation: 69 Stat. 695 (1955)
Title of Act: Presidential Libraries Act

Title of Legislative History: Cost of Former Presidents to U.S. Taxpayers: Hearing Before the Subcommittee on Treasury, Postal Service, and General Government of the Senate Committee on Appropriations and Subcommittee on Civil Service and General Services of the Senate Committee on Governmental Affairs, 96th Cong., 1st Sess. (1979)

Publication Date: 1980
Author: Subcommittee on Treasury, Postal Service, and General Government, Senate Committee on Appropriations; Subcommittee on Civil Service and General Services, Senate Committee on Governmental Affairs
Pages: iii, 328

L/C Card Number: 80-600792
OCLC No.: 5955650
SuDoc No.: Y4.Ap6/2:P92
CIS No.: 80-S181-8
UPA Citation: N/A
Relevant Bills: H.R.J. Res. 330 (84th Cong.), H.R.J. Res. 331 (84th Cong.), H.R.J. 332 (84th Cong.), S. 607 (85th Cong.), S. 609 (85th Cong.), H.R. 4638 (88th Cong.), S. 1373 (88th Cong.)

Supplementary material to these joint hearings held in 1979 includes the 1955 hearings on the Presidential Libraries Act, H.R.J. Res. 330 (84th Cong.), P.L. 84-859 (Sess. I), before a Special Subcommittee of the House Committee on Government Operations. Additional supplementary material to these 1979 hearings includes excerpts from Congressional reports and Congressional debate on the Presidential Libraries Act; Former Presidents Act of 1958, S. 607 (85th Cong.), P.L. 85-745; and the Presidential Transition Act of 1963, H.R. 4638 (88th Cong.), P.L. 88-277. Full citations to all reports and debates are provided.

Record No.: 084
Public Law No.: N/A
Bill No.: N/A
Statutes at Large Citation: Stat.: N/A
Title of Act: N/A

Title of Legislative History: Single Court of Patent Appeals, Legislative
                                 History, Study of Subcommittee on Patents,
                                 Trademarks, and Copyrights, 85th Congress,
                                 2ndSession, Pursuant to S. Res. 236, Study No.
                                 20,85th Cong., 2nd Sess. (Comm. Print 1958)
Publication Date: 1959
Author: Subcommittee on Patents, Trademarks, and Copyrights, Senate Committee on the Judiciary
Pages: viii, 55

L/C Card Number: 59-60963
OCLC No.: 16766255
SuDoc No.: Y4.J89/2:P27/3/no.20
CIS No.: Committee-Print: S0432
UPA Citation: N/A
Relevant Bills: H.R. 9084 (50th Cong.), S. 2141 (50th Cong.), H.R. 831 (51st Cong.), S. 1588 (51st Cong.), H.R. 8533 (53rd Cong.), S. 2613 (53rd Cong.), H.R. 7083 (55th Cong.), S. 4256 (55th Cong.), H.R. 5294 (56th Cong.), S. 1883 (56th Cong.), H.R. 9296 (58th Cong.), H.R. 10769 (58th Cong.), H.R. 13087 (58th Cong.), S. 2632 (58th Cong.), S. 4656 (58th Cong.), H.R. 8458 (59th Cong.), H.R. 12470 (59th Cong.), S. 1693 (59th Cong.), S. 3517 (59th Cong.), H.R. 14047 (60th Cong.), H.R. 19466 (60th Cong.), H.R. 20386 (60th Cong.), H.R. 21455 (60th Cong.), S. 3161 (60th Cong.), H.R. 14622 (61st Cong.), S. 4982 (61st Cong.), H.R. 9843 (62nd Cong.), H.R. 26277 (62nd Cong.), H.R. 5011 (65th Cong.), S. 4 (65th Cong.), H.R. 5012 (66th Cong.), S. 818 (66th Cong.), H.R. 12371 (74th Cong.), S. 3823 (74th Cong.), H.R. 5636 (75th Cong.), H.R. 5855 (75th Cong.), S. 475 (75th Cong.), H.R. 7187 (76th Cong.), S. 2687 (76th Cong.), S. 928 (77th Cong.), S. 3744 (84th Cong.)

This study is also available in the reprint *Research Studies in Patent Law*, (Buffalo: Hein, 1979). This study examines legislative proposals for a single court of patent appeals from the 50th - 76th Congresses (1887-1942). None of these proposals ever became law. The study is divided into two parts. "Early Proposals (1887-1921)" begins with a chart summarizing bills from the 50th - 66th Congresses (1887-1922). In addition to summarizing the bills' provisions for the court's membership, jurisdiction, and appeals from the court, the chart also provides the citations to any Congressional reports on these bills. The study then examines in detail bills from the 59th, 60th, 61st, 62nd, and 66th Congresses on which Congressional hearings were held. For each of these bills, the study summarizes and quotes the bill from the relevant Congressional hearings. For some bills, further Congressional action is described and Congressional reports are summarized and quoted. The second part "Recent Proposals (1936-57)" begins with a chart similar to the first chart, but summarizing the bills from the 74th - 84th Congresses (1935-1958). The study then examines in detail bills from the 75th and 76th Congresses on which Congressional hearings were held. These bills receive the same treatment as the bills examined in detail in the first part of the study. Full citations are provided. An appendix contains the text of the following bills: S. 1693 (59th Cong.), H.R. 12470 (59th Cong.), S. 475 (75th Cong.), and S. 3744 (84th Cong.).

Record No.: 085
Public Law No.: 85-726
Bill No.: S. 3880 (85th Cong.)
Statutes at Large Citation: 72 Stat. 731 (1958)
Title of Act: Federal Aviation Act of 1958

Title of Legislative History: Legislative History of Federal Aviation Act of
                                1958
Publication Date: 1960
Author: Federal Aviation Agency
Pages: 1243

L/C Card Number: 60-61760
OCLC No.: 1981034
SuDoc No.: FAA1.5:F31a
CIS No.: N/A
UPA Citation: N/A
Relevant Bills: S. 3880 (85th Cong.), H.R. 12616 (85th Cong.)

This three volume legislative history contains the full text of the House and Senate hearings and reports on S. 3880 (85th Cong.) which became the Federal Aviation Act of 1958 and H.R. 12616 (85th Cong.), its companion bill. Also included is the full text of the act itself, as well as the Senate Committee on Interstate and Foreign Commerce's comparative print which shows the differences between the Civil Aeronautics Act of 1938, P.L. 75-706, and the Federal Aviation Act of 1958. A chart indicates references to H.R. 12616 (85th Cong.) and S. 3880 (85th Cong.) in the *Congressional Record*.

Record No.: 086
Public Law No.: 85-836
Bill No.: S. 2888 (85th Cong.)
Statutes at Large Citation: 72 Stat. 997 (1958)
Title of Act: Welfare and Pension Plans Disclosure Act

Title of Legislative History: Legislative History of Welfare and Pension
                                 Plans Disclosure Act of 1958, as Amended by
                                 Public Law 87-420 of 1962
Publication Date: 1962
Author: Department of Labor, Office of the Solicitor
Pages: xxxvi, 568

L/C Card Number: 63-26
OCLC No.: 22128444
SuDoc No.: L21.5:W45
CIS No.: N/A
UPA Citation: N/A
Relevant Bills: S. 1122 (85th Cong.), S. 1813 (85th Cong.), S. 2137
    (85th Cong.), S. 2175 (85th Cong.), S. 1145 (85th Cong.), S. 2888 (85th
    Cong.), H.R. 4653 (85th Cong.), H.R. 487 (85th Cong.), H.R. 2437 (85th
    Cong.), H.R. 7802 (85th Cong.), H.R. 7960 (85th Cong.), H.R. 5994
    (85th Cong.), H.R. 6014 (85th Cong.), H.R. 6649 (85th Cong.), H.R.
    6513 (85th Cong.), H.R. 6650 (85th Cong.), H.R. 7607 (85th Cong.),
    H.R. 8004 (85th Cong.), S. 1944 (87th Cong.), H.R. 7234 (87th Cong.),
    H.R. 7235 (87th Cong.), H.R. 7040 (87th Cong.), H.R. 4929 (87th
    Cong.), H.R. 8723 (87th Cong.)

This comprehensive legislative history was compiled shortly after the Amendment of 1962, H.R. 8723 (87th Cong.), P.L. 87-420, which strengthened the original act. The introductory material contains separate indices to the 1957 and 1961 Congressional hearings, as well as a list of the persons and organizations whose testimony appears in the excerpted hearings. Also in the introductory material are an outline of the act as amended, the text of the act, and a list of the persons and organizations whose testimony appears in the included excerpted hearings. The history begins with a section on general background and history. The remaining sections correspond with sections of the act as amended. Each section consists of relevant excerpts from Congressional reports, debates, and hearings. Each section is prefaced with a detailed subject index. The history concludes with the criminal provisions codified from the Amendment of 1961 to Title 18 of the *United States Code*.

Record No.: 087
Public Law No.: 86-257
Bill No.: S. 1555 (86th Cong.)
Statutes at Large Citation: 73 Stat. 519 (1959)
Title of Act: Labor-Management Reporting and Disclosure Act of 1959

Title of Legislative History: Legislative History of Labor-Management
                                             Reporting and Disclosure Act of 1959
Publication Date: 1959
Author: National Labor Relations Board, Office of the General Counsel, Division of Law
Pages: liii, 1-967; liii, 968-1927

L/C Card Number: 60-60460
OCLC No.: 422197
SuDoc No.: LR1.5:L11/7/v.1,2
CIS No.: N/A
UPA Citation: N/A
Relevant Bills: S. 505 (86th Cong.), S. 748 (86th Cong.), H.R. 3540
        (86th Cong.), S. 1002 (86th Cong.), H.R. 4473 (86th Cong.), H.R. 4474
        (86th Cong.), S. 1137 (86th Cong.), S. 1311 (86th Cong.), S. 1384 (86th
        Cong.), S. 1385 (86th Cong.), S. 1386 (86th Cong.), S. 1387 (86th
        Cong.), S. 1555 (86th Cong.), H.R. 7265 (86th Cong.), H.R. 8400 (86th
        Cong.), H.R. 8342 (86th Cong.), H.R. 8490 (86th Cong.)

This two volume work contains the bills, reports, and debate which constitute the legislative history of the Labor-Management Reporting and Disclosure Act of 1959 or the Landrum-Griffin Act, S. 1555 (86th Cong.), P.L. 86-257. The introductory material includes a chronological statement of Congressional action, a table of cases referred to in reports and debate, and sectional and topical indexes to the amendments which the Landrum-Griffin Act made to the Labor-Management Relations Act of 1947, P.L. 80-101. Volume I contains the full text of the Landrum-Griffin Act, as well as the full text of several related bills introduced in the 86th Congress on labor-management reform legislation and their accompanying reports. Volume II contains relevant debate. It concludes with the text of the Labor-Management Relations Act of 1947, both before and after its amendment by the Labor-Management Reporting and Disclosure Act of 1959, as well as a table of the various bills' proposed amendments to the Labor-Management Relations Act of 1947.

Record No.: 088
Public Law No.: 86-257
Bill No.: S. 1555 (86th Cong.)
Statutes at Large Citation: 73 Stat. 519 (1959)
Title of Act: Labor-Management Reporting and Disclosure Act of 1959

Title of Legislative History: Legislative History of Labor Management
                                 Reporting and Disclosure Act of 1959: Titles I-
                                 VI
Publication Date: 1964
Author: Department of Labor, Office of the Solicitor, Division of
Labor-Management Laws
Pages: xlvii, 1138

L/C Card Number: 64-53
OCLC No.: 1534033
SuDoc No.: L21.5:L11/2
CIS No.: N/A
UPA Citation: N/A
Relevant Bills: S. 505 (86th Cong.), S. 748 (86th Cong.), S. 1002 (86th Cong.),
      S. 1311 (86th Cong.), S. 1137 (86th Cong.), H.R. 3540 (86th Cong.),
      H.R. 4473 (86th Cong.), S. 1555 (86th Cong.), H.R. 7265 (86th Cong.),
      H.R. 3302 (86th Cong.), S. 3974 (86th Cong.), H.R. 8342 (86th Cong.),
      H.R. 7680 (86th Cong.), H.R. 8400 (86th Cong.), S. 3068 (86th Cong.),
      S. 3571 (86th Cong.)

The introductory material to this legislative history includes the text of the
Labor-Management Reporting and Disclosure Act of 1959, S. 1555
(86th Cong.), P.L. 86-257, as well as indices to the 1959 Congressional
hearings on the various bills introduced in the 86th Congress which proposed
labor-management reform legislation. The main part of the history consists
of sections specifically concerned with each title of the Labor-Management
Reporting and Disclosure Act. The text of each of these sections includes a
quotation from the act followed by pertinent excerpts from the *Congressional
Record* and Congressional reports. Each section includes a subject index to its
text.

Record No.: 089
Public Law No.: 87-30
Bill No.: H.R. 3935 (87th Cong.)
Statutes at Large Citation: 75 Stat. 65 (1961)
Title of Act: Fair Labor Standards Amendments of 1961

Title of Legislative History: Legislative History of the Fair Labor Standards
                                 Amendments of 1961, P.L. 87-30, 87th
                                 Congress, H.R. 3935, 88th Cong., 1st Sess.
                                 (Comm. Print 1963)

Publication Date: 1963
Author: House Committee on Education and Labor
Pages: vi, 904

L/C Card Number:
OCLC No.: 11026957
SuDoc No.: Y4.Ed8/1:L11/24
CIS No.: Committee-Print: H1931
UPA Citation: N/A
Relevant Bills: H.R. 12677 (86th Cong.), H.R. 12853 (86th Cong.), S. 3758 (86th Cong.), H.R. 3935 (87th Cong.), H.R. 5900 (87th Cong.), S. 895 (87th Cong.), S. 1457 (87th Cong.)

This is a legislative history of the Fair Labor Standards Amendments of 1961, H.R. 3935 (87th Cong.), P.L. 87-30. This public law extended minimum wage protection to workers employed in large retail trade or service enterprises, as well as raising the minimum wage for workers already covered. The first chapter of the history, entitled "General and Background Matters," contains the legislative history documents which will be quoted in part in the later chapters of the history. The first chapter includes the text of H.R. 3935 (87th Cong.) as introduced, as reported to the House, as passed by the House, as reported to the Senate, as passed by the Senate, and as reported by the Conference committee. Each version of the bill is followed by an explanation of that version as excerpted from the *Congressional Record* or Congressional reports. Sometimes, the history will refer to the pages of the history on which the relevant bill or explanation appears within a fully reproduced Congressional report. Also included is the text as passed of P.L. 87-30. Next, the chapter contains the House, Senate, and Conference reports on H.R. 3935 (87th Cong.). This is followed by the House and Senate debate and passage, as excerpted from the *Congressional Record* or the Conference report. Coverage is given to the House and Senate debate and passage of H.R. 12677 (86th Cong.), a similar bill from the previous Congress. Next, the history includes the text, debate, and votes on the major substitutes for and major amendments to the main bills in the 87th and 86th Congresses. In addition, the first chapter includes the Congressional debate in the 87th and 86th Congresses on the need for the legislation. The first chapter concludes with discussions excerpted from the Congressional debate and Congressional reports on the treatment of small local businesses in the retail and service areas and on the constitutionality of the extension of minimum wage legislation to retail enterprises. The history includes the texts of the bills and amendments to them as they were separately printed or appeared in the *Congressional Record* or Congressional reports. Full citations to the permanent *Congressional Record* are provided for the quoted debate. The Congressional reports are reproduced in full, including their citations. When the history quotes from Congressional reports, it gives full citations to them. The remainder of the history consists of a section-by-section discussion of the Fair Labor Standards Amendments of 1961. This discussion has been excerpted from the Congressional debate and Congressional reports.

Record No.: 090
Public Law No.: 87-346
Bill No.: H.R. 6775 (87th Cong.)
Statutes at Large Citation: 75 Stat. 762 (1961)
Title of Act: To Amend the Shipping Act, 1916, as Amended, to Authorize
Ocean Common Carriers and Conferences Thereof Serving
the Foreign Commerce of the United States to Enter into
Effective and Fair Dual Rate Contracts with Shippers and
Consignees

Title of Legislative History: Index to Legislative History of Steamship
Conference Dual Rate Law, Public Law 87-346
(75 Stat. 762), S. Doc. 100, 87th Cong., 2nd Sess.
(1962)
Publication Date: 1962
Author: Senate Committee on Commerce
Pages: x, 482

L/C Card Number: 62-61993
OCLC No.: 2105146
SuDoc No.: Y1.1/2:Serial 12450
CIS No.: N/A
UPA Citation: N/A
Relevant Bills: H.R. 4299 (87th Cong.), H.R. 6775 (87th Cong.), S. 2154 (87th
Cong.)

This is a legislative history of H.R. 6775 (87th Cong.), P.L. 87-346, which
amended the Shipping Act, 1916, H.R. 15455 (64th Cong.), P.L. 64-260 to
explicitly permit groups of steamship operators or steamship conferences to
charge lower rates to customers who ship exclusively with them. The history
begins with the text of P.L. 87-346 as passed. The text has been divided into
thirty-four sections labeled title and A - GG. For the title and each section A -
GG, the Index first quotes that section as it appears in the public law. It then
traces that section's development through H.R. 4299 (87th Cong.) as
introduced; and H.R. 6775 (87th Cong.) as introduced, as reported to the
House, as passed by the House, as reported to the Senate, as passed by the
Senate, and as printed in the Conference report. The history quotes these bill
versions when necessary for clarity. Then, for each section, the history lists
the relevant page numbers from the House hearings on H.R. 4299 (87th Cong.)
and Senate hearings on H.R. 6775 (87th Cong.); House report on H.R. 6775
(87th Cong.); Senate report on H.R. 6775 (87th Cong.); Conference report on
H.R. 6775 (87th Cong.); and House and Senate debate on H.R. 4299 (87th
Cong.) and H.R. 6775 (87th Cong.) as it was printed in the *Congressional
Record*. Full citations to these documents are included in the introduction to
the work. The Index provides the page numbers of these documents as they
were originally separately published. After the Index, the work continues with
the texts of the relevant bills, Congressional reports, and Congressional
debate. This portion includes the texts of H.R. 4299 (87th Cong.) as introduced
and H.R. 6775 (87th Cong.) as introduced and reported to the House. In
addition, the history includes the House, Senate, and Conference reports on
H.R. 6775 (87th Cong.). Coverage is given to the House and Senate debate
and passage of H.R. 6775 (87th Cong.). The lengthy Senate debate focuses on

antitrust considerations. The history provides the *Congressional Record* daily edition pagination to this debate, but the pagination does not match the bound *Congressional Record*.

Record No.: 091
Public Law No.: 87-794
Bill No.: H.R. 11970 (87th Cong.)
Statutes at Large Citation: 76 Stat. 872 (1962)
Title of Act: Trade Expansion Act of 1962

Title of Legislative History: Legislative History of H.R. 11970, 87th
Congress, Trade Expansion Act of 1962, Public
Law 87-794, 90th Cong., 1st Sess. (Comm. Print
1967)
Publication Date: 1967
Author: House Committee on Ways and Means
Pages: xv, 1-1168; xv, 1169-2045

L/C Card Number: 67-61165
OCLC No.: 6671989
SuDoc No.: Y4.W36:T67/21/pts.1-2
CIS No.: Committee-Print: H3722, H3723
UPA Citation: N/A
Relevant Bills: H.R. 9900 (87th Cong.), H.R. 11970 (87th Cong.)

This two volume legislative history follows in chronological order the Congressional action which resulted in the Trade Expansion Act of 1962, H.R. 11970 (87th Cong.), P.L. 87-794. The introductory material includes a chronological table of the act's passage, as well as an alphabetical listing of members of Congress with references to floor debate. The history includes the full text of the public law, various versions of H.R. 9900 (87th Cong.) and H.R. 11970 (87th Cong.), and the Congressional reports and Congressional debate on these bills. Selections from relevant hearings are also included.

Record No.: 092
Public Law No.: 87-834
Bill No.: H.R. 10650 (87th Cong.)
Statutes at Large Citation: 76 Stat. 960 (1962)
Title of Act: Revenue Act of 1962

Title of Legislative History: Legislative History of H.R. 10650, 87th
Congress, Revenue Act of 1962, Public Law
87-834, 90th Cong., 1st Sess. (Comm. Print
1967)
Publication Date: 1967
Author: House Committee on Ways and Means
Pages: 1438;1439-2783;2785-3745;4558

L/C Card Number: 67-60940
OCLC No.: 900527
SuDoc No.: Y4.W36:R32/64/962/pts.1-4
CIS No.: Committee-Print: H1004,H1005,H1006,H1007
UPA Citation: N/A
Relevant Bills: H.R. 10650 (87th Cong.)

This four part compilation presents in chronological order the
Congressional action which resulted in the Revenue Act of 1962, H.R. 10650
(87th Cong.), P.L. 87-834.   The introductory material includes both an
alphabetical listing of members of Congress with references to relevant floor
debate and a chronological table of Congressional action. The history itself
begins with the complete text of the act.   It includes not only the
various versions of H.R. 10650 (87th Cong.), Congressional reports,
Congressional debate, Congressional press releases, and excerpts from
Congressional hearings, but also several Presidential communications and
Treasury Department documents.

Record No.: 093
Public Law No.: 88-38
Bill No.: S. 1409 (88th Cong.)
Statutes at Large Citation: 77 Stat. 56 (1963)
Title of Act: Equal Pay Act of 1963

Title of Legislative History: Legislative History of Equal Pay Act of 1963
(Amending Sec. 6 of Fair Labor Standards Act
of 1938, as Amended), P.L. 88-38, 88th
Congress, H.R. 6060 and S. 1409, 88th Cong.,
1st Sess. (Comm. Print 1963)
Publication Date: 1963
Author: House Committee on Education and Labor
Pages: v, 114

L/C Card Number: 64-61436
OCLC No.: 1655865
SuDoc No.: Y4.Ed8/1:P29/3
CIS No.: Committee-Print: H0534
UPA Citation: N/A

Relevant Bills: S. 1409 (88th Cong.), H.R. 6060 (88th Cong.), H.R. 3861 (88th Cong.), H.R. 4022 (88th Cong.), S. 882 (88th Cong.), S. 910 (88th Cong.)

This legislative history is divided into two main parts. The first part includes the text from the *Congressional Record* of several versions of the related bills S. 1409 (88th Cong.) and H.R. 6060 (88th Cong.), as well as some rejected amendments to these bills. Also included are the Senate and House reports on these bills and an examination of other proposed legislation on equal pay from the eighty-eighth Congress. The second part of the history consists of debate from the *Congressional Record* on S. 1409 (88th Cong.) and H.R. 6060 (88th Cong.).

Record No.: 094
Public Law No.: 88-272
Bill No.: H.R. 8363 (88th Cong.)
Statutes at Large Citation: 78 Stat. 19 (1964)
Title of Act: Revenue Act of 1964

Title of Legislative History: Legislative History of H.R. 8363, 88th Congress, Revenue Act of 1964, Public Law 88-272, 89th Cong., 2nd Sess. (Comm. Print 1966)
Publication Date: 1966
Author: House Committee on Ways and Means
Pages: 1405;1407-2494;2495-3543;4404

L/C Card Number: 67-60164
OCLC No.: 953733
SuDoc No.: Y4.W36:R32/64/pts.1-4
CIS No.: Committee-Print: H0979,H0980,H0981,H0982
UPA Citation: N/A
Relevant Bills: H.R. 8363 (88th Cong.)

The purpose of this compilation was to make available the full text of the documents relating to the passage of the Revenue Act of 1964, H.R. 8363 (88th Cong.), P.L. 88-272. The introductory material includes a chronological history of the legislation and alphabetical listings of members of Congress with cross references to floor debates. The compilation begins with the text of the act, then chronologically presents the relevant documents. These documents include: several versions of H.R. 8363 (88th Cong.); Congressional debate on this bill; and the House, Senate, and Conference reports on this bill. Also included are the President's 1963 tax message and congressional press releases. Appendix II is a comparison of provisions as passed by the House with previous law, Treasury recommendations, and various versions of H.R. 8363 (88th Cong.).

Record No.: 095
Public Law No.: 88-349
Bill No.: H.R. 6041 (88th Cong.)
Statutes at Large Citation: 78 Stat. 238 (1964)
Title of Act: To Amend the Prevailing Wage Section of the Davis-Bacon Act,
        as Amended; and Related Sections of the Federal Airport Act,
        as Amended; and the National Housing Act, as Amended

Title of Legislative History: Legislative History of the Act Amending the
        Prevailing Wage Section of the Davis-Bacon
        Act, as Amended, P.L. 88-349, 88th Congress,
        H.R. 6041, 88th Cong., 2nd Sess. (Comm. Print
        1964)
Publication Date: 1964
Author: House Committee on Education and Labor
Pages: v, 122

L/C Card Number: 65-60808
OCLC No.: 239747
SuDoc No.: Y4.Ed8/1:D29/5
CIS No.: Committee-Print: H4580
UPA Citation: N/A
Relevant Bills: H.R. 404 (88th Cong.), H.R. 6041 (88th Cong.)

This legislative history contains the text of H.R. 6041 (88th Cong.) as
introduced, as well as the House and Senate reports on the bill. Also
contained in this work are excerpts from the *Congressional Record* which cover
amendments to H.R. 6041 (92nd Cong.), its passage, and various debates
regarding that bill. A full citation to the daily edition of the *Congressional
Record* follows each excerpt. The history contains explanation and discussion
of specific provisions of H.R. 6041 (92nd Cong.). A quote from H.R. 6041 (92nd
Cong.) is followed by discussion of that provision excerpted from Congressional
reports, Congressional debate, and Congressional hearings. House hearings
were held in 1963 and 1964 to amend the Davis-Bacon Act are excerpted with
full citations.

Record No.: 096
Public Law No.: 88-352
Bill No.: H.R. 7152 (88th Cong.)
Statutes at Large Citation: 78 Stat. 241 (1964)
Title of Act: Civil Rights Act of 1964

Title of Legislative History: Legislative History of Titles 7 and 11 of Civil
        Rights Act of 1964
Publication Date: 1968
Author: Equal Employment Opportunity Commission
Pages: various

L/C Card Number: 68-62391
OCLC No.: 453662
SuDoc No.: Y3.Eq2:2C49/2
CIS No.: N/A
UPA Citation: N/A
Relevant Bills: H.R. 10144 (87th Cong.), H.R. 405 (88th Cong.), S. 1937 (88th
    Cong.), H.R. 7152 (88th Cong.), H.R. 3139 (88th Cong.)

This legislative history consists of four parts. Part I is a narrative history of
fair employment practice laws. Part II contains the texts of Title VII and Title
XI of the Civil Rights Act of 1964, H.R. 7152 (88th Cong.), P.L. 88-352, with
annotations to the legislative history. Part III contains the text of the relevant
Congressional reports. Part IV contains the Congressional debate on the two
titles. The Appendix contains a chart which lists the sponsor, subject, and
action taken on amendments to Title VII and Title XI which were adopted or
rejected by the House and Senate.

Record No.: 097
Public Law No.: 88-352
Bill No.: H.R. 7152 (88th Cong.)
Statutes at Large Citation: 78 Stat. 241 (1964)
Title of Act: Civil Rights Act of 1964

Title of Legislative History: Desegregation of Public Schools: Legislative
                                History of Title IV of the Civil Rights Act of
                                1964
Publication Date: 1967
Author: Raymond J. Celada of the Legislative Reference Service
Pages: 48

L/C Card Number: N/A
OCLC No.: 22534145
SuDoc No.: N/A
CIS No.: N/A
UPA Citation: UPA Film No.: MS: Reel No. 1; Frame No. 0278.LRS No.: LC
2701A; 389/38 A-181
Relevant Bills Bills: H.R. 7152 (88th Cong.), S. 1731 (88th Cong.)

This chronological narrative legislative history follows the Congressional
events which led to the enactment of Title IV of the Civil Rights Act of 1964,
H.R. 7152 (88th Cong.), P.L. 88-352. Footnotes provide extensive citations to
Congressional documents, Congressional reports, and Congressional debate.
The appendices include the text of Title IV, as well as several versions of H.R.
7152 (88th Cong.).

Record No.: 098
Public Law No.: 88-352
Bill No.: H.R. 7152 (88th Cong.)
Statutes at Large Citation: 78 Stat. 241 (1964)
Title of Act: Civil Rights Act of 1964

Title of Legislative History: Nondiscrimination in Federally Assisted
                                Programs: Legislative History and Analysis of
                                Title VI of the Civil Rights Act of 1964
Publication Date: 1965
Author: Raymond J. Celada of the Legislative Reference Service
Pages: 85

L/C Card Number: N/A
OCLC No.: 22221341
SuDoc No.: N/A
CIS No.: N/A
UPA Citation: UPA Film No.: MS Reel No.1; Frame No. 0064.LRS No.: E 185
G1; 336/38 A-116
Relevant Bills: H.R. 7152 (88th Cong.)

The largest part of this narrative history deals with the enactment of Title VI
of the Civil Rights Act of 1964, H.R. 7152 (88th Cong.), P.L. 88-352. The essay
quotes relevant documents and footnotes provide extensive citations to various
versions of H.R. 7152 (88th Cong.), Congressional reports, Congressional
documents, and Congressional debate. Also included are an analysis of Title
VI's Constitutional basis, a sectional analysis of Title VI, and an examination
of the title's administration. The appendices include the text of Title VI, as
well as samples of the Department of Health, Education, and Welfare
regulations for assuring compliance with Title VI.

Record No.: 099
Public Law No.: 88-379
Bill No.: S. 2 (88th Cong.)
Statutes at Large Citation: 78 Stat. 329 (1964)
Title of Act: Water Resources Research Act of 1964

Title of Legislative History: The Water Resources Research Act of 1964: An
                                Assessment, 94th Cong., 2nd Sess. (Comm. Print
                                1976)
Publication Date: 1976
Author: Subcommittee on Energy Research and Water Resources, Senate
Committee on Interior and Insular Affairs
Pages: vii, 142

L/C Card Number: 76-601676
OCLC No.: 2166936
SuDoc No.: Y4.In8/13:W29/27
CIS No.: 76-S442-14
UPA Citation: N/A
Relevant Bills: S. 3579 (87th Cong.), H.R. 2683 (88th Cong.), H.R. 2689
    (88th Cong.), H.R. 4048 (88th Cong.), H.R. 7234 (88th Cong.),
    H.R. 7239 (88th Cong.), H.R. 7258 (88th Cong.), S. 2 (88th
    Cong.), H.R. 3606 (89th Cong.), H.R. 5930 (89th Cong.), H.R.
    6282 (89th Cong.), H.R. 8916 (89th Cong.), S. 22 (89th Cong.), S. 1051
    (91st Cong.), S. 3553 (91st Cong.), H.R. 1400 (92nd Cong.), H.R. 3835
    (92nd Cong.), H.R. 6403 (92nd Cong.), H.R. 7293 (92nd Cong.), H.R.
    10203 (92nd Cong.), S. 121 (92nd Cong.), S. 219 (92nd Cong.), S. 2428
    (92nd Cong.)

Chapter III of this document is a narrative legislative history of the Water
Resources Research Act of 1964, S. 2 (88th Cong.), P.L. 88-379. The chapter
also briefly discusses a 1966 amendment to the act S. 22 (89th Cong.), P.L. 89-
404, and a 1971 amendment H.R. 10203 (92nd Cong.), P.L. 92-175. The
history begins by reviewing some of the events which led to water resources
research legislation in the 88th Congress. The chapter follows the progress of
S. 2 (88th Cong.) through Congress summarizing and quoting the Senate
hearings, Senate report, Senate debate, House hearings, House report, House
debate, and Conference report on that bill. The narrative pays close attention
to amendments to S. 2 (88th Cong.) accepted and rejected on the Senate and
House floors, as well as changes made to the text of S. 2 (88th Cong.) as
reported by the House committee. Footnotes provide full citations to all
summarized and/or quoted documents. Next, the chapter provides a similar,
but briefer legislative history treatment for two amendments to the Water
Resources Research Act of 1964: a 1966 amendment, S. 22 (89th Cong.), P.L.
89-404; and a 1971 amendment, H.R. 10203 (92nd Cong.), P.L. 92-175. In a
separate section for each public law, the history follows the chronological
progress of H.R. 3606 (89th Cong.) and H.R. 10203 (92nd Cong.) and their
related bills through Congress. Again, Congressional hearings, reports, and
debate are summarized and quoted with footnotes providing full citations to
all mentioned documents.

Record No.: 100
Public Law No.: 88-563
Bill No.: H.R. 8000 (88th Cong.)
Statutes at Large Citation: 78 Stat. 809 (1964)
Title of Act: Interest Equalization Tax Act

Title of Legislative History: Legislative History of H.R. 8000, 88th Congress,
                                Interest Equalization Tax Act, Public Law 88-
                                563, 89th Cong., 2nd Sess. (Comm. Print 1966)

Publication Date: 1966
Author: House Committee on Ways and Means
Pages: ix, 1257

L/C Card Number: 66-65708
OCLC No.: 2201739
SuDoc No.: Y4.W36:In8/29
CIS No.: Committee-Print: H0978
UPA Citation: N/A
Relevant Bills: H.R. 8000 (88th Cong.)

This compilation chronologically presents the documents produced by
Congress and the executive branch during the process of enacting the
Interest Equalization Tax Act, H.R. 8000 (88th Cong.), P.L. 88-563. The
introductory material includes an alphabetical listing of members of Congress
with cross references to floor debates, as well as a chronological table of action
on the legislation. Among the included documents are: the act; several
versions of H.R. 8000 (88th Cong.); a president's special message; a
Congressional press release; selections from Congressional hearings; the
Congressional reports; and the Congressional debate.

Record No.: 101
Public Law No.: 89-4
Bill No.: S. 3 (89th Cong.)
Statutes at Large Citation: 79 Stat. 5 (1965)
Title of Act: Appalachian Regional Development Act of 1965

Title of Legislative History: Summary and Analysis of the Legislative
                                History of the Appalachian Regional
                                Development Act of 1965 and Subsequent
                                Amendments: A Report, 99th Cong., 1st Sess.
                                (Comm. Print 1985)
Publication Date: 1985
Author: Senate Committee on the Environment and Public Works
Pages: ix, 68, [32]

L/C Card Number: 85-602961
OCLC No.: 11862230
SuDoc No.: Y4.P96/10:S.Prt.99-14
CIS No.: 85-S322-4
UPA Citation: N/A
Relevant Bills: S. 2782 (88th Cong.), S. 3 (89th Cong.), S. 602 (90th Cong.),   S.
        1072 (91st Cong.), S. 2317 (92nd Cong.), H.R. 4073 (94th   Cong.), H.R.
        8777 (95th Cong.), S. 65 (98th Cong.)

This is a legislative history of the Appalachian Regional Development Act of 1965 (ARDA), S. 3 (89th Cong.), P.L. 89-4.   It focuses on ARDA's development through subsequent amendments to P.L. 89-4.   The history begins with a short narrative essay on the Congressional activity which resulted in the original ARDA. Footnotes provide citations to bills, Congressional reports, Congressional hearings, and Congressional debate. Next, the history includes a section-by-section analysis of ARDA as passed in 1965. The following section provides brief narrative essays on the laws which amended ARDA from 1965-1975. Footnotes provide complete citations to public laws, bills, Congressional reports, Congressional hearings, and Congressional debate. These amending acts include: Appalachian Regional Development Act Amendment of 1967, S. 602 (90th Cong.), P.L. 90-103; Appalachian Regional Development Act Amendments of 1969, S. 1072 (91st Cong.), P.L. 91-123; Appalachian Regional Development Act Amendments of 1971, S. 2317 (92nd Cong.), P.L. 92-65; and the Regional Development Act of 1975, H.R. 4073 (94th Cong.), P.L. 94-188.   The final part of the legislative history covers ARDA's development from 1975-1984.

Record No.: 102
Public Law No.: 89-44
Bill No.: H.R. 8371 (89th Cong.)
Statutes at Large Citation: 79 Stat. 136 (1965)
Title of Act: Excise Tax Reduction Act of 1965

Title of Legislative History: Legislative History of H.R. 8371, 89th Congress, Excise Tax Reduction Act of 1965, Public Law 89-44, 89th Cong., 1st Sess. (Comm. Print 1965)
Publication Date: 1965
Author: House Committee on Ways and Means
Pages: xii, 935

L/C Card Number: 66-60382
OCLC No.: 1688533
SuDoc No.: Y4.W36:L52/4
CIS No.: Committee-Print: H0744
UPA Citation: N/A
Relevant Bills: H.R. 8371 (89th Cong.)

The compilation presents the documents produced by Congress and the Executive branch during the process of enacting the Excise Tax Reduction Act, H.R. 8371 (89th Cong.), P.L. 89-44.   The introductory material includes an alphabetical listing of members of Congress with cross references to debate, as well as a chart of items affected by the Act with cross references to the Act and the Congressional reports. Among the included documents are: the Act; several versions of H.R. 8371 (89th Cong.); the president's message; a Congressional press release; selections from Congressional hearings; the Congressional reports; and, the Congressional debate.

Record No.: 103
Public Law No.: 89-49
Bill No.: H.R. 8464 (89th Cong.)
Statutes at Large Citation: 79 Stat. 172 (1965)
Title of Act: To Provide, for the Period Beginning on July 1, 1965, and
              Ending on June 30, 1966, a Temporary Increase in the Public
              Debt Limit Set Forth in Section 21 of the Second Liberty Bond
              Act

Title of Legislative History: Legislative History of H.R. 8464, 89th
                               Congress, Bill to Provide Temporary Increase
                               in Public Debt Limit, Public Law 89-49, 89th
                               Cong., 1st Sess. (Comm. Print 1965)
Publication Date: 1965
Author: House Committee on Ways and Means
Pages: vii, 220

L/C Card Number: 65-62973
OCLC No.: 16720769
SuDoc No.: Y4.W36:L52/3
CIS No.: Committee-Print: H0700
UPA Citation: N/A
Relevant Bills: H.R. 8464 (89th Cong.)

This compilation chronologically presents the documents Congress produced in 1965 during the process of enacting legislation to provide a temporary increase in the public debt limit, H.R. 8464 (89th Cong.), P.L. 89-49. The introductory material includes an alphabetical listing of members of Congress with cross references to debate. The documents include: the act; several versions of H.R. 8464 (89th Cong.); Congressional hearings; Congressional reports; and, Congressional debate.

Record No.: 104
Public Law No.: 89-73
Bill No.: H.R. 3708 (89th Cong.)
Statutes at Large Citation: 79 Stat. 218 (1965)
Title of Act: Older Americans Act of 1965

Title of Legislative History: Older Americans Act of 1965, as Amended:
                                History and Related Acts
Publication Date: 1979
Author: Department of Health, Education, and Welfare, Office of Human
Development Services, Administration on Aging
Pages: viii, 173

L/C Card Number: 80-602137
OCLC No.: 5421966
SuDoc No.: HE23.3005:OL1/979
CIS No.: N/A
UPA Citation: N/A
Relevant Bills: H.R. 3708 (89th Cong.), H.R. 10730 (90th Cong.), H.R.
    11235 (91st Cong.), S. 1163 (92nd Cong.), S. 50 (93rd Cong.),
    H.R. 11105 (93rd Cong.), H.R. 3922 (94th Cong.), H.R. 6668
    (95th Cong.), H.R. 12255 (95th Cong.)

This publication provides a single source of information on the original Older
Americans Act of 1965, H.R. 3708 (89th Cong.), P.L. 89-73, and
eight subsequent amendments in the period 1967-1978: Amendment of 1967,
H.R. 10730 (90th Cong.), P.L. 90-42; Amendment of 1969, H.R. 11235 (91st
Cong.), P.L. 91-69; Amendment of 1972, S. 1163 (92nd Cong.), P.L. 92-258;
Amendment of 1973, S. 50 (93rd Cong.), P.L. 93-29; Amendment of 1974, H.R.
11105 (93rd Cong.), P.L. 93-351; Amendment of 1975, H.R. 3922 (94th Cong.),
P.L. 94-135; Amendment of 1977, H.R. 6668 (95th Cong.), P.L. 95-65;
Amendment of 1978, H.R. 12255 (95th Cong.), P.L. 95-478. The work is
divided into three parts. Part I contains the text of the act after the
Amendment of 1978 with footnotes which indicate how specific amendments
affected the text of the act. Part II contains excerpts of nineteen acts whose
implementation impinges on that of the Older Americans Act. Part III is a
three page narrative history of the action. No citations to Congressional
documents are included. A detailed index provides references to sections of the
act as amended through October 1978.

Record No.: 105
Public Law No.: 89-110
Bill No.: S. 1564 (89th Cong.)
Statutes at Large Citation: 79 Stat. 437 (1965)
Title of Act: Voting Rights Act of 1965

Title of Legislative History: The Voting Rights Act of 1965: Legislative
                                History AND The Voting Rights Amendments
                                of 1970 IN Voting Rights Act of 1965, as
                                Amended: History, Effects, and Alternatives

Publication Date: 1975
Author: Jerome J. Hanus, Paul M. Downing, and Donovan Gay of the
Congressional Research Service
Pages: 135

L/C Card Number: N/A
OCLC No.: 4796218
SuDoc No.: N/A
CIS No.: N/A
UPA Citation: UPA Film No.: MS 75-76 Supp., Reel No. II, Frame No. 0795;
CRS No.: E 185 D, 75-243 GGR
Relevant Bills Bills: H.R. 6400 (89th Cong.), H.R. 7896 (89th Cong.), S. 1564
    (89th   Cong.), H.R. 4249 (91st Cong.), H.R. 12695 (91st Cong.), S.   818
    (91st Cong.), S. 2029 (91st Cong.), S. 2456 (91st Cong.),   S. 2507 (91st
    Cong.)

Chapter II, found on pages 11-24 of this document, is entitled "The Voting
Rights Act of 1965: Legislative History". It is a narrative legislative history of
the Voting Rights Act of 1965, S. 1564 (89th Cong.), P.L. 89-110. Chapter III,
found on pages 25-37, of this document is entitled "The Voting Rights
Amendments of 1970: Legislative History". It is a legislative history of the
Voting Rights Act Amendments of 1970, H.R. 4249 (91st Cong.), P.L. 91-285.
These chapters are similarly organized, proceeding roughly chronologically,
but with separate sections discussing House and Senate action. They provide
detailed summaries and comparisons of relevant bill versions. Congressional
hearings and Congressional reports are noted, but not summarized in detail.
The chapters summarize amendments to the bills as proposed in the hearings
and amendments to the bills as reported from committees. Footnotes provide
full citations to these Congressional hearings and reports. Congressional
debate covering proposed and passed amendments and the votes on these
amendments is noted. The chapters also note the Congressional votes on the
relevant bills and the date of Congressional debate. Each chapter do notes
arguments in favor of and in opposition to the proposed legislation from the
Congressional hearings and Congressional debate without providing citations
to these documents. In addition, the chapters contain summaries of the
legislation as finally passed.

Record No.: 106
Public Law No.: 89-243
Bill No.: H.R. 4750 (89th Cong.)
Statutes at Large Citation: 79 Stat. 954 (1965)
Title of Act: Interest Equalization Tax Extension Act of 1965

Title of Legislative History: Legislative History of H.R. 4750, 89th
                                 Congress, Interest Equalization Tax Extension
                                 Act of 1965, Public Law 89-243, 89th Cong., 1st
                                 Sess. (Comm. Print 1965)

Publication Date: 1965
Author: House Committee on Ways and Means
Pages: vii, 583

L/C Card Number: 66-60450
OCLC No.: 7266826
SuDoc No.: Y4.W36:In8/25
CIS No.: Committee-Print: H2471
UPA Citation: N/A
Relevant Bills: H.R. 4750 (89th Cong.), H.R. 8000 (88th Cong.)

This legislative history chronologically presents the Congressional action which resulted in the enactment of the Interest Equalization Tax Extension Act of 1965, H.R. 4750 (89th Cong.), P.L. 89-243. The introductory material includes an alphabetical listing of members of Congress with references to Congressional debate on H.R. 4750 (89th Cong.) and the Conference report on this bill. The history begins with the text of the act. It also contains a presidential message, various versions of H.R. 4750 (89th Cong.), Congressional press releases, Congressional hearings, Congressional reports, and Congressional debate. Concluding the work is the text of the Interest Equalization Tax Act, H.R. 8000 (88th Cong.), P.L. 88-563.

Record No.: 107
Public Law No.: 89-272
Bill No.: S. 306 (89th Cong.)
Statutes at Large Citation: 79 Stat. 992 (1965)
Title of Act: Solid Waste Disposal Act

Title of Legislative History: Legislative History of the Solid Waste Disposal
                                Act, As Amended, 93rd Cong., 2nd Sess.
                                (Comm. Print 1974)
Publication Date: 1974
Author: Senate Committee on Public Works
Pages: viii, 503

L/C Card Number: 74-602836
OCLC No.: 1371583
SuDoc No.: Y4.P96/10:93-22
CIS No.: 74-S642-17
UPA Citation: N/A
Relevant Bills: S. 306 (89th Cong.), H.R. 5446 (93rd Cong.), H.R. 4306 (93rd Cong.), H.R. 4292 (93rd Cong.), H.R. 4674 (93rd Cong.), S. 489 (93rd Cong.), H.R. 11833 (91st Cong.), S. 2005 (91st Cong.), S. 4012 (91st Cong.), H.R. 15785 (90th Cong.), S. 3201 (90th Cong.)

This is a legislative history of the Solid Waste Disposal Act, S. 306 (89th Cong.), P.L. 89-272, as amended through 1974. The Solid Waste Disposal Act was Title II of the Clean Air Act Amendments of 1965. In the order of their appearance in the volume, the amending laws are: Solid Waste Disposal Act, One Year Extension, H.R. 5446 (93rd Cong.), P.L. 93-14; Resource Recovery Act of 1970, H.R. 11833 (91st Cong.), P.L. 91-512, Title I; National Materials Policy Act, H.R. 11833 (91st Cong.), P.L. 91-512, Title II; Solid Waste Disposal Act, Sixty Day Extension, S. 4012 (91st Cong.), P.L. 91-316; Solid Waste Disposal Act, One Year Extension, H.R. 15758 (90th Cong.), P.L. 90-574. The document includes the text of the Solid Waste Disposal Act, as amended to 1974. Chapters dedicated to the original and amending acts include the text of each act, Congressional debate, Congressional reports, excerpts from Congressional hearings, and versions of bills. The history concludes with a chart comparing sections of the laws which it examined, as well as a section by section index to the Solid Waste Disposal Act, as amended, with references to the relevant contained documents.

Record No.: 108
Public Law No.: 89-329
Bill No.: H.R. 9567 (89th Cong.)
Statutes at Large Citation: 79 Stat. 1219 (1965)
Title of Act: Higher Education Act of 1965

Title of Legislative History: Teacher Corps: Legislative History and
                                Selected Program Information
Publication Date: 1977
Author: Marcia Scott of the Congressional Research Service
Pages: 25

L/C Card Number: N/A
OCLC No.: N/A
SuDoc No.: N/A
CIS No.: N/A
UPA Citation: UPA Film No: MS 76-78 Supp., Reel No. XII, Frame No. 1036;
CRS No.: 77-104ED
Relevant Bills: S. 370 (89th Cong.), S. 1172 (89th Cong.), S. 600 (89th Cong.),
        H.R. 9627 (89th Cong.), H.R. 9833 (89th Cong.), S. 2302 (89th Cong.),
        H.R. 9928 (89th Cong.), H.R. 9567 (89th Cong.), H.R. 10943 (90th
        Cong.), S. 3769 (90th Cong.), H.R. 514 (91st Cong.), S. 659 (92nd Cong.),
        H.R. 69 (93rd Cong.), S. 2657 (94th Cong.)

This narrative legislative history provides a summary of the various bills which preceded the enactment of Title V, Part B of the Higher Education Act of 1965, S. 370 (89th Cong.), P.L. 89-329.   Relevant Congressional debate and Congressional hearings are summarized and cited.   In addition, the essay also briefly summarizes and explains the motivations for six subsequent acts which affected the Teachers Corps: Higher Education Act of 1965, Amendment and Extension of 1967, H.R.

10943 (90th Cong.), P.L. 90-35; Higher Education Act of 1965, Amendment of 1968, S. 3769 (90th Cong.), P.L. 90-575; Elementary and Secondary Education Act of 1965, Amendment and Extension of 1970, H.R. 514 (91st Cong.), P.L. 91-230; Higher Education Act of 1965, Amendment of 1972, S. 659 (92nd Cong.), P.L. 92-318; Elementary and Secondary Education Act of 1965, Extension and Amendment of 1974, H.R. 69 (93rd Cong.), P.L. 93-380; Higher Education Act of 1965, Amendment of 1976, S. 2657 (94th Cong.), P.L. 94-482.

Record No.: 109
Public Law No.: 89-368
Bill No.: H.R. 12752 (89th Cong.)
Statutes at Large Citation: 80 Stat. 38 (1966)
Title of Act: Tax Adjustment Act of 1966

Title of Legislative History: Legislative History of H.R. 12752, 89th Congress, Tax Adjustment Act of 1966, Public Law 89-368, 89th Cong., 2nd Sess. (Comm. Print 1966)
Publication Date: 1966
Author: House Committee on Ways and Means
Pages: xi, 1260

L/C Card Number: 66-62739
OCLC No.: 2188215
SuDoc No.: Y4.W36:T19/38
CIS No.: Committee-Print: H2135
UPA Citation: N/A
Relevant Bills: H.R. 12752 (89th Cong.)

The Congressional action leading to the enactment of the Tax Adjustment Act of 1966, H.R. 12752 (89th Cong.), P.L. 89-368 is presented chronologically in this legislative history. Introductory material includes an alphabetical listing of members of Congress with references to relevant debate, as well as a list of subjects affected by the act with references to the act and Congressional reports. The history begins with the full text of the act and includes excerpts from Presidential messages, reports, and tax recommendations. The full text of several versions of H.R. 12752 (89th Cong.) and the relevant Congressional press releases, Congressional hearings, Congressional reports, and Congressional debate also appear in the work. Concluding the work is a Congressionally prepared summary of the act. The appendices include a chronological table of Congressional action, as well as a summary of amendments which were rejected.

Record No.: 110
Public Law No.: 89-472
Bill No.: H.R. 15202 (89th Cong.)
Statutes at Large Citation: 80 Stat. 221 (1966)
Title of Act: To Provide, for the Period Beginning on July 1, 1966, and
               Ending on June 30, 1967, a Temporary Increase in the Public
               Debt Limit Set Forth in Section 21 of the Second Liberty Bond
               Act

Title of Legislative History: Legislative History of H.R. 15202, 89th
                               Congress (2nd Session), Bill to Provide
                               Temporary Increase in Public Debt Limit,
                               Public Law 89-472, and Legislative History of
                               H.R. 8464, 89th Congress (1st Session), Bill to
                               Provide Temporary Increase in Public Debt
                               Limit, Public Law 89-49, 89th Cong., 2nd Sess.
                               (Comm. Print 1966)
Publication Date: 1966
Author: House Committee on Ways and Means
Pages: various

L/C Card Number: 66-62992
OCLC No.: 139
SuDoc No.: Y4.W36:L52/3/966
CIS No.: Committee-Print: H3015
UPA Citation: N/A
Relevant Bills: H.R. 15202 (89th Cong.)

This legislative history chronologically presents the Congressional action
which resulted in the enactment of H.R. 15202 (89th Cong.), P.L. 89-472. The
introductory material includes an alphabetical listing of members of Congress
with references to Congressional debate. The legislative history begins
with the text of P.L. 89-472 and includes Congressional hearings, several
versions of H.R. 15202 (89th Cong.), Congressional reports, and Congressional
debate. The Joint Committee on Internal Revenue Taxation's estimates of
federal receipts for the fiscal years 1966 and 1967 concludes the work. This
volume also contains a reprint of the legislative history of H.R. 8464 (89th
Cong.), P.L. 89-49, To Provide a Temporary Increase in the Public Debt Limit.

Record No.: 111
Public Law No.: 89-487
Bill No.: S. 1160 (89th Cong.)
Statutes at Large Citation: 80 Stat. 250 (1966)
Title of Act: Freedom of Information Act

Title of Legislative History: Legislative History of the Public Information
Section of the Administrative Procedure Act --
The Freedom of Information Act IN U.S.--
Government Information Policies and
Practices Administration and Operation of the
Freedom of Information Act (Part 4): Hearings
Before the Subcommittee on Foreign
Operations and Government Information of the
House Committee on Government Operations,
92nd Cong., 2nd Sess. (1972)

Publication Date: 1972
Author: Subcommittee on Foreign Operations and Government
Information, House Committee on Government Operations
Pages: iv, 1005-1373

L/C Card Number: 70-614955
OCLC No.: 219010
SuDoc No.: Y4.G74/7:In3/12/pt.4
CIS No.: 72-H401-31
UPA Citation: N/A
Relevant Bills: S. 1663 (88th Cong.), S. 1666 (88th Cong.), S. 1160 (89th
Cong.), H.R. 5012 (89th Cong.), H.R. 5013 (89th Cong.), H.R. 5014 (89th
Cong.), H.R. 5015 (89th Cong.), H.R. 5016 (89th Cong.), H.R. 5017 (89th
Cong.), H.R. 5018 (89th Cong.), H.R 5019 (89th Cong.), H.R. 5020 (89th
Cong.), H.R. 5021 (89th Cong.), H.R. 5237 (89th Cong.), H.R. 5406 (89th
Cong.), H.R. 5520 (89th Cong.), H.R. 5583 (89th Cong.), H.R. 6172 (89th
Cong.), H.R. 6739 (89th Cong.), H.R. 7010 (89th Cong.), H.R. 7161 (89th
Cong.)

This narrative legislative history was included as pages 1367 - 1373 of
hearings held in 1972 before the House Subcommittee on Foreign Operations
and Government Information. The essay briefly examines prior freedom of
information legislation, then relates in detail the action which led to the
enactment of the Freedom of Information Act, S. 1160 (89th Cong.), P.L. 89-
487. Footnotes provide citations to bills, Congressional debate, Congressional
hearings, and Congressional reports. The Freedom of Information Act was
incorporated into Section 552 of Title 5 of the *United States Code* by P.L. 90-
23.

Record No.: 112
Public Law No.: 89-563
Bill No.: S. 3005 (89th Cong.)
Statutes at Large Citation: 80 Stat. 718 (1966)
Title of Act: National Traffic and Motor Vehicle Safety Act of 1966

Title of Legislative History: Federal Consumer Safety Legislation, Study of Scope and Adequacy of Automobile Safety, Flammable Fabrics, and Hazardous Substances Programs

Publication Date: 1970
Author: National Commission on Product Safety
Pages: xv, 213

L/C Card Number: 70-606730
OCLC No.: 118376
SuDoc No.: Y3.N21/25:2C76
CIS No.: N/A
UPA Citation: N/A
Relevant Bills: H.R. 5069 (83rd Cong.), S. 3379 (83rd Cong.), S. 1283 (86th Cong.), H.R. 13228 (89th Cong.), S. 3005 (89th Cong.), S. 3298 (89th Cong.), H.R. 5654 (90th Cong.), S. 1003 (90th Cong.), S. 1689 (91st Cong.)

The National Commission on Product Safety Act, S.J. Res. 33 (90th Cong.), P.L. 90-146, established the National Commission on Product Safety and charged it with conducting a comprehensive investigation into the scope and adequacy of federal consumer safety legislation. This document is a study the Commission had requested to be prepared by the Chief Counsel of the Federal Highway Administration. Its purpose was to examine the federal safety laws, as of 1970, for the three subject areas of automobiles, flammable fabrics, and hazardous household substances. The discussion in each of these areas begins with a section on the legislative history of the federal safety legislation in that area. The study examines these laws: National Traffic and Motor Vehicle Safety Act of 1966, S. 3005 (89th Cong.), P.L. 89-563; Flammable Fabrics Act, H.R. 5069 (83rd Cong.), P.L. 83-88; Flammable Fabrics Act, Amendment of 1954, S. 3379 (83rd Cong.), P.L. 83-629; Flammable Fabrics Act, Amendment of 1967, S. 1003 (90th Cong.), P.L. 90-189; Federal Hazardous Substances Labeling Act of 1960, S. 1283 (86th Cong.), P.L. 86-613; Child Protection Act of 1966, S. 3298 (89th Cong.), P.L. 89-756; and Child Protection and Toy Safety Act of 1969, S. 1689 (91st Cong.), P.L. 91-113. Each legislative history section includes numerous quotes from the relevant Congressional reports, Congressional debate, Congressional hearings, and public laws. Footnotes provide complete citations to all quoted documents.   After each legislative history, the study examines the implementation of the public law or laws in that area. Sometimes these sections on implementation will also include legislative history information, when discussing such topics as how the language of the acts has been interpreted.

Record No.: 113
Public Law No.: 89-601
Bill No.: H.R. 13712 (89th Cong.)
Statutes at Large Citation: 80 Stat. 830 (1966)
Title of Act: Fair Labor Standards Amendments of 1966

Title of Legislative History: Legislative History of Fair Labor Standards
Amendments of 1966, Public Law 89-601, 89th
Congress, H.R. 13712, 90th Cong., 2nd Sess.
(Comm. Print 1968)
Publication Date: 1968
Author: Senate Committee on Labor and Public Welfare
Pages: v, 205

L/C Card Number: 68-67122
OCLC No.: 3637
SuDoc No.: Y4.L11/2:F15/3
CIS No.: Committee-Print S1178
UPA Citation: N/A
Relevant Bills: H.R. 13712 (89th Cong.), H.R. 10518 (89th Cong.)

This legislative history contains the complete text of the Fair Labor Standards
Amendments of 1966, H.R. 13712 (89th Cong.), P.L. 89-601. It also contains
the Congressional reports on H.R. 13712 (89th Cong.) and its companion bill
H.R. 10518 (89th Cong.). The report provides both an alphabetical subject
index and a sectional index to the act. The indexes provide the page numbers
of the original Congressional reports and the Congressional reports as
reprinted in the legislative history, as well as the page numbers of the debate
in the *Congressional Record*.

Record No.: 114
Public Law No.: 89-719
Bill No.: H.R. 11256 (89th Cong.)
Statutes at Large Citation: 80 Stat. 1125 (1966)
Title of Act: Federal Tax Lien Act of 1966

Title of Legislative History: Legislative History of H.R. 11256, 89th
Congress, Federal Tax Lien Act of 1966, Public
Law 89-719, 89th Cong., 2nd Sess. (Comm.
Print 1966)
Publication Date: 1966
Author: House Committee on Ways and Means
Pages: ix, 783

L/C Card Number: 67-60165
OCLC No.: 953734
SuDoc No.: Y4.W36:T19/40
CIS No.: Committee-Print: H0977
UPA Citation: N/A
Relevant Bills: H.R. 11256 (89th Cong.), H.R. 11290 (89th Cong.)

This legislative history chronologically presents the Congressional
action which resulted in the enactment of the Federal Tax Lien Act of 1966,
H.R. 11256 (89th Cong.), P.L. 89-719. The introductory material includes
a chronological table of the legislation's progress, as well as an
alphabetical listing of members of Congress with cross references to
Congressional debate. The legislative history contains the full text of the act,
an American Bar Association Report, several versions of H.R. 11256 (89th
Cong.), Congressional press releases, Congressional hearings, Congressional
reports, and Congressional debate.

Record No.: 115
Public Law No.: 89-754
Bill No.: S. 3708 (89th Cong.)
Statutes at Large Citation: 80 Stat. 1255 (1966)
Title of Act: Demonstration Cities and Metropolitan Development Act of 1966

Title of Legislative History: Demonstration Cities and Metropolitan
                                 Development Act of 1966, P.L. 89-754, Together
                                 with a Brief Summary, Section-by-Section
                                 Analysis, Legislative History, and Conference
                                 Report, 89th Cong., 2nd Sess. (Comm. Print
                                 1966)
Publication Date: 1966
Author: House Committee on Banking and Currency
Pages: iii, 84

L/C Card Number: 67-60183
OCLC No.: 2581458
SuDoc No.: Y4.B22/1:C49/3
CIS No.: Committee-Print: H1905
UPA Citation: N/A
Relevant Bills: H.R. 12341 (89th Cong.), H.R. 12946 (89th Cong.), H.R.
    13064 (89th Cong.), H.R. 9256 (89th Cong.), H.R. 15890 (89th Cong.),
    S. 3711 (89th Cong.), S. 3708 (89th Cong.)

The document presents a one page chronological history of the enactment of
the Demonstration Cities and Metropolitan Development Act of 1966, S. 3708
(89th Cong.), P.L. 89-754. The history provides citations to Congressional

hearings, bills, reports, and debate. The Conference report and the full text of the act follow the history. Also included are a summary of the act's principal provisions and a section-by-section analysis of the act.

Record No.: 116
Public Law No.: 89-800
Bill No.: H.R. 17607 (89th Cong.)
Statutes at Large Citation: 80 Stat. 1508 (1966)
Title of Act: To Suspend the Investment Credit and the Allowance of
          Accelerated Depreciation in the Case of Certain Real Property

Title of Legislative History: Legislative History of H.R. 17607, 89th
                   Congress, Suspension of the Investment Credit
                   and the Allowance of Accelerated Depreciation
                   in the Case of Certain Real Property, P.L. 89-
                   800, 89th Cong., 2nd Sess. (Comm. Print 1966)
Publication Date: 1966
Author: House Committee on Ways and Means
Pages: ix, 1489

L/C Card Number: 67-60321
OCLC No.: 218307
SuDoc No.: Y4.W36:C86/2
CIS No.: Committee-Print: H0983
UPA Citation: N/A
Relevant Bills: H.R. 17607 (89th Cong.)

The legislative history presents the Congressional action which resulted in the enactment of H.R. 17607 (89th Cong.). The introductory material includes a chronological table of the legislation's progress through Congress, as well as an alphabetical listing of members of Congress with cross references to Congressional debate. The legislative history includes the full text of the act, President's message, several versions of the bill, Congressional press releases, Congressional hearings, Congressional reports, Congressional debate, and summary of the act.

Record No.: 117
Public Law No.: 89-809
Bill No.: H.R. 13103 (89th Cong.)
Statutes at Large Citation: 80 Stat. 1539 (1966)
Title of Act: Foreign Investors Tax Act of 1966

Title of Legislative History: Legislative History of H.R. 13103, 89th
                                 Congress, Foreign Investors Tax Act of 1966,
                                 Public Law 89-809, 90th Congress, 1st Session,
                                 90th Cong., 1st Sess. (Comm. Print 1967)
Publication Date: 1967
Author: House Committee on Ways and Means
Pages: x, 1162; x, 1163-2189

L/C Card Number: 67-61120
OCLC No.: 19431549
SuDoc No.: Y4.W36:F76in/7/pt.1-2
CIS No.: Committee-Print: H2981
UPA Citation: N/A
Relevant Bills: H.R. 5916 (89th Cong.), H.R. 11297 (89th Cong.), H.R. 13103
    (89th Cong.), H.R. 10 (89th Cong.), H.R. 11765 (89th Cong.), S. 1013
    (89th Cong.), H.R. 18230 (89th Cong.)

The legislative history chronologically details the Congressional action which
resulted in the enactment of the Foreign Investors Tax Act of 1966, H.R. 13103
(89th Cong.), P.L. 89-809, Title I. The introductory material includes a
chronological table of the legislation's progress through Congress, as well as an
alphabetical listing of members of Congress with cross references to
Congressional debate. The legislative history includes the full text of the act,
several versions of the several related bills, Congressional press releases, the
report of the Presidential Task Force on Promoting Increased Foreign
Investment in U.S. Corporate Securities and Increased Foreign Financing for
U.S. Corporations Operating Abroad, Congressional hearings, Congressional
reports, Congressional debate, and a Presidential statement. Also included is a
summary of the Presidential Election Campaign Fund Act which appeared as
Title III of P.L. 89-809. The appendices include versions of several bills which
became different sections of P.L. 89-809.

Record No.: 118
Public Law No.: 90-3
Bill No.: H.R. 4573 (90th Cong.)
Statutes at Large Citation: 81 Stat. 4 (1967)
Title of Act: To Provide, for the Period Ending on June 30, 1967, a
             Temporary Increase in the Public Debt Limit Set Forth in
             Section 21 of the Second Liberty Bond Act

Title of Legislative History: Legislative History of H.R. 4573, 90th
                                 Congress, 1st Session, To Provide Temporary
                                 Increase in Public Debt Limit, Public Law 90-
                                 3,and H.R. 10867, 90th Congress, 1st Session,
                                 To Increase Public Debt Limit Set Forth in Sec.
                                 21 of Second Liberty Bond Act, and for Other
                                 Purposes, Public Law 90-39, 90th Cong., 1st
                                 Sess. (Comm. Print 1967)

Publication Date: 1967
Author: House Committee on Ways and Means
Pages: xi, 1181

L/C Card Number: 67-62437
OCLC No.: 7602502
SuDoc No.: Y4.W36:D35/5
CIS No.: Committee-Print: H1046
UPA Citation: N/A
Relevant Bills: H.R. 4573 (90th Cong.), H.R. 10867 (90th Cong.), H.R. 10328
    (90th Cong.)

The legislative history includes the full text of the act, Congressional
press releases, Congressional hearings, several versions of H.R. 4573 (90th
Cong.), Congressional reports, and Congressional debate. The introductory
material includes a chronological table of the legislation's progress through
Congress, as well as an alphabetical listing of members of Congress with cross
references to Congressional debate. Part A of this document presents the
Congressional action which resulted in the enactment of H.R. 4573 (90th
Cong.), P.L. 90-3. The introductory material includes an alphabetical listing of
members of Congress with cross references to Congressional debate, as well as
a chronological table of the legislation's progress through Congress. Part B
chronologically presents the Congressional action which resulted in the
enactment of P.L. 90-39. The legislative history includes the full text of
the act, Congressional press releases, Congressional hearings, several
versions of H.R. 10867 (90th Cong.) and its related bill H.R. 10328 (90th
Cong.), Congressional reports, and Congressional debate.

Record No.: 119
Public Law No.: 90-23
Bill No.: H.R. 5357 (90th Cong.)
Statutes at Large Citation: 81 Stat. 54 (1967)
Title of Act: Freedom of Information Act

Title of Legislative History: Freedom of Information Act Source Book,
                                Legislative Materials, Cases, Articles, 93rd
                                Cong., 2nd Sess. (Comm. Print 1974)
Publication Date: 1974
Author: Subcommittee on Administrative Practice and Procedure, Senate
Committee on the Judiciary
Pages: v, 432

L/C Card Number: 74-601465
OCLC No.: 912056
SuDoc No.: Y4.J89/2:In3/10
CIS No.: 74-S522-6
UPA Citation: N/A

Relevant Bills: S. 1663 (88th Cong.), S. 1666 (88th Cong.), H.R. 5012 (89th Cong.), S. 1160 (89th Cong.), H.R. 5357 (90th Cong.)

Part one of this source book consists of a short narrative history of the Freedom of Information Act, H.R. 5357 (90th Cong.), P.L. 90-23. Footnotes provide complete citations to various Congressional documents. It is followed by a chronological table which summarizes the Freedom of Information Act's history and provides full citations to all relevant Congressional documents. Selected documents are included in full. Among these included documents are: the Freedom of Information Act as codified by law, H.R. 5357 (90th Cong.), P.L. 90-23, as well as selected Congressional reports and Congressional debate on this codification. Also included are selected Congressional reports and Congressional debate on the Freedom of Information Act before codification, S. 1160 (89th Cong.), P.L. 89-487. Part two of this source book lists court cases which involved the Freedom of Information Act. Part three is a selected bibliography of articles on the Freedom of Information Act. Part four consists of the Department of Justice's Freedom of Information Regulations, as of 1974.

Record No.: 120
Public Law No.: 90-26
Bill No.: H.R. 6950 (90th Cong.)
Statutes at Large Citation: 81 Stat. 57 (1967)
Title of Act: To Restore the Investment Credit and the Allowance of Accelerated Depreciation in the Case of Certain Real Property

Title of Legislative History: Legislative History of H.R. 6950, 90th Congress, To Restore Investment Credit and Allowance of Accelerated Depreciation in Case of Certain Real Property, Public Law 90-26, 90th Cong., 1st Sess. (Comm. Print 1967)
Publication Date: 1967
Author: House Committee on Ways and Means
Pages: xvi, 1250

L/C Card Number: 67-62201
OCLC No.: 7441046
SuDoc No.: Y4.W36:C86/4
CIS No.: Committee-Print: H2960
UPA Citation: N/A
Relevant Bills: H.R. 13103 (89th Cong.), H.R. 17607 (89th Cong.), H.R. 6950 (90th Cong.)

This legislative history sets forth the Congressional action which resulted in the enactment of H.R. 6950 (90th Cong.), P.L. 90-26. The investment credit and allowance of accelerated depreciation on certain real property had been suspended by H.R. 17607 (89th Cong.), P.L. 89-800. H.R. 6950 (90th Cong.), P.L. 90-26 restored this credit and allowance and also amended the Presidential Election Campaign Fund Act, H.R. 13103 (89th Cong.), P.L. 89-809, Title III. The introductory material includes a chronological table of the legislation's progress through Congress, as well as an alphabetical listing of members of Congress with cross references to debate. The history includes the full text of the act, President's message, several versions of H.R. 6950 (90th Cong.), Congressional press releases, Congressional hearings, Congressional reports, and Congressional debate.

Record No.: 121
Public Law No.: 90-59
Bill No.: H.R. 6098 (90th Cong.)
Statutes at Large Citation: 81 Stat. 145 (1967)
Title of Act: Interest Equalization Tax Extension Act of 1967

Title of Legislative History: Legislative History of H.R. 6098, 90th
                                 Congress, 1st Session, Interest Equalization
                                 Tax Extension Act of 1967, Public Law 90-59,
                                 and H.R. 4750, 89th Congress, 1st Session,
                                 Interest Equalization Tax Extension Act of
                                 1965, Public Law 89-243, 90th Cong., 1st Sess.
                                 (Comm. Print 1967)
Publication Date: 1967
Author: House Committee on Ways and Means
Pages: various

L/C Card Number: 67-62436
OCLC No.: 12728459
SuDoc No.: Y4.W36:In8/25/967
CIS No.: Committee-Print: H3009
UPA Citation: N/A
Relevant Bills: H.R. 8000 (88th Cong.), H.R. 4750 (89th Cong.), H.R. 3813 (90th Cong.), H.R. 6098 (90th Cong.)

Part I of this legislative history details the Congressional action which resulted in the enactment of the Interest Equalization Tax Extension Act of 1967, H.R. 6098 (90th Cong.), P.L. 90-59. The introductory material includes an alphabetical listing of members of Congress with cross references to Congressional debate, as well as a chronological table of the legislation's passage. The history includes the full text of the act, several versions of H.R. 6098 (90th Cong.) and its related bill H.R. 3813 (90th Cong.), Congressional press releases, Congressional hearings, Congressional reports, and Congressional debate. Part II chronologically presents the Congressional action which resulted in the enactment of the Interest Equalization Tax Extension Act of 1965, H.R. 4750 (89th Cong.), P.L. 89-243. The introductory material includes an alphabetical listing of members of Congress with cross references to Congressional debate. The history includes the full text of the act, President's message, several versions of H.R. 4750 (89th Cong.), Congressional press releases, Congressional hearings, Congressional reports, and Congressional debate. An appendix contains the full text of the Interest Equalization Tax Act, H.R. 8000 (88th Cong.), P.L. 88-563.

Record No.: 122
Public Law No.: 90-202
Bill No.: S. 830 (90th Cong.)
Statutes at Large Citation: 81 Stat. 602 (1967)
Title of Act: Age Discrimination in Employment Act of 1967

Title of Legislative History: Next Steps in Combating Age Discrimination
                                 in Employment with Special Reference to
                                 Mandatory Retirement Policy
Publication Date: 1977
Author: Senate Special Committee on Aging
Pages: 26

L/C Card Number: 77-603538
OCLC No.: 955399
SuDoc No.: Y4.Ag4:R31/7
CIS No.: N/A
UPA Citation: N/A
Relevant Bills: S. 788 (90th Cong.), S. 830 (90th Cong.)

This committee print contains several short essays which discuss various aspects of the Age Discrimination in Employment Act of 1967 (ADEA), S. 830 (90th Cong.), P.L. 90-202. Part I deals with the history, achievements, and shortcomings of the ADEA. It includes a brief narrative legislative history which provides complete citations to relevant Congressional hearings, Congressional reports, and Congressional debate. Part II presents arguments for and against mandatory retirement. Part III presents several different legislative approaches considered by Congress during the first six months of the 95th Congress, 1977, in response to the employment needs of older workers.

Record No.: 123
Public Law No.: 90-351
Bill No.: H.R. 5037 (90th Cong.)
Statutes at Large Citation: 82 Stat. 197 (1968)
Title of Act: Omnibus Crime Control and Safe Streets Act of 1968

Title of Legislative History: Index to Legislative History of Omnibus Crime
                                  Control and Safe Streets Act of 1968
Publication Date: 1973
Author: Department of Justice, Law Enforcement Assistance
Administration, Office of General Counsel
Pages: viii, 339

L/C Card Number: 73-601191
OCLC No.: 1073741
SuDoc No.: J1.2:C86/16
CIS No.: N/A
UPA Citation: N/A
Relevant Bills: H.R. 5037 (90th Cong.), S. 917 (90th Cong.)

The legislative history begins with several detailed indexes. The first index
provides citations to subjects as they were treated in Congressional reports
and Congressional debate. There are also indices to the views of individual
Senators and members of Congress in Congressional debate. The
Congressional activity which resulted in the enactment of the Omnibus Crime
Control and Safe Streets Act of 1968, H.R. 5037 (90th Cong.), P.L. 90-351 is
indexed chronologically. The legislative history includes: several versions of
H.R. 5037 (90th Cong.), excerpts from Congressional reports, and excerpts
from Congressional debate.

Record No.: 124
Public Law No.: 90-602
Bill No.: H.R. 10790 (90th Cong.)
Statutes at Large Citation: 82 Stat. 1173 (1968)
Title of Act: Radiation Control for Health and Safety Act of 1968

Title of Legislative History: Legislative History of Radiation Control for
                                  Health and Safety Act of 1968

Publication Date: 1975
Author: Department of Health, Education, and Welfare
Pages: ix, 1494

L/C Card Number: 84-601931
OCLC No.: 12104759
SuDoc No.: HE20.4102:L52/v.1,2
CIS No.: N/A
UPA Citation: N/A

Relevant Bills: H.R. 10790 (90th Cong.), H.R.J. Res. 280 (90th Cong.), H.R. 11107 (90th Cong.), H.R. 11101 (90th Cong.), S. 2067 (90th Cong.), S. 2075 (90th Cong.), H.R. 11365 (90th Cong.), H.R. 11401 (90th Cong.), H.R. 12092 (90th Cong.), H.R. 12185 (90th Cong.), H.R. 15156 (90th Cong.), H.R. 15196 (90th Cong.), H.R. 15985 (90th Cong.), S. 3211 (90th Cong.)

The two volume legislative history contains all of the documents produced by Congress during the enactment of the Radiation Control for Health and Safety Act of 1968, H.R. 10790 (90th Cong.), P.L. 90-602. The first volume has the documents Congress produced in 1967, and the second volume has the documents Congress produced in 1968. The introductory material consists of a chronological table of the legislation's progress which provides complete citations to all relevant Congressional documents. The legislative history consists of the full text of these documents in their chronological order. Among the included documents are: several versions of H.R. 10790 (90th Cong.) and its related bills; President's message; Congressional debate; Congressional hearings; and Congressional reports. The appendix consists of a subject index to the legislative history.

Record No.: 125
Public Law No.: 91-54
Bill No.: H.R. 10946 (91st Cong.)
Statutes at Large Citation: 83 Stat. 96 (1969)
Title of Act: Construction Safety Act

Title of Legislative History: Legislative History of Federal Construction Safety Act, 91st Cong., 1st Sess. (Comm. Print 1969)
Publication Date: 1969
Author: Senate Committee on Labor and Public Welfare
Pages: v, 105

L/C Card Number: 73-604470
OCLC No.: 52491
SuDoc No.: Y4.L11/2:C76
CIS No.: 71-S542-10
UPA Citation: N/A
Relevant Bills: H.R. 10946 (91st Cong.), S.1368 (91st Cong.)

This is a legislative history of the Construction Safety Act, H.R. 10946 (91st Cong.), P.L. 91-54. It is the public law that tightened the safety standards on federal and federally financed construction projects. Materials are presented in roughly chronological order. The history begins with the texts of H.R. 10946 (91st Cong.) and its related bill S. 1368 (91st Cong.) as they were introduced. It proceeds with the text of H.R. 10946 (91st Cong.) as reported

to the House, the House debate on H.R. 10946 (91st Cong.), and the text of
H.R. 10946 (91st Cong.) as passed by the House. Next, the history presents
H.R. 10946 (91st Cong.) as reported to the Senate and the Senate debate on
this bill. The text of several versions of the bills has been included. The
Congressional debate has been excerpted from the *Congressional Record*,
with the dates of the debate provided. The House and Senate reports on
H.R. 10946 (91st Cong.) directly precede the text of P.L. 91-54. The text of
P.L. 91-54 concludes the legislative history.

Record No.: 126
Public Law No.: 91-173
Bill No.: S. 2917 (91st Cong.)
Statutes at Large Citation: 83 Stat. 742 (1969)
Title of Act: Federal Coal Mine Health and Safety Act of 1969

Title of Legislative History: Legislative History of Federal Coal Mine
                                 Health and Safety Act of 1969 (Public Law 91-
                                 173) As Amended through 1974, Including
                                 Black Lung Amendments of 1972, 94th Cong.,
                                 1st Sess. (Comm. Print 1975)
Publication Date: 1975
Author: Senate Committee on Labor and Public Welfare
Pages: v, 1702; vi, 1703-3205

L/C Card Number: 76-600930
OCLC No.: 2819925
SuDoc No.: Y4.L11/2:C63/5/pt.1-2
CIS No.: 75-S542-21&22
UPA Citation: N/A
Relevant Bills: H.R. 13950 (91st Cong.), S. 355 (91st Cong.), S. 467 (91st
     Cong.), S. 1094 (91st Cong.), S. 1178 (91st Cong.), S. 1300 (91st Cong.),
     S. 1907 (91st Cong.), S. 2118 (91st Cong.), S. 2284 (91st Cong.), S. 2405
     (91st Cong.), S. 2917 (91st Cong.), H.R. 9212 (92nd Cong.), S. 2289
     (92nd Cong.), S. 2675 (92nd Cong.), S. 3940 (92nd Cong.)

The Congressional action which resulted in the enactment of the Federal
Coal Mine Health and Safety Act of 1969, S. 2917 (91st Cong.), P.L. 91-173,
and the Black Lung Benefits Act of 1972, H.R. 9212 (92nd Cong.), P.L. 92-303
is a two part legislative history. The first part presents the history of the
Federal Coal Mine Health and Safety Act of 1969. Its table of contents
chronologically lists the documents which the history contains the full text.
Among the included documents are several versions of S. 2917 (91st Cong.)
and its related bills, Congressional debate, Congressional reports, and the
public law. The second part consists of several appendices. Appendix I is
the legislative history of the Black Lung Benefits Act. Its table of contents

chronologically lists first the House and then the Senate documents for which the history contains the full text. Among the included documents are: several versions of H.R. 9212 (92nd Cong.) and its related bills; Congressional reports; Congressional debate; and the public law. Appendix II consists of the text of the Senate's related bills on the Federal Coal Mine Health and Safety Act of 1969. Appendix III consists of the excerpts from the bound *Congressional Record Daily Digest* for 1969, pertinent to the Federal Coal Mine Health and Safety Act of 1969.

Record No.: 127
Public Law No.: 91-190
Bill No.: S. 1075 (91st Cong.)
Statutes at Large Citation: 83 Stat. 852 (1970)
Title of Act: National Environmental Policy Act of 1969

Title of Legislative History: National Environmental Policy Act of 1969
                                (P.L. 91-190): Bibliography
Publication Date: 1976
Author: Steve Hughes of the Congressional Research Service
Pages: 263

L/C Card Number: N/A
OCLC No.: 5061980
SuDoc No.: N/A
CIS No.: N/A
UPA Citation: UPA Film No.: MS 76-78 Supp., Reel No. VI, Frame No. 212;
CRS No.: 77-41 EP
Relevant Bills: S. 1075 (91st Cong.)

This selective bibliography reflects a number of publications which have been regularly cited. Section A contains citations to Congressional documents such as Congressional hearings and Congressional reports. The citations refer to both the documents which comprise the early legislative history of the National Environmental Policy Act of 1969 (NEPA), S. 1075 (91st Cong.), P.L. 91-190, as well as its implementation and amendments. Section B provides citations to law journal articles which consider the extensive litigation on and judicial interpretation of NEPA. Section C provides citations to articles which consider NEPA issues. The journal articles are cross-disciplinary. Section D provides citations to policy papers and bibliographies which treat NEPA issues. Section E provides citations to journal articles and technical reports which address problems related to the preparation of environmental impact statements. An appendix provides citations to books and doctoral dissertations which treat NEPA issues.

Record No.: 128
Public Law No.: 91-375
Bill No.: H.R. 17070 (91st Cong.)
Statutes at Large Citation: 84 Stat. 719 (1970)
Title of Act: Postal Reorganization Act

Title of Legislative History: Explanation of Postal Reorganization Act and
                                Selected Background Material, Revised July
                                1975, 94th Cong., 1st Sess. (Comm. Print 1975)
Publication Date: 1975
Author: Senate Committee on Post Office and Civil Service
Pages: v, 314

L/C Card Number: 75-602302
OCLC No.: 1603929
SuDoc No.: Y4.P84/11:P84/25/975
CIS No.: 75-S622-3
UPA Citation: N/A
Relevant Bills: H.R. 17070 (91st Cong.), S. 3842 (91st Cong.)

This is a legislative history of the Postal Reorganization Act, H.R. 17070
(91st Cong.), P.L. 91-375. It begins with a short narrative summary of the
Postal Reorganization Act's provisions and then continues with the text of
P.L. 91-375. The Conference report and House report on H.R. 17070 (91st
Cong.), as well as the Senate report on S. 3842 (91st Cong.) are also
contained in this work. The history presents the President's message upon
transmitting the Administration's proposed bill H.R. 17070 (91st Cong.) to
Congress. The Senate Committee on Post Office and Civil Service's report
of its 1973-1974 investigation into the Postal Service concludes the work.
This report in part contains excerpts from and full citations to
Congressional postal oversight hearings held in 1973. The report also
provides evaluations of the Postal Service's organization and operations.

Record No.: 129
Public Law No.: 91-596
Bill No.: S. 2193 (91st Cong.)
Statutes at Large Citation: 84 Stat. 1590 (1970)
Title of Act: Occupational Safety and Health Act of 1970

Title of Legislative History: Legislative History of Occupational Safety and
                                Health Act of 1970 (S. 2193, P.L. 91-596), 92nd
                                Cong., 1st Sess. (Comm. Print 1971)
Publication Date: 1971
Author: Subcommittee on Labor, Senate Committee on Labor and Public
Welfare
Pages: vi, 1278

L/C Card Number: 77-614618
OCLC No.: 214239
SuDoc No.: Y4.L11/2:Sa1/5
CIS No.: 71-S542-17
UPA Citation: N/A
Relevant Bills: H.R. 843 (91st Cong.), H.R. 3809 (91st Cong.), H.R. 4294 (91st
    Cong.), H.R. 13373 (91st Cong.), H.R. 16785 (91st Cong.), H.R. 19200
    (91st Cong.), S. 2193 (91st Cong.), S. 2788 (91st Cong.), S. 4404 (91st
    Cong.)

The legislative history of the Occupational Safety and Health Act of 1970
(OSHA) contains primary source materials arranged in the chronological
order of their publication. Access to these materials is enhanced by the
table of contents and two indexes. The table of contents provides access by
bill number. There is a section-by-section index as well as a subject matter
index.

Record No.: 130
Public Law No.: 91-604
Bill No.: H.R. 17255 (91st Cong.)
Statutes at Large Citation: 84 Stat. 1676 (1970)
Title of Act: Clean Air Amendments of 1970

Title of Legislative History: Legislative History of Clean Air Amendments
                                of 1970 Together with a Section-by-Section
                                Index, 93rd Cong., 2nd Sess. (Comm. Prints
                                1974)
Publication Date: 1974
Author: Senate Committee on Public Works
Pages: vii, 791; iii, 795-1596

L/C Card Number: 74-601207
OCLC No.: 908971
SuDoc No.: Y4.P96/10:93-18/v.1-2
CIS No.: 74-S642-9; 74-5642-10
UPA Citation: N/A
Relevant Bills: H.R. 6518 (88th Cong.), S. 780 (90th Cong.), H.R. 17255 (91st
    Cong.), S. 3072 (91st Cong.), S. 3229 (91st Cong.), S. 3466 (91st Cong.),
    S. 3546 (91st Cong.), S. 4358 (91st Cong.)

This two volume work focuses on the Clean Air Amendments of 1970.
Included is the text of the Clean Air Act as amended through the technical
amendments made by P.L. 92-157 in 1971; the President's remarks upon
signing the 1970 amendments; and the text of the original Clean Air Act as
amended by the Air Quality Act of 1967. There is a tabular comparison by
section of the Clean Air Amendments of 1970 to S. 4358, H.R. 17255 and
prior existing law. A section-by-section index provides access to the
primary source materials.

Record No.: 131
Public Law No.: 91-644
Bill No.: H.R. 17825 (91st Cong.)
Statutes at Large Citation: 84 Stat. 1880 (1971)
Title of Act: Omnibus Crime Control Act of 1970

Title of Legislative History: Legislative History of the 1971 Amendments to
the Omnibus Crime Control and Safe Streets
Act of 1968

Publication Date: 1972
Author: Law Enforcement Assistance Administration
Pages: xvii, 104

L/C Card Number: N/A
OCLC No.: 1868401
SuDoc No.: J1.2:C86/12
CIS No.: N/A
UPA Citation: N/A
Relevant Bills: H.R. 5037 (90th Cong.), H.R. 17825 (91st Cong.)

This is a legislative history of the Omnibus Crime Control Act of 1970. It
begins with an index to P.L. 91-644 which explains which sections of this
law amended the Omnibus Crime Control and Safe Streets Act of 1968, and
which provides citations to the included Congressional documents. The
history includes several versions of H.R. 17825 (91st Cong.), as well as
excerpts from Congressional reports and Congressional debate. See
J1.2:C86/16, A Legislative History of the Omnibus Crime Control and Safe
Streets Act of 1968 (Record No.: 123), and J1.2:C86/19, A Legislative History
of the Crime Control Act of 1973 (Record No.: 145).

Record No.: 132
Public Law No.: 92-255
Bill No.: S. 2097 (92nd Cong.)
Statutes at Large Citation: 86 Stat. 65 (1972)
Title of Act: Drug Abuse Office and Treatment Act of 1972

Title of Legislative History: Legislative History of the Drug Abuse Office
and Treatment Act of 1972: Public Law 92-255,
March 21, 1972

Publication Date: 1972
Author: Executive Office of the President, Special Action Office for Drug
Abuse Prevention
Pages: 323

L/C Card Number: N/A
OCLC No.: 2490739
SuDoc No.: Pr Ex20.2: D84X
CIS No.: N/A
UPA Citation: N/A
Relevant Bills: H.R. 9264 (92nd Cong.), H.R. 12089 (92nd Cong.), S. 2097
    (92nd Cong.)

This legislative history is divided into six parts. Part One is an introduction
which presents chronologically Congress' action in passing the Drug
Abuse Office and Treatment Act of 1972. Part Two contains the President's
message upon transmitting the proposed legislation. Parts Three, Four
and Five contain respectively the primary materials relating to action in the
House, Senate and Conference Committee. Part Six contains the
President's remarks upon signing the law.

Record No.: 133
Public Law No.: 92-261
Bill No.: H.R. 1746 (92nd Cong.)
Statutes at Large Citation: 86 Stat. 103 (1972)
Title of Act: Equal Employment Opportunity Act of 1972

Title of Legislative History: Legislative History of Equal Employment
                                Opportunity Act of 1972 (H.R. 1746, P.L.92-261),
                                Amending Title 7 of Civil Rights Act of 1964,
                                92nd Cong., 2nd Sess. (Comm. Print 1972)
Publication Date: 1972
Author: Subcommittee on Labor, Senate Committee on Labor and Public
Welfare
Pages: xxii, 2067

L/C Card Number: 72-603494
OCLC No.: 553984
SuDoc No.: Y4.L11/2:Em7/21
CIS No.: 72-S542-28
UPA Citation: N/A
Relevant Bills: H.R. 7152 (88th Cong.), H.R. 1746 (92nd Cong.), H.R.
    6760 (92nd Cong.), H.R. 9247 (92nd Cong.), S. 2515 (92nd Cong.), S.
    2617 (92nd Cong.)

This is the legislative history of the Equal Employment Opportunity Act of
1972. This public law amended Title VII of the Civil Rights Act of 1964.
Four indices are included: a Congressional debate index; a subject matter
index; a bill index; and, a bill amendment index. Appendices include the
text of P.L. 92-261; changes made by P.L. 92-261 to Title VII; the original text
of Title VII; and a comparison of the original Title VII to several bills.

Record No.: 134
Public Law No.: 92-261
Bill No.: H.R. 1746 (92nd Cong.)
Statutes at Large Citation: 86 Stat. 103 (1972)
Title of Act: Equal Employment Opportunity Act of 1972

Title of Legislative History: Equal Employment Opportunity Act of 1972:
                                Legislative History
Publication Date: 1977
Author: Paul M. Downing of the Congressional Research Service
Pages: 100

L/C Card Number: N/A
OCLC No.: 4879966
SuDoc No.: N/A
CIS No.: N/A
UPA Citation: UPA Film No.: MS 76-78 Supp., Reel No. III, Frame No.
0004; CRS No.: 77-100G
Relevant Bills: H.R. 10065 (89th Cong.), H.R. 6228 (91st Cong.), H.R. 13517
    (91st Cong.), H.R. 17555 (91st Cong.), S. 2453 (91st Cong.), S. 2806 (91st
    Cong.), H.R. 1746 (92nd Cong.), H.R. 9247 (92nd Cong.), S. 2515 (92nd
    Cong.), S. 2617 (92nd Cong.)

This publication is a narrative legislative history in five sections. The
first section briefly examines equal employment opportunity legislation
before the 91st Congress. The remaining sections track the equal
employment opportunity legislation in the 91st and 92nd Congresses. The
text of the sections gives citations to relevant bills, Congressional hearings,
Congressional reports, and Congressional debate. The text of the Equal
Employment Opportunity Act of 1972 is reprinted. A subject index is
included.

Record No.: 135
Public Law No.: 92-463
Bill No.: H.R. 4383 (92nd Cong.)
Statutes at Large Citation: 86 Stat. 770 (1972)
Title of Act: Federal Advisory Committee Act

Title of Legislative History: Federal Advisory Committee Act (Public Law
                                92-463) Sourcebook, Legislative History, Texts,
                                and Other Documents, 95th Cong., 2nd Sess.
                                (Comm. Print 1978)
Publication Date: 1978
Author: Subcommittee on Energy, Nuclear Proliferation, and Federal
Services, Senate Committee on Governmental Affairs
Pages: ix, 394

L/C Card Number: 79-601033
OCLC No.: 4239327
SuDoc No.: Y4.G74/9:Ad9/3
CIS No.: 78-S402-19
UPA Citation: N/A
Relevant Bills: H.R. 3378 (85th Cong.), H.R. 7390 (85th Cong.), S. 3067 (91st
    Cong.), H.R. 4383 (92nd Cong.), S. 1637 (92nd Cong.), S. 1964 (92nd
    Cong.), S. 2064 (92nd Cong.), S. 3529 (92nd Cong.), S. 5 (94th Cong.),
    H.R. 8979 (95th Cong.), S. 1329 (95th Cong.), S. 1838 (95th Cong.), S.
    1847 (95th Cong.), S. 2088 (95th Cong.)

This publication on the Federal Advisory Committee Act begins with an
essay on the background and history of the Act. Reprinted are the texts of
the original Act, and the Act as amended by the Sunshine Act. Reprints of
other primary materials are divided into six sections. The first presents
background materials from the 85th Congress. The second, third and
fourth sections contain, respectively, primary materials relating to action
in the Senate, House, and Conference Committee during the 91st and 92d
Congresses. The fifth section reprints several executive orders and the
sixth section contains summaries of cases decided under the act. A
bibliography which provides citations to journal articles, monographs and
Congressional documents is included. This publication concludes with the
text of several bills from the 95th Congress (none of which passed) which
would have amended the Federal Advisory Committee Act.

Record No.: 136
Public Law No.: 92-473
Bill No.: H.R. 15376 (92nd Cong.)
Statutes at Large Citation: 86 Stat. 789 (1972)
Title of Act: Service Contract Act of 1965, Amendment of 1972

Title of Legislative History: Legislative History of Service Contract Act
                                Amendments of 1972 (H.R. 15376, Public Law
                                92-473), Approved Oct. 9, 1972, 92nd Cong., 2nd
                                Sess. (Comm. Print 1972)
Publication Date: 1972
Author: Subcommittee on Labor, Senate Committee on Labor and Public
Welfare
Pages: v, 84

L/C Card Number: 73-600637
OCLC No.: 596765
SuDoc No.: Y4.L11/2:Se6/6
CIS No.: 73-S542-4
UPA Citation: N/A
Relevant Bills: H.R. 15376 (92nd Cong.), S. 3827 (92nd Cong.)

The legislative history of the Service Contract Act Amendments of 1972, H.R. 15376 (92nd Cong.), P.L. 92-473 contains multiple versions of H.R. 15376 (92nd Cong.), and a version of its related bill S. 3827 (92nd Cong.), as well as the Congressional debate. The history concludes with the text of the 1972 amendments. It also contains H. Rept. 92-1251 on H.R. 15376 and S. Rept. 92-1131 on H.R. 15376.

Record No.: 137
Public Law No.: 92-500
Bill No.: S. 2770 (92nd Cong.)
Statutes at Large Citation: 86 Stat. 816 (1972)
Title of Act: Federal Water Pollution Control Act Amendments of 1972

Title of Legislative History: Legislative History of Water Pollution Control
                                 Act Amendments of 1972 Together with
                                 Section-by-Section Index, 93rd Cong., 1st Sess.
                                 (Comm. Print 1973)
Publication Date: 1973
Author: Senate Committee on Public Works
Pages: v, 1110; iii, 1113-1766

L/C Card Number: 73-601377
OCLC No.: 14422037
SuDoc No.: Y4.P96/10:93-1/v.1-2
CIS No.: 73-S642-3; 73-S642-4
UPA Citation: N/A
Relevant Bills: H.R. 11896 (92nd Cong.), S. 2770 (92nd Cong.)

This is a legislative history of the Federal Water Pollution Control Act Amendments of 1972. The following primary sources are reprinted in reverse chronological order: P.L. 92-500; documents relating to the presidential veto and veto override; excerpts from the Conference Report on S. 2770 (92d Cong.); House and Senate debate on the Conference Report; the main House bill on water pollution control, H.R. 11896 (92d Cong.); and the Senate Report and debate on S. 2770 (92d Cong.). A chart lists each section of P.L. 92-500 by title and number and the corresponding sections of H.R. 11896 (92d Cong.), S. 2770 (92d Cong.), and the Federal Water Pollution Control Act. A section-by-section index is included.

Record No.: 138
Public Law No.: 92-517
Bill No.: S. 4062 (92nd Cong.)
Statutes at Large Citation: 86 Stat. 999 (1972)
Title of Act: National Capital Area Transit Act of 1972

Title of Legislative History: Legislative History of S. 4062 (Public Law 92-
517) Providing for Acquisition of Mass Transit
Bus Systems Engaged in Regular Route
Operations in National Capital Area, 92nd
Cong., 2nd Sess. (Comm. Print 1972)

Publication Date: 1972
Author: Senate Committee on the District of Columbia
Pages: v, 394

L/C Card Number: 73-600783
OCLC No.: 596789
SuDoc No.: Y4.D63/2:B96/3
CIS No.: 73-S302-3
UPA Citation: N/A
Relevant Bills: H.R. 16119 (92nd Cong.), H.R. 16659 (92nd Cong.), H.R. 16724
(92nd Cong.), S. 3966 (92nd Cong.), S. 4062 (92nd Cong.)

The legislative history of the National Capital Area Transit Act of 1972,
begins with a table which chronologically presents the Congressional
action which resulted in the passage of the Act. It concludes with the text of
the act as passed.

Record No.: 139
Public Law No.: 92-574
Bill No.: H.R. 11021 (92nd Cong.)
Statutes at Large Citation: 86 Stat. 1234 (1972)
Title of Act: Noise Control Act of 1972

Title of Legislative History: Legislative History of Noise Control Act of 1972,
Together with Section-by-Section Index, 93rd
Cong., 2nd Sess. (Comm. Print 1974)

Publication Date: 1974
Author: Senate Committee on Public Works
Pages: v, 680

L/C Card Number: 75-601448
OCLC No.: 2131280
SuDoc No.: Y4.P96/10:93-23
CIS No.: 75-S642-1
UPA Citation: N/A
Relevant Bills: H.R. 5275 (92nd Cong.), H.R. 5388 (92nd Cong.), H.R. 11021
(92nd Cong.), S. 1016 (92nd Cong.), S. 3342 (92nd Cong.)

The work begins with the full text of the Noise Control Act of 1972. In
addition to the standard primary sources relating to H.R. 11021 (92d Cong.)
and its related bill S. 3342 (92d Cong.), hearings on the Administration's
bills are included. A section-by-section index provides access to the primary
source materials.

Record No.: 140
Public Law No.: 92-576
Bill No.: S. 2318 (92nd Cong.)
Statutes at Large Citation: 86 Stat. 1251 (1972)
Title of Act: Longshoremen's and Harbor Workers' Compensation Act
        Amendments of 1972

Title of Legislative History: Legislative History of the Longshoremen's and
        Harbor Workers' Compensation Act
        Amendments of 1972 (S. 2318, Public Law 92-
        576), 92nd Cong., 2nd Sess. (Comm. Print 1972)
Publication Date: 1972
Author: Subcommittee on Labor, Senate Committee on Labor and Public
Welfare
Pages: v, 648

L/C Card Number: 72-603688
OCLC No.: 584609
SuDoc No.: Y4.L11/2:L86/5
CIS No.: Committee-Print: S4386
UPA Citation: N/A
Relevant Bills: S. 2917 (91st Cong.), H.R. 3505 (92nd Cong.), H.R. 9212 (92nd
        Cong.), H.R. 11071 (92nd Cong.), H.R. 12006 (92nd Cong.), H.R. 15023
        (92nd Cong.), H.R. 16562 (92nd Cong.), H.R. 16725 (92nd Cong.), H.R.
        17090 (92nd Cong.), S. 525 (92nd Cong.), S. 1547 (92nd Cong.), S. 2318
        (92nd Cong.)

Three of the four components of a legislative history are provided in this
work on the Longshoremen's and Harbor Workers' Compensation Act
Amendments of 1972: multiple versions of the pertinent bills;
Congressional reports; and Congressional debates. In addition, an
appendix provides the text of several other related bills; the
Longshoremen's and Harbor Workers' Compensation Act Amendments of
1972; and the Black Lung Benefits Act of 1972 as amended by the Federal
Coal Mine Health and Safety Act of 1969.

Record No.: 141
Public Law No.: 92-583
Bill No.: S. 3507 (92nd Cong.)
Statutes at Large Citation: 86 Stat. 1280 (1972)
Title of Act: Coastal Zone Management Act of 1972

Title of Legislative History: Legislative History of the Coastal Zone
        Management Act of 1972, As Amended in 1974
        and 1976 with a Section-by-Section Index, 94th
        Cong., 2nd Sess. (Comm. Print 1976)

Publication Date: 1976
Author: Senate Committee on Commerce; Senate National Ocean Policy Study
Pages: viii, 1117

L/C Card Number: 77-600822
OCLC No.: 2669397
SuDoc No.: Y4.C73/2:C63/7
CIS No.: 76-S262-20
UPA Citation: N/A
Relevant Bills: H.R. 14845 (91st Cong.), H.R. 15099 (91st Cong.), H.R. 16155
    (91st Cong.), S. 2802 (91st Cong.), S. 3183 (91st Cong.), S. 3460 (91st
    Cong.), H.R. 2492 (92nd Cong.), H.R. 2493 (92nd Cong.), H.R. 3615
    (92nd Cong.), H.R. 9229 (92nd Cong.), H.R. 14146 (92nd Cong.), S. 582
    (92nd Cong.), S. 638 (92nd Cong.), S. 3507 (92nd Cong.), H.R. 16215
    (93rd Cong.), S. 3922 (93rd Cong.), H.R. 3981 (94th Cong.), S. 586 (94th
    Cong.)

This three part publication provides a legislative history of the Coastal Zone Management Act of 1972. Part I, covering this Act, includes an essay on Congressional action during the 91st and 92d Congresses which has citations to relevant government publications and a chronological table of the legislation's progress through Congress. A section-by-section index provides access to the primary materials reprinted here. Part II covers the Coastal Zone Management Act Amendments of 1974 and is limited to the text of the amendments, Congressional reports and debate, and a section-by-section index. Part III covers the Coastal Zone Management Act Amendments of 1976. This part includes an essay on Congressional action, reprints of Congressional reports and debate, and a section-by-section index.

Record No.: 142
Public Law No.: 92-603
Bill No.: H.R. 1 (92nd Cong.)
Statutes at Large Citation: 86 Stat. 1329 (1972)
Title of Act: Social Security Amendments of 1972

Title of Legislative History: Legislative History of Professional Standards
                                Review Organization: Provisions of the Social
                                Security Act Amendments: Legislation
                                Through October 25, 1977
Publication Date: 1978
Author: Department of Health, Education, and Welfare, Health Care Financing Administration, Health Standards and Quality Bureau
Pages: 86

L/C Card Number: N/A
OCLC No.: 3697475
SuDoc No.: HE22.202:L52
CIS No.: N/A
UPA Citation: N/A
Relevant Bills: H.R. 1 (92nd Cong.), H.R. 10284 (94th Cong.), H.R. 3 (95th
    Cong.), S. 143 (95th Cong.)

This is a legislative history of amendments to the Social Security Act that
pertain to Professional Standards Review Organizations (PSROs). The
relevant sections of three laws are reprinted: the Social Security
Amendments of 1972; Social Security Amendment of 1975; and the
Medicare-Medicaid Anti-Fraud and Abuse Amendments. Selected
legislative history materials relating to these laws are provided.

Record No.: 143
Public Law No.: 92-603
Bill No.: H.R. 1 (92nd Cong.)
Statutes at Large Citation: 86 Stat. 1329 (1972)
Title of Act: Social Security Amendments of 1972

Title of Legislative History: Legislative History of the Supplemental
                                Security Income (SSI) Program: 1969-1972
Publication Date: 1977
Author: Martha S. Proskauer of the Congressional Research Service
Pages: 87

L/C Card Number: N/A
OCLC No.: N/A
SuDoc No.: N/A
CIS No.: N/A
UPA Citation: UPA Film No.: MS 76-78 Supp., Reel No. XII, Frame No. 840;
CRS No.: 77-69 ED.
Relevant Bills: H.R. 14173 (91st Cong.), H.R. 16311 (91st Cong.), H.R. 17550
    (91st Cong.), H.R. 1 (92nd Cong.)

This is a legislative history essay on the Social Security Amendments of
1972. Although the various bills considered provisions for a "Family
Assistance Plan" which would have replaced the Aid to Families with
Dependent Children program, the law as passed was limited to reforming
programs for the aged, blind, and disabled adults. This publication traces
the legislation only in regard to the programs for adults. The essay
chronologically traces the bills' progress through Congress. Much of the
narrative summarizes the different versions of these bills and their
amendments, concentrating on their provisions for benefit levels, funding
and eligibility. Selected Congressional reports and hearings are quoted or
summarized. The publication concludes with the text of P.L. 92-603.

Record No.: 144
Public Law No.: N/A
Bill No.: N/A
Statutes at Large Citation: 84 Stat. 2086 (1970)
Title of Act: Reorganization Plan No. 3 of 1970

Title of Legislative History: Legal Compilation, Statutes and Legislative
                               History, Executive Orders, Regulations,
                               Guidelines and Reports
Publication Date: 1973-1974
Author: Environmental Protection Agency
Pages: various

L/C Card Number: 73-602602
OCLC No.: 800286
SuDoc No.: EP1.5
CIS No.: N/A
UPA Citation: N/A
Relevant Bills: H.R. 17255 (91st Cong.), H.R. 9727 (92nd Cong.), H.R. 10729
    (92nd Cong.), H.R. 11021 (92nd Cong.), S. 2770 (92nd Cong.)

The goal of this forty volume legislative history was to create a useful
compilation of the legal authority under which the Environmental
Protection Agency (EPA) operates. Some of the statutes which provide the
EPA with the specific authority for controlling pollution include: Clean Air
Amendments of 1970, Water Pollution Control Act Amendments of 1972,
Federal Environmental Pesticide Control Act of 1972, Noise Control Act of
1972; and the Marine Protection, Research, and Sanctuaries Act of 1972.
The main part of the set covers the creation of the EPA in 1970 through the
92nd Cong., 1st Sess., 1971. Also included are a number of pre-1970 statutes
which were transferred to the EPA's administration or referred to in post-
1970 acts which the EPA administers. The first supplement covers the 92nd
Cong., 2nd Sess., 1972. The second supplement covers the 93rd Cong., 1st
Sess., 1973. There is a separately bound table of contents to the main part of
the set and the first supplement. The set is divided into eight subject areas:
General, Air, Water, Solid, Waste, Pesticides, Radiation, and Noise. Each
subject area is organized in a four part scheme. The mnemonic scheme is
continued in the supplements. Statutes are listed "1.1, 1.2, 1.3...". A codified
version of a statute appears as 1.1. The public laws composing that statute
appear as "1.1a, 1.1b, 1.1c...". The history includes not only statutes
primarily concerned with EPA, but also statutes which touch only
tangentially upon the EPA. However, only that part of each public law
relevant to the EPA is included. Each public law is followed by its legislative
history. The legislative histories consist of the relevant parts of the
Congressional reports and Congressional debate. Reorganization plans,
such as the one which established the EPA are included in the "1.1, 1.2,
1.3..." numbering scheme. Reorganization plans are followed by the
relevant Presidential messages. The history provides full citations to all
documents. Executive orders, regulations, and guidelines and reports
continue the mnemonic device established.

Relevant Public Laws included in this set: National Environmental Policy
Act of 1969, P.L. 91-190; Environmental Quality Improvement Act of 1970,

P.L. 91-224; Amortization of Pollution Control Facilities, P.L. 91-172; Department of Transportation Act, P.L. 89-670; Federal Highway Act of 1968, P.L. 90-495; Federal Highway Act of 1970, P.L. 91-605; Airport and Airway Development Act of 1970, P.L. 91-258; The Administration of Disaster Assistance, P.L. 91-606; Amendments to Interest on Certain Government Obligations, Int. Revenue Code, P.L. 90-364; Revenue Act of 1971, P.L. 92-178; Uniform Relocation Assistance and Real Property Acquisition Policies Act of 1970, P.L. 91-646; Codification of 5 U.S.C. § 301, P.L. 89-554; The Public Health Service Act, P.L. 78-410; National Mental Health Act, P.L. 79-487; National Heart Act, P.L. 80-655; National Dental Research Act, P.L. 80-755; Public Health Service Act Amendments, P.L. 80-781; Career Compensation Act of 1949, P.L. 81-351; Amendment to Title 13 U.S. Code, P.L. 83-740; National Health Survey Act, P.L. 84-652; An Act of Implementing §25(b) of the Organic Act of Guam, P.L. 84-896; Amendments to §314(c) of the Public Health Service Act, P.L. 85-544; Health Amendments of 1959, P.L. 86-105; International Health Research Act of 1960, P.L. 86-610; Hawaii Omnibus Act, P.L. 86-624; Amendments to §301(d) of the Public Health Service Act, P.L. 86-798; 1960 Amendments to Title III of the Public Health Service Act, P.L. 86-720; Community Health Service and Facilities Act of 1961, P.L. 87-395; Extension of Application of Certain Laws to American Samoa, P.L. 87-688; Amendments to Title IV of the Public Health Service Act, P.L. 87-838; Graduate Public Health Training Amendments of 1964, P.L. 88-497; Community Health Services Extension Amendments, P.L. 89-109; Amendments to Public Health Service Act, P.L. 89-115; Comprehensive Health Planning and Public Health Services Amendments of 1966, P.L. 89-749; Partnership for Health Amendments of 1967, P.L. 90-174; Health Manpower of 1968, P.L. 90-490; Public Health Training Grants Act, P.L. 91-208; Medical Facilities Construction and Modernization Amendments of 1970; Public Health Service Drug Abuse Research, P.L. 91-513; Heart Disease, Cancer, Stroke and Kidney Disease Amendments of 1970, P.L. 91-515; Comprehensive Alcohol Abuse and Alcoholism Prevention, Treatment and Rehabilitation Act of 1970, P.L 91-616; The Davis-Bacon Act, P.L. 71-798; Amendment to the Act of March 3, 1931, August 30, 1935, P.L. 74-403; An Act to Require the Payment of Prevailing Rates of Wages on Federal Public Works in Alaska and Hawaii, P.L. 76-633; Amendments to Davis-Bacon Act, P.L. 88-349; To Authorize Certain Administrative Expenses in the Government Service, P.L. 79-600; To Amend the Federal Property and Administrative Services Act of 1949; P.L. 81-744; Small Business Opportunities Act, P.L. 85-800; Administrative Expenses Act, P.L. 79-600; Amendments to the 1946 Travel Expense Act; P.L. 84-189; Enactment of Title 5, *United States Code*, "Government Organization and Employees"; P.L. 89-554; Increase Maximum Rates Per Diem Allowance for Government Employees, P.L. 91-114; Disclosure of Information, June 25, 1948, P.L. 80-772; Agricultural Environmental and Consumer Protection Programs Appropriation, P.L. 92-399; Air Pollution Act of July 14, 1955, P.L. 84-159; Extension of §5-a of Air Pollution Act of July 14, 1955, P.L. 86-365; Motor Vehicle Exhaust Study Act of June 8, 1960, P.L. 86-493; Amendment of Act of July 14, 1955, P.L. 87-761; The Clean Air Act, P.L. 88-206; Motor Vehicle Air Pollution Control Act, and Solid Waste Disposal Act, P.L. 89-272; Clean Air Amendments of 1966, P.L. 89-675; Air Quality Act of 1967, P.L. 90-148; Authorization for Fuel and Vehicle Research, P.L. 91-137; Extension of Clean Air Act, July 10, 1970, P.L. 91-316; Clean Air Amendments of 1970, December 31, 1970, P.L. 91-604; Technical

Amendments to the Clean Air Act, November 18, 1971, P.L. 92-157; Contracts: Acquisition, Construction or Furnishing of Test Facilities and Equipment Act of July 16, 1952, P.L. 82-557; Record on Review and Enforcement of Agency Orders, P.L. 85-791; Highway Safety Act of 1966, P.L. 89-564; Federal Aid Highway Act of 1970, P.L. 91-605; Federal Salary Act, as amended, General Schedule, P.L. 89-554; Registers, Individuals Receiving Compensation, September 11, 1967, P.L. 90-83; Postal Revenue and Federal Salary Act of 1967, P.L. 90-206; The Federal Aviation Act of 1958, P.L. 85-726; Occupational Safety and Health Act of 1970, P.L. 91-604; Amendments to the Fish and Wildlife Act of 1956, P.L. 92-159; Airport and Airway Programs, P.L. 92-174; Noise Control Act of 1972, P.L. 92-574; Secretaries of Treasury and Labor Shall Make Regulations for Contractors and Subcontractors, P.L. 73-324; Regulations Governing Contractors and Subcontractors Amendments to Act, P.L. 81-72; Regulations Governing Contractors and Subcontractors Amendment of 1958, P.L. 85-800; Motor Vehicle Information and Cost Savings Act, P.L. 92-513; River and Harbor Act of 1886, P.L. 49-929; New York Harbor Act of 1888, P.L. 50-469; River and Harbor Act of 1890, P.L. 51-907; River and Harbor Act of 1894, P.L. 53-299; River and Harbor Act of 1899, P.L. 55-425; Supplemental Appropriations Act of 1971, P.L. 91-665; The Water Pollution Control Act, P.L. 80-845; Water Pollution Control Act Extension P.L. 82-845; Water Pollution Control Act of 1956, P.L. 84-660; Alaska's Water Pollution Control Act Amendments, P.L. 86-70; Hawaii's Water Pollution Control Act Amendments, P.L. 86-624; The Federal Water Pollution Control Act of 1961, P.L. 87-88; The Water Quality Act of 1965, P.L. 89-234; The Clean Water Restoration Act of 1966, P.L. 89-753; The Water Quality Improvement Act of 1970, P.L. 91-224; Rivers and Harbors Act of 1970, P.L. 91-611; Extension of Authorized Funds for Federal Water Pollution Control Act of 1971, P.L. 9250; Extension of Federal Water Pollution Control Act of 1971, P.L. 92-137; Extension of Certain Provisions of Federal Water Pollution Control Act of 1971, P.L. 92-240; The Oil Pollution Control Act of 1961, P.L. 87-167; 1966 Amendments to the Oil Pollution Act of 1961, P.L. 89-551; To Authorize Certain Administrative Expenses in the Government Services and for Other Purposes, P.L. 79-600; An Act to Codify, Revise and Amend the Laws Relating to the Judiciary, P.L. 61-475; Act to Amend the Judicial Code and to Further Define the Jurisdiction of Circuit Courts of Appeal and of the Supreme Court and for Other Purposes, P.L. 68-415; An Act in Reference to Writs of Error, P.L. 70-10; 1934 Amendments to 1893 Act, P.L. 73-298; Customs Enforcement Act of 1935, P.L. 74-238; 1938 Amendments to §§91, 92 of Title 46 U.S.C., P.L. 75-656; Customs Simplification Act of 1954, P.L. 83-768; Outer Continental Shelf Lands Act, P.L. 82-212; Act to Enact Title 5, *United States Code*, P.L. 89-554; To Amend Section 552 of Title 5, *United States Code*, P.L. 90-23; Act to Amend Title 5, 10 and 37, *United States Code* to Codify Recent Laws, P.L. 90-623; Higher Education Act of 1965, P.L. 89-329; Higher Education Amendments of 1968, P.L. 90-575; Higher Education Amendments of 1970, P.L. 91-230; Water Resources Planning Act, P.L. 89-80; Rivers and Harbors Act of 1970, P.L. 91-611; Water Resources Planning Act Amendments of 1971, P.L. 92-27; Appalachian Regional Development Act of 1965, P.L. 89-4; 1969 Amendments to the Appalachian Regional Development Act, P.L. 91-123; Airport and Airway Development and Revenue Act of 1970, P.L. 91-258; Appalachian Regional Development Act Amendments of 1971, P.L. 92-65; To Amend the Act of March 10, 1934, P.L. 79-732; To Amend the Act of March 10, 1934, P.L. 80-697; To Amend the Act of March 10, 1934, as amended, P.L. 85-624; Federal Water Project Recreation Act, P.L. 89-72; Public Works and Economic Development Act of 1965; P.L. 89-136; River and Harbor Act of 1910, P.L. 61-245; New York Harbor Act of 1888, P.L. 50-496; River and Harbor Act of 1894, P.L. 53-299; 1908 Amendments to 1894 Act, P.L. 60-152; 1909 Amendments to 1908 Act, P.L. 60-231; Repealing Certain Obsolete Provisions of Law Relating to the Naval Service, P.L. 81-144; 1952 Amendments to the New York Harbor Act of 1888, P.L. 82-526; 1958 Amendments to Act of 1888, P.L. 85-802; Rural Development Act of 1972, P.L. 92-419; Commerce Department Maritime Programs, P.L. 92-402; Marine Resources and Engineering Development Act of 1966, P.L. 92-583; The Solid Waste Disposal Act, P.L. 89-272; One-Year Extension of Solid Waste Disposal Authorization, P.L. 90-574; Extension of Solid Waste Disposal Act, P.L. 91-316; The Resource Recovery Act of 1970, P.L. 91-512; Housing Act of 1954, P.L. 83-560; Housing Act of 1956, P.L. 84-1020; Housing Act of 1957, P.L. 85-104; Housing Act of 1959, P.L. 86-372; Area Development Act, P.L. 87-27; Housing Act of 1961, P.L. 87-70; Housing Act of 1964, P.L. 88-560; Appalachian Regional Development Act of 1965, P.L. 89-4; Housing and Urban Development Act of 1965, P.L. 89-117; Demonstration Cities and Metropolitan Development Act of 1966, P.L. 89-754; Housing and Urban Development Acts, Obsolete References, P.L. 90-19; Appalachian Regional Development Act, Amendments of 1967, P.L. 90-103; Housing and Urban Development Act of 1968, P.L. 90-448; Housing and Urban Development Act of 1969, P.L. 91-152; Technical Amendments of the Housing act of 1954, P.L. 91-606; Model Cities and Metropolitan Development Programs, P.L. 91-609; Definition of Executive Agency, P.L. 89-554; Rates of Pay for Labor, P.L. 73-325; Act to Amend Title XVIII, Title XXVIII, and Other Purposes, May 24, 1949, P.L. 81-72; Small Business Procurement Procedures Act, P.L. 85-800; The Insecticide Act, P.L. 61-152; Federal Insecticide, Fungicide, and Rodenticide Act, P.L. 80-104; Nematocide, Plant Regulator, Defoliant and Desiccant Amendments of 1959, P.L. 86-139; Additional Time for Registration of Certain Nematocides, Plant Regulators, Defoliants and Desiccants, P.L. 87-10; Food Additives Transitional Provision Amendment of 1961, P.L. 87-19; Amendments to the Federal Insecticide, Fungicide, and Rodenticide Act, P.L. 88-305; Food Additives Transitional Provision Amendment of 1964, P.L. 88-625; Organized Crime Control Act of 1969, P.L. 91-452; Poison Prevention Packaging Act of 1970, P.L. 91-601; Food, Drug, and Cosmetic Act, 1906; P.L. 59-384; Federal Food, Drug, and Cosmetic Act, P.L. 75-717; Food Additives Amendments of 1958, P.L. 85-929; Color Additives Amendments of 1960, P.L. 86-618; Administrative Agency Proceedings Act, P.L. 85-791; Amendments to Food Additives, P.L. 86-546; Drug Amendments of 1962, P.L. 87-781; Heart Disease, Cancer, Stroke, and Kidney Disease Amendments of 1970, P.L. 91-515; Comprehensive Health Manpower Training Act of 1979, P.L. 92-157; Federal Environmental Pesticide Control Act of 1972, P.L. 92-516; Pesticide Research Act, P.L. 85-582; Fish and Wildlife Studies, P.L. 86-279; Protection of Fish and Wildlife From Pesticides, P.L. 89-232; Pesticide Research, P.L. 90-394; Agricultural Research Service, Department of Agriculture and Related Agencies Appropriation Act of 1965, P.L. 88-573; Poison Prevention Packaging Act of 1970, P.L. 91-601; Federal Environmental Pesticide Control Act of 1972, P.L. 92-516; Administrative Procedure in Hearings Act, P.L. 79-404; Administrative Procedure in Hearings Amendments, P.L. 89-554; Uniform Review, Records and Enforcement Orders Amendments, P.L. 85-791; Appeals To and/or From the Circuit Court of Appeals, P.L. 61-475; Judicial

Code Amendments of 1925, P.L. 68-415; Writs of Error Abolished Amendments, P.L. 70-10; District of Columbia Court of Appeals Act, P.L. 73-298; Court of Appeals Review Act, P.L. 80-773; Federal Food, Drug and Cosmetic Act, P.L. 75-717; Federal Adulterated Food Amendments, P.L. 83-518; Food Additives Amendment of 1958, P.L. 85-929; Color Additive Amendments of 1960, P.L. 86-618; Animal Drugs in Feeds Amendments of 1968, P.L. 90-399; Federal Food, Drug, and Cosmetic Act Amendments of 1962, P.L. 87-781; National Advisory Council Amendments, P.L. 87-781; National Advisory Council Amendments, P.L. 91-515; Federal Food, Drug, and Cosmetic Act - Regulations and Hearings, P.L. 75-717; Judicial Code, Definition, Amendments, P.L. 80-773; Federal Food, Drug and Cosmetic Act Amendments of 1954, P.L. 83-335; 1956 Federal Food Drug, and Cosmetic Amendments, P.L. 84-905; Abbreviated Records on Review Act, P.L. 85-791; 1960 Amendments to Federal Food, Drug, and Cosmetic Act, P.L. 86-618; Federal Food, Drug, and Cosmetic Act Penalties, P.L. 75-717; 1951 Amendments to Federal Food, Drug, and Cosmetic Act, P.L. 82-215; Food Coloring Amendments of 1960, P.L. 86-618; Drug Abuse Control Amendments of 1965, P.L. 89-74; Federal Food, Drug, and Cosmetic Act LSD Amendments, P.L. 90-639; Comprehensive Drug Abuse Prevention and Control Act, P.L. 91-513; Armed Forces Research and Development Act, P.L. 82-557; Armed Forces Procurement Amendments of 1956, P.L. 84-1028; Rule Making, June 11, 1946, P.L. 97-404; Administrative Procedure and Rule Making, P.L. 89-554; Judicial Interim Relief and Review of Agencies Acts, P.L. 79-404; Judicial Interim Relief and Review of Agency Amendments, P.L. 89-554; Judicial Interim Relief and Review of Agencies Acts, P.L. 79-404; Judicial Interim Relief and Review of Agency Amendments, P.L. 89-554; The Water Quality Improvement Act of 1970, P.L. 91-224; Federal Water Pollution Control Act Amendments of 1972, P.L. 92-500; Atomic Energy Act of 1946, P.L. 79-585; Amendments to Atomic Energy Act of 1954, P.L. 84-722; 1956 Amendments to the Atomic Energy Act of 1954, P.L. 84-1006; 1957 Amendments to the Atomic Energy Act of 1954, P.L. 85-162; Amendments to the Atomic Energy Act of 1954, P.L. 85-256; Amendments to the Atomic Energy Act of 1964, P.L. 85-287; Amendments to the Atomic Energy Act of 1964, P.L. 85-479; Government Employees Training Act, P.L. 85-507; Amendment to the Atomic Energy Act of 1954, P.L. 85-602; Amendments to Atomic Energy Act of 1954, P.L. 85-681; Amendments to Atomic Energy Act of 1954, P.L. 85-744; Amendments to the Atomic Energy Act of 1954, P.L. 86-300; Amendments to Atomic Energy Act of 1954, P.L. 86-373; Amendment to Atomic Energy Act of 1954, P.L. 87-206; To Amend the Tariff Act of 1930, and Certain Related Laws, P.L. 87-456; To Amend the Atomic Energy Act of 1954, P.L. 87-615; To Adjust Postal Rates, P.L. 87-793; To Amend the Atomic Energy Act of 1954, P.L. 88-394; 1964 Amendments to the Atomic Energy Act of 1954, P.L. 88-489; To Amend Section 170 of the Atomic Energy Act of 1954, P.L. 89-645; To Amend the Atomic Energy Act of 1954, P.L. 90-190; Atomic Energy Act Amendments, P.L. 91-560; Atomic Energy Commission Appropriation Authorization. P.L. 92-84; Armed Forces Research and Development, P.L. 82-577; Armed Services Procurement Amendments of 1956, P.L. 84-1028; Foreign Assistance Act of 1961, P.L. 87-195; Foreign Assistance Act of 1963, P.L. 88-205; The Resource Recovery Act of 1970, P.L. 91-512; Noise Pollution and Abatement Act of 1970, P.L. 91-604; Federal Water Pollution Control Act

Amendments of 1972, P.L. 92-500; Marine Protection, Research, and Sanctuaries Act of 1972, P.L. 92-532; Federal Environmental Pesticide Control Act of 1972, P.L. 92-516; Noise Control Act of 1972, P.L. 92-574.

Record No.: 145
Public Law No.: 93-83
Bill No.: H.R. 8152 (93rd Cong.)
Statutes at Large Citation: 87 Stat. 197 (1973)
Title of Act: Crime Control Act of 1973

Title of Legislative History: Indexed Legislative History of Crime Control
                                Act of 1973
Publication Date: 1973
Author: Department of Justice, Law Enforcement Assistance Administration, Office of General Counsel
Pages: xxii, 347

L/C Card Number: 73-603559
OCLC No.: 897799
SuDoc No.: J1.2:C86/19
CIS No.: N/A
UPA Citation: N/A
Relevant Bills: H.R. 5037 (90th Cong.), H.R. 8152 (93rd Cong.)

The legislative history begins with a detailed section-by-section index to the Crime Control Act of 1973. Following this index, the full text of the referenced documents appears in the chronological order of Congressional action. The legislative history concludes with a summary of how the Crime Control Act of 1973 amended the Omnibus Crime Control and Safe Streets Act of 1968, H.R. 5037 (90th Cong.), P.L. 90-351. See also Record No. 123 and Record No. 131.

Record No.: 146
Public Law No.: 93-95
Bill No.: S. 1423 (93rd Cong.)
Statutes at Large Citation: 87 Stat. 314 (1973)
Title of Act: To Amend the Labor Management Relations Act, 1947, to
              Permit Employer Contributions to Jointly Administered Trust
              Funds Established by Labor Organizations to Defray Costs of
              Legal Services

Title of Legislative History: Legislative History of Joint Labor-Management
                                Trust Funds for Legal Services, P.L. 93-95, S.
                                1423, 93rd Cong., 2nd Sess. (Comm. Print 1974)
Publication Date: 1974
Author: Subcommittee on Labor, Senate Committee on Labor and Public
Welfare
Pages: v, 151

L/C Card Number: 74-600735
OCLC No.: 842773
SuDoc No.: Y4.L11/2:L52/6
CIS No.: 74-S542-3
UPA Citation: N/A
Relevant Bills: H.R. 77 (93rd Cong.), S. 1423 (93rd Cong.)

The legislative history chronologically presents the Congressional action
which resulted in the enactment of the Labor Management Relations Act of
1947 Amendments of 1973. The history includes several versions of S. 1423
(93rd Cong.) and its companion bill H.R. 77 (93rd Cong.), as well as the
Congressional reports and Congressional debate on these bills. The history
concludes with the text of P.L. 93-95.

Record No.: 147
Public Law No.: 93-112
Bill No.: H.R. 8070 (93rd Cong.)
Statutes at Large Citation: 87 Stat. 355 (1973)
Title of Act: Rehabilitation Act of 1973

Title of Legislative History: Appendix A: Legislative and Judicial History o
                                f Section 504 of the Rehabilitation Act of 1973
                                Pertaining to Transportation for Handicapped
                                Persons IN Urban Transportation for
                                Handicapped Persons: Alternative Federal
                                Approaches
Publication Date: 1979
Author: Congressional Budget Office
Pages: xvi, 113

L/C Card Number: 79-604142
OCLC No.: 6089807
SuDoc No.: Y10.12:H19/981
CIS No.: 79-J932-39
UPA Citation: N/A
Relevant Bills: H.R. 8070 (93rd Cong.)

The legislative history is contained in Appendix A of Urban Transportation
for Handicapped Persons: Alternative Federal Approaches. It is a reprint
of the Congressional Research Service's (CRS) Section 504 of the

Rehabilitation Act of 1973 Pertaining to Transportation for Handicapped Persons as amended by the Update of Report Entitled Section 504 of the Rehabilitation Act of 1973 and Transportation for Handicapped Persons, dated July 30, 1979. Although it is a reprint of a CRS publication, it is not included in the UPA microfilm set. Section 504 prohibits discriminations against the handicapped by any program receiving federal financial assistance. The publication focuses on the law's impact on recipient of financial assistance from the Department of Transportation. It is noted that the legislative histories of the Act, its amendments, and a related law do not provide much that is relevant to section 504. Commentary on the use of legislative history as well as several related court cases is included. The history concludes by noting that as the time of publication (1979) the Department of Transportation' s regulations under Section 504 were being challenged in court.

Record No.: 148
Public Law No.: 93-148
Bill No.: H.R.J. Res. 542 (93rd Cong.)
Statutes at Large Citation: 87 Stat. 555 (1973)
Title of Act: War Powers Resolution

Title of Legislative History: The War Powers Resolution: A Special Study of the Committee on Foreign Affairs, 97th Cong., 2nd Sess. (Comm. Print 1982)
Publication Date: 1982
Author: House Committee on Foreign Affairs
Pages: xv, 292

L/C Card Number: 82-602327
OCLC No.: 8442136
SuDoc No.: Y4.F76/1:W19/11
CIS No.: 82-H382-13
UPA Citation: N/A
Relevant Bills: H.R. 17598 (91st Cong.), H.R. 17762 (91st Cong.), H.R. 18205 (91st Cong.), H.R. 18539 (91st Cong.), H.R. 18654 (91st Cong.), H.R. Con. Res. 199 (91st Cong.), H.R. Con. Res. 611 (91st Cong.), H.R.J. Res. 1151 (91st Cong.), H.R.J. Res. 1302 (91st Cong.), H.R.J. Res. 1355 (91st Cong.), H.R. Res. 1064 (91st Cong.), H.R. Res. 1120 (91st Cong.), S. 3964 (91st Cong.), H.R.J. Res. 1 (92nd Cong.), H.R.J. Res. 669 (92nd Cong.), S. 731 (92nd Cong.), S. 1880 (92nd Cong.), S. 2956 (92nd Cong.), S.J. Res. 18 (92nd Cong.), S.J. Res. 59 (92nd Cong.), H.R.J. Res. 2 (93rd Cong.), H.R.J. Res. 542 (93rd Cong.), S. 440 (93rd Cong.)

The House Committee on Foreign Affairs study attempts to explain why and how the War Powers Resolution was enacted and what it has meant. The study begins by examining the Tonkin Gulf Resolution. It continues to examine the effect of the War Powers Resolution on international incidents through 1982. The study's chief value as a legislative history lies in its examination of war powers legislation in the 91st, 92nd, and 93rd Congresses. The narrative essay has footnotes which provide extensive citations to relevant bills, Congressional hearings, Congressional reports, and Congressional debate. The study concludes with the text of the War Powers Resolution. After November 7, 1973, the terms "War Powers Resolution" and "War Powers Act" are one and the same.

Record No.: 149
Public Law No.: 93-191
Bill No.: H.R. 3180 (93rd Cong.)
Statutes at Large Citation: 87 Stat. 737 (1973)
Title of Act: To Amend Title 39, United States Code, to Clarify the Proper Use of the Franking Privilege by Members of Congress

Title of Legislative History: Franking Privilege for Members of Congress, Public Law 93-191 (Effective Dec. 18, 1973) Compilation of Legislative History, 93rd Cong., 1st Sess. (Comm. Print 1973)
Publication Date: 1973
Author: House Committee on Post Office and Civil Service
Pages: ix, 172

L/C Card Number: 74-600578
OCLC No.: 899019
SuDoc No.: Y4.P84/10:F85/2
CIS No.: 74-H622-1
UPA Citation: N/A
Relevant Bills: H.R. 3180 (93rd Cong.)

This is a legislative history of legislation clarifying the franking or postage privileges of members of Congress, H.R. 3180 (93rd Cong.), P.L. 93-191. It contains the text of P.L. 93-191, as well as several versions of H.R. 3180 (93rd Cong.), Congressional reports, and Congressional debate.

Record No.: 150
Public Law No.: 93-198
Bill No.: S. 1435 (93rd Cong.)
Statutes at Large Citation: 87 Stat. 774 (1973)
Title of Act: District of Columbia Self-Government and Governmental Reorganization Act

Title of Legislative History: Home Rule for the District of Columbia, 1973-
1974: Background and Legislative History of
H.R. 9056, H.R. 9682, and Related Bills
Culminating in the District of Columbia Self-
Government and Governmental
Reorganization Act, 93rd Cong., 2nd Sess.
(Comm. Print 1974)
Publication Date: 1976
Author: House Committee on the District of Columbia
Pages: vii, 3952

L/C Card Number: 85-601586
OCLC No.: 2561380
SuDoc No.: Y4.D63/1:93-S-4/chap.1-6
CIS No.: 76-H302-8; 76-H302-9; 76-H302-10; 76-H302-11
UPA Citation: N/A
Relevant Bills: H.R. 6186 (93rd Cong.), H.R. 9056 (93rd Cong.), H.R. 9215
(93rd Cong.), H.R. 9598 (93rd Cong.), H.R. 9617 (93rd Cong.), H.R.
9682 (93rd Cong.), H.R. 10597 (93rd Cong.), H.R. 10692 (93rd Cong.),
H.R. 10693 (93rd Cong.), H.R. 12109 (93rd Cong.), H.R. 15791 (93rd
Cong.), S. 1435 (93rd Cong.)

This four volume work in six chapters provides legislative history materials
for the District of Columbia Self-Government and Governmental
Reorganization Act. In addition to the standard sources, there is extensive
coverage of markup sessions. Chapter One contains the House
Subcommittee on Government Operations markup sessions from May and
June 1973. Included are several discussion drafts, as well as the
transcripts of the sessions. Chapter Two contains the House Committee on
the District of Columbia's markup sessions of July 1973. Included are
session transcripts as well as multiple bill versions and the Committee's
Report. Chapters Three and Four concern the House and Senate bills
respectively. Chapters Three and Four concern the House and Senate bills,
respectively. Chapter Five addresses the Conference Committee actions,
reprints the text of P.L. 93-198, and provides the Conference Agenda in its
appendix. Chapter Six is a legislative history of three 1974 laws which
affected P.L. 93-198: the District of Columbia Revenue Act of 1947,
Amendment of 1974; the District of Columbia Self-Government and
Governmental Reorganization Act, Amendments of 1974; and P.L. 93-395.
Each chapter concludes with a general index. Some chapters also provide
an index to the various versions of the bills discussed in that chapter. A
general index covering the complete work is included.

Record No.: 151
Public Law No.: 93-198
Bill No.: S. 1435 (93rd Cong.)
Statutes at Large Citation: 87 Stat. 774 (1973)
Title of Act: District of Columbia Self-Government and Governmental
Reorganization Act

Title of Legislative History: Legislative History of the District of Columbia
Self-Government and Governmental
Reorganization Act, S. 1435 (Public Law 93-
198), 93rd Cong., 1st Sess. (Comm. Prints 1973)
Publication Date: 1974
Author: Senate Committee on the District of Columbia
Pages: vi, 860; vi, 861-2063

L/C Card Number: 74-601920
OCLC No.: 1010456
SuDoc No.: Y4.D63/2:Se4/pt.1-2
CIS No.: 74-S302-3&4
UPA Citation: N/A
Relevant Bills: H.R. 6186 (93rd Cong.), H.R. 9056 (93rd Cong.), H.R. 9682
(93rd Cong.), H.R. 10692 (93rd Cong.), H.R. 10693 (93rd Cong.), H.R.
12109 (93rd Cong.), S. 1435 (93rd Cong.)

This is a legislative history of the District of Columbia Self-Government and
Governmental Reorganization Act and two 1974 laws which affected that
Act: the District of Columbia Revenue Act of 1947, Amendment of 1974; and
the District of Columbia Self-Government Act, Amendment of 1974.   In
addition to selected legislative history materials, the President's statement
on signing P.L. 93-198 and the text of all three Acts are included.

Record No.: 152
Public Law No.: 93-205
Bill No.: S. 1983 (93rd Cong.)
Statutes at Large Citation: 87 Stat. 884 (1973)
Title of Act: Endangered Species Act of 1973

Title of Legislative History: A Legislative History of the Endangered
Species Act of 1973, as Amended in 1976, 1977,
1978, 1979, and 1980: Together with a Section-
by-Section Index, 97th Cong., 2nd Sess.
(Comm. Print 1982)
Publication Date: 1982
Author: Senate Committee on the Environment and Public Works
Pages: xiii, 1506

L/C Card Number: 82-602255
OCLC No.: 8492249
SuDoc No.: Y4.P96/10:97-6
CIS No.: 82-S322-4
UPA Citation: N/A
Relevant Bills: H.R. 9424 (89th Cong.), H.R. 11363 (91st Cong.), H.R. 37 (93rd
Cong.), S. 1983 (93rd Cong.), H.R. 8092 (94th Cong.), H.R. 10229 (94th
Cong.), S. 229 (94th Cong.), S. 3122 (94th Cong.), H.R. 6405 (95th
Cong.), H.R. 14104 (95th Cong.), S. 1316 (95th Cong.), S. 2899 (95th
Cong.), H.R. 2218 (96th Cong.), H.R. 4388 (96th Cong.), H.R. 6839 (96th
Cong.), S. 1143 (96th Cong.)

This is a legislative history of the Endangered Species Act of 1973, as amended through 1980. Selected legislative history materials are provided for the Act and the following amendments: Amendments of 1976 (P.L. 94-325); Amendments of 1976 (P.L. 94-359); Amendments of 1977; Amendments of 1978; Energy and Water Development Appropriation Act, 1980; Amendments of 1979; and Amendment of 1980. A section-by-section index provides access to the materials. Although hearings are not represented, an annotated bibliography of relevant hearings is provided. Included is the Endangered Species Act of 1973, as amended through 1980 and codified in Title 16 of the *United States Code*. The history concludes with a bibliography of journal articles and government documents on the Endangered Species Act. Annotations are provided for the journal articles.

Record No.: 153
Public Law No.: 93-253
Bill No.: H.R. 8245 (93rd Cong.)
Statutes at Large Citation: 88 Stat. 50 (1974)
Title of Act: Reorganization Plan No. 2 of 1973, amendments

Title of Legislative History: Legislative History of 1974 Amendments of
Section 2680(h) of Federal Tort Claims Act
(Intentional Torts) IN Amendments to the
Federal Tort Claims Act, S. 2117: Part I, Joint
Hearing Before the Subcommittee on Citizens
and Shareholders Rights and Remedies and
the Subcommittee on Administrative Practice
and Procedure of the Senate Committee on the
Judiciary, 95th Cong., 2nd Sess. (1978)
Publication Date: 1978
Author: Subcommittee on Citizens and Shareholders Rights and Remedies, Subcommittee on Administrative Practice and Procedure, Senate Committee on the Judiciary
Pages: iv, 351

L/C Card Number: 78-602681
OCLC No.: 4129358
SuDoc No.: Y4.J89/2:T63/2/pt.1-2
CIS No.: 78-S521-36; 79-S521-14
UPA Citation: N/A
Relevant Bills: H.R. 8245 (93rd Cong.), H.R. 10439 (93rd Cong.), S. 2117 (95th Cong.)

Legislative history materials relating to the 1974 Amendment of Section 2680(h) of the Federal Tort Claims Act (Intentional Torts) are contained in the appendix to Amendments to the Federal Tort Claims Act, S. 2117, Part I. There is a list of primary sources compiled by the Congressional

Research Service; a reprint of the Senate Report; and House debate from March 5, 1974. Also included in the appendix is a law review article on P.L. 93-253 which includes an examination of its legislative history; and several court opinions and one appellate brief from famous tort claims cases against the federal government. An index to the hearing and its appendix is in Part II.

Record No.: 154
Public Law No.: 93-259
Bill No.: S. 2747 (93rd Cong.)
Statutes at Large Citation: 88 Stat. 55 (1974)
Title of Act: Fair Labor Standards Amendments of 1974

Title of Legislative History: Legislative History of the Fair Labor Standards Amendments of 1974 (Public Law 93-259), 94th Cong., 2nd Sess. (Comm. Print 1976)
Publication Date: 1976
Author: Subcommittee on Labor, Senate Committee on Labor and Public Welfare
Pages: xlix, 2512

L/C Card Number: 77-600796
OCLC No.: 2395075
SuDoc No.: Y4.L11/2:F15/3/974/v.1-2
CIS No.: 76-S542-22 & 23
UPA Citation: N/A
Relevant Bills: H.R. 7935 (93rd Cong.), H.R. 12435 (93rd Cong.), S. 1725 (93rd Cong.), S. 1861 (93rd Cong.), S. 2727 (93rd Cong.), S. 2747 (93rd Cong.)

This is a legislative history of the Fair Labor Standards Amendments of 1974. The history begins with five indices: a subject index; a table of cases; an index to the remarks of Representatives and Senators; an index to the procedural history of P.L. 93-259; and, a section-by-section index. The section-by-section index indicates where specific subjects are treated in P.L. 93-259 and in the Fair Labor Standards Act as it appeared before and after P.L. 93-259. The legislative history itself is arranged strictly chronologically. It includes multiple versions of and amendments to H.R. 7935 (93rd Cong.) and its related bill S. 1725 (93rd Cong.). The history also includes Congressional debates and reports. H.R. 7935 (93rd Cong.) passed both houses but was vetoed by the President. The President's veto message is provided. This veto triggered another round of legislative activity. The history includes multiple versions of and amendments to S. 2747 (93rd Cong.) and its related bill H.R. 12435 (93rd Cong.). The history concludes with the text of P.L. 93-259, as well as the text of the Fair Labor Standards Act as amended to 1974 with the changes made by P.L. 93-259 shown in italics.

Record No.: 155
Public Law No.: 93-319
Bill No.: H.R. 14368 (93rd Cong.)
Statutes at Large Citation: 88 Stat. 246 (1974)
Title of Act: Energy Supply and Environmental Coordination Act of 1974

Title of Legislative History: A Legislative History of the Energy Supply and
                               Environmental Coordination Act of 1974,
                               Together With A Section-By-Section Index, 94th
                               Cong., 2nd Sess. (Comm. Prints 1976)
Publication Date: 1976
Author: Senate Committee on Public Works
Pages: viii, 1471; iv, 1475-3046

L/C Card Number: 76-603055
OCLC No.: 2577138
SuDoc No.: Y4.P96/10:94-7/v.1-2
CIS No.: 76-S642-6; 76-S642-7
UPA Citation: N/A
Relevant Bills: H.R. 11450 (93rd Cong.), H.R. 11882 (93rd Cong.), H.R. 13834
       (93rd Cong.), H.R. 14368 (93rd Cong.), S. 921 (93rd Cong.), S. 2589
       (93rd Cong.), S. 2680 (93rd Cong.), S. 2772 (93rd Cong.), S. 3267 (93rd
       Cong.), S. 3287 (93rd Cong.)

This is a legislative history of the Energy Supply and Environmental
Coordination Act of 1974. The text of P.L. 93-319 and the President's
remarks upon signing the law open this work. Selected primary materials
are provided for H.R. 14368 (93d Cong.) and other related bills, including the
Energy Emergency Act, S. 2589 (93d Cong.) which was vetoed by the
President. The Energy Supply and Environmental Coordination Act
originated in the Energy Emergency Act. The President's veto message is
included. The appendices include a table that shows where sections of P.L.
93-319 appeared in the major bills leading to its passage and a table that
shows which sections of the Clean Air Act Amendments of 1970 were
affected by P.L. 93-319. A section-by-section index provides access to the
materials reprinted in this publication.

Record No.: 156
Public Law No.: 93-319
Bill No.: H.R. 14368 (93rd Cong.)
Statutes at Large Citation: 88 Stat. 246 (1974)
Title of Act: Energy Supply and Environmental Coordination Act of 1974

Title of Legislative History: Environmental Protection Affairs of 93rd
                               Congress, 94th Cong., 1st Sess. (Comm. Print
                               1975)
Publication Date: 1975
Author: Senate Committee on Public Works
Pages: x, 330

L/C Card Number: 75-601686
OCLC No.: 1501751
SuDoc No.: Y4.P96/10:94-2
CIS No.: 75-S642-7
UPA Citation: N/A
Relevant Bills: H.R. 1059 (93rd Cong.), H.R. 4873 (93rd Cong.), H.R. 5368
    (93rd Cong.), H.R. 5395 (93rd Cong.), H.R. 5450 (93rd Cong.), H.R.
    6452 (93rd Cong.), H.R. 8637 (93rd Cong.), H.R. 8860 (93rd Cong.),
    H.R. 9726 (93rd Cong.), H.R. 10955 (93rd Cong.), H.R. 11450 (93rd
    Cong.), H.R. 12859 (93rd Cong.), H.R. 13176 (93rd Cong.), H.R. 13747
    (93rd Cong.), H.R. 13906 (93rd Cong.), H.R. 14368 (93rd Cong.), H.R.
    15223 (93rd Cong.), H.R. 15382 (93rd Cong.), H.R. 15472 (93rd Cong.),
    H.R. 15560 (93rd Cong.), H.R. 16045 (93rd Cong.), H.R. 16901 (93rd
    Cong.), S. 386 (93rd Cong.), S.433 (93rd Cong.), S. 502 (93rd Cong.), S.
    1086 (93rd Cong.), S. 1351 (93rd Cong.), S. 1735 (93rd Cong.), S. 1888
    (93rd Cong.), S. 2589 (93rd Cong.), S. 2772 (93rd Cong.), S. 2846 (93rd
    Cong.), S. 3035 (93rd Cong.), S. 3231 (93rd Cong.), S. 3679 (93rd Cong.),
    S. 3934 (93rd Cong.)

The document contains twelve chapters: Air Quality, Health Effects of Air
Pollution, and Water Pollution and Ocean Dumping. Each chapter
discusses the Congressional activity during the 93rd Congress on that
chapter's subject. Each chapter is similarly organized. Most chapters
contain sections on "legislation enacted" and "legislative proposals" and
conclude with a bibliography of Congressional documents from the 93rd
Congress. The sections on legislation describe bills and public laws or
discuss and selectively quote bill versions and Congressional hearings.
Footnotes provide complete citations. The bibliographies of Congressional
documents provide full citations to Congressional reports, documents,
committee prints, and hearings. Lists of selected supporting documents,
such as documents from the executive branch and journal articles are
provided in various chapters. The chapters also frequently cite and discuss
relevant reports by the Environmental Protection Agency. The laws for
which the chapters provide legislative history information include: Energy
Supply and Environmental Coordination Act of 1974; Safe Drinking Water
Act; Agriculture and Consumer Protection Act of 1973; National Mass
Transportation Assistance Act of 1974; and Agriculture-Environmental
and Consumer Protection Appropriation Act, 1975.

Record No.: 157
Public Law No.: 93-344
Bill No.: H.R. 7130 (93rd Cong.)
Statutes at Large Citation: 88 Stat. 297 (1974)
Title of Act: Congressional Budget and Impoundment Control Act of 1974

Title of Legislative History: Congressional Budget and Impoundment
                               Control Act of 1974, Public Law 93-344,
                               Legislative History, S. 1541 - H.R. 7130, 93rd
                               Cong., 2nd Sess. (Comm. Print 1974)
Publication Date: 1974
Author: Senate Committee on Government Operations
Pages: xxi, 2111

L/C Card Number: 75-600588
OCLC No.: 1231102
SuDoc No.: Y4.G74/6:B85/8
CIS No.: 75-S402-1
UPA Citation: N/A
Relevant Bills: H.R. 7130 (93rd Cong.), S. 1541 (93rd Cong.)

This is a legislative history of the Congressional Budget and Impoundment
Control Act of 1974. The Table of Contents serves to track the legislative
action and refer the user to the reprinted primary materials. There is
detailed coverage of the numbered and floor amendments to H.R. 7130 (93d
Cong.) and its related bill S. 1541 (93d Cong.). The Table of Contents plays
an important gathering function for these amendments by indicating what
pages of the debate contain action on a given amendment, even if the
amendment was introduced, debated, and agreed to or rejected on different
dates. Selected legislative history materials are reprinted in chronological
order. This publication concludes with the text of the Congressional Budget
and Impoundment Control Act of 1974 and a name index.

Record No.: 158
Public Law No.: 93-344
Bill No.: H.R. 7130 (93rd Cong.)
Statutes at Large Citation: 88 Stat. 297 (1974)
Title of Act: Congressional Budget and Impoundment Control Act of 1974

Title of Legislative History: Congressional Budget and Impoundment
                               Control Act of 1974 (Public Law 93-344),
                               Legislative History (H.R. 7130 -- S. 1541), 96th
                               Cong., 1st Sess. (Comm. Print 1979)
Publication Date: 1979
Author: House Committee on the Budget
Pages: iii, 415

L/C Card Number: 79-601417
OCLC No.: 5073857
SuDoc No.: Y4.B85/3:Im7/2
CIS No.: 79-H262-8
UPA Citation: N/A
Relevant Bills: H.R. 7130 (93rd Cong.), S. 1541 (93rd Cong.)

This is a legislative history of the Congressional Budget and Impoundment Control Act of 1974. It contains the Congressional reports on H.R. 7130 (93rd Cong.) and its companion bill S. 1541 (93rd Cong.); Congressional debate on H.R. 7130; and the text of P.L. 93-344. Also included are Congressional reports from the 94th Congress on the "Implementation of New Congressional Budget Procedures for Fiscal Year 1976."

Record No.: 159
Public Law No.: 93-344
Bill No.: H.R. 7130 (93rd Cong.)
Statutes at Large Citation: 88 Stat. 297 (1974)
Title of Act: Congressional Budget and Impoundment Control Act of 1974

Title of Legislative History: Index to the Legislative History of the
                               Congressional Budget and Impoundment
                               Control Act of 1974

Publication Date: 1980
Author: Barbara and Ken LePoer of the Congressional Budget Office
Pages: xi, 481

L/C Card Number: 80-603388
OCLC No.: 6729482
SuDoc No.: Y10.2:C76/2/ind.
CIS No.: 80-J932-33
UPA Citation: N/A
Relevant Bills: H.R. 98 (93rd Cong.), H.R. 630 (93rd Cong.), H.R. 2443 (93rd
     Cong.), H.R. 2842 (93rd Cong.), H.R. 4053 (93rd Cong.), H.R. 5388
     (93rd Cong.), H.R. 7130 (93rd Cong.), H.R. 8480 (93rd Cong.), H.R.
     8762 (93rd Cong.), H.R. 8876 (93rd Cong.), H.R. 9879 (93rd Cong.), S.
     40 (93rd Cong.), S. 373 (93rd Cong.), S. 565 (93rd Cong.), S. 703 (93rd
     Cong.), S. 758 (93rd Cong.), S. 846 (93rd Cong.), S. 905 (93rd Cong.), S.
     1030 (93rd Cong.), S. 1213 (93rd Cong.), S. 1214 (93rd Cong.), S. 1215
     (93rd Cong.), S. 1392 (93rd Cong.), S. 1414 (93rd Cong.), S. 1516 (93rd
     Cong.), S. 1541 (93rd Cong.), S. 1641 (93rd Cong.), S. 1648 (93rd Cong.)

The index to the legislative history of the Congressional Budget and Impoundment Control Act of 1974, H.R. 7130 (93rd Cong.), P.L. 93-344 covers ten volumes. These ten volumes include six volumes of hearings held in 1973 and 1974; the interim and final reports of the Joint Study Committee on Budget Control; and legislative histories of P.L. 93-344 by the Senate Committee on Government Operations and by the Congressional Research Service. The index provides access by the names of persons who testified or were mentioned in testimony at the hearings, budgetary terms, bills, amendments to bills, Congressional reports, and sections of P.L. 93-344. The index provides two numbers for each subject term. The first two digits of the first number indicate the volumes. The next four digits indicate the page of that volume on which the subject appears. The second number indicates reel and frame for a two reel microfilm set of the ten indexed volumes.

Record No.: 160
Public Law No.: 93-344
Bill No.: H.R. 7130 (93rd Cong.)
Statutes at Large Citation: 88 Stat. 297 (1974)
Title of Act: Congressional Budget and Impoundment Control Act of 1974

Title of Legislative History: Impoundment Control Act of 1974: Legislative
                              History and Implementation
Publication Date: 1976
Author: Allen Schick of the Congressional Research Service
Pages: 116

L/C Card Number: N/A
OCLC No.: 24470518
SuDoc No.: N/A
CIS No.: N/A
UPA Citation: UPA Film No.: MS 75-76 Supp., Reel No.II, Frame No. 0407.
CRS No.: HJ8 U.S.A. 76-45S
Relevant Bills: H.R. 5193 (93rd Cong.), H.R. 7130 (93rd Cong.), H.R. 8480
              (93rd Cong.), S. 373 (93rd Cong.), S. 1541 (93rd Cong.), S. 3034 (93rd
              Cong.)

This Congressional Research Service document includes legislative history information on the Impoundment Control Act of 1974. The Act appeared as Title X of the Congressional Budget and Impoundment Control Act of 1974. The "Summary and Background" portion of the document includes a discussion of the legislative history of the Impoundment Control Act. An essay compares the relevant bills from the 93rd Congress and provides citations to relevant Congressional debate and Congressional reports. The "Section-by-Section Analysis" portion of the document includes a legislative history discussion for each section of the act. These discussions also compare bills from the 93rd Congress and cite relevant Congressional debate and Congressional reports. In addition, the document contains information on the act's implementation in fiscal years 1975 and 1976.

Record No.: 161
Public Law No.: 93-360
Bill No.: S. 3203 (93rd Cong.)
Statutes at Large Citation: 88 Stat. 395 (1974)

Title of Act: To Amend the National Labor Relations Act to Extend its
          Coverage and Protection to Employees of Nonprofit Hospitals

Title of Legislative History: Legislative History of Coverage of Nonprofit
                   Hospitals under National Labor Relations Act,
                   1974, Public Law 93-360, S. 3203, 93rd Cong.,
                   2nd Sess. (Comm. Print 1974)
Publication Date: 1974
Author: Subcommittee on Labor, Senate Committee on Labor and Public
Welfare
Pages: v, 467

L/C Card Number: 74-603342
OCLC No.: 3206065
SuDoc No.: Y4.L11/2:H79/4/974
CIS No.: 74-S542-33
UPA Citation: N/A
Relevant Bills: H.R. 1236 (93rd Cong.), H.R. 13676 (93rd Cong.), H.R. 13678
     (93rd Cong.), S. 794 (93rd Cong.), S. 2292 (93rd Cong.), S. 3088 (93rd
     Cong.), S. 3203 (93rd Cong.)

This is a legislative history of the laws which extended the coverage of the
National Labor Relations Act to nonprofit hospital workers. The history
concludes with the text of P.L. 93-360. The Appendix includes the text of the
Labor Management Relations Act of 1947, as amended by P.L. 93-360 and
the text of several related bills.

Record No.: 162
Public Law No.: 93-378
Bill No.: S. 2296 (93rd Cong.)
Statutes at Large Citation: 88 Stat. 476 (1974)
Title of Act: Forest and Rangeland Renewable Resources Planning Act of
          1974

Title of Legislative History: Compilation of the Forest and Rangeland
                   Renewable Resources Act of 1974, 96th Cong.,
                   1st Sess. (Comm. Print 1979)
Publication Date: 1979
Author: Senate Committee on Agriculture, Nutrition, and Forestry
Pages: vi, 1508

L/C Card Number: 79-604178
OCLC No.: 5836471
SuDoc No.: Y4.Ag8/3:F76/2
CIS No.: 79-S162-23
UPA Citation: N/A

Relevant Bills: H.R. 15283 (93rd Cong.), S. 2296 (93rd Cong.), H.R. 15069 (94th Cong.), S. 3091 (94th Cong.), H.R. 6362 (95th Cong.), H.R. 11777 (95th Cong.), H.R. 11778 (95th Cong.), H.R. 11779 (95th Cong.), S. 1360 (95th Cong.), S. 3033 (95th Cong.), S. 3034 (95th Cong.), S. 3035 (95th Cong.)

This volume contains legislative history materials for the following six public laws: Forest and Rangeland Renewable Resources Planning Act of 1974; National Forest Management Act of 1976 S. 3091 (94th Cong.), P.L. 94-588; National Forest Management Act of 1976, Amendment of 1978, S. 1360 (95th Cong.), P.L. 95-233; Cooperative Forestry Assistance Act of 1978 H.R. 11777 (95th Cong.), P.L. 95-313; Forest and Rangeland Renewable Resources Research Act of 1978 H.R. 11778 (95th Cong.), P.L. 307; and Renewable Resources Extension Act of 1978 H.R. 11779 (95th Cong.), P.L. 95-306. Each of the first three public laws is treated in its own chapter. The second three public laws are treated in a single chapter. Selected primary sources are reprinted. The materials for each public law conclude with the President's statement upon signing the enrolled bill into law and the text of that public law.

Related Public Laws: P.L. 93-378; P.L. 95-233; P.L. 95-313; P.L. 95-307; P.L. 95-306.

Record No.: 163
Public Law No.: 93-383
Bill No.: S. 3066 (93rd Cong.)
Statutes at Large Citation: 88 Stat. 633 (1974)
Title of Act: Housing and Community Development Act of 1974

Title of Legislative History: Compilation of the Housing and Community Development Act of 1974, 93rd Cong., 2nd Sess. (Comm. Print 1974)

Publication Date: 1974
Author: Subcommittee on Housing, House Committee on Banking and Currency
Pages: v, 753

L/C Card Number: 74-602837
OCLC No.: 1160829
SuDoc No.: Y4.B22/1:H81/71
CIS No.: 74-H242-6
UPA Citation: N/A
Relevant Bills: H.R. 15361 (93rd Cong.), S. 3066 (93rd Cong.)

This document contains materials relevant to the legislative history of the Housing and Community Development Act of 1974. P.L. 93-383 established a program of community development grants. It affected many aspects of housing and housing assistance. Title VI of P.L. 93-383 may be cited as the National Mobile Home Construction and Safety Standards Act of 1974, and

Title VII as the Consumer Home Mortgage Assistance Act of 1974. The document begins with the text of P.L. 93-383. The document continues with a detailed section-by-section summary of P.L. 93-383. Selected primary sources are reprinted.

Record No.: 164
Public Law No.: 93-406
Bill No.: H.R. 2 (93rd Cong.)
Statutes at Large Citation: 88 Stat. 829 (1974)
Title of Act: Employee Retirement Income Security Act of 1974
Title of Legislative History: Legislative History of the Employee Retirement Income Security Act of 1974: Public Law 93-406, 94th Cong., 2nd Sess. (Comm. Print 1976)
Publication Date: 1976
Author: Subcommittee on Labor, Senate Committee on Labor and Public Welfare
Pages: xlix, 5322

L/C Card Number: 77-600583
OCLC No.: 2349652
SuDoc No.: Y4.L11/2:R31/10/v.1-3
CIS No.: 76-S542-13&14&15
UPA Citation: N/A
Relevant Bills: H.R. 2 (93rd Cong.), H.R. 462 (93rd Cong.), H.R. 4200 (93rd Cong.), H.R. 9824 (93rd Cong.), H.R. 12481 (93rd Cong.), H.R. 12855 (93rd Cong.), H.R. 12906 (93rd Cong.), S. 4 (93rd Cong.), S. 1179 (93rd Cong.), S. 1557 (93rd Cong.), S. 1631 (93rd Cong.)

This is a legislative history of the Employee Retirement Income Security Act of 1974. The publication begins with nine indices to the Congressional documents included in the legislative history. These indices cover the following broad subject areas: definitions; reporting and disclosure; participation and vesting; funding; fiduciary responsibility; termination insurance; enforcement; Internal Revenue Code; and miscellaneous. Selected primary sources are reprinted. The text of P.L. 93-406 is included in the history.

Record No.: 165
Public Law No.: 93-409
Bill No.: H.R. 11864 (93rd Cong.)
Statutes at Large Citation: 88 Stat. 1069 (1974)
Title of Act: Solar Heating and Cooling Demonstration Act of 1974

Title of Legislative History: Energy Research and Development
Administration, Statutes and Legislative
Histories, Volume I, Solar Heating and
Cooling Demonstration Act of 1974, Public Law
93-409, 95th Cong., 2nd Sess. (Comm. Print
1978)

Publication Date: 1978
Author: Subcommittee on Advanced Energy Technologies and Energy
Conservation Research, Development and Demonstration, House
Committee on Science and Technology
Pages: vii, 428

L/C Card Number: 78-601563
OCLC No.: 3803657
SuDoc No.: Y4.Sci2:95/Y
CIS No.: 78-H702-13
UPA Citation: N/A
Relevant Bills: H.R. 10952 (93rd Cong.), H.R. 11864 (93rd Cong.), S. 2650
(93rd Cong.), S. 2658 (93rd Cong.)

The legislative history of the Solar Heating and Cooling Demonstration
Act of 1974, begins with a chronology of the Congressional action which led
to the passage of the Act. This chart lists the dates of introduction of bills,
dates of committee action on bills, dates of Congressional hearings, dates of
Congressional debate, and dates and citations of Congressional reports.
The history then continues with the text of P.L. 93-409. Selected primary
sources are reprinted. This volume is Volume I of a five volume set. The
other volumes are described under other record numbers. See also Record
Numbers 166 (vol. II), 169 (vol. III), 172 (vol. IV), and 192 (vol. V).

Record No.: 166
Public Law No.: 93-410
Bill No.: H.R. 14920 (93rd Cong.)
Statutes at Large Citation: 88 Stat. 1079 (1974)
Title of Act: Geothermal Energy Research, Development, and
Demonstration Act of 1974

Title of Legislative History: Energy Research and Development
Administration, Statutes and Legislative
Histories, Volume II, Geothermal Energy
Research, Development, and Demonstration
Act of 1974, Public Law 93-410, 95th Cong., 2nd
Sess. (Comm. Print 1978)

Publication Date: 1978
Author: Subcommittee on Advanced Energy Technologies and Energy
Conservation Research, Development and Demonstration, House
Committee on Science and Technology
Pages: vii, 257

L/C Card Number: 78-601563
OCLC No.: 3803657
SuDoc No.: Y4.Sci2:95/Z
CIS No.: 78-H702-14
UPA Citation: N/A
Relevant Bills: H.R. 8628 (93rd Cong.), H.R. 9658 (93rd Cong.), H.R. 11212
    (93rd Cong.), H.R. 14172 (93rd Cong.), H.R. 14920 (93rd Cong.), S. 2465
    (93rd Cong.)

The legislative history of the Geothermal Energy Research, Development,
and Demonstration Act of 1974 begins with a chronology of the
Congressional action which led to the passage of the Act. This chart lists
the dates of introduction of bills, dates of committee action on bills, dates of
Congressional hearings, dates of Congressional debate, and dates and
citations of Congressional reports. The history then continues with the text
of P.L. 93-410. Selected primary sources are reprinted. This volume is
Volume II of a five volume set. Other volumes are described under other
record numbers. See also Record Numbers 165 (vol. I), 169 (vol. III), 172
(vol. IV) and 192 (vol. V).

Record No.: 167
Public Law No.: 93-415
Bill No.: S. 821 (93rd Cong.)
Statutes at Large Citation: 88 Stat. 1109 (1974)
Title of Act: Juvenile Justice and Delinquency Prevention Act of 1974

Title of Legislative History: Indexed Legislative History of Juvenile Justice
                and Delinquency Prevention Act of 1974
Publication Date: 1974
Author: Department of Justice, Law Enforcement Assistance
Administration, Office of General Counsel
Pages: xxiii, 440

L/C Card Number: 75-601524
OCLC No.: 1677333
SuDoc No.: J1.2:L52/2/974
CIS No.: N/A
UPA Citation: N/A
Relevant Bills: H.R. 15276 (93rd Cong.), S. 821 (93rd Cong.)

The legislative history of the Juvenile Justice and Delinquency Prevention
Act of 1974 begins with a section-by-section index to the Act. For each
section of the Act, the index provides citations to the relevant Congressional
documents included in the history: bills, Congressional reports, and

Congressional debate. The introductory material also includes a chronological table of prior federal governmental activity concerning juvenile delinquency, as well as a chronological table of Congressional activity in the 93rd Congress which led to the enactment of the Act. The text of P.L. 93-415 is included.

Record No.: 168
Public Law No.: 93-443
Bill No.: S. 3044 (93rd Cong.)
Statutes at Large Citation: 88 Stat. 1263 (1974)
Title of Act: Federal Election Campaign Act Amendments of 1974

Title of Legislative History: Legislative History of Federal Election
                               Campaign Act Amendments of 1974

Publication Date: 1977
Author: Federal Election Commission
Pages: v, 1223

L/C Card Number: N/A
OCLC No.: 3466451
SuDoc No.: Y3.El2/3:2L52/974
CIS No.: N/A
UPA Citation: N/A
Relevant Bills: H.R. 16090 (93rd Cong.), S. 3044 (93rd Cong.)

The legislative history presents chronologically the Congressional action which led to the enactment of the Federal Election Campaign Act Amendments of 1974. Selected primary sources are reprinted. Also included are the President's remarks on signing S. 3044 (93rd Cong.) into law and the text of P.L. 93-443. The history concludes with a detailed subject index and an index to the days of the relevant Congressional debate.

Record No.: 169
Public Law No.: 93-473
Bill No.: S. 3234 (93rd Cong.)
Statutes at Large Citation: 88 Stat. 1431 (1974)
Title of Act: Solar Energy Research, Development, and Demonstration Act
              of 1974

Title of Legislative History: Energy Research and Development
                               Administration: Statutes and Legislative
                               Histories, Volume III, Solar Energy Research
                               Development and Demonstration Act of 1974,
                               Public Law 93-473, 95th Cong., 2nd Sess.
                               (Comm. Print 1978)

Publication Date: 1978
Author: Subcommittee on Advanced Energy Technologies and Energy
Conservation Research, Development and Demonstration, House
Committee on Science and Technology
Pages: vii, 245

L/C Card Number: 78-601563
OCLC No.: 3803657
SuDoc No.: Y4.Sci2:95/AA
CIS No.: 78-H702-15
UPA Citation: N/A
Relevant Bills: H.R. 15612 (93rd Cong.), H.R. 16371 (93rd Cong.), S. 3234
     (93rd Cong.)

The legislative history of the Solar Energy Research, Development, and
Demonstration Act of 1974 begins with a chronology of the Congressional
action which led to the passage of P.L. 93-473. This chart lists the dates of
introduction of bills, dates of Congressional hearings, dates of
Congressional debate, and dates and citations of Congressional reports.
The history then continues with the text of P.L. 93-473. Selected primary
sources are reprinted. This volume is Volume III of a five volume set.
Other volumes are described under other record numbers. See also Record
Numbers 165 (vol. I), 166 (vol. II), 172 (vol. IV) and 192 (vol. V).

Record No.: 170
Public Law No.: 93-502
Bill No.: H.R. 12471 (93rd Cong.)
Statutes at Large Citation: 88 Stat. 1561 (1974)
Title of Act: Freedom of Information Act, Amendment of 1974

Title of Legislative History: Freedom of Information Act and Amendments
                               of 1974 (P.L. 93-502), Source Book, Legislative
                               History, Texts, and Other Documents, 94th
                               Cong., 1st Sess. (Comm. Print 1975)
Publication Date: 1975
Author: Subcommittee on Government Information and Individual Rights,
House Committee on Government Operations; Subcommittee on
Administrative Practice and Procedure, Senate Committee on the Judiciary
Pages: ix, 571

L/C Card Number: 75-601607
OCLC No.: 1501738
SuDoc No.: Y4.G74/7:In3/16
CIS No.: 75-H402-6
UPA Citation: N/A
Relevant Bills: S. 1160 (89th Cong.), H.R. 5357 (90th Cong.), H.R. 12471 (93rd
    Cong.), S. 2543 (93rd Cong.)

This is a legislative history of the Freedom of Information Act
Amendments of 1974. The history begins with Congressional reports
analyzing the administration of the Freedom of Information Act until 1972.
Selected primary sources are reprinted. The appendices include the text of
H.R. 12471 (93rd Cong.), as well as the Presidential message upon vetoing
this bill. The appendices also include the texts of the original Freedom of
Information Act; the Freedom of Information Act as codified by law; the
Freedom of Information Act Amendments of 1974; and the Freedom of
Information Act as amended by P.L. 93-502. The history concludes with an
appendix containing the Attorney General's memoranda on the
implementation of P.L 93-502.

Record No.: 171
Public Law No.: 93-523
Bill No.: S. 433 (93rd Cong.)
Statutes at Large Citation: 88 Stat. 1660 (1974)
Title of Act: Safe Drinking Water Act

Title of Legislative History: A Legislative History of the Safe Drinking
                               Water Act: Together with a Section-by-Section
                               Index, 97th Cong., 2nd Sess. (Comm. Print
                               1982)
Publication Date: 1982
Author: Senate Committee on the Environment and Public Works
Pages: vi, 1103

L/C Card Number: 82-602254
OCLC No.: 8491626
SuDoc No.: Y4.P96/10:97-9
CIS No.: 82-S322-5
UPA Citation: N/A
Relevant Bills: H.R. 13002 (93rd Cong.), S. 433 (93rd Cong.), H.R. 6827 (95th
    Cong.), S. 1528 (95th Cong.), H.R. 3509 (96th Cong.), H.R. 8117 (96th
    Cong.), S. 1146 (96th Cong.)

This is a legislative history of the Safe Drinking Water Act and its 1977, 1979
and 1980 Amendments (P.L. 95-190, P.L. 96-63, P.L. 96-502). The legislative
history begins with the text of the Safe Drinking Water Act, as amended. A
chapter is dedicated to each public law. Each chapter contains the text of a

public law, and relevant bills, Congressional reports, and Congressional debate. Excerpts from Congressional hearings are also included. The history concludes with a section-by-section index to the Safe Drinking Water Act, as amended. For each section of the act, the index provides citations to the relevant documents included in the history.

Record No.: 172
Public Law No.: 93-577
Bill No.: S. 1283 (93rd Cong.)
Statutes at Large Citation: 88 Stat. 1878 (1974)
Title of Act: Federal Nonnuclear Energy Research and Development Act
     of 1974

Title of Legislative History: Energy Research and Development
                               Administration: Statutes and Legislative
                               Histories, Vol. IV, Federal Nonnuclear Energy
                               Research and Development Act of 1974, as
                               Amended, Public Law 93-577, 95th Cong., 2nd
                               Sess. (Comm. Print 1978)
Publication Date: 1978
Author: Subcommittee on Advanced Energy Technologies and Energy Conservation Research, Development and Demonstration, House Committee on Science and Technology
Pages: v, 757

L/C Card Number: 78-601563
OCLC No.: 3803657
SuDoc No.: Y4.Sci2:95/PP
CIS No.: 78-H702-33
UPA Citation: N/A
Relevant Bills: H.R. 13565 (93rd Cong.), S. 1283 (93rd Cong.), S. 826 (95th Cong.), S. 1340 (95th Cong.)

The legislative history of the Federal Nonnuclear Energy Research and Development Act of 1974 begins with a chronological table of the Congressional action which led to the enactment of the Act. The history contains the text of P.L. 93-577. Selected primary sources are reprinted. The Appendix includes the text of laws which affected the implementation of the Act; Sections 205 and 657 of the Department of Energy Organization Act; and the Department of Energy Act of 1978 -- Civilian Applications. This volume is Volume IV of a five volume set. Other volumes are described under other record numbers. See also Record Numbers 165 (vol. I), 166 (vol. II), 169 (vol. III), and 192 (vol. V).

Record No.: 173
Public Law No.: 93-579
Bill No.: S. 3418 (93rd Cong.)
Statutes at Large Citation: 88 Stat. 1896 (1974)
Title of Act: Privacy Act of 1974

Title of Legislative History: Legislative History of the Privacy Act of 1974, S.
3418 (Public Law 93-579): Source Book on
Privacy, 94th Cong., 2nd Sess. (Comm. Print
1976)
Publication Date: 1976
Author: Senate Committee on Government Operations; Subcommittee on
Government Information and Individual Rights, House Committee on
Government Operations
Pages: xii, 1458

L/C Card Number: 76-603293
OCLC No.: 2580606
SuDoc No.: Y4.G74/6:L52/3
CIS No.: 76-S402-22
UPA Citation: N/A
Relevant Bills: H.R. 1281 (93rd Cong.), H.R. 7677 (93rd Cong.), H.R. 12206
(93rd Cong.), H.R. 13872 (93rd Cong.), H.R. 14493 (93rd Cong.), H.R.
16373 (93rd Cong.), S. 1688 (93rd Cong.), S. 2542 (93rd Cong.), S. 2810
(93rd Cong.), S. 2963 (93rd Cong.), S. 3116 (93rd Cong.), S. 3418 (93rd
Cong.), S. 3633 (93rd Cong.)

The legislative history of the Privacy Act of 1974, S. 3418 (93rd Cong.), P.L.
93-579 presents the major bills which would comprise the law. The history
includes several versions of S. 3418 (93rd Cong.) and a markup session
transcript on this bill. It also includes several versions of the related bill
H.R. 16373 (93rd Cong.) and the Congressional reports on both these bills.
The history then presents P.L. 93-579, additional bills concerning privacy
from the 93rd Congress, and the Congressional debate on S. 3418
(93rd Cong.) and H.R. 16373 (93rd Cong.). As a source book, the history
includes explanatory newspaper and law review articles on the Privacy
Act, as well as a bibliography on the Privacy Act which provides citations to
law review articles, books, and government documents. The Appendix
includes selected cases regarding the personal privacy exception to the
Freedom of Information Act, H.R. 5357 (90th Cong.), P.L. 90-23.

Record No.: 174
Public Law No.: 93-619
Bill No.: S. 754 (93rd Cong.)
Statutes at Large Citation: 88 Stat. 2076 (1975)
Title of Act: Speedy Trial Act of 1974

Title of Legislative History: Legislative History of Title I of the Speedy Trial
                               Act of 1974
Publication Date: 1980
Author: Anthony Partridge of the Federal Judicial Center
Pages: v, 384

L/C Card Number: 80-604161
OCLC No.: 7125280
SuDoc No.: Ju13.2:L52
CIS No.: N/A
UPA Citation: N/A
Relevant Bills: H.R. 14822 (91st Cong.), S. 3936 (91st Cong.), H.R. 7107 (92nd
       Cong.), S. 895 (92nd Cong.), H.R. 17409 (93rd Cong.), S. 754 (93rd
       Cong.), S. 961 (96th Cong.), S. 1028 (96th Cong.)

The legislative history of the Speedy Trial Act of 1974 and the Speedy Trial
Act Amendments of 1979, S. 961 (96th Cong.), P.L. 96-43 begins with a
chronological list of the major legislative history materials. The remainder
of the publication is divided into three parts. Part One is an essay which
addresses the broader purposes of the legislation. Part Two is a section-by-
section analysis of the Speedy Trial Act as codified. Each section of the act
is reprinted and followed by excerpts from relevant Congressional
documents. Part Three presents the text of Title I of the Speedy Trial Act as
it appears in P.L. 93-619 and as it appeared in the major bills: H.R. 7107 (92d
Cong.); S. 895 (92d Cong.); H.R. 17409 (93d Cong.); and S. 754 (93d Cong.).

Record No.: 175
Public Law No.: 94-12
Bill No.: H.R. 2166 (94th Cong.)
Statutes at Large Citation: 89 Stat. 26 (1975)
Title of Act: Tax Reduction Act of 1975

Title of Legislative History: Tax Reduction Act of 1975, P.L. 94-12, (H.R.
                               2166): The Legislative Development of Each
                               Provision, Including Those Items Not Adopted
Publication Date: 1975
Author: Susan L. Drake, Jane G. Gravelle, and Harold A. Kohnen of the
Congressional Research Service
Pages: xi, 58

L/C Card Number: N/A
OCLC No.: 24647097
SuDoc No.: N/A
CIS No.: N/A
UPA Citation: UPA Film No.: MS 75-76 Supp., Reel No. VI, Frame No.
0029.CRS No.: HJ 4625 U.S.A. 75-108E
Relevant Bills: H.R. 2166 (94th Cong.)

The Congressional Research Service document on the Tax Reduction Act of 1975 provides legislative history information for this Act. The document begins with a summary of P.L. 94-12. The document's introduction is a short essay which follows H.R. 2166 (94th Cong.) as it progresses through Congress. The essay notes the dates of committee action, pertinent passage dates, and Congressional hearings and provides citations to the Congressional reports. The greatest part of the document consists of a subject analysis of P.L. 94-12. For each subject heading, subsections describe relevant information from any or all of the following: pre-P.L. 94-12 law; the Administration's proposal; H.R. 2166 (94th Cong.) as passed by the House, testimony of the Secretary of the Treasury before the Senate Finance Committee; the Senate Finance Committee's version of H.R. 2166 (94th Cong.); H.R. 2166 (94th Cong.) as passed by the Senate; and P.L. 94-12. The document concludes with excerpts from the House Ways and Means Committee Republican members' proposal and the   Joint Economic Committee's recommendations.

Record No.: 176
Public Law No.: 94-29
Bill No.: S. 249 (94th Cong.)
Statutes at Large Citation: 89 Stat. 97 (1975)
Title of Act: Securities Acts Amendments of 1975

Title of Legislative History: Legislative History of Securities Acts
                                  Amendments of 1975, 94th Cong., 1st Sess.
                                  (Comm. Print 1975)
Publication Date: 1975
Author: House Committee on Interstate and Foreign Commerce
Pages: ii, 315

L/C Card Number: 75-602966
OCLC No.: 1743780
SuDoc No.: Y4.In8/4:Se2/24
CIS No.: 75-H502-17
UPA Citation: N/A
Relevant Bills: H.R. 9323 (73rd Cong.), H.R. 340 (93rd Cong.), H.R. 5050
     (93rd Cong.), H.R. 4111 (94th Cong.), S. 249 (94th Cong.)

The legislative history of the Securities Acts Amendments of 1975 contains the Conference report on S. 249 (94th Cong.), the explanatory statement of the Conference committee, and the House report on H.R. 4111 (94th Cong.). The Conference report contains the text of S. 249 (94th Cong.), the Senate's amendment in nature of a substitute for the Senate bill and the House amendment. The House amendment in turn had also been a substitute. The Conference committee's explanatory statement notes the differences between the Senate bill, House amendment, and the substitute agreed to in conference. The House report on H.R. 4111 (94th Cong.) contains the text of H.R. 4111 (94th Cong.) as reported with amendments. The House later passed H.R. 4111 (94th Cong.) with further amendments before it passed S. 249 (94th Cong.) in lieu of it. The House report contains a discussion of the bill's major provisions, as well as agency reports and minority views on the bill. The House report also shows the changes made by H.R. 4111 (94th Cong.) to existing laws, particularly the Securities Exchange Act of 1934.

Record No.: 177
Public Law No.: 94-71
Bill No.: H.R. 7767 (94th Cong.)
Statutes at Large Citation: 89 Stat. 395 (1975)
Title of Act: Veterans Disability Compensation and Survivor Benefits Act of 1975

Title of Legislative History: Veterans Disability Compensation and Survivor Benefits Act of 1975: Hearing on S. 1597 and Related Bills Before the Subcommittee on Compensation and Pensions of the Senate Committee on Veterans' Affairs, 94th Cong., 1st Sess. (1975)
Publication Date: 1975
Author: Subcommittee on Compensation and Pensions, Senate Committee on Veterans' Affairs
Pages: v, 492

L/C Card Number: 75-602955
OCLC No.: 1859483
SuDoc No.: Y4.V64/4:D63/4
CIS No.: 75-S761-11
UPA Citation: N/A
Relevant Bills: H.R. 7767 (94th Cong.), S. 110 (94th Cong.), S. 770 (94th Cong.), S. 1432 (94th Cong.), S. 1597 (94th Cong.)

This 1975 hearing contain materials relevant to the legislative history of the Veterans Disability Compensation and Survivor Benefits Act of 1975. P.L. 94-71 increased disability compensation for disabled veterans and their survivors. The appendices to these hearings include the text of H.R. 7767 (94th Cong.) as passed by the House, as well as the House report on H.R. 7767 (94th Cong.). The appendices also include an excerpt from the final Senate debate and passage of a compromise version of H.R. 7767 (94th Cong.). This excerpt summarizes the differences between the House and Senate versions of the bill. Also included is the text of P.L. 94-71. In addition, the appendices also include the text as reported of the main Senate bill to increase disability compensation, S. 1597 (94th Cong.), and the Senate report on this bill. The body of the hearing includes the text of S. 1597 (94th Cong.) as introduced, as well as the introductory statement of its sponsor. This statement explains that increases in compensation were necessary because of cost of living increases. Also included is the Veterans' Administration agency report on S. 1597 (94th Cong.). In addition, the body of the hearing includes the texts as introduced of S. 110 (94th Cong.), S. 770 (94th Cong.), and S. 1432 (94th Cong.). These were additional bills concerning veterans disability compensation. Each of these bills is followed by the Veterans' Administration and Office of Management and Budget agency reports on that bill. Other than H.R. 7767 (94th Cong.), none of these bills became public law.

Record No.: 178
Public Law No.: 94-82
Bill No.: H.R. 2559 (94th Cong.)
Statutes at Large Citation: 89 Stat. 419 (1975)
Title of Act: Executive Salary Cost-of-Living Adjustment Act

Title of Legislative History: Documentary History of Federal Pay
                                Legislation, 1975, 94th Cong., 2nd Sess.
                                (Comm. Print 1976)
Publication Date: 1976
Author: Senate Committee on Post Office and Civil Service
Pages: iv, 534

L/C Card Number: 76-601553
OCLC No.: 2271649
SuDoc No.: Y4.P84/11:P29/10/975
CIS No.: 76-S622-3
UPA Citation: N/A
Relevant Bills: H.R. 2559 (94th Cong.), S. Res. 239 (94th Cong.)

Part One of this document chronologically presents the Congressional action which led to the enactment of the Executive Salary Cost-of-Living Adjustment Act. It includes a draft of proposed legislation, a Congressional report, Congressional debate, and the text of P.L. 94-82. Part Two presents the history of Executive Order 11883, federal pay comparability adjustment of October 1975. Part Three presents the text of several major studies released in 1975 by the executive branch concerning federal salaries. Part Four presents the text of federal pay laws through February 18, 1975, as codified.

Record No.: 179
Public Law No.: 94-123
Bill No.: H.R. 8240 (94th Cong.)
Statutes at Large Citation: 89 Stat. 669 (1975)
Title of Act: Veterans' Administration Physician and Dentist Pay
              Comparability Act of 1975

Title of Legislative History: Veterans' Administration Physician Pay
                              Comparability Act of 1975: Hearings on S. 1711
                              and Related Bills Before the Subcommittee on
                              Health and Hospitals of the Senate Committee
                              on Veterans' Affairs
Publication Date: 1975
Author: Subcommittee on Health and Hospitals, Senate Committee on
Veterans' Affairs
Pages: vi, 682

L/C Card Number: 75-603659
OCLC No.: 2072640
SuDoc No.: Y4.V64/4:V64/6
CIS No.: 76-S761-1
UPA Citation: N/A
Relevant Bills: H.R. 8240 (94th Cong.), S. 1507 (94th Cong.), S. 1711 (94th
    Cong.)

These 1975 hearings and their appendices contain legislative history
materials relevant to the Veterans Administration Physician and Dentist
Pay Comparability Act of 1975. P.L. 94-123 provided for special pay and
incentives for Veterans' Administration (VA) physicians, dentists, and
other medical personnel in order to help with their recruitment and
retention. The Appendices include selected primary sources for this Act as
well as for the bill being considered, S. 1711 (94th Cong.). The text of P.L. 94-
123 is reprinted. The body of the hearings includes the text of S. 1711 (94th
Cong.) as introduced as well as the introductory remarks of its sponsor.
These remarks include, as insertions, excerpts from 1975 House Hearings
on VA recruitment and retention of medical staff. Also reprinted are
agency reports on S. 1711 (94th Cong.) from the VA and the Office of
Management and Budget. The text of another bill, S. 1507 (94th Cong.), to
increase pay for VA medical personnel and a report by the VA on that bill
are also included. The hearings also provide an early draft bill by the VA to
increase pay for Veterans' Administration medical personnel.

Record No.: 180
Public Law No.: 94-135
Bill No.: H.R. 3922 (94th Cong.)
Statutes at Large Citation: 89 Stat. 713 (1975)
Title of Act: Older Americans Amendments of 1975

Title of Legislative History: Older Americans Amendments of 1975 (A
                               Compilation of P.L. 94-135, Accompanying
                               Reports, and Related Acts), 95th Cong., 2nd
                               Sess. (Comm. Print 1978)

Publication Date: 1978
Author: Subcommittee on Aging, Senate Committee on Human Resources
Pages: vii, 362

L/C Card Number: N/A
OCLC No.: 4245292
SuDoc No.: N/A
CIS No.: 78-S412-1
UPA Citation: N/A
Relevant Bills: H.R. 3708 (89th Cong.), H.R. 3922 (94th Cong.), S. 1425 (94th
    Cong.)

The legislative history of the Older Americans Amendments of 1975 begins
with the text of P.L. 94-135. It contains the Conference and House reports on
H.R. 3922 (94th Cong.), as well as the Senate report on the related bill S. 1425
(94th Cong.). The Conference report provides the text of the Conference
substitute version of H.R. 3922 (94th Cong.) and explains the differences
between the House bill, Senate amendment, and Conference substitute
versions of H.R. 3922 (94th Cong.). The Senate report presents the text of S.
1425 (94th Cong.) as reported from Committee. The history concludes with
the text of the Older Americans Act of 1965, as amended by P.L. 94-135 and
previous acts, as well as the text of excerpts from several related acts also
amended by P.L. 94-135.

Record No.: 181
Public Law No.: 94-163
Bill No.: S. 622 (94th Cong.)
Statutes at Large Citation: 89 Stat. 871 (1975)
Title of Act: Energy Policy and Conservation Act

Title of Legislative History: Statutory Authority for the Administrator of
                                 the Environmental Protection Agency to Modify
                                 Automobile Fuel Economy Test Procedures in
                                 Automobile Fuel Economy, EPA Oversight:
                                 Hearings Before a Subcommittee of the House
                                 Committee on Government Operations, 96th
                                 Cong., 2nd Sess. (1980)
Publication Date: 1980
Author: Raymond Natter, Legislative Attorney, American Law Division,
Library of Congress, Congressional Research Service
Pages: pp. 93-106

L/C Card Number: 80-601926
OCLC No.: 6333376
SuDoc No.: Y4.G74/7:Au8/7
CIS No.: 80-H401-40
UPA Citation: N/A
Relevant Bills: H.R. 2633 (94th Cong.), H.R. 7014 (94th Cong.), S. 622 (94th
    Cong.), S. 1883 (94th Cong.)

The legislative history of Section 301 of the Energy Policy and Conservation Act was prepared by the Congressional Research Service (CRS) at the request of the House Committee on Government Operations.Section 301 provided that the Environmental Protection Agency (EPA) could test the fuel economy of passenger vehicles by the procedures used by the EPA in 1975 or by procedures which yield comparable results. The Committee wanted to determine whether Section 301 authorized the EPA to promulgate new test procedures which significantly differed from the 1975 procedures. The Committee had CRS examine the legislative history of the Energy Policy and Conservation Act in light of this question. The legislative history is divided into two parts. One section deals with the House, the other with the Senate. The section on the House focuses on H.R. 7014 (94th Cong.), the main House bill.This bill contained the House's language on testing procedures. In attempting to determine the legislative intent behind Section 301, the history quotes from the House report on H.R. 7014 (94th Cong.); and from House hearings on a related bill and on the energy crisis. In the Senate section, the history focuses on S. 1883 (94th Cong.). This bill contained the Senate's language on testing procedures. This bill was later incorporated into S. 622 (94th Cong.). In attempting to determine the legislative intent behind Section 301, the history quotes from the text of S. 1883 (94th Cong.) as it was reported to and passed by the Senate, as well asquoting from the Senate report on S. 1883 (94th Cong.). In addition, the history indicates that the Conference report on S. 622 (94th Cong.) was examined, but shed no light on the legislative intent behind Section 301.

Record No.: 182
Public Law No.: 94-165
Bill No.: H.R. 8773 (94th Cong.)
Statutes at Large Citation: 89 Stat. 977 (1975)
Title of Act: Department of the Interior and Related Agencies
                Appropriation Act, 1976

Title of Legislative History: Legislative History: ERDA Appropriations for
                               Fiscal Year 1976 Contained in P.L. 94-165: An
                               Act Making Appropriations for the
                               Department of the Interior & Related Agencies
                               for the Fiscal Year Ended 6/30/76, & the Period
                               Ending 9/30/76
Publication Date: 1976
Author: M. Joey Stechschulte and Shelley G. Prosser of the Energy Research and Development Administration
Pages: ix, 1850

L/C Card Number: N/A
OCLC No.: 2366162
SuDoc No.: ER1.2:L52/v.1-4
CIS No.: N/A
UPA Citation: N/A
Relevant Bills: H.R. 8773 (94th Cong.)

This is a legislative history of the Energy Research and Development Administration Appropriations for fiscal year 1976 as contained in the Department of the Interior and Related Agencies Appropriation Act, 1976. The history begins with a chronological table which presents the Congressional action which led to the enactment of P.L. 94-165. The history contains several versions of H.R. 8773 (94th Cong.), as well as the Congressional reports, Congressional hearings, and Congressional debate on this bill. The history also includes the text of P.L. 94-165.

Record No.: 183
Public Law No.: 94-168
Bill No.: H.R. 8674 (94th Cong.)
Statutes at Large Citation: 89 Stat. 1007 (1975)
Title of Act: Metric Conversion Act of 1975

Title of Legislative History: Metric Conversion Act of 1975 -- Legislative
                                History and Implementation 1970-1978
Publication Date: 1978
Author: Dorothy M. Bates and Edith Fairman Cooper of the Congressional Research Service
Pages: 87

L/C Card Number: N/A
OCLC No.: N/A
SuDoc No.: N/A
CIS No.: N/A
UPA Citation: UPA Film No.: MS 78-79 Supp., Reel No. IX, Frame No. 0648.CRS No.: 78-192 SPR
Relevant Bills: H.R. 12555 (92nd Cong.), S. 2483 (92nd Cong.), H.R. 5749 (93rd Cong.), H.R. 11035 (93rd Cong.), S. 100 (93rd Cong.), H.R. 254 (94th Cong.), H.R. 492 (94th Cong.), H.R. 627 (94th Cong.), H.R. 6154 (94th Cong.), H.R. 6177 (94th Cong.), H.R. 6264 (94th Cong.), H.R. 7353 (94th Cong.), H.R. 8674 (94th Cong.), S. 100 (94th Cong.), S. 1882 (94th Cong.)

The Congressional Research Service document contains two chapters which form a narrative legislative history of the efforts in the 92nd, 93rd, and 94th Congresses to pass metric conversion legislation. In 1975, the Metric Conversion Act of 1975 was passed. The narrative describes the Congressional action chronologically. The text provides bill numbers and footnotes provide complete citations to relevant Congressional reports, hearings, and debate. The text compares the relevant bills and quotes Congressional debate and Congressional hearings. The appendices include the text of P.L. 94-168 and excerpts from the testimony of the director of the National Bureau of Standards at Congressional hearings held in 1975. Also included in the appendices is a chronology of events concerning metric conversion which includes the Congressional action leading to P.L. 94-168. The appendices conclude with a list of selected references which include Congressional documents, journal articles and other sources.

Record No.: 184
Public Law No.: 94-265
Bill No.: H.R. 200 (94th Cong.)
Statutes at Large Citation: 90 Stat. 331 (1976)
Title of Act: Fishery Conservation and Management Act of 1976

Title of Legislative History: A Legislative History of the Fishery
Conservation and Management Act of 1976,
Together with a Section-by-Section Index, 94th
Cong., 2nd Sess. (Comm. Print 1976)
Publication Date: 1976
Author: Senate Committee on Commerce; Senate National Ocean Policy Study
Pages: v, 1176

L/C Card Number: 76-603603
OCLC No.: 2622285
SuDoc No.: Y4.C73/2:F53/13
CIS No.: 76-S262-17
UPA Citation: N/A
Relevant Bills: H.R. 200 (94th Cong.), S. 961 (94th Cong.)

This is a legislative history of the Fishery Conservation and Management Act of 1976. The history begins with the text of P.L. 94-265. Selected primary sources are reprinted. The history concludes with a section-by-section index to the reprinted materials.

Record No.: 185
Public Law No.: 94-282
Bill No.: H.R. 10230 (94th Cong.)
Statutes at Large Citation: 90 Stat. 459 (1976)
Title of Act: National Science and Technology Policy, Organization, and
Priorities Act of 1976

Title of Legislative History: A Legislative History of the National Science
and Technology Policy, Organization, and
Priorities Act of 1976, 95th Cong., 1st Sess.
(Comm. Print 1977)

Publication Date: 1977
Author: Senate Committee on Commerce, Science, and Transportation; Senate Committee on Human Resources
Pages: vi, 824

L/C Card Number: 77-602169
OCLC No.: 3084066
SuDoc No.: Y4.C73/7:N21s
CIS No.: 77-S262-8
UPA Citation: N/A
Relevant Bills: H.R. 34 (92nd Cong.), S. 32 (92nd Cong.), S. 1261 (92nd Cong.), H.R. 2272 (93rd Cong.), S. 32 (93rd Cong.), S. 1686 (93rd Cong.), S. 2495 (93rd Cong.), H.R. 4461 (94th Cong.), H.R. 7830 (94th Cong.), H.R. 9058 (94th Cong.), H.R. 10230 (94th Cong.), S. 32 (94th Cong.)

This is a legislative history of the National Science and Technology Policy, Organization, and Priorities Act of 1976. The materials are presented in reverse chronological order. It begins with the text of P.L. 94-282 and continues with chapters on the Senate and House action on national science and technology policy bills from the 94th, 93d and 92d Congresses. Selected bills, debates and reports are reprinted. In addition, tables of contents from relevant hearings are selectively provided.

Record No.: 186
Public Law No.: 94-283
Bill No.: S. 3065 (94th Cong.)
Statutes at Large Citation: 90 Stat. 475 (1976)
Title of Act: Federal Election Campaign Act Amendments of 1976

Title of Legislative History: Legislative History of Federal Election Campaign Act Amendments of 1976
Publication Date: 1977
Author: Federal Election Commission
Pages: v, 1198

L/C Card Number: 77-604848
OCLC No.: 3466487
SuDoc No.: Y3.El2/3:2L52/976
CIS No.: N/A
UPA Citation: N/A
Relevant Bills: H.R. 12406 (94th Cong.), S. 2911 (94th Cong.), S. 2912 (94th Cong.), S. 2918 (94th Cong.), S. 2953 (94th Cong.), S. 2980 94th Cong.), S. 2987 (94th Cong.), S. 3065 (94th Cong.)

The legislative history presents chronologically the Congressional action which led to the enactment of the Federal Election Campaign Act

Amendments of 1976. The history includes Congressional hearings on earlier bills, as well as the texts of S. 3065 (94th Cong.) and its companion bill H.R. 12406 (94th Cong.); and the Congressional debate and reports on S. 3065 (94th Cong.) and H.R. 12406 (94th Cong.). Also included are the President's remarks on signing S. 3065 (94th Cong.) into law and the text of P.L. 94-283. The history concludes with a detailed subject index.

Record No.: 187
Public Law No.: 94-324
Bill No.: S. 2529 (94th Cong.)
Statutes at Large Citation: 90 Stat. 720 (1976)
Title of Act: Veterans Housing Amendments Act of 1976

Title of Legislative History: Review of Veterans Housing and Insurance
                                 Programs: Hearings on Veterans Housing and
                                 Insurance Programs Together with S. 2529, S.
                                 1911, and Related Bills Before the
                                 Subcommittee on Housing and Insurance of
                                 the Senate Committee on Veterans' Affairs,
                                 94th Cong., 1st & 2nd Sess. (1975 & 1976)
Publication Date: 1976
Author: Subcommittee on Housing and Insurance, Senate Committee on Veterans' Affairs
Pages: vi, 904

L/C Card Number: 77-600529
OCLC No.: 2622315
SuDoc No.: Y4.V64/4:H81/2
CIS No.: 76-S761-7
UPA Citation: N/A
Relevant Bills: S. 1911 (94th Cong.), S. 1991 (94th Cong.), S. 2159 (94th
       Cong.), S. 2200 (94th Cong.), S. 2529 (94th Cong.), S. 2776 (94th Cong.)

These hearings contain legislative history materials relevant to the Veterans Housing Amendments of 1976. P.L. 94-324 liberalized the home loan program for mobile home purchases and offered home loan program benefits to those who served in the armed forces between 1947 and 1950. In addition to selected legislative history materials on S. 2529, there are reprints of Veterans' Administration (VA) reports on the bill and an amendment. Several other bills dealing with veterans' housing and insurance benefit programs are reprinted: S. 1911 (94th Cong.); S. 1991 (94th Cong.); S. 2159 (94th Cong.); S. 2200 (94th Cong.); and S. 2776 (94th Cong.). A majority of the bills are followed by the relevant VA's reports. There is an Office of Management and Budget report on S. 1911 (94th Cong.). The first appendix contains the Senate Report on S. 1911 (94th Cong). This bill did not become law. The second appendix contains the text of S. 2529 (94th

Cong.) as reported; a section-by-section analysis of the bill; a description of how S. 2529 (94th Cong.) would change the veterans' housing benefits programs are codified; and the VA's report on S. 2529 (94th Cong.) as reported. The third appendix contains the text of P.L. 94-324.

Record No.: 188
Public Law No.: 94-399
Bill No.: H.R. 11009 (94th Cong.)
Statutes at Large Citation: 90 Stat. 1205 (1976)
Title of Act: To Provide for an Independent Audit of the Financial
                Condition of the Government of the District of Columbia

Title of Legislative History: Legislative History of Public Law 94-399 (H.R.
                                11009 and S. 3608): To Provide for an
                                Independent Audit of the Financial Condition
                                of the Government of the District of Columbia
                                and to Establish a Temporary Commission on
                                Financial Oversight of the District of Columbia
                                94th Cong., 2nd Sess. (Comm. Print 1976)
Publication Date: 1976
Author: Senate Committee on the District of Columbia
Pages: v, 122

L/C Card Number: 76-603410
OCLC No.: 2652002
SuDoc No.: Y4.D63/2:L52/2
CIS No.: 76-S302-5
UPA Citation: N/A
Relevant Bills: H.R. 11009 (94th Cong.), S. 3608 (94th Cong.)

This is a legislative history of a public law which provided for the improvement of the financial system of the District of Columbia after home rule had been established, P.L. 94-399. The history begins with a chronological chart showing the progress of H.R. 11009 (94th Cong.) and its related bill S. 3608 (94th Cong.) through Congress. The chart provides the dates of hearings and debate and includes the report numbers of the Congressional reports. Selected primary sources are reprinted. The history concludes with the text of P.L. 94-399.

Record No.: 189
Public Law No.: 94-409
Bill No.: S. 5 (94th Cong.)
Statutes at Large Citation: 90 Stat. 1241 (1976)
Title of Act: Government in the Sunshine Act

Title of Legislative History: Government in the Sunshine Act, S.5 (Public
                                Law 94-409): Source Book, Legislative History,
                                Texts, and Other Documents, 94th Cong., 2nd
                                Sess. (Comm. Print 1976)

Publication Date: 1976
Author: Senate Committee on Government Operations; House Committee
on Government Operations
Pages: viii, 832

L/C Card Number: 77-601931
OCLC No.: 3092617
SuDoc No.: Y4.G74/6:G74/7
CIS No.: 77-S402-15
UPA Citation: N/A
Relevant Bills: S. 3881 (92nd Cong.), H.R. 4 (93rd Cong.), H.R. 10000 (93rd
       Cong.), S. 260 (93rd Cong.), H.R. 5075 (94th Cong.), H.R. 9868 (94th
       Cong.), H.R. 10315 (94th Cong.), H.R. 11007 (94th Cong.), H.R. 11656
       (94th Cong.), S. 5 (94th Cong.)

This legislative history of the Government in the Sunshine Act begins with
a brief essay on the Congressional action in the 92nd, 93rd, and 94th
Congresses which resulted in the enactment of the Sunshine Act. This
essay's footnotes provide complete citations to mentioned Congressional
documents. The introductory material also includes the text of P.L. 94-409.
Selected primary sources are reprinted. Unlike most source books, this one
does not contain materials other than Congressional documents.

Record No.: 190
Public Law No.: 94-409
Bill No.: S. 5 (94th Cong.)
Statutes at Large Citation: 90 Stat. 1241 (1976)
Title of Act: Government in the Sunshine Act

Title of Legislative History: An Interpretive Guide to the Government in
                                the Sunshine Act
Publication Date: 1978
Author: Richard K. Berg and Stephen H. Klitzman of the Administrative
Conference of the United States, Office of the Chairman
Pages: xvi, 134

L/C Card Number: 78-602321
OCLC No.: 3957762
SuDoc No.: Y3.Ad6:8Su7
CIS No.: N/A
UPA Citation: N/A

Relevant Bills: S. 3881 (92nd Cong.), S. 260 (93rd Cong.), H.R. 9868 (94th Cong.), H.R. 10315 (94th Cong.), H.R. 11656 (94th Cong.), S. 5 (94th Cong.)

This document offers the perspective of the Administrative Conference of the United States on the open meeting provisions of the Government in the Sunshine Act. The Administrative Conference is an independent agency whose function is to furnish advice and assistance on problems of administrative procedure to the agencies and Congress. The document begins with a short chronological table of the act's legislative history and a list of full citations to the relevant Congressional documents. In the main part of the document, the Administrative Conference offers its interpretation of the open meeting provisions of Section 3 of the Act, codified at Section 552b of Title 5 of the *United States Code*. The text of each subsection is followed by the Administrative Conference's interpretation of that section. In addition to providing citations to agency regulations, footnotes provide citations to Congressional documents. The appendices include the text of P.L. 94-409; a chart of proposed and final agency regulations for implementing the open meeting provisions; and a chart of how the definition of "meeting" evolved in S. 5 (94th Cong.) and related bills.

Record No.: 191
Public Law No.: 94-412
Bill No.: H.R. 3884 (94th Cong.)
Statutes at Large Citation: 90 Stat. 1255 (1976)
Title of Act: National Emergencies Act

Title of Legislative History: The National Emergencies Act (Public Law 94-412): Source Book, Legislative History, Texts, and Other Documents, 94th Cong., 2nd Sess. (Comm. Print 1976)
Publication Date: 1976
Author: Senate Committee on Government Operations; Senate Special Committee on National Emergencies and Delegated Emergency Powers
Pages: ix, 360

L/C Card Number: 81-603104
OCLC No.: 2671118
SuDoc No.: Y4:G74/6:N21 em/2
CIS No.: 76-S402-25
UPA Citation: N/A
Relevant Bills: H.R. 16668 (93rd Cong.), S. 3957 (93rd Cong.), H.R. 3884 (94th Cong.), S. 977 (94th Cong.)

This is a legislative history of the National Emergencies Act. Part One contains a narrative essay on the historical need for the Act. Part Two contains the initial authorizing resolution, interim report (93rd Congress) and final report (94th Congress) of the Senate's Special Committee on National Emergencies and Delegated Emergency Powers.

Part III contains related bills, Congressional reports, and Congressional debate. The history concludes with the text of the law as enacted. Appendix A presents the text of proclamations of natural emergency which were terminated by P.L. 94-412. Appendix B is a bibliography of periodical articles, books, and government documents related to the National Emergencies Act.

Record No.: 192
Public Law No.: 94-413
Bill No.: H.R. 8800 (94th Cong.)
Statutes at Large Citation: 90 Stat. 1260 (1976)
Title of Act: Electric and Hybrid Vehicle Research, Development, and
           Demonstration Act of 1976

Title of Legislative History: Energy Research and Development
                               Administration: Statutes and Legislative
                               Histories, Volume V, Electric and Hybrid
                               Vehicle Research, Development, and
                               Demonstration Act of 1976, Public Law 94-413,
                               95th Cong., 2nd Sess, (Comm. Print 1978)
Publication Date: 1978
Author: Subcommittee on Advanced Energy Technologies and Energy Conservation Research, Development, and Demonstration, House Committee on Science and Technology
Pages: vii, 386

L/C Card Number: 78-601563
OCLC No.: 5051914
SuDoc No.: Y4.Sci2:95/EE
CIS No.: 78-H702-34
UPA Citation: N/A
Relevant Bills: H.R. 5470 (94th Cong.), H.R. 8800 (94th Cong.), S. 1632 (94th
           Cong.)

The legislative history of the Electric and Hybrid Vehicle Research, Development, and Demonstration Act of 1976 provides the text of the law. The history continues with the President's message upon vetoing H.R. 8800 (94th Cong.) and the Conference report on H.R. 8800 (94th Cong.). The history includes H.R. 8800 (94th Cong.) as reported from the House committee, as well as the House report on this bill. The history also includes the text of the related bill S. 1632 (94th Cong.) as reported from the Senate committee, as well as the Senate report on S. 1632 (94th Cong.). The Appendix includes the Senate and House debate on overriding the Presidential veto, as well as other debate on H.R. 8800 (94th Cong.). This volume is Volume V of a five volume set. Note that Volume 1 is Record Number 165, Volume 2 is Record Number 166, Volume 3 is Record Number 169, and Volume 4 is Record Number 172.

Record No.: 193
Public Law No.: 94-421
Bill No.: H.R. 8603 (94th Cong.)
Statutes at Large Citation: 90 Stat. 1303 (1976)
Title of Act: Postal Reorganization Act Amendments of 1976

Title of Legislative History: H.R. 8603, Postal Reorganization Act,
                               Amendments of 1976: Public Law 94-421:
                               Legislative History, 94th Cong., 2nd Sess.
                               (Comm. Print 1976)
Publication Date: 1976
Author: House Committee on Post Office and Civil Service
Pages: iii, 557

L/C Card Number: 77-600621
OCLC No.: 2850317
SuDoc No.: Y4.P84/10:P84/52
CIS No.: 76-H622-14
UPA Citation: N/A
Relevant Bills: H.R. 8603 (94th Cong.)

This is a legislative history of the Postal Reorganization Act Amendments
of 1976, H.R. 8603 (94th Cong.), P.L. 94-421. The history begins with the text
of P.L. 94-421. The history contains several versions of H.R. 8603 (94th
Cong.), as well as the Congressional reports and Congressional debate on
this bill.

Record No.: 194
Public Law No.: 94-432
Bill No.: H.R. 14298 (94th Cong.)
Statutes at Large Citation: 90 Stat. 1369 (1976)
Title of Act: Veterans and Survivors Pension Adjustment Act of 1976

Title of Legislative History: Veterans and Survivors Pension Reform Act:
                               Hearings on S. 2635 and Related Bills Before
                               the Subcommittee on Compensation and
                               Pensions of the Senate Committee on Veterans'
                               Affairs, 94th Cong., 1st Sess. (1975)
Publication Date: 1976
Author: Subcommittee on Compensation and Pensions, Senate Committee
on Veterans' Affairs
Pages: v, 1079

L/C Card Number: 77-600654
OCLC No.: 2682115
SuDoc No.: Y4.V64/4:V64/8
CIS No.: 77-S761-1
UPA Citation: N/A

Relevant Bills: H.R. 10355 (94th Cong.), H.R. 14298 (94th Cong.), S. 880 (94th Cong.), S. 1406 (94th Cong.), S. 2635 (94th Cong.)

The compiled documents include the text of bills, hearings, debates, and the law as passed for the Veterans and Survivors Pensions Adjustment Act of 1976. In addition, the compilation contains the internal agency reports on the bills.

Record No.: 195
Public Law No.: 94-433
Bill No.: H.R. 14299 (94th Cong.)
Statutes at Large Citation: 90 Stat. 1374 (1976)
Title of Act: Veterans Disability Compensation and Survivor Benefits Act of 1976

Title of Legislative History: Veterans Disability Compensation and Survivor Benefits Act of 1976: Hearing on S. 3596 (94th Cong.) Before the Subcommittee on Compensation and Pensions of the Senate Committee on Veterans' Affairs, 94th Cong., 2nd Sess. (1976)
Publication Date: 1976
Author: Subcommittee on Compensation and Pensions, Senate Committee on Veterans' Affairs
Pages: iv, 513

L/C Card Number: 76-603729
OCLC No.: 2630931
SuDoc No.: Y4.V64/4:V64/7
CIS No.: 76-S761-8
UPA Citation: N/A
Relevant Bills: H.R. 14299 (94th Cong.), S. 2331 (94th Cong.), S. 3596 (94th Cong.)

The publication of the 1976 hearings contain materials related to the Veterans Disability Compensation and Survivor Benefits Act of 1976. It includes the texts of bills introduced and related as well as the report from the Congressional Budget Office.

Record No.: 196
Public Law No.: 94-469
Bill No.: S. 3149 (94th Cong.)
Statutes at Large Citation: 90 Stat. 2003 (1976)
Title of Act: Toxic Substances Control Act

Title of Legislative History: Legislative History of the Toxic Substances
Control Act, Together with a Section-by-Section
Index, 94th Cong., 2nd Sess. (Comm. Print
1976)
Publication Date: 1976
Author: House Committee on Interstate and Foreign Commerce
Pages: vii, 801

L/C Card Number: 77-601318
OCLC No.: 2720172
SuDoc No.: Y4.In8/4:T66
CIS No.: 77-H502-3
UPA Citation: N/A
Relevant Bills: H.R. 14032 (94th Cong.), S. 3149 (94th Cong.)
The legislative history of the Toxic Substances Control Act is comprised of
text and appendices. The text is set out in chapters as follows: Chapter I
has the text of the act as passed and the President's message; Chapter II
contains the texts of the Senate documents, the bill, the report, and the
debates; Chapter III gives the House bill version and its report and debate;
and Chapter IV has the Conference Committee report and comparison of
the various sections. Appendix I is the 1971 report from the Council on
Environmental Quality. Appendix II is a bibliography of the legislative
activities associated with proposals to control toxic substances. The history
concludes with a section-by-section index.

Record No.: 197
Public Law No.: 94-488
Bill No.: H.R. 13367 (94th Cong.)
Statutes at Large Citation: 90 Stat. 2341 (1976)
Title of Act: State and Local Fiscal Assistance Amendments of 1976

Title of Legislative History: General Revenue Sharing: An Overview of the
1972 Act and a Legislative History of the State
and Local Fiscal Assistance Amendments of
1976 (P.L. 94-488)
Publication Date: 1977
Author: Maureen McBreen of the Congressional Research Service
Pages: 28

L/C Card Number: N/A
OCLC No.: N/A
SuDoc No.: N/A
CIS No.: N/A
UPA Citation: UPA Film No.: MS 76-78 Supp., Reel No. X, Frame No. 0576.
CRS No.: 77-3E
Relevant Bills: H.R. 6558 (94th Cong.), H.R. 13367 (94th Cong.), S. 1625 (94th
Cong.)

This Congressional Research Service study examines the legislative history of the State and Local Fiscal Assistance Amendments of 1976. The study notes the dates of introduction and sponsors of the administration's proposal in the House and in the Senate. The basic provisions of the law are summarized.

Record No.: 198
Public Law No.: 94-502
Bill No.: S. 969 (94th Cong.)
Statutes at Large Citation: 90 Stat. 2383 (1976)
Title of Act: Veterans' Education and Employment Assistance Act of 1976

Title of Legislative History: Veterans' Education and Employment
                                 Assistance Act of 1976: Hearings on S. 969 and
                                 Related Bills Before the Subcommittee on
                                 Readjustment, Education, and Employment of
                                 the Senate Committee on Veterans' Affairs,
                                 94th Cong., 1st Sess. (1975)
Publication Date: 1976
Author: Subcommittee on Readjustment, Education, and Employment, Senate Committee on Veterans' Affairs
Pages: various

L/C Card Number: 77-601521
OCLC No.: 2881738
SuDoc No.: Y4.V64/4:Ed8/6/pt.1-4
CIS No.: 77-S761-4&5&6&7
UPA Citation: N/A
Relevant Bills: H.R. 9576 (94th Cong.), S. 817 (94th Cong.), S. 836 (94th
     Cong.), S. 969 (94th Cong.), S. 1371 (94th Cong.), S. 1805 (94th Cong.),
     S. 2100 (94th Cong.), S. 2365 (94th Cong.), S. 2487 (94th Cong.), S. 2789
     (94th Cong.), S. 2995 (94th Cong.), S. 3225 (94th Cong.)

The appendices and texts of these 1975 hearings contain legislative history materials relevant to the legislative history of the Veterans' Education and Employment Assistance Act of 1976. The provisions to increase veterans' educational assistance allowances and to establish a Post-Vietnam Era Veterans' Educational Assistance program are included in the documentation. The appendices to the hearings contain lengthy excerpts from the Senate report. The final debate on S. 969 (94th Cong.) in both the Senate and House is also included. The appendices conclude with the text of the Act. In addition, the text of the hearings includes the texts as introduced of several Senate bills from the 94th Congress on veterans' education benefits. The Veterans' Administration agency report is provided.

Record No.: 199
Public Law No.: 94-519
Bill No.: H.R. 14451 (94th Cong.)
Statutes at Large Citation: 90 Stat. 2451 (1976)
Title of Act: Federal Property and Administrative Services Act of 1949,
               Amendment of 1976

Title of Legislative History: Distribution of Federal Surplus Property to
                               State and Local Organizations: Source book:
                               Amendments to the Federal Property and
                               Administrative Services Act of 1949 Made by
                               Public Law 94-519 (with Regulations and
                               Statutes), 94th Cong., 2nd Sess. (Comm. Print
                               1976)
Publication Date: 1976
Author: House Committee on Government Operations
Pages: v, 181

L/C Card Number: 77-601267
OCLC No.: 3768278
SuDoc No.: Y4.G74/7:Su7/13
CIS No.: 77-H402-1
UPA Citation: N/A
Relevant Bills: H.R. 14451 (94th Cong.)

The document contains legislative history materials relevant to a 1976
amendment to the Federal Property and Administrative Services Act of
1949. The document begins with the text of the law and continues with the
amendments through 1976. The document concludes with text of the
pertinent federal regulations as of 1976, as well as texts of related statutes.

Record No.: 200
Public Law No.: 94-553
Bill No.: S. 22 (94th Cong.)
Statutes at Large Citation: 90 Stat. 2541 (1976)
Title of Act: Copyrights, 1976

Title of Legislative History: Legislative History: The Mathias Amendment
                               and Section 118(e) of the Copyright Act of 1976
                               IN Public Broadcasting Report, 96th Cong.,
                               2nd Sess. (Comm. Print 1980)
Publication Date: 1980
Author: Subcommittee on Courts, Civil Liberties, and the Administration of
Justice, House Committee on the Judiciary
Pages: vii, 107

L/C Card Number: 82-602117
OCLC No.: 6584379
SuDoc No.: Y4.J89/1:B78
CIS No.: 80-H522-8
UPA Citation: N/A
Relevant Bills: S. 1361 (93rd Cong.), H.R. 2223 (94th Cong.), S. 22 (94th
    Cong.)

A legislative history of Section 118(e) of the Copyright Act of 1976 appears as
pages 6-25, Part Two of this document. This narrative legislative history
provides citations to the relevant bills, Congressional hearings,
Congressional reports, and Congressional debate. Other parts of this
document specifically deal with the sample voluntary licensing agreement
approved in 1979 by the Copyright Office and publishing industry
associations.

Record No.: 201
Public Law No.: 94-559
Bill No.: S. 2278 (94th Cong.)
Statutes at Large Citation: 90 Stat. 2641 (1976)
Title of Act: Civil Rights Attorney's Fees Awards Act of 1976

Title of Legislative History: Civil Rights Attorney's Fees Awards Act of
                               1976: Public Law 94-559, S. 2278/ Source Books,
                               Legislative History, Texts, and Other
                               Documents, 94th Cong., 2nd Sess. (Comm.
                               Print 1976)
Publication Date: 1976
Author: Subcommittee on Constitutional Rights, Senate Committee on the
Judiciary
Pages: xvii, 313

L/C Card Number: 77-601298
OCLC No.: 2834427
SuDoc No.: Y4.J89/2:C49/22
CIS No.: 77-S522-5
UPA Citation: N/A
Relevant Bills: H.R. 15460 (94th Cong.), S. 2278 (94th Cong.)

This is a legislative history of the Civil Rights Attorneys' Fees Awards Act
of 1976, S. 2278 (94th Cong.), P.L. 94-559. Its introductory material includes
a subject index, speaker's index to Congressional debate, table of cases cited
in the legislative history, and text of P.L. 94-559. The appendix includes the
text of statutes covered or amended, citations to cases awarding attorney's
fees under the private attorney general concept, index to key votes, and text
of federal attorney's fees statutes.

Record No.: 202
Public Law No.: 94-579
Bill No.: S. 507 (94th Cong.)
Statutes at Large Citation: 90 Stat. 2743 (1976)
Title of Act: Federal Land Policy and Management Act of 1976

Title of Legislative History: Legislative History of the Federal Land Policy
and Management Act of 1976 (Public Law 94-
579), 95th Cong., 2nd Sess. (Comm. Print 1978)

Publication Date: 1978
Author: Senate Committee on Energy and Natural Resources
Pages: xxiv, 1779

L/C Card Number: 78-601778
OCLC No.: 4106770
SuDoc No.: Y4.En2:95-99
CIS No.: 78-S312-10
UPA Citation: N/A
Relevant Bills: H.R. 7211 (92nd Cong.), S. 921 (92nd Cong.), S. 2401 (92nd
Cong.), S. 424 (93rd Cong.), S. 1041 (93rd Cong.), H.R. 13777 (94th
Cong.), S. 507 (94th Cong.)

The legislative history of the Federal Land Policy and Management Act
begins with a topical index and the text of the law. The main part of the
legislative history consists of chapters which cover 94th Congress Senate
action, House action, and Conference committee action. The chapter on
conference action has a staff print in alternating typeface which reveals the
agreements or compromises between the House and Senate revisions. The
legislative history concludes with the text of some related and similar bills
from three separate Congresses.

Record No.: 203
Public Law No.: 94-579
Bill No.: S. 507 (94th Cong.)
Statutes at Large Citation: 90 Stat. 2743 (1976)
Title of Act: Federal Land Policy and Management Act of 1976

Title of Legislative History: Let's Trade: The Land Exchange Provisions of
the Federal Land Policy and Management Act
IN Workshop on Public Land Acquisition and
Alternatives, 97th Cong., 1st Sess. (Comm.
Print 1981)

Publication Date: 1981
Author: Senate Committee on Energy and Natural Resources
Pages: xii, 1029

L/C Card Number: 81-603896
OCLC No.: 8117039
SuDoc No.: Y4.En2:97-34
CIS No.: 81-S312-11
UPA Citation: N/A
Relevant Bills: H.R. 7211 (92nd Cong.), S. 921 (92nd Cong.), S. 2401 (92nd
        Cong.), S. 424 (93rd Cong.), H.R. 13777 (94th Cong.), S. 507 (94th
        Cong.)

The document is a compilation of prepared remarks by the chief counsel for
the minority of the Senate Committee on Energy and Natural Resources. A
large part of these remarks form a narrative legislative history of the land
exchange provisions of the Federal Land Policy and Management Act of
1976. The remarks follow Congress-by-Congress development of legislation.
The remarks summarize and quote the relevant bills and Congressional
reports. The remarks trace relevant bill versions and Senate, House, and
Conference reports.

Record No.: 204
Public Law No.: 94-580
Bill No.: S. 2150 (94th Cong.)
Statutes at Large Citation: 90 Stat. 2795 (1976)
Title of Act: Resource Conservation and Recovery Act of 1976

Title of Legislative History: Environmental Protection Affairs of the
                                Ninety-Fourth Congress, 95th Cong., 1st Sess.
                                (Comm. Print 1977)
Publication Date: 1977
Author: Senate Committee on the Environment and Public Works
Pages: ix, 723

L/C Card Number: N/A
OCLC No.: 3549684
SuDoc No.: Y4.P96/10:95-3
CIS No.: 77-S322-4
UPA Citation: N/A
Relevant Bills: H.R. 2633 (94th Cong.), H.R. 2932 (94th Cong.), H.R. 3118
        (94th Cong.), H.R. 3130 (94th Cong.), H.R. 3787 (94th Cong.), H.R. 5487
        (94th Cong.), H.R. 6218 (94th Cong.), H.R. 7108 (94th Cong.), H.R. 9294
        (94th Cong.), H.R. 9560 (94th Cong.), H.R. 10363 (94th Cong.), H.R.
        10498 (94th Cong.), H.R. 11510 (94th Cong.), H.R. 12380 (94th Cong.),
        H.R. 12704 (94th Cong.), H.R. 12944 (94th Cong.), H.R. 13339 (94th
        Cong.), H.R. 14862 (94th Cong.), H.R. 14965 (94th Cong.), S. 521 (94th
        Cong.), S. 946 (94th Cong.), S. 1474 (94th Cong.), S. 1744 (94th Cong.),
        S. 1754 (94th Cong.), S. 2150 (94th Cong.), S. 2162 (94th Cong.), S. 2578
        (94th Cong.), S. 2710 (94th Cong.), S. 3037 (94th Cong.), S. 3038 (94th
        Cong.), S. 219 (94th Cong.), S. 3622 (94th Cong.)

The history is divided into chapters to explain and analyze the individual components of environmental protection efforts by Congress. Each chapter discusses Congressional activity during he 94th Congress. The chapters contain sections on legislation enacted, legislative proposals, and a bibliography of Congressional documents. One of the documents' three appendices discusses the legislative activity relating to the National Environmental Policy Act of 1969 (NEPA). It provides legislative history information for the 1975 amendment to NEPA.

Record No.: 205
Public Law No.: 94-581
Bill No.: H.R. 2735 (94th Cong.)
Statutes at Large Citation: 90 Stat. 2842 (1976)
Title of Act: Veterans Omnibus Health Care Act of 1976

Title of Legislative History:　Senate Legislative History of the Veterans Omnibus Health Care Act of 1976 IN Veterans Omnibus Health Care Act of 1976: Hearings before the Subcommittee on Health and Hospitals of the Senate Committee on Veterans' Affairs, 94th Cong., 2nd Sess. (1976)

Publication Date: 1977
Author: Subcommittee on Health and Hospitals, Senate Committee on Veterans' Affairs
Pages: vi, 586; vi, 587-1332

L/C Card Number: 77-601067
OCLC No.: 2764886
SuDoc No.: Y4.V64/4:V64/17/pt.1-2
CIS No.: 77-S761-2&3
UPA Citation: N/A
Relevant Bills: H.R. 1547 (94th Cong.), H.R. 2735 (94th Cong.), H.R. 3348 (94th Cong.), H.R. 10268 (94th Cong.), H.R. 10394 (94th Cong.), S. 531 (94th Cong.), S. 2636 (94th Cong.), S. 2771 (94th Cong.), S. 2856 (94th Cong.), S. 2868 (94th Cong.), S. 2908 (94th Cong.)

A legislative history of the Veterans' Omnibus Health Care Act of 1976 is included in Appendix II. In addition, the history includes lengthy excerpts from the Senate report on S. 2908 and a section-by-section analysis of it. The Veterans' Administration and Office of Management and Budget agency reports are provided. The history concludes with the text of the Act.

Record No.: 206
Public Law No.: N/A
Bill No.: S. Res. 400 (94th Cong.)
Statutes at Large Citation: N/A
Title of Act: To Establish a Standing Committee of the Senate on
            Intelligence Activities

Title of Legislative History: To Create a Senate Select Committee on
                Intelligence: A Legislative History of Senate
                Resolution 400

Publication Date: 1976
Author: William N. Raiford of the Congressional Research Service
Pages: 189

L/C Card Number: N/A
OCLC No.: 24526011
SuDoc No.: N/A
CIS No.: N/A
UPA Citation: UPA Film No.: MS 75-76 Supp., Reel No. IV, Frame No. 232;
CRS No. 76-149 F, JX 1015 L
Relevant Bills: S. Res. 400 (94th Cong.)

This is a legislative history of S. Res. 400 (94th Cong.) which established the
Senate Select Committee on Intelligence. The history's Introduction is a
short summary of the Senate action which led to the passage of S. Res. 400
(94th Cong.). For example, the Introduction summarizes the
recommendations of the Select Committee to Study Governmental
Operations with respect to Intelligence Activities (94th Cong.) or Church
Committee. The history contains six chapters and five appendices. Chapter
I provides a brief overview of resolutions from earlier Congresses which
had attempted to establish Congressional oversight of intelligence activities.
Chapter II summarizes proposals from the 94th Congress to create
intelligence oversight committees. Chapter III summarizes the action on
S. Res. 400 (94th Cong.) by the Senate Government Operations Committee,
Senate Judiciary Committee, and Senate Committee on Rules and
Administration. Chapter III summarizes and quotes from the
Committees' hearings and reports. Chapter III summarizes three versions
as it was reported from the Government Operations Committee; as it was
marked-up but not reported from the Committee on Rules and
Administration; and as reported by the Committee on Rules and
Administration (Cannon Amendment.). Chapter IV summarizes the
Senate Armed Services Committee's hearings on the fourth version, known
as the "Cannon Compromise." Chapter V presents the text of the Cannon
Compromise, a section-by-section analysis, and other pertinent remarks
from the Senate debate. Chapter V does indicate the *Congressional
Record* citations for the analysis and debate. Chapter VI presents the text of
the law as passed. The appendices contain copies of the reports by the
Senate Committee on Government Operations and Senate Committee on
Rules and Administration. The appendices also contain a bibliography of

the relevant Senate hearings, Senate report, and Senate debate, as well as a chronology of the Congressional activity which led to the passage of S. Res. 400 (94th Cong.).

Record No.: 207
Public Law No.: 95-30
Bill No.: H.R. 3477 (95th Cong.)
Statutes at Large Citation: 91 Stat. 126 (1977)
Title of Act: Tax Reduction and Simplification Act of 1977

Title of Legislative History: Impact of the Administration's Tax Stimulus
                                Package on Small Business and Examination
                                of Employment Tax Credit Alternatives:
                                Hearing Before the Senate Select Committee on
                                Small Business, 95th Cong., 1st Sess. (1977)
Publication Date: 1977
Author: Senate Select Committee on Small Business
Pages: iv, 456

L/C Card Number: 77-604723
OCLC No.: 3553527
SuDoc No.: Y4.Sm1/2:T19/11
CIS No.: 77-S721-35
UPA Citation: N/A
Relevant Bills: H.R. 3477 (95th Cong.)

The February 22, 1977 Senate hearings contain many legislative history materials relevant to Title II of the Tax Reduction and Simplification Act of 1977. Title II established a tax credit or businesses which created new jobs or hired certain new employees. The legislative history materials appear in the exhibits or appendices to these hearings. These materials include the text of H.R. 3477 (95th Cong.) as passed by the House and Senate, as well as the House and Senate reports on H.R. 3477 (95th Cong.). It is limited to those parts of the bills and reports which deal with the new jobs tax credit. The materials also include a section-by-section analysis of the new jobs tax credit and a side-by-side comparison of the House and Senate versions. In addition, the materials include the Senate debate on H.R. 3477 (95th Cong.) as excerpted from the *Congressional Record*. Included as excerpts from the *Congressional Record* are some amendments to the new jobs credit portion of H.R. 3477 (95th Cong.). The materials provide several statements by the Secretary of the Treasury and president of the National Small Business Association excerpted from earlier and later 1977 Congressional hearings. Included are materials the Congressional committees used to evaluate the new jobs tax credit such as a study of employment tax credits as a policy tool and a summary of administration's economic stimulus program.

Record No.: 208
Public Law No.: 95-95
Bill No.: H.R. 6161 (95th Cong.)
Statutes at Large Citation: 91 Stat. 685 (1977)
Title of Act: Clean Air Act Amendments of 1977

Title of Legislative History: Environmental Protection Affairs of the
                                 Ninety-Fifth Congress, 96th Cong., 1st Sess.
                                 (Comm. Print 1979)
Publication Date: 1979
Author: Senate Committee on the Environment and Public Works
Pages: vi, 697

L/C Card Number: 79-603401
OCLC No.: 5727659
SuDoc No.: Y4.P96/10:96-5
CIS No.: 79-S322-11
UPA Citation: N/A
Relevant Bills: S. 1075 (91st Cong.), H.R. 2 (95th Cong.), H.R. 3199 (95th
     Cong.), H.R. 3209 (95th Cong.), H.R. 5146 (95th Cong.), H.R. 6161 (95th
     Cong.), H.R. 7073 (95th Cong.), H.R. 7878 (95th Cong.), H.R. 8444 (95th
     Cong.), H.R. 11226 (95th Cong.), H.R. 2647 (95th Cong.), H.R. 13311
     (95th Cong.), S. 7 (95th Cong.), S. 252 (95th Cong.), S. 682 (95th Cong.),
     S. 1617 95th Cong.), S. 1678 (95th Cong.), S. 1952 (95th Cong.), S. 2380
     (95th Cong.), S. 2704 (95th Cong.), S. 3083 (95th Cong.)

The document contains fourteen chapters devoted to major legislation
enacted, legislative proposals, bibliography of additional readings, and
bibliography of Congressional documents. The chapters are narrative
essays which discuss bill versions, hearings, floor debate, and reports. The
bibliographies of additional readings give access to journal articles,
executive documents, and books. The bibliographies of Congressional
documents provide full citations to Congressional reports, documents, bills,
and hearings. Most chapters discuss several laws. Laws are discussed in
more than one chapter. The most discussed laws include: Clean Air
Amendments of 1977, H.R. 6161 (95th Cong.), P.L. 95-95; Clean Water Act of
1977, H.R. 3199 (95th Cong.), P.L. 95-217; Surface Mining Control and
Reclamation Act of 1977, H.R. 2 (95th Cong.), P.L. 95-87; Water Research
and Development Act of 1978, S. 2704 (95th Cong.), P.L. 95-467; Port and
Tanker Safety Act of 1978, S. 682 (95th Cong.), P.L. 95-474; Federal Pesticide
Act of 1978, S. 1678 (95th Cong.), P.L. 95-396; Quiet Communities Act of 1978,
S. 3083 (95th Cong.), P.L. 95-609; Powerplant and Industrial Fuel Use Act of
1978, H.R. 5146 (95th Cong.), P.L. 95-620; National Ocean Pollution
Research and Development and Monitoring Planning Act of 1978, S. 1617
(95th Cong.), P.L. 95-273; and Intervention on the High Seas Act,
Amendment of 1978, S. 2380 (95th Cong.), P.L. 95-302. Appendix A contains
a list of the 296 laws passed during the 95th Congress which were
concerned with energy, environment, and natural resources. Each public
law entry lists the House report, the Senate report, passage in the
Congressional Record, and the Presidential statement, and a description of
the legislation. Appendix B provides an annotated guide to public laws of

the 95th Congress relating to the National Environmental Policy Act (NEPA), S.1075 (91st Cong.), P.L. 91-190. Each law's annotation explains how that law impacted NEPA. Appendix B also contains abstracts of NEPA-related bills of the 95th Congress which did not pass, as well as a bibliography of Congressional documents on these NEPA-related laws and bills.

Record No.: 209
Public Law No.: 95-95
Bill No.: H.R. 6161 (95th Cong.)
Statutes at Large Citation: 91 Stat. 685 (1977)
Title of Act: Clean Air Act Amendments of 1977

Title of Legislative History: A Legislative History of the Clean Air Act
                                  Amendments of 1977: A Continuation of the
                                  Clean Air Act Amendments of 1970: Together
                                  with a Section-By-Section Index, 95th Cong.,
                                  2nd Sess. (Comm. Print 1978)
Publication Date: 1979-1980
Author: Senate Committee on the Environment and Public Works
Pages: 7514

L/C Card Number: 74-601207
OCLC No.: 5301790
SuDoc No.: Y4.P96/10:95-16/v.3-8
CIS No.: 79-S322-12&13&14; 80-S322-2&4&5
UPA Citation: N/A
Relevant Bills: H.R. 2633 (94th Cong.), H.R. 2650 (94th Cong.), H.R. 3118 (94th Cong.), H.R. 4369 (94th Cong.), H.R. 7704 (94th Cong.), H.R. 10498 (94th Cong.), H.R. 11501 (94th Cong.), H.R. 12954 (94th Cong.), S. 3219 (94th Cong.), H.R. 2380 (95th Cong.), H.R. 4151 (95th Cong.), H.R. 6161 (95th Cong.), S. 251 (95th Cong.), S. 252 (95th Cong.), S. 253 (95th Cong.), S. 697 (95th Cong.), S. 714 (95th Cong.), S. 719 (95th Cong.), S. 919 (95th Cong.), S. 1053 (95th Cong.)

The legislative history of the Clean Air Act Amendments of 1977, H.R. 6161 covers the Congressional action in the 94th and 95th Congresses which resulted in P.L. 95-95. The history begins with the text of the Clean Air Act as amended through P.L. 95-95 and the text of P.L. 95-95. The history then continues with the Conference report on H.R. 6161 (95th Cong.) and the Congressional debate on this Conference report. From the Senate of the 95th Congress, the history contains S. 252 (95th Cong.) as reported, as well as the Senate debate and Senate report on this bill. From the House of the 95th Congress, the history contains H.R. 6161 (95th Cong.) as introduced and reported, as well as the House report and House debate on this bill. The legislative history continues with a side-by-side comparison of H.R. 6161

(95th Cong.), S. 252 (95th Cong.), and S. 3219 (94th Cong.). The legislative history materials from the 94th Congress begin with the Conference report on S. 3219 (94th Cong.) and the Senate debate on this Conference report. From the Senate of the 94th Congress, the history contains S. 3219 (94th Cong.) as reported, as well as the Senate report and Senate debate on this bill. From the House of the 94th Congress, the history contains H.R. 10498 (94th Cong.) as reported, as well as the House report and House debate on this bill. The legislative history continues with a side-by-side comparison of H.R. 10498 (94th Cong.) and S. 3219 (94th Cong.). The history also includes the text of the Clean Air Act as amended prior to P.L. 95-95.A section-by-section index provides citations to the Congressional documents included in the history which refer to each section. In addition, the history contains the text of at least one version of a number of bills.

Record No.: 210
Public Law No.: 95-115
Bill No.: H.R. 6111 (95th Cong.)
Statutes at Large Citation: 91 Stat. 1048 (1977)
Title of Act: Juvenile Justice Amendments of 1977

Title of Legislative History: Indexed Legislative History of the "Juvenile
                                Justice Amendments of 1977"
Publication Date: 1980
Author: Department of Justice, Office of Justice Assistance, Research, and Statistics
Pages: xvi, 406

L/C Card Number: 75-601524
OCLC No.: 6475539
SuDoc No.: J1.2:In2/8
CIS No.: N/A
UPA Citation: N/A
Relevant Bills: S. 821 (93rd Cong.), H.R. 6111 (95th Cong.), S. 1021 (95th Cong.), S. 1218 (95th Cong.)

This is a legislative history of the Juvenile Justice and Delinquency Act of 1974, Amendments of 1977. The history begins with a section-by-section index to the Juvenile Justice and Delinquency Act of 1974, as amended through 1977. For each section of the Act, the index provides citations to Congressional documents included in the legislative history. The history includes several versions of H.R. 6111 (94th Cong.) and its related bill S. 1021 (94th Cong.), as well as the Congressional reports and Congressional debate on these bills. The text of the administration bill S. 1218 (94th Cong.) is also included. The history also includes the text of the Juvenile Justice and Delinquency Prevention Act of 1974, as amended through 1977. The statement of the President upon signing H.R. 6111 (94th Cong.) into law, as well as the post-signing statements of the senator who sponsored S. 1021 (94th Cong.) and of the chairman of the Senate Subcommittee to Investigate Juvenile Delinquency. The appendix contains the text of the Juvenile Justice and Delinquency Prevention Act of 1974, S. 821 (93rd Cong.), P.L. 93-415.

Record No.: 211
Public Law No.: 95-116
Bill No.: H.R. 6502 (95th Cong.)
Statutes at Large Citation: 91 Stat. 1062 (1977)
Title of Act: To Amend Title 38 of the United States Code to Provide an Automobile Assistance Allowance and to Provide Automotive Adaptive Equipment to Veterans of World War I

Title of Legislative History: Veterans Health Care Amendments Act of 1977: Hearing on S. 1693 and H.R. 6502 Before the Subcommittee on Health and Readjustment of the Senate Committee on Veterans' Affairs, 95th Cong., 1st Sess. (1977)
Publication Date: 1977
Author: Subcommittee on Health and Readjustment, Senate Committee on Veterans' Affairs
Pages: iv, 389

L/C Card Number: 78-600922
OCLC No.: 3718977
SuDoc No.: Y4.V64/4:H34/8
CIS No.: 78-S761-5
UPA Citation: N/A
Relevant Bills: H.R. 5027 (95th Cong.), H.R. 6502 (95th Cong.), S. 1693 (95th Cong.)

The appendices and text of these 1977 hearings include legislative history materials relevant to H.R. 6502 (95th Cong.), P.L. 95-116.P.L. 95-116 which extended the automobile assistance allowance and automotive adaptive equipment veterans' benefit programs to veterans of World War I. The appendices include the text of H.R. 6502 (95th Cong.) as reported to the Senate, as well as the House and Senate reports. The appendices also include the text of the law. In addition, the appendices contain materials on Title III of H.R. 5027 (95th Cong.). H.R. 5027 (95th Cong.) was a broader veterans' medical benefits bill. Its Title III had been derived from S. 1693 (95th Cong.) and provided for veterans' benefit programs in readjustment professional counseling; preventive healthcare; drug and alcohol treatment; and, rehabilitation. The appendices include the text of Title III of H.R. 5027 (95th Cong.) as reported to the Senate, as well as those parts of the Senate report on H.R. 5027 (95th Cong.) which concerned Title III of that bill. Also included is the final Senate debate and passage of the Senate version of H.R. 5027 (95th Cong.). The text of the hearings includes S. 1693

(95th Cong.) as introduced, as well as the introductory statement of its sponsor. The citation to this statement also indicates its date and pagination in the daily *Congressional Record*. The text of the hearings also includes H.R. 6502 (95th Cong.) as passed by the House, as well as the Veterans' Administration's agency report.

Record No.: 212
Public Law No.: 95-117
Bill No.: H.R. 1862 (95th Cong.)
Statutes at Large Citation: 91 Stat. 1063 (1977)
Title of Act: Veterans Disability Compensation and Survivor Benefits Act of
         1977

Title of Legislative History: Veterans Disability Compensation and
                Survivor Benefits Act of 1977: Hearing on S.
                1703 and Related Bills Before the Subcommittee
                on Compensation and Pension of the Senate
                Committee on Veterans' Affairs, 95th Cong.,
                1st Sess. (1977)
Publication Date: 1977
Author: Subcommittee on Compensation and Pension, Senate Committee
on Veterans' Affairs
Pages: iv, 419

L/C Card Number: 78-600916
OCLC No.: 3785983
SuDoc No.: Y4.V64/4:V64/7/977
CIS No.: 78-S761-2
UPA Citation: N/A
Relevant Bills: H.R. 1862 (95th Cong.), H.R. 6501 (95th Cong.), H.R. 7345
      (95th Cong.), S. 13 (95th Cong.), S. 379 (95th Cong.), S. 1141 (95th
      Cong.), S. 1642 (95th Cong.), S. 1703 (95th Cong.)

The Appendices to this Hearing contain legislative history materials for both the Veterans Disability Compensation and Survivor Benefits Act of 1977 and the Veterans and Survivors Pension Adjustment Act of 1977. The materials relevant to P.L. 95-117 include the text of H.R. 1862 (95th Cong.) as reported by the Senate committee, the Senate report, and the Congressional debate on H.R. 1682 (95th Cong.). The materials conclude with the text of the public law. The materials relevant to P.L. 95-204 include the text of H.R. 7345 as reported by the Senate committee, the Senate report on H.R. 7345, and the Congressional debate, concluding with the text of the public law. The Hearing documents contain material pertinent to the history of these public laws. Materials relevant to P.L. 95-117 include H.R. 1862 (95th Cong.) as referred to the Senate committee, as well as the House and Veterans' Administration's reports on H.R. 1862 (95th Cong.). Materials relevant to P.L. 95-204 include H.R. 7345 (95th Cong.) as referred to the Senate committee, as well as the House and Veterans' Administration's reports on

H.R. 7345 (95th Cong.). The text of the Hearing also includes the texts of several other related bills as referred to the Senate committee: S. 1703 (95th Cong.), S. 1642 (95th Cong.), S. 1141 (95th Cong.), S. 13 (95th Cong.), S. 379 (95th Cong.), and H.R. 6501 (95th Cong.). The Hearing documents contain testimony and written statements on the issue of the need for changes in veterans' benefits.

Record No.: 213
Public Law No.: 95-128
Bill No.: H.R. 6655 (95th Cong.)
Statutes at Large Citation: 91 Stat. 1111 (1977)
Title of Act: Housing and Community Development Act of 1977

Title of Legislative History: Compilation of the Housing and Community
                                Development Act of 1977, 95th Cong., 1st Sess.
                                (Comm. Print 1977)
Publication Date: 1977
Author: Subcommittee on Housing and Community Development, House Committee on Banking, Finance, and Urban Affairs
Pages: v, 362

L/C Card Number: N/A
OCLC No.: 3656211
SuDoc No.: Y4.B22/1:H81/69
CIS No.: 77-H242-15
UPA Citation: N/A
Relevant Bills: H.R. 6655 (95th Cong.), S. 1523 (95th Cong.)

This is a legislative history of the Housing and Community Development Act of 1977, H.R. 6655 (95th Cong.), P.L. 95-128. The history begins with the text of P.L. 95-128. The text of the Act is followed by a summary. The history also contains the Conference committee's joint explanatory statement excerpted from the Conference committee's report on H.R. 6655 (95th Cong.). The House report on H.R. 6655 (95th Cong.), and the Senate report on S. 1523 (95th Cong.) are included.

Record No.: 214
Public Law No.: 95-142
Bill No.: H.R. 3 (95th Cong.)
Statutes at Large Citation: 91 Stat. 1175 (1977)
Title of Act: Medicare-Medicaid Anti-Fraud and Abuse Amendments

Title of Legislative History: Summary of Medicare-Medicaid Anti-Fraud
and Abuse Amendments, H.R. 3, 95th
Congress, Public Law 95-142, and Medicare
and Medicaid Reimbursement for Rural
Health Clinic Services, H.R. 8422 (H.R. 2504),
95th Congress, Public Law 95-210, 95th Cong.,
1st Sess. (Comm. Print 1977)
Publication Date: 1977
Author: House Committee on Ways and Means
Pages: v, 15

L/C Card Number: 78-601327
OCLC No.: 3601983
SuDoc No.: Y4.W36:WMCP95-59
CIS No.: 77-H782-99
UPA Citation: N/A
Relevant Bills: H.R. 3 (95th Cong.), H.R. 422 (95th Cong.), H.R. 2504 (95th
Cong.), H.R. 8422 (95th Cong.), H.R. 8543 (95th Cong.), S. 143 (95th
Cong.)

This is a legislative history of the Medicare-Medicaid Anti-Fraud and
Abuse Amendments (P.L. 95-142) and the legislation which provided for
reimbursement for rural health clinic services (P.L. 95-210). The history
contains both a chronological chart and a section-by-section summary for
each law. Each chart chronologically follows the Congressional action
which resulted in each public law. The charts provide citations to bills and
Congressional reports and provide dates of Congressional hearings,
Congressional action, and Congressional debate. The section-by-section
summaries provide very brief summaries of each section of the laws.

Record No.: 215
Public Law No.: 95-151
Bill No.: H.R. 3744 (95th Cong.)
Statutes at Large Citation: 91 Stat. 1245 (1977)
Title of Act: Fair Labor Standards Amendments of 1977

Title of Legislative History: Legislative History of the Fair Labor Standards
Amendments of 1977, 96th Cong., 1st Sess.
(Comm. Print 1979)
Publication Date: 1979
Author: Senate Committee on Labor and Human Resources
Pages: vi, 827

L/C Card Number: 81-603095
OCLC No.: 7324581
SuDoc No.: Y4.L11/4:F15
CIS No.: 79-S542-3
UPA Citation: N/A

Relevant Bills: H.R. 3744 (95th Cong.), S. 1871 (95th Cong.)

The legislative history of the Fair Labor Standards Amendments of 1977 chronologically presents its materials, dividing them by date and chamber. The history focuses on H.R. 3744 (95th Cong.) and its related bill S. 1871 (95th Cong.). The history includes the text of H.R. 3744 (95th Cong.) as introduced, as reported to the House, as passed by the House, as reported to the Senate, and as passed by the Senate. The history gives the House, Senate, and Conference reports on H.R. 3744 (95th Cong.), as well as the House debate on H.R. 3744 (95th Cong.). The Conference report provides a joint explanatory statement which compares the House bill, Senate amendment, and Conference agreement versions of H.R. 3744 (95th Cong.). In addition, the history includes the text of S. 1871 (95th Cong.) as introduced and as reported to the Senate. The history includes the Senate report on S. 1871 (95th Cong.), as well as the Senate debate on S. 1871 (95th Cong.). The history sets out the numerous amendments to S. 1871 (95th Cong.). The text of these amendments are included as they were separately printed or as they appeared in the *Congressional Record*. The history provides overall citations to where the House and Senate debate appears in the *Congressional Record*, but does not provide internal pagination, although some of the excerpts are long. These excerpts include articles and reports inserted into the *Congressional Record*. The history has procedural statements excerpted from the *Congressional Record*, such as statements that a bill was reported favorably from committee or statements which record the votes on amendments. The history concludes with the text of P.L. 95-151.

Record No.: 216
Public Law No.: 95-164
Bill No.: S. 717 (95th Cong.)
Statutes at Large Citation: 91 Stat. 1290 (1977)
Title of Act: Federal Mine Safety and Health Amendments Act of 1977

Title of Legislative History: Legislative History of the Federal Mine Safety and Health Act of 1977, 95th Cong., 2nd Sess. (Comm. Print 1978)

Publication Date: 1978
Author: Subcommittee on Labor, Senate Committee on Human Resources
Pages: vi, 1406

L/C Card Number: 78-602811
OCLC No.: 4252705
SuDoc No.: Y4.H88:M66/2
CIS No.: 78-S412-9
UPA Citation: N/A
Relevant Bills: H.R. 2060 (95th Cong.), H.R. 4287 (95th Cong.), S. 717 (95th Cong.)

The legislative history of the Federal Mine Safety and Health Amendments Act of 1977 is presented in chronological order. It focuses on S. 717 (95th Cong.) and its companion bill H.R. 4287 (95th Cong.). The history contains the text of S. 717 as introduced, as reported, as passed by the Senate, and as passed by the House. The history provides the text from the *Congressional Record* of some of the numbered amendments to S. 717. The history has a section-by-section analysis of S. 717, the Senate report on S. 717, and the Conference report on S. 717 . Excerpts from the Senate and House debate on S. 717 reprinted in the *Congressional Record* are given. In addition, the history includes the text of H.R. 4287 as introduced and reported. The House report on H.R. 4287, as well as excerpts from the House debate on H.R. 4287 is given. The history concludes with the text of P.L. 95-164.

Record No.: 217
Public Law No.: 95-216
Bill No.: H.R. 9346 (95th Cong.)
Statutes at Large Citation: 91 Stat. 1509 (1977)
Title of Act: Social Security Amendments of 1977

Title of Legislative History: Legislative History of Titles I-XX of the Social Security Act, Vol. XVIII, 95th Congress, 1977-1978
Publication Date: 1980
Author: Social Security Administration, Office of Operational Policy and Procedures, Office of Regulations, Division of Technical Documents and Privacy, Technical Documents Branch
Pages: various

L/C Card Number: 82-642935
OCLC No.: 8006388
SuDoc No.: HE3.5/3:977-78/v.18
CIS No.: N/A
UPA Citation: N/A
Relevant Bills: H.R. 3 (95th Cong.), H.R. 1404 (95th Cong.), H.R. 3387 (95th Cong.), H.R. 3477 (95th Cong.), H.R. 4975 (95th Cong.), H.R. 4976 (95th Cong.), H.R. 5322 (95th Cong.), H.R. 8200 (95th Cong.), H.R. 8422 (95th Cong.), H.R. 8423 (95th Cong.), H.R. 8811 (95th Cong.), H.R. 9346 (95th Cong.), H.R. 12370 (95th Cong.), H.R. 13511 (95th Cong.), H.R. 13655 (95th Cong.), S. 143 (95th Cong.), S. 2266 (95th Cong.), S. 2474 (95th Cong.), S. 2534 (95th Cong.).

The volume contains the legislative histories of each of the thirteen public laws passed during the Ninety-Fifth Congress which in any way affected or added to any of the twenty titles of the Social Security Act. These public laws include the Social Security Amendments of 1977, H.R. 9346 (95th Cong.), P.L. 95-216 and the Medicare-Medicaid Anti-Fraud and Abuse Amendments, H.R. 3 (95th Cong.), P.L. 95-142.Each public law receives the same treatment. Each legislative history begins with a "Finder's Aid" cover sheet. This finder's aid lists the subjects covered by the public law and indicates in which sections of the Social Security Act and public law and which pages of STATUTES AT LARGE and the relevant Congressional reports these subjects are discussed. The Finder's Aid is followed by the text of the public law. The public law indicates the STATUTES AT LARGE pagination. The public law is followed by the relevant House, Senate, and Conference reports. The histories contain selected Congressional reports. The histories include only the relevant pages from other Congressional reports. The histories consist of photocopies of documents.

Record No.: 218
Public Law No.: 95-217
Bill No.: H.R. 3199 (95th Cong.)
Statutes at Large Citation: 91 Stat. 1566 (1977)
Title of Act: Clean Water Act of 1977

Title of Legislative History: Legislative History of the Clean Water Act of 1977: A Continuation of the Legislative History of the Federal Water Pollution Control Act: Together with a Section-by-Section Index, 95th Cong., 2nd Sess. (Comm. Print 1978)
Publication Date: 1978
Author: Senate Committee on the Environment and Public Works
Pages: ix, 551; iv, 555-1505

L/C Card Number: 73-601377
OCLC No.: 4383494
SuDoc No.: Y4.P96/10:95-14/v.3-4
CIS No.: 78-S322-9&10
UPA Citation: N/A
Relevant Bills: H.R. 3199 (95th Cong.), S. 1952 (95th Cong.)

This is a legislative history of the Clean Water Act of 1977. The Clean Water Act of 1977 amended the Federal Water Pollution Control Act (FWPCA), S. 2770 (92nd Cong.), P.L. 92-500. This two volume legislative history constitutes volumes three and four of a larger legislative history of the FWPCA. Volumes 3 and 4 are continuously numbered in one sequence, starting from page one. The history is divided into four chapters. These four chapters present legislative history materials in roughly reverse chronological order. Chapter I contains the text of the Clean Water Act of 1977, as well as the text of the FWPCA as amended by the Clean Water Act of 1977, and the President's message upon signing H.R. 3199 into law. Chapter II contains the Conference report on H.R. 3199 and the House and Senate debate excerpted from the *Congressional Record* on this Conference report. Chapter III contains the text of S. 1952 as reported to the Senate, the Senate report on S. 1952, and the Senate debate on S. 1952. Chapter III also contains the administration testimony excerpted from June 1977 Senate hearings on amending the FWPCA. Chapter IV contains H.R. 3199 as introduced and reported, as well as the House report and House debate on H.R. 3199 (95th Cong.). Chapter IV also contains the administration testimony excerpted from House hearings on amending the FWPCA held in September 1977. Citations are given to Congressional reports. The history provides three appendices which consist of three tables. The first table shows section-by-section the amendments made to the FWPCA by P.L. 95-217. The second table compares the sections of P.L. 95-217, the FWPCA, H.R. 3199 (95th Cong.) as reported, and S. 1952 (95th Cong.) as reported. The third table shows where selected topics appear in the sections of P.L. 95-217, the FWPCA, H.R. 3199 (95th Cong.) as reported, and S. 1952 (95th Cong.) as reported. The history concludes with a bibliography and a section-by-section index. The Bibliography lists the House and Senate hearings, reports, prints, and debates from the 93rd and 94th Congresses which focused on amending the FWPCA. The Section-by-Section Index lists each section of the Clean Water Act of 1977 as discussed and where the discussion appears in the history.

Record No.: 219
Public Law No.: 95-239
Bill No.: H.R. 4544 (95th Cong.)
Statutes at Large Citation: 92 Stat. 95 (1978)
Title of Act: Black Lung Benefits Reform Act of 1977

Title of Legislative History: Black Lung Benefits Reform Act and Black Lung Benefits Revenue Act of 1977, 96th Cong., 1st Sess. (Comm. Print 1979)
Publication Date: 1979
Author: House Committee on Education and Labor
Pages: vii, 1241

L/C Card Number: 80-600817
OCLC No.: 6018354
SuDoc No.: Y4.Ed8/1:B56/8
CIS No.: 79-H342-16
UPA Citation: N/A
Relevant Bills: H.R. 3476 (93rd Cong.), H.R. 8834 (93rd Cong.), H.R. 8835 (93rd Cong.), H.R. 13367 (93rd Cong.), H.R. 16448 (93rd Cong.), H.R. 17178 (93rd Cong.), S. 3952 (93rd Cong.), H.R. 7 (94th Cong.), H.R. 8 (94th Cong.), H.R. 2913 (94th Cong.), H.R. 3333 (94th Cong.), H.R. 10760 (94th Cong.), S. 3183 (94th Cong.), H.R. 1532 (95th Cong.), H.R. 4389 (95th Cong.), H.R. 4544 (95th Cong.), H.R. 5322 (95th Cong.), H.R. 13167 (95th Cong.), S. 1538 (95th Cong.), S. 1656 (95th Cong.)

This is a legislative history of the Black Lung Benefits Reform Act of 1977 (P.L. 95-239); the Black Lung Benefits Revenue Act of 1977 (P.L. 95-227); and clarifying amendments to the Black Lung Benefits Revenue Act of 1977

(P.L. 95-488). The history chronologically presents the relevant legislative history materials for each public law. The history includes the relevant bills as introduced and reported; the House, Senate, and Conference reports on these bills; and, the House and Senate debate on these bills. The history concludes with the text of the Black Lung Benefits Act as it appeared as Title IV of the Federal Mine Safety and Health Act of 1977, S. 717 (95th Cong.), P.L. 95-164. The Appendix to the history consists of excerpts from a speech by a staff employee of the House Subcommittee on Labor Standards concerning the legislative history of the black lung reform efforts.

Record No.: 220
Public Law No.: 95-242
Bill No.: H.R. 8638 (95th Cong.)
Statutes at Large Citation: 92 Stat. 120 (1978)
Title of Act: Nuclear Non-Proliferation Act of 1978

Title of Legislative History: Legislative History of the Nuclear
Nonproliferation Act of 1978, H.R. 8638 (Public
Law 95-242), 96th Cong., 1st Sess. (Comm.
Print 1979)

Publication Date: 1979
Author: Subcommittee on Energy, Nuclear Proliferation, and Federal Services, Senate Committee on Governmental Affairs
Pages: vii, 974

L/C Card Number: 79-603774
OCLC No.: 5369578
SuDoc No.: Y4.G74/9:N88/6
CIS No.: 79-S402-16
UPA Citation: N/A
Relevant Bills: H.R. 15419 (94th Cong.), S. 1439 (94th Cong.), S. 3770 (94th Cong.), H.R. 17 (95th Cong.), H.R. 4409 (95th Cong.), H.R. 6910 (95th Cong.), H.R. 8638 (95th Cong.), S. 897 (95th Cong.), S. 1432 (95th Cong.)

This is a legislative history of the Nuclear Nonproliferation Act of 1978 (P.L. 95-242). The history begins with the text of the Act and includes a list of nonproliferation bills introduced in the 94th Congress and a discussion of these bills. The history also provides a list of nonproliferation bills introduced in the 95th Congress and the text of several of these bills, including several versions of the major bills, H.R. 8638 (95th Cong.) and S. 897 (95th Cong.). The history lists hearings from the 94th and 95th Congresses on nuclear nonproliferation legislation, but includes no excerpts from these hearings. The history lists relevant Congressional reports from the 94th and 95th Congresses and includes the text of the House report on H.R. 8638 (95th Cong.) and the Senate report on S. 897 (95th

Cong.). The history lists citations to the *Congressional Record* for relevant debate in the 95th Congress and includes the text of this debate. From the executive branch, the history includes: notable executive branch correspondence, President's statement upon signing H.R. 8638 (95th Cong.) into law, and Presidential statements on nuclear nonproliferation. The history concludes with a chronology of the act. The chronology provides citations to the *Congressional Record* for such Congressional action as debate, insertions into the Record, bill introductions, bill amendments, and reports on bills.

Record No.: 221
Public Law No.: 95-250
Bill No.: H.R. 3813 (95th Cong.)
Statutes at Large Citation: 92 Stat. 163 (1978)
Title of Act: To Amend the Act of October 2, 1968, an Act to Establish a
Redwood National Park in the State of California

Title of Legislative History: Legislative History of the Redwood National
Park Expansion Act of 1978 (Public Law 95-
250), 95th Cong., 2nd Sess. (Comm. Print 1978)
Publication Date: 1978
Author: Subcommittee on National Parks and Insular Affairs, House Committee on Interior and Insular Affairs
Pages: v, 395

L/C Card Number: 79-601532
OCLC No.: 5170326
SuDoc No.: Y4.In8/14:R24/5
CIS No.: 78-H442-7
UPA Citation: N/A
Relevant Bills: H.R. 3813 (95th Cong.), S. 1976 (95th Cong.)

The legislative history of the 1978 Act (P.L. 95-250) is divided into four chapters. Chapter I contains the text of H.R. 3813 as introduced, reported, and passed; the House reports; and, House debate on this bill. Chapter II contains the text of the companion bill (S. 1976) as introduced, reported, and passed; the Senate reports; and, Senate debate on this bill. Chapter III has the text of H.R. 3813 as passed by the Senate, Conference report; and, the Congressional debate on the Conference report. Chapter IV gives the text of P.L. 95-250, as well as the text of the act to establish a Redwood National Park, S. 2515 (90th Cong.), (P.L. 90-545) which P.L. 95-250 modified. The history provides continuous pagination, although the original pagination of the included documents is also retained. The original pagination for the Congressional debate is from the *Congressional Record* daily edition.

Record No.: 222
Public Law No.: 95-367
Bill No.: H.R. 6669 (95th Cong.)
Statutes at Large Citation: 92 Stat. 601 (1978)
Title of Act: National Climate Program Act

Title of Legislative History: National Climate Program Act of 1978:
                                Background and Legislative History IN
                                Implementation of the Climate Act: Hearing
                                Before the Subcommittee on Natural Resources
                                and Environment of the House Committee on
                                Science and Technology, 96th Cong., 1st Sess.
                                (1979)
Publication Date: 1979
Author: Subcommittee on Natural Resources and Environment, House
Committee on Science and Technology
Pages: vii, 228

L/C Card Number: 80-600777
OCLC No.: 5983243
SuDoc No.: Y4.Sci.2:96/40
CIS No.: 80-H701-3
UPA Citation: N/A
Relevant Bills: H.R. 10013 (94th Cong.), H.R. 13736 (94th Cong.), H.R. 783
    (95th Cong.), H.R. 3399 (95th Cong.), H.R. 4468 (95th Cong.), H.R. 5722
    (95th Cong.), H.R. 6380 (95th Cong.), H.R. 6669 (95th Cong.), S. 421
    (95th Cong.), S. 1652 (95th Cong.), S. 1980 (95th Cong.), S. 2092 (95th
    Cong.)

A legislative history of the National Climate Program Act, H.R. 6669 (95th
Cong.), P.L. 95-367, appears as pages 190-228 of this hearing. The essay
chronologically follows Congressional action. The essay's footnotes provide
complete citations to bills, Congressional hearings, Congressional reports,
and Congressional debate. The appendices include a bibliography of
government documents, books, and journal articles concerning climatic
change and variability and the National Climate Program Act. The
appendices also give the text of P.L. 95-367.

Record No.: 223
Public Law No.: 95-393
Bill No.: H.R. 7819 (95th Cong.)
Statutes at Large Citation: 92 Stat. 808 (1978)
Title of Act: Diplomatic Relations Act

Title of Legislative History: Legislative History of the Diplomatic Relations
                                Act, 96th Cong., 1st Sess. (Comm. Print 1979)

Publication Date: 1979
Author: Senate Committee on Foreign Relations
Pages: v, 793

L/C Card Number: 79-602912
OCLC No.: 5180420
SuDoc No.: Y4.F76/2:L52/5
CIS No.: 79-S382-32
UPA Citation: N/A
Relevant Bills: H.R. 1484 (95th Cong.), H.R. 1535 (95th Cong.), H.R. 1536
     (95th Cong.), H.R. 2701 (95th Cong.), H.R. 2702 (95th Cong.), H.R. 2703
     (95th Cong.), H.R. 3409 (95th Cong.), H.R. 3841 (95th Cong.), H.R. 5182
     (95th Cong.), H.R. 6133 (95th Cong.), H.R. 7046 (95th Cong.), H.R. 7309
     (95th Cong.), H.R. 7679 (95th Cong.), H.R. 7819 (95th Cong.), H.R. 8364
     (95th Cong.), H.R. 8683 (95th Cong.), S. 476 (95th Cong.), S. 477 (95th
     Cong.), S. 478 (95th Cong.), S. 1256 (95th Cong.), S. 1257 (95th Cong.)

This is a legislative history of the Diplomatic Relations Act. The principal
purpose of this law was to complement the 1961 Vienna Convention on
Diplomatic Relations, 23 U.S.T. 3229, T.I.A.S. No. 7502. The history begins
with the text of P.L. 95-393, the Department of State regulations
implementing P.L. 95-393, and a short essay on the history of the concept of
diplomatic immunity.   The history also includes Congressional debate on
H.R. 7819 (95th Cong.) as well as Congressional reports on H.R. 7819 (95th
Cong.) and the related bill H.R. 7679 (95th Cong.). The Congressional
hearings on H.R. 7819 (95th Cong.) and its related bills are also included.
In addition, the history contains the text of the diplomatic immunity bills
from the 95th Congress. The history concludes with the text of the Vienna
Convention on Diplomatic Relations and the Report of the United States
Delegation to the United Nations Conference on Diplomatic Intercourse and
Immunities.

Record No.: 224
Public Law No.: 95-396
Bill No.: S. 1678 (95th Cong.)
Statutes at Large Citation: 92 Stat. 819 (1978)
Title of Act: Federal Pesticide Act of 1978

Title of Legislative History: Federal Pesticide Act of 1978, 95th Cong., 2nd
                      Sess. (Comm. Print 1978)
Publication Date: 1979
Author: Senate Committee on Agriculture, Nutrition, and Forestry
Pages: v, 233

L/C Card Number:
OCLC No.: 5120597
SuDoc No.: Y4.Ag8/3:P43/3
CIS No.: 79-S162-5
UPA Citation: N/A

Relevant Bills: H.R. 1237 (80th Cong.), S. 1678 (95th Cong.)

This is a legislative history of the Federal Pesticide Act of 1978. The history begins with the statement of the sponsor of S. 1678 (95th Cong.) upon the Senate's consideration of the Conference report on the bill. The history continues with the joint explanatory statement of the Conference committee comparing the Senate bill, House amendment, and Conference substitute. The history includes the text of the Federal Pesticide Act of 1978, as well as a section-by-section analysis of the act which summarizes its provisions and how they amended the Federal Insecticide, Fungicide, and Rodenticide Act (FIFRA), H.R. 1237 (80th Cong.), P.L. 80-104. The next section of the history typographically shows the changes made to FIFRA by the Federal Pesticide Act of 1978. The history also contains a section-by-section analysis of FIFRA as amended through the Federal Pesticide Act of 1978 which summarizes FIFRA. The history concludes with an excerpt from the Senate report on S. 1678 (95th Cong.) entitled "Committee Consideration." This excerpt chronologically summarizes the Congressional action which resulted in the Federal Pesticide Act of 1978. Appendix I is an essay on the history of pesticide regulation. Appendix II is a chart which offers side-by-side summaries of FIFRA before and after its amendment by the Federal Pesticide Act of 1978.

Record No.: 225
Public Law No.: 95-405
Bill No.: S. 2391 (95th Cong.)
Statutes at Large Citation: 92 Stat. 865 (1978)
Title of Act: Futures Trading Act of 1978

Title of Legislative History: Futures Trading Act of 1978, 95th Cong., 2nd
                               Sess. (Comm. Print 1978)
Publication Date: 1979
Author: Senate Committee on Agriculture, Nutrition, and Forestry
Pages: v, 164

L/C Card Number: 79-602904
OCLC No.: 6015121
SuDoc No.: Y4.Ag8/3:F98
CIS No.: 79-S162-13
UPA Citation: N/A
Relevant Bills: H.R. 13113 (93rd Cong.), S. 2391 (95th Cong.), S. 2758 (95th
    Cong.)

The legislative history of the Futures Trading Act of 1978 begins with a summary of S. 2931 (95th Cong.) as agreed to by the Conference committee, as well as the joint explanatory statement of the Conference committee excerpted from the Conference report. The history then presents the text of P.L. 95-405. The next section of the history presents the text of the Commodity Exchange Act as amended to 1974 and codified at Chapter 1 of

Title 7 of the UNITED STATES CODE. The deletions and additions made by P.L. 95-405 are shown using fonts. The history also includes a section-by-section analysis of the Futures Trading Act of 1978 which offers a narrative explanation of each section of the act. The history concludes with excerpts from Congressional reports on evaluating the Commodity Futures Trading Commission Act of 1974, H.R. 13113 (93rd Cong.), P.L. 93-463, and the Commodity Futures Trading Commission. The appendices include lists of the names and addresses of commodity exchanges, commodities for which the Commodity Futures Trading Commission has approved trading; and, a glossary of terms used in commodity futures trading.

Record No.: 226
Public Law No.: 95-405
Bill No.: S. 2391 (95th Cong.)
Statutes at Large Citation: 92 Stat. 865 (1978)
Title of Act: Futures Trading Act of 1978

Title of Legislative History: Background of the 1978 Disclosure
                                 Amendments to the Commodity Futures
                                 Trading Commission Act of 1974 IN
                                 Commodity Futures Trading Commission
                                 Oversight: Hearing Before the Subcommittee
                                 on Commerce, Consumer, and Monetary
                                 Affairs of the House Committee on
                                 Government Operations, 97th Cong., 2nd Sess.
                                 (1982)
Publication Date: 1982
Author: Subcommittee on Commerce, Consumer, and Monetary Affairs, House Committee on Government Operations
Pages: x, 1471

L/C Card Number: 82-602035
OCLC No.: 8522115
SuDoc No.: Y4.G74/7:C73/22
CIS No.: 82-H401-30
UPA Citation: N/A
Relevant Bills: H.R. 5676 (67th Cong.), H.R. 11843 (67th Cong.), H.R. 6772 (74th Cong.), S.J. Res. 170 (80th Cong.), H.R. 13094 (90th Cong.), H.R. 13113 (93rd Cong.), H.R. 10285 (95th Cong.), S. 2391 (95th Cong.)

The legislative history of the Futures Trading Act of 1978 appears as pages 1041-1056 of the hearing documents. The history focuses on the disclosure provisions of the act which prohibit the Commodity Futures Trading Commission from publicly disclosing outside of a Commission administrative proceeding the market position of any trader. The history also examines the disclosure provisions in P.L. 95-405's predecessors: Future Trading Act of 1921, H.R. 5676 (67th Cong.), P.L. 67-66; Grain Futures Act of 1922, H.R. 11843 (67th Cong.), P.L. 67-331; Commodity

Exchange Act of 1936, H.R. 6772 (74th Cong.), P.L. 74-675; Commodity Exchange Act of 1936, Amendment of 1947, S.J. Res. 170 (80th Cong.), P.L. 80-392; Commodity Exchange Act of 1936, Amendment of 1968, H.R. 13094 (90th Cong.), P.L. 90-258; and Commodity Futures Trading Commission Act of 1974, H.R. 13113 (93rd Cong.), P.L. 93-463. The essay discusses and/or quotes relevant law review articles, public acts, code sections, bills, Congressional debate, Congressional reports, and Congressional hearings.

Record No.: 227
Public Law No.: 95-454
Bill No.: S. 2640 (95th Cong.)
Statutes at Large Citation: 92 Stat. 1111 (1978)
Title of Act: Civil Service Reform Act of 1978

Title of Legislative History: Legislative History of the Civil Service Reform Act of 1978, 96th Cong., 1st Sess. (Comm. Print 1979)
Publication Date: 1979
Author: House Committee on Post Office and Civil Service
Pages: iii, 2016

L/C Card Number: 85-601592
OCLC No.: 5590572
SuDoc No.: Y4.P84/10:C49/12/v.1-2
CIS No.: 79-H622-11&12
UPA Citation: N/A
Relevant Bills: H.R. 11280 (95th Cong.), S. 2640 (95th Cong.)

The legislative history of the Civil Service Reform Act of 1978 is a two volume set. Volume One contains several versions of H.R. 11280, the House's proposed Civil Service Reform Act of 1978, as well as the House report and House debate. Volume One also includes the House debate on S. 2640 and S. 2640 as passed by the House. Volume Two contains several versions of S. 2640, the Senate report, the debate, and the Conference committee's report on S. 2640 (95th Cong.). Volume Two concludes with some post-enactment statements by Representatives on the House floor concerning the Civil Service Reform Act of 1978.

Record No.: 228
Public Law No.: 95-476
Bill No.: H.R. 12028 (95th Cong.)
Statutes at Large Citation: 92 Stat. 1497 (1978)
Title of Act: Veterans' Housing Benefits Act of 1978

Title of Legislative History: Veterans' Housing, Burial, and Cemetery
                                Programs: Hearing Before the Subcommittee
                                on Housing, Insurance, and Cemeteries of the
                                Senate Committee on Veterans' Affairs, 95th
                                Cong., 2nd Sess. (1978)
Publication Date: 1978
Author: Subcommittee on Housing, Insurance, and Cemeteries, Senate
Committee on Veterans' Affairs
Pages: v, 702

L/C Card Number: 79-600985
OCLC No.: 4579014
SuDoc No.: Y4.V64/4:H81/3
CIS No.: 79-S761-4
UPA Citation: N/A
Relevant Bills: H.R. 4341 (95th Cong.), H.R. 10268 (95th Cong.), H.R. 10269
     (95th Cong.), H.R. 10356 (95th Cong.), H.R. 11009 (95th Cong.), H.R.
     12028 (95th Cong.), H.R. 12257 (95th Cong.), H.R. 12258 (95th Cong.),
     S. 1556 (95th Cong.), S. 1643 (95th Cong.), S. 2870 (95th Cong.)

The appendices to these hearings include many documents relevant to the
legislative history of the Veterans' Housing Benefits Act of 1978, H.R. 12028
(95th Cong.), P.L. 95-476. This Act contained provisions concerning home
loans, education loans, burial benefits, and cemetery programs.   The
documents are presented chronologically, but without comment.   H.R.
12028 was the bill finally passed.   It contained provisions which had
originally appeared in a number of other bills. The appendices include the
text of H.R. 12028 as introduced, as reported from the House committee, as
reported from the Senate committee, and as the compromise bill which
became law as it appeared in both the *Congressional Record* and as
separately printed. The appendices also include the House report on H.R.
12028 and excerpts from the Senate report on H.R. 12028. The House report
has the Veterans' Administration agency reports on four bills whose
provisions were incorporated into H.R. 12028 : H.R. 11009, H.R. 10356 , H.R.
10269, and H.R. 10268. Both the House and Senate reports show how their
bill versions would change Title 38 of the *United States Code*.   The
appendices also include a comparison of the House bill, Senate
amendment,   and   compromise   agreement   reprinted   from   the
Congressional Record. In addition, the appendices include the texts as
reported from the House committees and House reports on H.R. 12257 and
H.R. 12258. These related bills had provisions similar to provisions of H.R.
12028 (95th Cong.) as signed into law.   The text of the hearings gives the
texts as introduced of S. 1643 (95th Cong.), S. 1556 (95th Cong.), and S. 2870
(95th Cong.), as well as the Veterans' Administration agency reports on
these bills. The hearings also provide the text of H.R. 4341 (95th Cong.) as
reported from the House committee, as well as the House report on the bill.
The hearings focus on these bills, although there is some discussion of
veterans' housing, burial, and cemetery programs in general. The
appendices conclude with the text of P.L. 95-476.

Record No.: 229
Public Law No.: 95-479
Bill No.: H.R. 11886 (95th Cong.)
Statutes at Large Citation: 92 Stat. 1560 (1978)
Title of Act: Veterans' Disability Compensation and Survivors' Benefits Act
        of 1978

Title of Legislative History: Veterans' Disability Compensation and
                                Survivors' Benefits Act of 1978: Hearing on S.
                                2828, S. 1929, S. 3187, S. 379 and H.R. 6501, and
                                H.R. 11888 Before the Subcommittee on
                                Compensation and Pension of the Senate
                                Committee on Veterans' Affairs, 95th Cong.,
                                2nd Sess. (1978)
Publication Date: 1978
Author: Subcommittee on Compensation and Pension, Senate Committee
on Veterans' Affairs
Pages: iv, 308

L/C Card Number: 79-601168
OCLC No.: 4761946
SuDoc No.: Y4.V64/4:V64/7/978
CIS No.: 79-S761-6
UPA Citation: N/A
Relevant Bills: H.R. 6501 (95th Cong.), H.R. 11886 (95th Cong.), H.R. 11888
        (95th Cong.), S. 379 (95th Cong.), S. 1929 (95th Cong.), S. 2828 (95th
        Cong.), S. 3187 (95th Cong.)

The Hearing includes the text of several bills as referred to the Senate
committee: S. 2828, S. 1929, S. 3187, S. 379, H.R. 6501, and H.R. 11888. Also
included are the House report on H.R. 6501 (95th Cong.) and House report
on H.R. 11888 (95th Cong.).The Appendices to this Hearing include
legislative history materials for the Veterans' Disability Compensation and
Survivors' Benefits Act of 1978. The Appendices include the Senate's debate
on passing H.R. 11886, as well as the text as amended and passed by the
Senate. The appendices also include the text of the related bill S. 2828 as
reported from the Senate committee and excerpts from the Senate report.
The Appendices conclude with the text of P.L. 95-479. The text of the
Hearing itself contains material pertinent to the history of P.L. 95-479.

Record No.: 230
Public Law No.: 95-495
Bill No.: H.R. 12250 (95th Cong.)
Statutes at Large Citation: 92 Stat. 1649 (1978)

Title of Act: To Designate the Boundary Waters Canoe Area Wilderness, to
               Establish the Boundary Waters Canoe Area Mining Protection
               Area

Title of Legislative History: Legislative History of the Boundary Waters
                               Canoe Area Wilderness (P.L. 95-495), 95th
                               Cong., 2nd Sess. (Comm. Print 1978)
Publication Date: 1979
Author: Subcommittee on National Parks and Insular Affairs, House
Committee on Interior and Insular Affairs
Pages: v, 318

L/C Card Number: 84-603601
OCLC No.: 4897736
SuDoc No.: N/A
CIS No.: 79-H442-1
UPA Citation: N/A
Relevant Bills: H.R. 2820 (95th Cong.), H.R. 8722 (95th Cong.), H.R. 12250
    (95th Cong.), S. 3242 (95th Cong.)

This is a legislative history of the public law which redesignated the
Boundary Waters Canoe Area a wilderness area and clarified the
permissible uses of the Boundary Waters Canoe Wilderness Area. The
legislative history is divided into chapters on House action, Senate action,
Conference action, and executive action. The materials within each chapter
are presented in chronological order.The chapter on House action includes
H.R. 12250 (95th Cong.) as introduced, as well as the remarks of its sponsor
on its introduction. This chapter also includes H.R. 12250 as reported to the
House, as well as the House report on H.R. 12250. This chapter concludes
with the House debate and passage of H.R. 12250. The chapter on Senate
action includes H.R. 12250 as reported to the Senate, as well as the Senate
report on H.R. 12250. This chapter concludes with the Senate debate and
passage of H.R. 12250 (95th Cong.). The Senate debate includes the insertion
of a chart comparing the law before amendment, with the House bill, and
with the Senate bill. The chapter on Conference action includes the
Conference report, as well as the House and Senate debate of and
agreement to this Conference report. The history includes the bills and
reports as separately printed and with full citations. The included debate
consists of photocopies of the daily *Congressional Record*, including the
daily edition's pagination. The history concludes with the text of P.L. 95-
495.

Record No.: 231
Public Law No.: 95-504
Bill No.: S. 2493 (95th Cong.)
Statutes at Large Citation: 92 Stat. 1705 (1978)
Title of Act: Airline Deregulation Act of 1978

Title of Legislative History: Legislative History of the Airline Deregulation
Act of 1978, 96th Cong., 1st Sess. (Comm. Print
1979)
Publication Date: 1979
Author: House Committee on Public Works and Transportation
Pages: vi, 990

L/C Card Number: 79-602919
OCLC No.: 5348239
SuDoc No.: Y4.P96/11:96-5
CIS No.: 79-H642-5
UPA Citation: N/A
Relevant Bills: S. 2229 (85th Cong.), S. 3880 (85th Cong.), H.R. 14465 (91st
Cong.), H.R. 6010 (95th Cong.), H.R. 12611 (95th Cong.), S. 2493 (95th
Cong.)

The legislative history of the Airline Deregulation Act of 1978 begins with
the text of P.L. 95-504. It shows by changing the typographical font how the
Airline Deregulation Act of 1978 amended: the Federal Aviation Act of 1958
(P.L. 85-726); Federal Aviation Act of 1958, Amendment of 1977 (P.L. 95-163);
Airport and Airway Development Act of 1970, (P.L. 91-258); and a 1957 act
on government guaranteed aircraft purchase loans, (P.L. 85-307). The
history also includes S. 2493 and its related bill H.R. 12611, as well as the
Congressional reports and Congressional debate on these bills.

Record No.: 232
Public Law No.: 95-507
Bill No.: H.R. 11318 (95th Cong.)
Statutes at Large Citation: 92 Stat. 1757 (1978)
Title of Act: Small Business Act, Amendment of 1978

Title of Legislative History: Government Procurement from Small and
Small Disadvantaged Businesses (Public Law
95-507 and Accompanying Reports), 96th
Cong., 2nd Sess. (Comm. Print 1980)
Publication Date: 1980
Author: House Committee on Small Business
Pages: v, 165

L/C Card Number: 80-602069
OCLC No.: 6509326
SuDoc No.: Y4.Sm1:G74/3
CIS No.: 80-H722-6
UPA Citation: N/A
Relevant Bills: H.R. 11318 (95th Cong.)

This is a legislative history of H.R. 11318 which amended the Small
Business Act, (P.L. 83-163) and Small Business Investment Act of 1958

(P.L. 85-699). The legislative history begins with the text of P.L. 95-507. It also contains the House report, Senate reports, and Conference report on H.R. 11318.

Record No.: 233
Public Law No.: 95-520
Bill No.: H.R. 5029 (95th Cong.)
Statutes at Large Citation: 92 Stat. 1820 (1978)
Title of Act: Veterans' Administration Programs Extension Act of 1978

Title of Legislative History: Veterans' Disability Compensation and Survivors' Benefits Act of 1978: Hearing on S. 2828, S. 1929, S. 3187, S. 379 and H.R. 6501, and H.R. 11888 Before the Subcommittee on Compensation and Pension of the Senate Committee on Veterans' Affairs, 95th Cong., 2nd Sess. (1978)
Publication Date: 1978
Author: Subcommittee on Compensation and Pensions, Senate Committee on Veterans' Affairs
Pages: iv, 308

L/C Card Number: 79-601168
OCLC No.: 4761946
SuDoc No.: Y4.V64/4:V64/7/978
CIS No.: 79-S761-6
UPA Citation: N/A
Relevant Bills: H.R. 5029 (95th Cong.), H.R. 6501 (95th Cong.), H.R. 11888 (95th Cong.), S. 379 (95th Cong.), S. 1929 (95th Cong.), S. 2828 (95th Cong.), S. 3187 (95th Cong.)

The records from the 1978 hearings of the Subcommittee on Compensation and Pensions contain legislative history materials relevant to the Veterans' Administration Programs Extension Act of 1978, H.R. 5029 (95th Cong.), P.L. 95-520.P.L. 95-520, among other provisions, included provisions which extended medical benefits for veterans in the Philippines and elsewhere outside the fifty states and provisions which continued veterans readjustment appointments within the federal civil service. The appendices to the hearings give H.R. 5029 (95th Cong.) as reported to the Senate, as well as the Senate report on H.R. 5029 (95th Cong.). The appendices provide the Senate debate on H.R. 5029 (95th Cong.). The citation to this debate includes the dates of debate and its pagination in the daily *Congressional Record*. The appendices conclude with the text of P.L. 95-520. The text of the hearings includes the texts as introduced of several related bills: S. 2828 (95th Cong.), S. 1929 (95th Cong.), S. 3187 (95th Cong.), and S. 379 (95th

Cong.). Also provided are the texts as passed by the House of H.R. 6501 (95th Cong.) and H.R. 11888 (95th Cong.), as well as the House reports on them. Most of the Senate bills are followed by the introductory statements of their sponsors and/or the Veterans' Administration's agency reports on them. The citations to the introductory statements include their dates and pagination in the daily *Congressional Record*.

Record No.: 234
Public Law No.: 95-521
Bill No.: S. 555 (95th Cong.)
Statutes at Large Citation: 92 Stat. 1824 (1978)
Title of Act: Ethics in Government Act of 1978

Title of Legislative History: Office of Government Ethics and Federal Post-Employment Restrictions: Legislative History of Titles IV and V of the Ethics in Government Act of 1979, as Amended, 96th Cong., 2nd Sess. (Comm. Print 1980)
Publication Date: 1980
Author: Senate Committee on Governmental Affairs
Pages: vi, 304

L/C Card Number: 80-603840
OCLC No.: 7738629
SuDoc No.: Y4.G74/9:G74/3
CIS No.: 80-S402-19
UPA Citation: N/A
Relevant Bills: H.R. 1 (95th Cong.), H.R. 6954 (95th Cong.), H.R. 13850 (95th Cong.), S. 555 (95th Cong.), S. 869 (96th Cong.)

This is a legislative history of Titles IV and V of the Ethics in Government Act of 1978 (P.L. 95-521), and the Ethics in Government Act of 1978, Amendment of 1979, (P.L. 96-28) which amended Title V. The history begins with the President's message upon transmitting a draft of the Administration's proposed legislation "The Ethics in Government Act of 1977". The history continues with the text of Title IV of the Ethics in Government Act of 1978 and the text of Title V of the Ethics in Government Act of 1978, as amended by P.L. 96-28. The history then separately treats Title IV, Title V, and P.L. 96-28. For each, the history presents relevant excerpts from Congressional reports and bills. For each, the history gives the Congressional debate. Also included are the text of Title V of P.L. 95-521 as passed and the text of P.L. 96-28. The Appendix consists of a background study: Senate Committee on Government Operations, Study of Federal Regulations, S. Doc. No. 25, 95th Cong., 1st Sess. (1977).

Record No.: 235
Public Law No.: 95-555
Bill No.: S. 995 (95th Cong.)
Statutes at Large Citation: 92 Stat. 2076 (1978)
Title of Act: Pregnancy Discrimination Act

Title of Legislative History: Legislative History of the Pregnancy
                                Discrimination Act of 1978: Public Law 95-555,
                                96th Cong., 2nd Sess. (Comm. Print 1980)
Publication Date: 1980
Author: Senate Committee on Labor and Human Resources
Pages: vi, 212

L/C Card Number: 80-602871
OCLC No.: 6503803
SuDoc No.: Y4.L11/4:P91/3
CIS No.: 80-S542-10
UPA Citation: N/A
Relevant Bills: H.R. 5055 (95th Cong.), H.R. 6075 (95th Cong.), S. 995 (95th
    Cong.)

The legislative history chronologically relates the Congressional action
which led to the Pregnancy Discrimination Act of 1978. The Table of
Contents notes and provides dates for each Congressional action. The
history contains several versions of S. 995 and its major related bill H.R.
6075, as well as the Congressional reports and Congressional debate on both
these bills. A version of H.R. 5055 is also included. The history contains
quotations from the *Congressional Record* noting hearings on all three of
these bills. The history concludes with the text of P.L. 95-555.

Record No.: 236
Public Law No.: 95-566
Bill No.: S. 2539 (95th Cong.)
Statutes at Large Citation: 92 Stat. 2402 (1978)
Title of Act: Middle Income Student Assistance Act

Title of Legislative History: Federal Student Assistance: Legislative
                                History, 95th Congress, 2nd Session
Publication Date: 1979
Author: James B. Stedman of the Congressional Research Service
Pages: 26

L/C Card Number: N/A
OCLC No.: N/A
SuDoc No.: N/A
CIS No.: N/A
UPA Citation: UPA Film No.: MS 78-79 Supp., Reel No. XI, Frame No.
0808.CRS No.: 79-6 EPW

Relevant Bills: H.R. 3946 (95th Cong.), H.R. 10854 (95th Cong.), H.R. 11274 (95th Cong.), H.R. 12050 (95th Cong.), H.R. 12929 (95th Cong.), H.R. 13511 (95th Cong.), H.R. Con. Res. 559 (95th Cong.), H.R. Con. Res. 683 (95th Cong.), S. 1753 (95th Cong.), S. 2473 (95th Cong.), S. 2538 (95th Cong.), S. 2539 (95th Cong.), S. Con. Res. 80 (95th Cong.), S. Con. Res. 104 (95th Cong.), S. Res. 524 (95th Cong.)

This is a legislative history of the Middle Income Student Assistance Act and the appropriations which first funded it, H.R. 12929 (P.L. 95-480). The history is divided into five chronological charts: Authorizing Legislation -- Amendments to Existing Aid Programs; Authorizing Legislation -- Tax Credits; First Concurrent Resolution on the Budget -- FY 1979; Second Concurrent Resolution on the Budget -- FY 1979; and Appropriations Legislation. Each of these chronological charts follows Congressional activity in a different legislative path. These paths eventually converged with the passage of the Middle Income Student Assistance Act and the appropriations to fund it. Each chart entry consists of a date and a short summary of Congressional action on that date, such as a bill's introduction, reporting, debate, amendment, or passage. Entries summarize bills' provisions and estimated costs.

Record No.: 237
Public Law No.: 95-588
Bill No.: H.R. 10173 (95th Cong.)
Statutes at Large Citation: 92 Stat. 2497 (1978)
Title of Act: Veterans' and Survivors' Pension Improvement Act of 1978

Title of Legislative History: Veterans' and Survivors' Pension Improvement Act of 1978: Hearing on S. 2384 Before the Senate Committee on Veterans' Affairs, 95th Cong., 2nd Sess. (1978)
Publication Date: 1978
Author: Senate Committee on Veterans' Affairs
Pages: iv, 789

L/C Card Number: 79-600705
OCLC No.: 4561629
SuDoc No.: Y4.V64/4:V64/19
CIS No.: 79-S761-3
UPA Citation: N/A
Relevant Bills: H.R. 10173 (95th Cong.), S. 2384 (95th Cong.)

This hearing serves as a legislative history of the Veterans' and Survivors' Pension Improvement Act of 1978. The hearing was printed after the passage of the act. An appendix includes the text of P.L. 95-588. The history provides the text as referred to committee of S. 2384 (95th Cong.), a bill related to H.R. 10173 (95th Cong.). The appendices include amendments to

S. 2384 (95th Cong.), S. 2384 as reported from committee, and excerpts from the Senate report on S. 2384 (95th Cong.). The appendices give H.R. 10173 (95th Cong.), the House and Conference reports on H.R. 10173 (95th Cong.), and the Congressional debate on this bill. The hearings also present testimony, written statements, and questions and answers on S. 2384 (95th Cong.).

Record No.: 238
Public Law No.: 95-591
Bill No.: H.R. 13500 (95th Cong.)
Statutes at Large Citation: 92 Stat. 2523 (1978)
Title of Act: Presidential Records Act of 1978

Title of Legislative History: Materials Relating to Legislative History of
                                Presidential Records Act of 1978 IN
                                Presidential Records Act of 1978: Hearings on
                                H.R. 10998 and Related Bills Before the
                                Subcommittee on Government Information
                                and Individual Rights of the Senate Committee
                                on Government Operations, 95th Cong., 2nd
                                Sess. (1978)
Publication Date: 1978
Author: Subcommittee on Government Information and Individual Rights,
House Committee on Government Operations
Pages: v, 896

L/C Card Number: 79-603668
OCLC No.: 5269633
SuDoc No.: Y4.G74/7:P92/5
CIS No.: 79-H401-36
UPA Citation: N/A
Relevant Bills: H.R. 9130 (95th Cong.), H.R. 10998 (95th Cong.), H.R. 11001
    (95th Cong.), H.R. 13364 (95th Cong.), H.R. 13500 (95th Cong.), H.R.
    14249 (95th Cong.), S. 2596 (95th Cong.), S. 3494 (95th Cong.)

Appendix 25 to these hearings is entitled "Materials Relating to Legislative History of Presidential Records Act of 1978." Appendix 25 begins with an essay which relates in chronological fashion the Congressional action which led to the enactment of the Presidential Records Act of 1978. The essay provides complete citations to relevant hearings. The attachments to this essay include the text of several bills as introduced and referred to committee: H.R. 9130, H.R. 13364, and H.R. 14249. The appendix also gives the main bill H.R. 13500 as reported from committee, as well as the House report on this bill. The hearings contain the text of H.R. 10998 and H.R. 11001, both as introduced. The history concludes with the text of P.L. 95-591.

The Appendices are as follows: Appendix A - Amendment No. 1743 to S.2384, March 22, 1978; Appendix B - Amendment No. 1934 to S.2384, May 4,

1978; Appendix C - H.R. 10173, an act, June 29, 1978; Appendix D - H. Rept. No. 95-1225 on H.R. 10173, May 31, 1978; Appendix E - S. 2384, July 17, 1978; Appendix F - excerpts from S. Rept. No. 95-1016 on S. 2384, July 17, 1978; Appendix G - excerpts from the *Congressional Record* on the passage of the Senate amendments; Appendix H - S. Conf. Rept. No. 95-1329 on H.R. 10173, October 12, 1978; Appendix I - excerpts from the *Congressional Record* on the passage of the conference rept. to H.R. 10173, October 12, 1978; and Appendix J - P.L. 95-588.

Record No.: 239
Public Law No.: 95-625
Bill No.: S. 791 (95th Cong.)
Statutes at Large Citation: 92 Stat. 3467 (1978)
Title of Act: National Parks and Recreation Act of 1978

Title of Legislative History: Legislative History of the National Parks and Recreation Act of 1978 (Public Law 95-625), 95th Cong., 2nd Sess. (Comm. Print 1978)

Publication Date: 1978
Author: Subcommittee on National Parks and Insular Affairs, House Committee on Interior and Insular Affairs
Pages: v, 986

L/C Card Number: 84-603600
OCLC No.: 4912784
SuDoc No.: Y4.In8/14:L52
CIS No.: 79-H442-6
UPA Citation: N/A
Relevant Bills: H.R. 6900 (95th Cong.), H.R. 9601 (95th Cong.), H.R. 12536 (95th Cong.), S. 491 (95th Cong.), S. 791 (95th Cong.), S. 2876 (95th Cong.)

The legislative history of the National Parks and Recreation Act of 1978 is divided into chapters which represent the Congressional actions: Chapter I contains the Bill as introduced, a statement of the administration's official position from the November 28, 1977 hearing before the Subcommittee on National Parks and Insular Affairs, the House Report, and the considerations and passage activities of the House; Chapter II gives the Senate report, the statement from the July 21, 1978 hearing from the Committee on Energy and National Resources; Chapter III provides several of the bills as amended by the House, and Senate consideration and action; Chapter IV has the text of the law and the President's statement upon signing; Chapter V concludes with a summary listing of the National Park System units which were affected by the Act.

Record No.: 240
Public Law No.: 96-22
Bill No.: S. 7 (96th Cong.)
Statutes at Large Citation: 93 Stat. 47 (1979)
Title of Act: Veterans' Health Care Amendments of 1979

Title of Legislative History: Veterans' Health Care Amendments of 1979:
                               Hearing on S. 7 Before the Senate Committee
                               on Veterans' Affairs, 96th Cong., 1st Sess.
                               (1979)
Publication Date: 1979
Author: Senate Committee on Veterans' Affairs
Pages: iii, 601

L/C Card Number: 79-603844
OCLC No.: 5524786
SuDoc No.: Y4.V64/4:H34/11
CIS No.: 79-S761-12
UPA Citation: N/A
Relevant Bills: S. 7 (96th Cong.)

The Appendices to this 1979 Hearing include legislative history materials
on the Veterans' Health Care Amendments of 1979. It includes the Senate
debate, excerpts from the Conference Report, and the rest of the Act. The
hearing text gives the Bill as introduced, the remarks, and the Agency
Report.

Record No.: 241
Public Law No.: 96-88
Bill No.: S. 210 (96th Cong.)
Statutes at Large Citation: 93 Stat. 668 (1979)
Title of Act: Department of Education Organization Act

Title of Legislative History: Legislative History of Public Law 96-88,
                               Department of Education Organization Act,
                               96th Cong., 2nd Sess. (Comm. Print 1980)
Publication Date: 1980
Author: Senate Committee on Governmental Affairs
Pages: 1860

L/C Card Number: 80-602063
OCLC No.: 6284765
SuDoc No.: Y4.G74/9:Ed8/3/pt.1-2
CIS No.: 80-S402-7&8
UPA Citation: N/A
Relevant Bills: H.R. 13343 (95th Cong.), H.R. 13778 (95th Cong.), S. 991 (95th
    Cong.), H.R. 2444 (96th Cong.), S. 210 (96th Cong.), S. 510 (96th Cong.)

The legislative history of the Department of Education Organization Act begins with the text of P.L. 96-88. The remainder is divided into four sections: Senate Action, House Action, Conference Action, and Executive Action. The Senate Action portion contains the various versions of the Bill, the Report, and the debate from the 95th Congress. These same materials are provided from the 96th Congress. The Administrative Bill (Executive) is added to this section. The House Action covers all legislative activities of the House for the 95th and 96th Congresses, i.e., various versions of the Bill, Reports and debates. Conference Action includes a comparison of S. 210 and the House Amendments of July 11, 1979. This section also includes the Conference report on S. 210 (96th Cong.) and the Congressional debate. Executive Action contains the President's message on transmitting its administration bill to Congress and the President's statement upon signing into law.

Record No.: 242
Public Law No.: 96-153
Bill No.: H.R. 3875 (96th Cong.)
Statutes at Large Citation: 93 Stat. 1101 (1979)
Title of Act: Housing and Community Development Amendments of 1979

Title of Legislative History: Compilation of the Housing and Community
Development Amendments of 1979, 96th Cong.,
2nd Sess. (Comm. Print 1980)
Publication Date: 1980
Author: Subcommittee on Housing and Community Development, House Committee on Banking, Finance, and Urban Affairs
Pages: v, 1123

L/C Card Number: N/A
OCLC No.: 6298887
SuDoc No.: Y4.B22/1:H81/70/979
CIS No.: 80-H242-8
UPA Citation: N/A
Relevant Bills: H.R. 3875 (96th Cong.), S. 903 (96th Cong.), S. 1064 (96th Cong.), S. 1149 (96th Cong.)

The volume is a legislative history of the Housing and Community Development Amendments of 1979. It begins with the text of P.L. 96-153. The history includes a section-by-section narrative summary of the Housing and Community Development Amendments of 1979, as well as the joint explanatory statement of the Conference Committee excerpted from the Conference report comparing the House's version of H.R. 3875 (96th Cong.) and the Senate amendments to it. The history contains H.R. 3875 as passed by the House and as passed by the Senate. The House debate on H.R. 3875 is included, as is the Senate debate on S. 903, S. 1064, S. 1149, and H.R. 3875. Also included are the House report on H.R. 3875 and the Senate reports on S. 903, S. 1064, and S. 1149.

Record No.: 243
Public Law No.: 96-157
Bill No.: S. 241 (96th Cong.)
Statutes at Large Citation: 93 Stat. 1167 (1979)
Title of Act: Justice System Improvement Act of 1979

Title of Legislative History: Indexed Legislative History of the "Justice
System Improvement Act of 1979"
Publication Date: 1980
Author: Department of Justice, Office of Justice Assistance, Research, and
Statistics, Office of General Counsel
Pages: Li, 903

L/C Card Number: 81-600752
OCLC No.: 7286758
SuDoc No.: J1.2:In2/9
CIS No.: N/A
UPA Citation: N/A
Relevant Bills: H.R. 5037 (90th Cong.), H.R. 2061 (96th Cong.), S. 241 (96th
Cong.)

This is a legislative history of the Justice System Improvement Act of 1979.
The history begins with a section-by-section index to Title I of the Omnibus
Crime Control and Safe Streets Act of 1968, H.R. 5037 (90th Cong.), P.L. 90-
351, as amended by the Justice System Improvement Act of 1979 and earlier
laws. The references under each section are to the legislative history
materials, such as bills and Congressional reports. The history contains S.
241 (96th Cong.) as introduced, as reported by Committee, as passed by
Senate, and as reported by Conference. The history also contains the Senate
and House debate, the Senate report, and the Conference reports on this
bill. This history also provides materials on the related bill H.R. 2061 (96th
Cong.). The history gives H.R. 2061 as reported and as passed, as well as
the House report and House debate on this bill. The history concludes with
the text of P.L. 96-157.

Record No.: 244
Public Law No.: 96-205
Bill No.: H.R. 3756 (96th Cong.)
Statutes at Large Citation: 94 Stat. 84 (1980)
Title of Act: To Authorize Appropriations for Certain Insular Areas of the
United States

Title of Legislative History: Legislative History of the Omnibus Insular
Areas Act of 1979-1980 (H.R. 3756) (Public Law
96-205), 96th Cong., 2nd Sess. (Comm. Print
1980)

Publication Date: 1980
Author: Subcommittee on National Parks and Insular Affairs, House Committee on Interior and Insular Affairs
Pages: v, 185

L/C Card Number: 80-602286
OCLC No.: 6389409
SuDoc No.: Y4.In8/14:L52/2
CIS No.: 80-H442-6
UPA Citation: N/A
Relevant Bills: H.R. 3756 (96th Cong.)

This is a legislative history of Congressional actions which were concerned with the insular areas of the United States, H.R. 3756 (96th Cong.), P.L. 96-205. It provides several versions of H.R. 3756, as well as the House and Senate reports on this bill. The history includes the House and Senate passage of H.R. 3756, excerpted from the *Congressional Record*. The history notes, but does not include hearings before the Senate Committee on Energy and Natural Resources. The history concludes with the text of P.L. 96-205.

Record No.: 245
Public Law No.: 96-212
Bill No.: S. 643 (96th Cong.)
Statutes at Large Citation: 94 Stat. 102 (1980)
Title of Act: Refugee Act of 1980

Title of Legislative History: Review of U.S. Refugee Resettlement Programs and Policies: A Report, 96th Cong., 2nd Sess. (Comm. Print 1980)
Publication Date: 1980
Author: Senate Committee on the Judiciary
Pages: viii, 342

L/C Card Number: 80-603884
OCLC No.: 6990183
SuDoc No.: Y4.J89/2:R25/17/980
CIS No.: 80-S522-10
UPA Citation: N/A
Relevant Bills: H.R. 3056 (95th Cong.), H.R. 7175 (95th Cong.), H.R. 2816 (96th Cong.), S. 643 (96th Cong.)

This committee print examines refugee assistance and resettlement policy, specifically the Refugee Act of 1980, S. 643 (96th Cong.), P.L. 96-212. The document begins with a brief examination of pre-1980 refugee admission and assistance legislation and programs. The document then proceeds to examine in detail the Refugee Act of 1980. First, an essay examines the major issues which Congress addressed during the development of the Refugee Act and their resolution. Second, another essay examines the legislative history of the Refugee Act of 1980. This essay is divided into three sections: Senate Action, House Action, and Conference Action. Within each section, Congressional action is chronologically followed. Both the major issues and legislative history essays quote and provide complete citations in their footnotes to the relevant Congressional hearings, Congressional reports, and Congressional debate. The main part of the document concludes with a section-by-section summary of the Refugee Act of 1980. The Appendix includes the text of P.L. 96-212, as well as the Conference report on S. 643 (96th Cong.). The Appendix also provides a report prepared by a private foundation, the New TransCentury Foundation, for the Social Security Administration of the Department of Health, Education, and Welfare. This 229 page report reviews existing refugee resettlement programs implemented in the United States and abroad. Based on this research, the report makes findings and recommendations for the future of refugee resettlement in the United States.

Record No.: 246
Public Law No.: 96-265
Bill No.: H.R. 3236 (96th Cong.)
Statutes at Large Citation: 94 Stat. 441 (1980)
Title of Act: Social Security Disability Amendments of 1980

Title of Legislative History: Disability Amendments of 1980 -- H.R. 3236: Provisions Relating to Disability Insurance, Public Law 96-265 Enacted June 9, 1980, 96th Cong., 2nd Sess. (Comm. Print 1980)
Publication Date: 1980
Author: Subcommittee on Social Security, House Committee on Ways and Means
Pages: iii, 59

L/C Card Number: 81-603633
OCLC No.: 6653244
SuDoc No.: Y4.W36:WMCP96-64
CIS No.: 80-H782-41
UPA Citation: N/A
Relevant Bills: H.R. 15630 (94th Cong.), H.R. 8076 (95th Cong.), H.R. 12972 (95th Cong.), H.R. 14084 (95th Cong.), H.R. 2054 (96th Cong.), H.R. 2854 (96th Cong.), H.R. 3236 (96th Cong.), H.R. 3464 (96th Cong.), S. 591 (96th Cong.)

This is a legislative history of the Social Security Disability Amendments of 980, Titles I and III, which are the titles dealing with disability insurance. The history begins with a narrative section-by-section summary of the disability insurance provisions of P.L. 96-265. For each section, the summary examines prior law, the Senate bill, Conference action, and effective date of the law. The history also includes a narrative essay on the legislative history of H.R. 3236 (96th Cong.) and other disability bills before the Social Security Subcommittee in previous Congresses. After a brief survey of the history of the disability insurance program, the essay concentrates on the bills introduced in the 94th - 96th Congresses to change the disability insurance program. The legislative history also contains the text of P.L. 96-265, Titles I and III. The history concludes with three tables. The first two tables show the estimated effect of disability insurance expenditures by provision and the change in the actuarial balance of the disability insurance program over the long range. The third table takes all individual subjects within the Act given the appropriate citation to: Statutes at Large, House Reports, Senate Reports and the Conference Reports.

Record No.: 247
Public Law No.: 96-294
Bill No.: S. 932 (96th Cong.)
Statutes at Large Citation: 94 Stat. 611 (1980)
Title of Act: Energy Security Act

Title of Legislative History: Compilation of the Energy Security Act of 1980, and 1980 Amendments to the Defense Production Act of 1950, 96th Cong., 2nd Sess. (Comm. Prints 1980)
Publication Date: 1980
Author: House Committee on Banking, Finance, and Urban Affairs
Pages: v, 2252

L/C Card Number: 80-603878
OCLC No.: 7137615
SuDoc No.: Y4.B22/1:En2/10/pt.1-3
CIS No.: 80-H242-13&14&15
UPA Citation: N/A
Relevant Bills: H.R. 9176 (81st Cong.), H.R. 3930 (96th Cong.), S. 932 (96th Cong.)

This is a legislative history of the Energy Security Act. Many of the titles within the Energy Security Act have individual popular names: Title I, Part A, Defense Production Act Amendments of 1980; Title I, Part B, United States Synthetic Fuels Corporation Act of 1980; Title III, Biomass Energy and Alcohol Fuels Act of 1980; Title IV, Renewable Energy Resources Act of 1980; Title V, Solar Energy and Energy Conservation Act of 1980; Title VI, Geothermal Energy Act of 1980; Title VII, Acid Precipitation Act of 1980. The history begins with the text of P.L. 96-294. It continues with a short summary of the Act and the joint explanatory statement of the Conference committee which notes the differences between several versions of S. 932 (96th Cong.). The history contains the House and Senate debate on this Conference report. The history includes the text of the Defense Production

Act of 1950, H.R. 9176 (81st Cong.), P.L. 81-774, as amended to 1980, codified at 50 U.S.C. app. S. 2061 et seq.. The original act is followed by a list of all the public laws passed during 1951-1980 which extended or amended it. The history includes House debate on H.R. 3930, a related bill of S. 932, the Senate debate on S. 932, and S. 932 as passed by both the House and Senate. Also provided are the House report on H.R. 3930 and the Senate reports on S. 932.

Record No.: 248
Public Law No.: 96-345
Bill No.: H.R. 5892 (96th Cong.)
Statutes at Large Citation: 94 Stat. 1139 (1980)
Title of Act: Wind Energy Systems Act of 1980

Title of Legislative History: Legislative History of the Wind Energy Systems Act of 1980 IN Wind Energy Systems Act of 1980, Hearings Before the Subcommittee on Energy Development and Applications of the House Committee on Science and Technology, 96th Cong., 1st Sess. (1979)

Publication Date: 1980
Author: Subcommittee on Energy Development and Applications, House Committee on Science and Technology
Pages: iv, 429

L/C Card Number: 80-603413
OCLC No.: 7097043
SuDoc No.: Y4.Sci2:96/137
CIS No.: 80-H701-92
UPA Citation: N/A
Relevant Bills: H.R. 3558 (96th Cong.), H.R. 5892 (96th Cong.)

A legislative history of the Wind Energy Systems Act of 1980, H.R. 5892 (96th Cong.), P.L. 96-345, appears as pages 273 - 429 of these hearings, Appendix II: Legislative History of the Wind Energy Systems Act of 1980. This legislative history contains H.R. 3558 as introduced, which was a bill related to H.R. 5892, as well as H.R. 5892, both as introduced and as reported. The history also contains the House, Senate, and Conference reports on H.R. 5892. The Department of Energy's views are included as its wind program planning outline prepared at the request of the Subcommittee on Energy Development and Applications and the Department's answers to questions submitted by the Subcommittee. The history concludes with the text of P.L. 96-345.

Record No.: 249
Public Law No.: 96-510
Bill No.: H.R. 7020 (96th Cong.)
Statutes at Large Citation: 94 Stat. 2767 (1980)
Title of Act: Comprehensive Environmental Response, Compensation, and
          Liability Act of 1980

Title of Legislative History: A Legislative History of the Comprehensive
                    Environmental Response, Compensation, and
                    Liability Act of 1980 (Superfund), Public Law
                    96-510: Together with a Section-by-Section
                    Index, 97th Cong., 2nd Sess. (Comm. Prints
                    1982)
Publication Date: 1983
Author: Senate Committee on the Environment and Public Works
Pages: xii,824; iii,1114; iii,398

L/C Card Number: 83-602641
OCLC No.: 9843530
SuDoc No.: Y4.P96/10:97-14/v.1-3
CIS No.: 83-S322-5&6&7
UPA Citation: N/A
Relevant Bills: H.R. 85 (96th Cong.), H.R. 4566 (96th Cong.), H.R. 4571 (96th
          Cong.), H.R. 7020 (96th Cong.), S. 1325 (96th Cong.), S. 1341 (96th
          Cong.), S. 1480 (96th Cong.)

This is a legislative history of the Comprehensive Environmental Response,
Compensation, and Liability Act of 1980 (Superfund). The Table of Contents
includes a guide to texts of bills and amendments. The history begins with
the text of P.L. 96-510 and the President's remarks on signing H.R. 7020 into
law. It contains S. 1480 as introduced and reported. S. 1480 was substituted
for the language of H.R. 7020 and this bill was passed by both Houses. The
history contains the Administration testimony on S. 1480 excerpted from
1979 Senate hearings on the bill. The history provides the Senate report and
the Senate and House debate. It gives H.R. 7020 as introduced, as reported,
and as passed by the House. The history also includes the House report on
H.R. 7020, as well as the House debate on this bill. The history provides
legislative history materials on the related bill H.R. 85 (96th Cong.) as
introduced, as reported, and as passed by the House. The history gives the
House report and debate on this bill. Appendix I and Appendix II to the
history include the texts of additional bills and printed amendments.
Appendix III consists of statements inserted into the *Congressional Record*
after the final passage of H.R. 7020. Appendix IV is a bibliography of the
relevant Congressional documents: hearings, reports, committee prints,
and miscellaneous documents. The history concludes with a table and a
section-by-section index. The table compares the sections of P.L. 96-510, S.
1480 as reported, H.R. 7020 as passed by the House, H.R. 7020 as reported,
H.R. 85 as passed by the House, and H.R. 85 as reported. The Section-by-
Section Index lists the relevant Congressional documents for each section
of P.L. 96-510 and where the relevant passages appear in the pages of the
legislative history.

Record No.: 250
Public Law No.: 96-586
Bill No.: H.R. 7306 (96th Cong.)
Statutes at Large Citation: 94 Stat. 3381 (1980)
Title of Act: To Provide for the Orderly Disposal of Certain Other Federal
Lands in Nevada and for the Acquisition of Certain Other
Lands in the Lake Tahoe Basin

Title of Legislative History: Legislative History of Lake Tahoe Preservation
Act (H.R. 7306) (Public Law 96-586), 96th Cong.,
2nd Sess. (Comm. Print 1980)
Publication Date: 1981
Author: Subcommittee on National Parks and Insular Affairs, House
Committee on Interior and Insular Affairs
Pages: v, 115

L/C Card Number: 81-601826
OCLC No.: 7502577
SuDoc No.: Y4.In8/14:L52/3
CIS No.: 81-H442-5
UPA Citation: N/A
Relevant Bills: H.R. 7306 (96th Cong.), H.R. 8235 (96th Cong.)

The legislative history documents concerning the preservation of the Lake
Tahoe area includes several versions of H.R. 7306 (96th Cong.), as well as
the House and Senate reports on this bill. The report of the Department
of the Interior on H.R. 7306 is given. The history includes the House
and Senate consideration and passage of H.R. 7306. In addition, the history
contains post-enactment statements from the House and Senate floors
concerning the meaning of H.R. 7306. The text of the related law, the 1980
Amendment to the Tahoe Regional Planning Compact, H.R. 8235, P.L. 96-
551, is also provided.

Record No.: 251
Public Law No.: 97-37
Bill No.: H.R. 1100 (97th Cong.)
Statutes at Large Citation: 95 Stat. 935 (1981)
Title of Act: Former Prisoner of War Benefits Act of 1981

Title of Legislative History: Former Prisoners of War Benefits Act of 1981:
Hearing on S. 251, S. 468, S. 670 and Related
Bills Before the Senate Committee on Veterans'
Affairs, 97th Cong., 1st sess. (1981)
Publication Date: 1981
Author: Senate Committee on Veterans' Affairs
Pages: iv, 398

L/C Card Number: 81-603730
OCLC No.: 7996399
SuDoc No.: Y4.V64/4:F76/981
CIS No.: 81-S761-13
UPA Citation: N/A
Relevant Bills: H.R. 1100 (97th Cong.), S. 251 (97th Cong.), S. 468 (97th
    Cong.), S. 670 (97th Cong.)

The appendices to these hearings comprise a legislative history of the
Former Prisoner of War Benefits Act of 1981. The history includes H.R.
1100 and the related bill S. 468, both as reported from committee. The
history provides the House report on H.R. 1100 (97th Cong.), as well as
excerpts from the Senate report on S. 468 (97th Cong.). The Senate action is
given. The appendices conclude with the text of P.L. 97-37. The hearing
itself includes the texts of S. 251 (97th Cong.), S. 468 (97th Cong.) and S. 670
(97th Cong.), all as referred to committee. The hearings materials
document the testimony, written statements, and questions and answers on
these bills.

Record No.: 252
Public Law No.: 98-473
Bill No.: H.R.J. Res. 648 (98th Cong.)
Statutes at Large Citation: 98 Stat. 1837 (1984)
Title of Act: Victims of Crime Act of 1984

Title of Legislative History: Indexed Legislative History of the Victims of
                                Crime Act of 1984
Publication Date: 1985
Author: Department of Justice, Office of Justice Programs, Office of
General Counsel
Pages: xxi, 231

L/C Card Number: 85-602933
OCLC No.: 12675358
SuDoc No.: J1.2:In2/10
CIS No.: N/A
UPA Citation: N/A
Relevant Bills: H.R. 3498 (98th Cong.), H.R. 5124 (98th Cong.), H.R. 5690
    (98th Cong.), H.R.J. Res. 648 (98th Cong.), S. 2423 (98th Cong..)

This is a legislative history of the Victims of Crime Act of 1984, Title II,
Chapter XIV. All of Title II of P.L. 98-473 is called the Comprehensive
Crime Control Act of 1984. The history is preceded by a section-by-section
index to the Act. For each section of the Act, the index lists the relevant
Congressional documents and where their relevant passages appear in the
pages of the history. The history contains the legislative history materials
in the chronological order of their publication. The history begins with the

text of the Final Report of the President's Task Force on Victims of Crime. The history continues with the text of S. 2423 as introduced and reported, as well as the Senate report and debate on this bill. The history includes the text of the compromise bill H.R. 5690 (98th Cong.) as introduced, as well as House debate. The history provides the text of the Conference bill (H.R.J. Res 648) as introduced, as well as House and Senate debate. The history concludes with the text of the Victims of Crime Act of 1984.

Record No.: 253
Public Law No.: 99-499
Bill No.: H.R. 2005 (99th Cong.)
Statutes at Large Citation: 100 Stat. 1613 (1986)
Title of Act: Superfund Amendments and Reauthorization Act of 1986

Title of Legislative History: A Legislative History of the Superfund Amendments and Reauthorization Act of 1986 (Public Law 99-499): Together with a Section-By-Section Index, 101st Cong., 2nd Sess. (Comm. Print 1990)
Publication Date: 1990
Author: Senate Committee on the Environment and Public Works
Pages: xvi, 5704

L/C Card Number: 90-602790
OCLC No.: 22736298
SuDoc No.: Y4.P96/10:S.Prt. 101-120/v.1-7
CIS No.: 90-S322-3&4&5&6&7&8&9
UPA Citation: N/A
Relevant Bills: H.R. 2005 (99th Cong.), H.R. 2817 (99th Cong.), H.R. 3852 (99th Cong.), S. 51 (99th Cong.)

This is a legislative history of the Superfund Amendments and Reauthorization Act (SARA) of 1986. The prefatory material includes a concise summary of P.L. 99-499's convoluted history. The history begins with the text of P.L. 99-499 as passed. Next, the history presents legislative history materials on S. 51, the main Senate Superfund amendments bill. This includes text of the Bill, Committee Reports, and debates. Also included is a Joint Committee on Taxation committee print which summarizes various Senate bills' approaches to financing Superfund. Since tax bills must originate in the House, the Senate substituted the text of S. 51 into H.R. 2005. The history provides the text of H.R. 2005 as passed by the Senate. The history gives the text of H.R. 2817 as introduced, as reported (from five House committees), and the reports from these committees on S. 51. A Joint Committee on Taxation committee print which summarizes various House bills' approaches to financing Superfund is added. The third division of documents presents materials on the compromise, i.e.. clean bill H.R. 3852. The House debate and substituted language is given, with the text as passed set out. The history cites to all the included Congressional hearings, reports, and debates. The appendices to the history include an appendix containing statements inserted into the *Congressional Record* after SARA's passage which commented upon or clarified certain SARA provisions. The history concludes with a Section-by-Section Index.

Record No.: 254
Public Law No.: 100-4
Bill No.: H.R. 1 (100th Cong.)
Statutes at Large Citation: 101 Stat. 7 (1987)
Title of Act: Water Quality Act of 1987

Title of Legislative History: A Legislative History of the Water Quality Act of 1987 (Public Law 100-4): Including Public Law 97-440; Public Law 97-117; Public Law 96-483; and Public Law 96-148 Together with a Section-by-Section Index, 100th Cong., 2nd Sess. (Comm. Print 1988)

Publication Date: 1988
Author: Senate Committee on the Environment and Public Works
Pages: xii, 2768

L/C Card Number: 89-601375
OCLC No.: 19003432
SuDoc No.: Y4.P96/10:S.Prt. 100-144/v.1-4
CIS No.: 88-S322-4&5&6&7
UPA Citation: N/A
Relevant Bills: S. 901 (96th Cong.), S. 2725 (96th Cong.), H.R. 4503 (97th Cong.), H.R. 7159 (97th Cong.), H.R. 3282 (98th Cong.), S. 431 (98th Cong.), S. 2006 (98th Cong.), H.R. 1 (100th Cong.)

This is a legislative history of the Water Quality Act of 1987 and four earlier water pollution control acts: 1983 amendments to the Federal Water Pollution Control Act (FWPCA), H.R. 7159 (97th Cong.), P.L. 97-440; Municipal Wastewater Treatment Construction Grant Amendments of 1981, H.R. 4503 (97th Cong.), P.L. 97-117; 1980 amendments to the FWPCA, S. 2725 (96th Cong.), P.L. 96-483; and 1979 amendments to the Clean Water Act of 1977, S. 901 (96th Cong.), P.L. 96-148. The history begins with the text of the FWPCA as amended, as well as the text of P.L. 100-4 itself. The history includes the Senate and House debate on H.R. 1 (100th Cong.), the President's message upon vetoing H.R. 1 (100th Cong.) as passed by Congress, and the Senate's and House's debate upon overriding the veto. H.R. 1 (100th Cong.) was identical to proposed legislation passed unanimously by the 99th Congress, but vetoed by the President. Next, the history presents materials on the legislation proposed in the 99th Congress,

H.R. 8 (99th Cong.) and S. 1128 (99th Cong.). The history includes the texts of H.R. 8 and S. 1128 as reported, as well as the House and Senate reports and debate on these bills. The history provides the Conference report on S. 1128 and the House's and Senate's debate and passage of the Conference report, as well as the President's message upon his pocket veto. For each of the earlier public laws, the documents of the text of the law, Congressional debate, and Congressional bills as reported. For some of the applicable public laws, the history includes Administration testimony excerpted from applicable Congressional hearings. The reports retain their original pagination, but the hearings do not. For the debate, the history provides citations to the daily or bound *Congressional Record*. A Section-by-Section Index is added.

Record No.: 255
Public Law No.: 100-379
Bill No.: S. 2527 (100th Cong.)
Statutes at Large Citation: 102 Stat. 890 (1988)
Title of Act: Worker Adjustment and Retraining Notification Act

Title of Legislative History: Legislative History of S. 2527, 100th Congress, Worker Adjustment and Retraining Notification Act, Public Law 100-379, 101st Cong., 2nd Sess (Comm. Print 1990)
Publication Date: 1990
Author: Subcommittee on Labor-Management Relations, House Committee on Education and Labor
Pages: iii, 847

L/C Card Number: 90-600644
OCLC No.: 21186014
SuDoc No.: Y4.Ed 8/1:101-K
CIS No.: 90-H342-1
UPA Citation: N/A
Relevant Bills: H.R. 1616 (99th Cong.), H.R. 3 (100th Cong.), H.R. 1122 (100th Cong.), S. 538 (100th Cong.), S. 1420 (100th Cong.), S. 2527 (100th Cong.)

The legislative history of the Worker Adjustment and Retraining Notification Act (WARN) begins with the text of the act. It includes the regulations promulgated under WARN, with the cites to the *Federal Register*. The history includes the Senate and House debates and votes on S. 2527 and the text of the bill as introduced. Historical information on the vetoed H.R. 3 with its plant closing notification provisions is provided. The President's veto message, the Senate debate on sustaining the Veto, and the House debate on the overriding the Veto are given. Documents from the earlier Senate debate action on S. 1420 are included. The text of H.R. 1122 and S. 538 are set out along with the other legislative history materials.

Record No.: 256
Public Law No.: 101-336
Bill No.: S. 933 (101st Cong.)
Statutes at Large Citation: 104 Stat. 327 (1990)
Title of Act: Americans with Disabilities Act of 1990

Title of Legislative History: Legislative History of Public Law 101-336, the
                                Americans with Disabilities Act, 101st Cong.,
                                2nd Sess. (Comm. Print 1990)
Publication Date: 1990
Author: House Committee on Education and Labor
Pages: 924; 925-1819; 1821-3081

L/C Card Number: 91-600580
OCLC No.: 23368329
SuDoc No.: Y4.Ed 8/1:102-A, B, & C
CIS No.: 91-H342-1&2&3
UPA Citation: N/A
Relevant Bills: H.R. 4498 (100th Cong.), S. 2345 (100th Cong.), H.R. 2273
   (101st Cong.), S. 933 (101st Cong.)

This is a three volume legislative history of the Americans with Disabilities
Act of 1990, S. 933 (101st Cong.), P.L. 101-336. Volume One contains the text
of the relevant Congressional reports, the Conference and Senate reports,
the House report and the relevant Congressional debates. The full text of
each report is reproduced, including its title page. In addition, Volume One
contains the texts of the regulations, statutes, and court cases which were
cited in the Congressional reports. All citations are to primary source
materials. A time table of the effective dates of the sections of the Act is
added. It concludes with the text of various tax statutes as amended by P.L.
101-336. Volumes Two and Three contain the text of ten hearings on S. 933
(101st Cong.) and H.R. 2273 (101st Cong.) and similar bills from the
previous Congress, H.R. 4498 (100th Cong.) and S. 2345 (100th Cong.).
These hearings were held between September 1988 and September 1989
before several committees, but most often before the Subcommittee on Select
Education of the House Committee on Education and Labor. The full text of
each hearing is reproduced including its title page.

Record No.: 257
Public Law No.: 101-433
Bill No.: S. 1511 (101st Cong.)
Statutes at Large Citation: 104 Stat. 978 (1990)
Title of Act: Older Workers Benefit Protection Act

Title of Legislative History: Legislative History of the Older Workers
                                Benefit Protection Act (S. 1511 and Related
                                Bills), 102nd Cong., 1st Sess. (Comm. Print
                                1991)

Publication Date: 1991
Author: Senate Committee on Labor and Human Resources
Pages: iv, 711; iv, 711-1266

L/C Card Number: 91-601752
OCLC No.: 24114183
SuDoc No.: Y4.L11/4: S.Prt. 102-33/Pt.1-2
CIS No.: 91-S542-3&4
UPA Citation: N/A
Relevant Bills: H.R. 1432 (101st Cong.), H.R. 3200 (101st Cong.), H.R. 5759
    (101st Cong.), S. 54 (101st Cong.), S. 1511 (101st Cong.)

The two volume legislative history of the Older Workers Benefit Protection
Act begins with the text of the Act. It provides all the components of a
legislative history across the 101st Congress related to the Act. Included
with the history are the texts of September 1989 Senate and House hearings
on age discrimination in employee benefit plans. The hearings are fully
reproduced, including their title pages with the appropriate Tables of
Contents. The history also includes the texts of S. 1511 (101st Cong.) and
H.R. 3200 (101st Cong.) as introduced. The history then covers the earlier
bills S. 54 (101st Cong.) and H.R. 1432 (101st Cong.). The history includes the
House report on H.R. 1432, Senate report on S. 54, and the April and March
1989 House and Senate hearings on waiving rights under the ADEA.

Author Index

Author	Record Number
Bates, Dorothy M., Congressional Research Service	183
Berg, Richard K., Office of the Chairman, Administrative Conference of the United States	190
Berger, Caruthers	016
Berger, Caruthers	028
Bird, David, Congressional Research Service	055
Boehlert, C. Richard, Office of Saline Water, Department of Interior	073
Bogsch, Arpad	027
Caudill, Christopher K., Environment and Natural Resources Policy Division, Congressional Research Service	099
Celada, Raymond J., Legislative Reference Service	097
Celada, Raymond J., Legislative Reference Service	098
Chilson, Hatfield	004
Civil Aeronautics Administration, Department of Commerce	062
Congressional Budget Office	147
Congressional Budget Office, LePoer, Barbara	159
Congressional Budget Office, LePoer, Ken	159
Congressional Research Service	077
Congressional Research Service	152
Congressional Research Service	223
Congressional Research Service, American Law Division, Ackerman, David M.	076
Congressional Research Service, American Law Division, Weimer, Douglas Reid	101

Author	Record Number
Congressional Research Service, Environmental Policy Division, Simmons, Malcolm M.	218
Congressional Research Service, Fiori, Patricia	055
Congressional Research Service, Fulton, Joseph F.	043
Congressional Research Service, Gay, Donovan	105
Congressional Research Service, Giordano-Evans, Angela M.	029
Congressional Research Service, Gravelle, Jane G.	175
Congressional Research Service, Hanus, Jerome J.	105
Congressional Research Service, Hughes, Steve	127
Congressional Research Service, Kohnen, Harold A.	175
Congressional Research Service, Kramer, Donna S.	220
Congressional Research Service, McBreen, Maureen	197
Congressional Research Service, McMurtry, Virginia A.	135
Congressional Research Service, Moore, Charlotte J.	245
Congressional Research Service, Natural Resources Policy Division, Copeland, Claudia	171
Congressional Research Service, Ocean and Coastal Resources Project, Lee, Martin R.	141
Congressional Research Service, Ocean and Coastal Resources Project, Zilberberg, Mark	184
Congressional Research Service, Proskauer, Martha S.	143
Congressional Research Service, Raiford,William N.	206
Congressional Research Service, Relyea, Harold C.	189
Congressional Research Service, Relyea, Harold C.	191
Congressional Research Service, Schick, Allen	160
Congressional Research Service, Science Policy Research Division	139

Author	Record Number
Congressional Research Service, Science Policy Research Division	165
Congressional Research Service, Science Policy Research Division	166
Congressional Research Service, Science Policy Research Division	169
Congressional Research Service, Science Policy Research Division	172
Congressional Research Service, Science Policy Research Division	192
Congressional Research Service, Scott, Marcia	108
Congressional Research Service, Stedman, James B.	236
Congressional Research Service, Sullivan, John H.	148
Congressional Research Service, Wason, James R.	047
Congressional Research Service, Williams, Grover S.	066
Congressional Research Service, Yadlosky, Elizabeth	055
Congressional Research Service, Zaritsky, Howard M.	079
Consultant to the Senate Special Committee on Aging, Rosenblum, Marc	122
Conway, Margaret M., Legislative Reference Service	075
Conway, Margaret M., Legislative Reference Service	084
Cooper, Edith Fairman, Congressional Research Service	183
Copeland, Claudia, Environment and Natural Resources Policy Division, Congressional Research Service	254
Copeland, Claudia, Natural Resources Policy Division, Congressional Research Service	171
Corry, Catherine S., Legislative Reference Service	039
Corry, Catherine S., Legislative Reference Service	071
Coulter, Raymond C., Office of Saline Water, Department of Interior	073

Author	Record Number
Dunne, Elizabeth K.	017
Edwards, Victor L.	074
Edwards, Victor L., Legislative Reference Service	034
Edwards, Victor L., Legislative Reference Service	070
Energy Research and Development Administration, Prosser, Shelly G.	182
Energy Research and Development Administration, Stechschule, M. Joey	182
Environment and Natural Resources Policy Division, Congressional Research Service	155
Environment and Natural Resources Policy Division, Congressional Research Service	196
Environment and Natural Resources Policy Division, Congressional Research Service, Caudill, Christopher K.	099
Environment and Natural Resources Policy Division, Congressional Research Service, Copeland, Claudia	254
Environment and Natural Resources Policy Division, Congressional Research Service, Hagen, Lillian S.	253
Environment and Natural Resources Policy Division, Congressional Research Service, Reisch, Mark E. Anthony	249
Environment and Natural Resources Policy Division, Congressional Research Service, Viessman, Warren	099
Environmental Policy Division, Congressional Research Service	130
Environmental Policy Division, Congressional Research Service	137
Environmental Policy Division, Congressional Research Service	156
Environmental Policy Division, Congressional Research Service	209
Environmental Policy Division, Congressional Research Service, Reisch, Mark E. Anthony	107

Author	Record Number
House Committee on Foreign Affairs	148
House Committee on Government Operations	189
House Committee on Government Operations	199
House Committee on Government Operations, Subcommittee on Commerce, Consumer, and Monetary Affairs	226
House Committee on Government Operations, Subcommittee on Environment, Energy, and Natural Resources	181
House Committee on Government Operations, Subcommittee on Foreign Operations and Government Information	111
House Committee on Government Operations, Subcommittee on Government Information and Individual Rights	081
House Committee on Government Operations, Subcommittee on Government Information and Individual Rights	170
House Committee on Government Operations, Subcommittee on Government Information and Individual Rights	173
House Committee on Government Operations, Subcommittee on Government Information and Individual Rights	238
House Committee on House Administration	173
House Committee on Interior and Insular Affairs	004
House Committee on Interior and Insular Affairs, Subcommittee on National Parks and Insular Affairs	221
House Committee on Interior and Insular Affairs, Subcommittee on National Parks and Insular Affairs	230
House Committee on Interior and Insular Affairs, Subcommittee on National Parks and Insular Affairs	239
House Committee on Interior and Insular Affairs, Subcommittee on National Parks and Insular Affairs	244

Author	Record Number
House Committee on Interior and Insular Affairs, Subcommittee on National Parks and Insular Affairs	250
House Committee on International Relations, Subcommittee on International Trade and Commerce	030
House Committee on Interstate and Foreign Commerce	035
House Committee on Interstate and Foreign Commerce	176
House Committee on Interstate and Foreign Commerce	196
House Committee on Interstate and Foreign Commerce, Counsel to the Special Subcommittee on Investigations, Manelli, David J.	038
House Committee on Interstate and Foreign Commerce, Special Subcommittee on Investigations	038
House Committee on Interstate and Foreign Commerce, Subcommittee on Communications	052
House Committee on Merchant Marine and Fisheries	051
House Committee on Post Office and Civil Service	149
House Committee on Post Office and Civil Service	193
House Committee on Post Office and Civil Service	227
House Committee on Public Works and Transportation	231
House Committee on Science and Technology, Subcommittee on Advanced Energy Technologies and Energy Conservation Research, Development, and Demonstration	165
House Committee on Science and Technology, Subcommittee on Advanced Energy Technologies and Energy Conservation Research, Development, and Demonstration	166
House Committee on Science and Technology, Subcommittee on Advanced Energy Technologies and Energy Conservation Research, Development, and Demonstration	169

Author	Record Number
House Committee on Ways and Means	109
House Committee on Ways and Means	110
House Committee on Ways and Means	114
House Committee on Ways and Means	116
House Committee on Ways and Means	117
House Committee on Ways and Means	118
House Committee on Ways and Means	120
House Committee on Ways and Means	121
House Committee on Ways and Means	214
House Committee on Ways and Means, Subcommittee on Social Security	246
Hubbard, F. Morse, Counsel to the Joint Committee on Internal Revenue Taxation	080
Hughes, Steve, Congressional Research Service	127
Jibrin, Barbara H., Legislative Reference Service	039
Joint Committee on Internal Revenue Taxation	080
Kaminstein, Abraham L.	010
Kaplan, Benjamin, Dr.	015
Klitzman, Stephen H., Office of the Chairman, Administrative Conference of the United States	190
Kohnen, Harold A., Congressional Research Service	175
Kramer, Donna S., Congressional Research Service	220
Latman, Alan	012
Latman, Alan	020
Law Enforcement Assistance Administration	131
Law Enforcement Assistance Administration, Department of Justice, Office of General Counsel	123

Author	Record Number
McBreen, Maureen, Congressional Research Service	197
McMurtry, Virginia A., Congressional Research Service	135
Moore, Charlotte J., Congressional Research Service	245
Morton, Perry W.	004
National Commission on Product Safety	112
National Institute of Law Enforcement and Criminal Justice	003
National Labor Relations Board	048
National Labor Relations Board	049
National Labor Relations Board	064
National Labor Relations Board, Office of the General Counsel, Division of Law	087
Natural Resources Policy Division, Congressional Research Service, Copeland, Claudia	171
New York University Law Review	007
Ocean and Coastal Resources Project, Congressional Research Service, Lee, Martin R.	141
Ocean and Coastal Resources Project, Congressional Research Service, Zilberberg, Mark	184
Office of General Counsel, Department of Justice, Office of Justice Assistance, Research, and Statistics, Greenwood, Karen S.	243
Office of General Counsel, Federal Alcohol Control Administration, Russell, W.A.	050
Office of General Counsel, Law Enforcement Assistance Administration, Department of Justice	123
Office of General Counsel, Law Enforcement Assistance Administration, Department of Justice	145
Office of General Counsel, Law Enforcement Assistance Administration, Department of Justice	167

Author	Record Number
Office of General Counsel, Law Enforcement Assistance Administration, Department of Justice	210
Office of General Counsel, Office of Justice Programs, Department of Justice	252
Office of Human Development Services, Department of Health, Education, and Welfare, Administration on Aging	104
Office of Justice Assistance, Research, and Statistics, Department of Justice	210
Office of Justice Assistance, Research, and Statistics, Department of Justice, Office of General Counsel, Greenwood, Karen S.	243
Office of Justice Programs, Department of Justice, Office of General Counsel	252
Office of Legislative Counsel, Senate	035
Office of Legislative Services, Food and Drug Administration	072
Office of Operational Policy and Procedures, Social Security Administration, Office of Regulations, Divison of Technical Documents and Privacy, Technical Documents Branch	217
Office of Regulations, Social Security Administration, Office of Operational Policy and Procedures, Division of Technical Documents and Privacy, Technical Documents Branch	217
Office of Saline Water, Department of Interior	073
Office of Saline Water, Department of Interior, Boehlert, C. Richard	073
Office of Saline Water, Department of Interior, Coulter, Raymond C.	073
Office of the Chairman, Administrative Conference of the United States	190
Office of the Chairman, Administrative Conference of the United States, Berg, Richard K.	190
Office of the Chairman, Administrative Conference of the United States, Klitzman, Stephen H.	190

Author	Record Number
Office of the General Counsel, National Labor Relations Boards, Division of Law	087
Office of the Solicitor, Department of Labor	086
Office of the Solicitor, Department of Labor, Division of Labor-Management Laws	088
Office of the Solicitor, Department of Labor, Division of Wage Determinations	042
Office of the Solicitor, Department of Labor, Randle, Claire	093
Partridge, Anthony, Federal Judicial Center	174
Proskauer, Martha S., Congressional Research Service	143
Prosser, Shelley G., Energy Research and Development Administration	182
Public Health Service, Department of Health, Education, and Welfare, Food and Drug Administration	054
Public Land Law Review Commission	001
Raiford, William N., Congressional Research Service	206
Railroad Retirement Board, Schreiber, David B.	053
Randle, Claire, Office of the Solicitor, Department of Labor	093
Reisch, Mark E. Anthony, Environment and Natural Resources Policy Division, Congressional Research Service	249
Reisch, Mark E. Anthony, Environmental Policy Division, Congressional Research Service	107
Relyea, Harold C., Congressional Research Service	189
Relyea, Harold C., Congressional Research Service	191
Ringer, Barbara A.	021
Ringer, Barbara A.	026
Rosenblum, Marc, Consultant to the Senate Special Committee on Aging	122

Author	Record Number
Russell, W.A., Office of General Counsel, Federal Alcohol Control Administration	050
Schick, Allen, Congressional Research Service	160
Schreiber, David B., Railroad Retirement Board	053
Schwaneberg, Robert, Federal Judicial Center	069
Science Policy Research Division, Congressional Research Service	139
Science Policy Research Division, Congressional Research Service	165
Science Policy Research Division, Congressional Research Service	166
Science Policy Research Division, Congressional Research Service	169
Science Policy Research Division, Congressional Research Service	172
Science Policy Research Division, Congressional Research Service	192
Scott, Marcia, Congressional Research Service	108
Select Subcommittee to Review WASP Bills, House Committee on Veterans' Affairs	057
Selective Service System	056
Senate Committee on Agriculture, Nutrition, and Forestry	162
Senate Committee on Agriculture, Nutrition, and Forestry	224
Senate Committee on Agriculture, Nutrition, and Forestry	225
Senate Committee on Agriculture, Nutrition, and Forestry, Subcommittee on Foreign Agricultural Policy	077
Senate Committee on Appropriations, Subcommittee on Treasury, Postal Service, and General Government	083
Senate Committee on Banking and Currency	041

Author	Record Number
Senate Committee on Banking, Housing, and Urban Affairs, Subcommittee on Securities	046
Senate Committee on Commerce	090
Senate Committee on Commerce	141
Senate Committee on Commerce	184
Senate Committee on Commerce, Science, and Transportation	185
Senate Committee on Energy and Natural Resources	202
Senate Committee on Energy and Natural Resources	203
Senate Committee on Energy and Natural Resources, Subcommittee on Energy and Mineral Resources	033
Senate Committee on Energy and Natural Resources, Subcommittee on Energy Conservation and Supply	061
Senate Committee on Finance, Subcommittee on Taxation and Debt Management Generally	060
Senate Committee on Foreign Relations	223
Senate Committee on Government Operations	157
Senate Committee on Government Operations	173
Senate Committee on Government Operations	189
Senate Committee on Government Operations	191
Senate Committee on Governmental Affairs	234
Senate Committee on Governmental Affairs	241
Senate Committee on Governmental Affairs, Subcommittee on Civil Service and General Services	083
Senate Committee on Governmental Affairs, Subcommittee on Energy, Nuclear Proliferation, and Federal Services	135
Senate Committee on Governmental Affairs, Subcommittee on Energy, Nuclear Proliferation, and Federal Services	220

Author	Record Number
Senate Committee on Human Resources	185
Senate Committee on Human Resources, Subcommittee on Aging	180
Senate Committee on Human Resources, Subcommittee on Labor	216
Senate Committee on Interior and Insular Affairs	076
Senate Committee on Interior and Insular Affairs, Subcommittee on Energy Research and Water Resources	099
Senate Committee on Labor and Human Resources	215
Senate Committee on Labor and Human Resources	235
Senate Committee on Labor and Human Resources	257
Senate Committee on Labor and Public Welfare	113
Senate Committee on Labor and Public Welfare	125
Senate Committee on Labor and Public Welfare	126
Senate Committee on Labor and Public Welfare, Subcommittee on Labor	036
Senate Committee on Labor and Public Welfare, Subcommittee on Labor	037
Senate Committee on Labor and Public Welfare, Subcommittee on Labor	065
Senate Committee on Labor and Public Welfare, Subcommittee on Labor	129
Senate Committee on Labor and Public Welfare, Subcommittee on Labor	133
Senate Committee on Labor and Public Welfare, Subcommittee on Labor	136
Senate Committee on Labor and Public Welfare, Subcommittee on Labor	140
Senate Committee on Labor and Public Welfare, Subcommittee on Labor	146

Author	Record Number
Senate Committee on Labor and Public Welfare, Subcommittee on Labor	154
Senate Committee on Labor and Public Welfare, Subcommittee on Labor	161
Senate Committee on Labor and Public Welfare, Subcommittee on Labor	164
Senate Committee on Post Office and Civil Service	128
Senate Committee on Post Office and Civil Service	178
Senate Committee on Public Works	107
Senate Committee on Public Works	130
Senate Committee on Public Works	137
Senate Committee on Public Works	139
Senate Committee on Public Works	155
Senate Committee on Public Works	156
Senate Committee on Rules and Administration	032
Senate Committee on the District of Columbia	138
Senate Committee on the District of Columbia	151
Senate Committee on the District of Columbia	188
Senate Committee on the Environment and Public Works	101
Senate Committee on the Environment and Public Works	152
Senate Committee on the Environment and Public Works	171
Senate Committee on the Environment and Public Works	204
Senate Committee on the Environment and Public Works	208
Senate Committee on the Environment and Public Works	209

Author	Record Number
Senate Committee on the Judiciary, Subcommittee on Patents, Trademarks, and Copyrights	010
Senate Committee on the Judiciary, Subcommittee on Patents, Trademarks, and Copyrights	011
Senate Committee on the Judiciary, Subcommittee on Patents, Trademarks, and Copyrights	012
Senate Committee on the Judiciary, Subcommittee on Patents, Trademarks, and Copyrights	013
Senate Committee on the Judiciary, Subcommittee on Patents, Trademarks, and Copyrights	014
Senate Committee on the Judiciary, Subcommittee on Patents, Trademarks, and Copyrights	015
Senate Committee on the Judiciary, Subcommittee on Patents, Trademarks, and Copyrights	016
Senate Committee on the Judiciary, Subcommittee on Patents, Trademarks, and Copyrights	017
Senate Committee on the Judiciary, Subcommittee on Patents, Trademarks, and Copyrights	018
Senate Committee on the Judiciary, Subcommittee on Patents, Trademarks, and Copyrights	019
Senate Committee on the Judiciary, Subcommittee on Patents, Trademarks, and Copyrights	020
Senate Committee on the Judiciary, Subcommittee on Patents, Trademarks, and Copyrights	021
Senate Committee on the Judiciary, Subcommittee on Patents, Trademarks, and Copyrights	022
Senate Committee on the Judiciary, Subcommittee on Patents, Trademarks, and Copyrights	023
Senate Committee on the Judiciary, Subcommittee on Patents, Trademarks, and Copyrights	024
Senate Committee on the Judiciary, Subcommittee on Patents, Trademarks, and Copyrights	025
Senate Committee on the Judiciary, Subcommittee on Patents, Trademarks, and Copyrights	026

Author	Record Number
Senate Committee on Veterans' Affairs, Subcommittee on Compensation and Pensions	233
Senate Committee on Veterans' Affairs, Subcommittee on Health and Hospitals	179
Senate Committee on Veterans' Affairs, Subcommittee on Health and Hospitals	205
Senate Committee on Veterans' Affairs, Subcommittee on Health and Readjustment	211
Senate Committee on Veterans' Affairs, Subcommittee on Housing and Insurance	187
Senate Committee on Veterans' Affairs, Subcommittee on Housing, Insurance, and Cemeteries	228
Senate Committee on Veterans' Affairs, Subcommittee on Readjustment, Education, and Employment	198
Senate National Ocean Policy Study	141
Senate National Ocean Policy Study	184
Senate Select Committee on Small Business	207
Senate Special Committee on Aging	122
Senate Special Committee on National Emergencies and Delegated Emergency Powers	191
Senate, Office of Legislative Counsel	035
Sharp, Freeman W., American Law Section, Legislative Reference Service	031
Simmons, Malcolm M., Environmental Policy Division, Congressional Research Service	218
Social Security Administration, Office of Operational Policy and Procedures, Office of Regulations, Division of Technical Documents and Privacy, Technical Documents Branch	217
Special Action Office for Drug Abuse Prevention	132
Special Subcommittee on Investigations, House Committee on Interstate and Foreign Commerce	038

Author	Record Number
Stechschulte, M. Joey, Energy Research and Development Administration	182
Stedman, James B., Congressional Research Service	236
Strauss, William S.	018
Strauss, William S.	019
Strauss, William S.	022
Strauss, William S.	024
Subcommittee on Administrative Practice and Procedure, Senate Committee on the Judiciary	119
Subcommittee on Administrative Practice and Procedure, Senate Committee on the Judiciary	153
Subcommittee on Administrative Practice and Procedure, Senate Committee on the Judiciary	170
Subcommittee on Advanced Energy Technologies and Energy Conservation Research, Development, and Demonstration, House Committee on Science and Technology	165
Subcommittee on Advanced Energy Technologies and Energy Conservation Research, Development, and Demonstration, House Committee on Science and Technology	166
Subcommittee on Advanced Energy Technologies and Energy Conservation Research, Development, and Demonstration, House Committee on Science and Technology	169
Subcommittee on Advanced Energy Technologies and Energy Conservation Research, Development, and Demonstration, House Committee on Science and Technology	172
Subcommittee on Advanced Energy Technologies and Energy Conservation Research, Development, and Demonstration, House Committee on Science and Technology	192
Subcommittee on Aging, Senate Committee on Human Resources	180

Author	Record Number
Subcommittee on Citizens and Shareholders Rights and Remedies, Senate Committee on the Judiciary	153
Subcommittee on Civil Service and General Services, Senate Committee on Governmental Affairs	083
Subcommittee on Commerce, Consumer, and Monetary Affairs, House Committee on Government Operations	226
Subcommittee on Communications, House Committee on Interstate and Foreign Commerce	052
Subcommittee on Compensation and Pensions, Senate Committee on Veterans' Affairs	177
Subcommittee on Compensation and Pensions, Senate Committee on Veterans' Affairs	194
Subcommittee on Compensation and Pensions, Senate Committee on Veterans' Affairs	195
Subcommittee on Compensation and Pensions, Senate Committee on Veterans' Affairs	212
Subcommittee on Compensation and Pensions, Senate Committee on Veterans' Affairs	229
Subcommittee on Compensation and Pensions, Senate Committee on Veterans' Affairs	233
Subcommittee on Constitutional Rights, Senate Committee on the Judiciary	201
Subcommittee on Courts, Civil Liberties, and the Administration of Justice, House Committee on the Judiciary	200
Subcommittee on Crime, House Committee on the Judiciary	045
Subcommittee on Economic Stabilization, House Committee on Banking, Finance, and Urban Affairs	068
Subcommittee on Energy and Mineral Resources, Senate Committee on Energy and Natural Resources	033
Subcommittee on Energy Conservation and Supply, Senate Committee on Energy and Natural Resources	061

Author	Record Number
Subcommittee on Housing and Community Development, House Committee on Banking, Finance, and Urban Affairs	213
Subcommittee on Housing and Community Development, House Committee on Banking, Finance, and Urban Affairs	242
Subcommittee on Housing and Insurance, Senate Committee on Veterans' Affairs	187
Subcommittee on Housing, House Committee on Banking and Currency	163
Subcommittee on Housing, Insurance, and Cemeteries, Senate Committee on Veterans' Affairs	228
Subcommittee on International Trade and Commerce, House Committee on International Relations	030
Subcommittee on Labor, Senate Committee on Human Resources	216
Subcommittee on Labor, Senate Committee on Labor and Public Welfare	036
Subcommittee on Labor, Senate Committee on Labor and Public Welfare	037
Subcommittee on Labor, Senate Committee on Labor and Public Welfare	065
Subcommittee on Labor, Senate Committee on Labor and Public Welfare	129
Subcommittee on Labor, Senate Committee on Labor and Public Welfare	133
Subcommittee on Labor, Senate Committee on Labor and Public Welfare	136
Subcommittee on Labor, Senate Committee on Labor and Public Welfare	140
Subcommittee on Labor, Senate Committee on Labor and Public Welfare	146
Subcommittee on Labor, Senate Committee on Labor and Public Welfare	154

Author	Record Number
Subcommittee on Patents, Trademarks, and Copyrights, Senate Committee on the Judiciary	014
Subcommittee on Patents, Trademarks, and Copyrights, Senate Committee on the Judiciary	015
Subcommittee on Patents, Trademarks, and Copyrights, Senate Committee on the Judiciary	016
Subcommittee on Patents, Trademarks, and Copyrights, Senate Committee on the Judiciary	017
Subcommittee on Patents, Trademarks, and Copyrights, Senate Committee on the Judiciary	018
Subcommittee on Patents, Trademarks, and Copyrights, Senate Committee on the Judiciary	019
Subcommittee on Patents, Trademarks, and Copyrights, Senate Committee on the Judiciary	020
Subcommittee on Patents, Trademarks, and Copyrights, Senate Committee on the Judiciary	021
Subcommittee on Patents, Trademarks, and Copyrights, Senate Committee on the Judiciary	022
Subcommittee on Patents, Trademarks, and Copyrights, Senate Committee on the Judiciary	023
Subcommittee on Patents, Trademarks, and Copyrights, Senate Committee on the Judiciary	024
Subcommittee on Patents, Trademarks, and Copyrights, Senate Committee on the Judiciary	025
Subcommittee on Patents, Trademarks, and Copyrights, Senate Committee on the Judiciary	026
Subcommittee on Patents, Trademarks, and Copyrights, Senate Committee on the Judiciary	027
Subcommittee on Patents, Trademarks, and Copyrights, Senate Committee on the Judiciary	028
Subcommittee on Patents, Trademarks, and Copyrights, Senate Committee on the Judiciary	034
Subcommittee on Patents, Trademarks, and Copyrights, Senate Committee on the Judiciary	039

Popular Name Index

Popular Name	Record Number
Agricultural Trade Development and Assistance Act of 1954	077
Agricultural Trade Development and Assistance Act of 1954, Amendment of 1959	077
Agricultural Trade Development and Assistance Act of 1954, Amendment of 1964	077
Agricultural Trade Development and Assistance Act of 1954, Amendment of 1968	077
Agriculture and Consumer Protection Act of 1973	156
Agriculture-Environmental and Consumer Protection Appropriation Act, 1972	144
Agriculture-Environmental and Consumer Protection Appropriation Act, 1973	144
Agriculture-Environmental and Consumer Protection Appropriation Act, 1974	144
Agriculture-Environmental and Consumer Protection Appropriation Act, 1975	156
Air Commerce Act of 1926	035
Air Pollution Control Act	144
Air Pollution Control Act, Amendment of 1959	144
Air Quality Act of 1967	130
Air Quality Act of 1967	144
Airline Deregulation Act of 1978	231
Airport and Airway Development Act of 1970	144
Airport and Airway Development Act of 1970	231
Airport and Airway Development Act of 1970, Amendment of 1971	144
Airport Development Acceleration Act of 1973	144
Alaska Omnibus Act	144
Alaska's Water Pollution Control Amendments	144

Popular Name	Record Number
Amending the Laws Granting Pensions to the Soldiers and Sailors of the War of Eighteen Hundred and Twelve, and their Widows	040
Amending the Statutes of the United States as to Procedure in the Patent Office and in the Courts with Regard to the Granting of Letters Patent for Inventions and with Regard to Interfering Patents	034
Amending the Statutes of the United States as to Procedure in the Patent Office and in the Courts with Regard to the Granting of Letters Patent for Inventions and with Regard to Interfering Patents	075
Amendment to the Act of March 3, 1931, August 30, 1935	144
Amendment to Title 13 U.S. Code	144
Amendments to Interest on Certain Government Obligations, Int. Rev. Code	144
Americans with Disabilities Act of 1990	256
Amortization of Pollution Control Facilities	144
Animal Drug Amendments of 1968	054
Animal Drug Amendments of 1968	144
Anti-Smuggling Act	144
Appalachian Regional Development Act Amendments of 1967	101
Appalachian Regional Development Act Amendments of 1967	144
Appalachian Regional Development Act Amendments of 1969	101
Appalachian Regional Development Act Amendments of 1969	144
Appalachian Regional Development Act Amendments of 1971	101
Appalachian Regional Development Act Amendments of 1971	144
Appalachian Regional Development Act of 1965	101

Popular Name	Record Number
Atomic Energy Act of 1954, Amendment of 1965	144
Atomic Energy Act of 1954, Amendment of 1966	144
Atomic Energy Act of 1954, Amendment of 1967	144
Atomic Energy Act of 1954, Amendment of 1970	144
Atomic Energy Act of 1954, Amendment of 1971	144
Authorization for Fuel and Vehicle Research	144
Authorizing the President, or Such Office or Agency as He May Designate, to Conclude and Give Effect to Agreements for the Settlement of Intercustodial Conflicts Involving Enemy Property	031
Bank Holding Company Act Amendments of 1970	046
Bank Holding Company Act of 1956	046
Banking Act of 1933	046
Bankruptcy Reform Act of 1978	217
Biomass Energy and Alcohol Fuels Act of 1980	247
Black Lung Benefits Act of 1972	126
Black Lung Benefits Act of 1972	140
Black Lung Benefits Reform Act of 1977	219
Black Lung Benefits Revenue Act of 1977	219
Career Compensation Act of 1949	144
Carriers and Employees Tax Act	053
Carriers Taxing Act of 1937	053
Central Intelligence Agency Act of 1949	066
CERCLA	249
Child Protection Act of 1966	112
Child Protection and Toy Safety Act of 1969	112
Civil Aeronautics Act of 1938	085

Popular Name	Record Number
Civil Rights Act of 1964, Title IV	097
Civil Rights Act of 1964, Title VI	098
Civil Rights Act of 1964, Title VII	096
Civil Rights Act of 1964, Title VII	133
Civil Rights Act of 1964, Title XI	096
Civil Rights Attorney's Fees Awards Act 0f 1976	201
Civil Service Reform Act of 1978	227
Clarke-McNary Act (Reforestation)	001
Clean Air Act	130
Clean Air Act	144
Clean Air Act Amendments of 1966	144
Clean Air Act Amendments of 1970	130
Clean Air Act Amendments of 1970	144
Clean Air Act Amendments of 1970	155
Clean Air Act Amendments of 1977	208
Clean Air Act Amendments of 1977	209
Clean Air Act, Amendment of 1962	144
Clean Air Act, Amendment of 1963	144
Clean Air Act, Amendment of 1965	107
Clean Air Act, Amendment of 1969	144
Clean Air Act, Amendment of 1970	144
Clean Air Act, Amendment of 1971	144
Clean Air Act, Amendment of 1973	144
Clean Water Act	254
Clean Water Act of 1977	208

Popular Name	Record Number
Clean Water Act of 1977	218
Clean Water Act of 1977, Amendment of 1979	254
Clean Water Restoration Act of 1966	144
Coastal Zone Management Act Amendments of 1976	141
Coastal Zone Management Act of 1972	141
Coastal Zone Management Act of 1972	144
Coastal Zone Management Act of 1972, Amendment of 1974	141
Codification 5 U.S.C. §301	144
Coinage Act of 1873	002
Color Additive Amendments of 1960	054
Color Additive Amendments of 1960	144
Commerce Department Maritime Programs	144
Commodity Exchange Act	225
Commodity Exchange Act of 1936	226
Commodity Exchange Act of 1936, Amendment of 1947	226
Commodity Exchange Act of 1936, Amendment of 1968	226
Commodity Futures Trading Commission Act of 1974	225
Commodity Futures Trading Commission Act of 1974	226
Communications Act Amendments, 1952	038
Communications Act of 1934	003
Communications Act of 1934	038
Communications Act of 1934	052

Popular Name	Record Number
Copyright Act of 1909	025
Copyright Act of 1909	026
Copyright Act of 1909	027
Copyright Act of 1909	028
Copyright Act of 1909, Amendment of 1912	007
Copyright Act of 1909, Amendment of 1912	018
Copyright Act of 1909, Amendment of 1912	020
Copyright Act of 1909, Amendment of 1940	026
Copyright Act of 1909, Amendment of 1952	014
Copyright Act of 1909, Amendment of 1952	018
Copyright Act of 1909, Amendment of 1952	020
Copyright Act of 1909, Amendment of 1954	006
Copyright Act of 1976, Section 118(e)	200
Court of Appeals Review Act	144
Crime Control Act of 1973	145
Current Tax Payment Act of 1943	058
Customs Enforcement Act of 1935	144
Customs Simplification Act of 1954	144
Davis-Bacon Act	042
Davis-Bacon Act	043
Davis-Bacon Act	044
Davis-Bacon Act	144
Davis-Bacon Act, Amendment of 1935	042
Davis-Bacon Act, Amendment of 1935	043
Davis-Bacon Act, Amendment of 1935	044

Popular Name	Record Number
Davis-Bacon Act, Amendment of 1935	144
Davis-Bacon Act, Amendment of 1960	043
Davis-Bacon Act, Amendment of 1960	044
Davis-Bacon Act, Amendment of 1964	043
Davis-Bacon Act, Amendment of 1964	044
Davis-Bacon Act, Amendment of 1964	095
Davis-Bacon Act, Amendment of 1964	144
Dawes Act (Indian Allotments)	001
Declaring that Certain Acts of Congress, Joint Resolutions, and Proclamations Shall Be Construed as if the War Had Ended and the Present or Existing Emergency Expired	030
Defense Production Act Amendments of 1951	068
Defense Production Act Amendments of 1952	068
Defense Production Act Amendments of 1953	068
Defense Production Act Amendments of 1955	068
Defense Production Act Amendments of 1974	068
Defense Production Act Amendments of 1975	068
Defense Production Act Amendments of 1980	068
Defense Production Act Amendments of 1980	247
Defense Production Act Extension Amendments of 1977	068
Defense Production Act of 1950	068
Defense Production Act of 1950	247
Defense Production Act of 1950, Amendment of 1951	068
Defense Production Act of 1950, Amendment of 1955	068

Popular Name	Record Number
Department of Energy Act of 1978 -- Civilian Applications	172
Department of Energy Organization Act	172
Department of the Interior and Related Agencies Appropriation Act, 1976	182
Department of Transportation Act	144
Desert Land Act of 1877	001
Desert Land Act of 1877	004
Diplomatic Relations Act	223
Disaster Relief Act of 1970	144
Disclosure of Information Act, June 25, 1948	144
District of Columbia Court of Appeals Act	144
District of Columbia Revenue Act of 1947, Amendment f 1974	150
District of Columbia Revenue Act of 1947, Amendment of 1974	151
District of Columbia Self-Government and Governmental Reorganization Act	150
District of Columbia Self-Government and Governmental Reorganization Act	151
District of Columbia Self-Government and Governmental Reorganization Act, Amendment of 1974	150
District of Columbia Self-Government and Governmental Reorganization Act, Amendment of 1974	151
Drug Abuse Control Amendments of 1965	144
Drug Abuse Office and Treatment Act of 1972	132
Drug Amendments of 1962	054
Drug Amendments of 1962	144
Drug Listing Act of 1972	054

Popular Name	Record Number
Dry Milk Solids Act	054
Durham-Humphrey Act (Drug Prescriptions)	054
Durham-Humphrey Act (Drug Prescriptions)	072
Economy Act	040
Education Amendments of 1972	029
Education Amendments of 1972	108
Education Amendments of 1974	029
Electric and Hybrid Vehicle Research, Development, and Demonstration Act of 1976	192
Elementary and Secondary Education Act of 1965, Amendment of 1970	108
Elementary and Secondary Education Act of 1965, Amendment of 1970	144
Elementary and Secondary Education Act of 1965, Amendment of 1974	108
Emergency Banking Relief Act	030
Emergency Livestock Credit Act of 1974	156
Employee Retirement Income Security Act of 1974	164
Employment Stabilization Act of 1931	041
Enactment of Title 5 United States Code, "Government Organization and Employees"	144
Endangered Species Act Amendments of 1978	152
Endangered Species Act of 1973	152
Endangered Species Act of 1973, Amendment of 1976	152
Endangered Species Act of 1973, Amendment of 1977	152
Endangered Species Act of 1973, Amendment of 1979	152

Popular Name	Record Number
Fair Labor Standards Amendments of 1966	113
Fair Labor Standards Amendments of 1974	154
Fair Labor Standards Amendments of 1977	215
Federal Adulterated Food Amendments	144
Federal Advisory Committee Act	135
Federal Airport Act	062
Federal Alcohol Administration Act	050
Federal Anti-Injunction Act	037
Federal Aviation Act of 1958	085
Federal Aviation Act of 1958	144
Federal Aviation Act of 1958	231
Federal Aviation Act of 1958, Amendment of 1977	231
Federal Coal Mine Health and Safety Act of 1969	126
Federal Coal Mine Health and Safety Act of 1969	140
Federal Election Campaign Act Amendments of 1974	168
Federal Election Campaign Act Amendments of 1976	186
Federal Environmental Pesticide Control Act of 1972	144
Federal Food, Drug, and Cosmetic Act	054
Federal Food, Drug, and Cosmetic Act, Amendment of 1941	054
Federal Food, Drug, and Cosmetic Act, Amendment of 1947	054
Federal Food, Drug, and Cosmetic Act, Amendment of 1948	054
Federal Food, Drug, and Cosmetic Act, Amendment of 1949	054

Popular Name	Record Number
Federal Water Pollution Control Act, Amendment of 1973	144
Federal Water Pollution Control Act, Amendment of 1974	144
Federal Water Pollution Control Act, Amendment of 1977	218
Federal Water Pollution Control Act, Amendment of 1980	254
Federal Water Pollution Control Act, Amendment of 1983	254
Federal Water Power Act	004
Federal Water Project Recreation Act	144
Federal Youth Corrections Act	069
Federal-Aid Highway Act of 1968	144
Federal-Aid Highway Act of 1970	144
Federal-Aid Highway Act of 1973	144
Federal-Aid Highway Act of 1973	156
Federal-Aid Highway Amendments of 1974	156
Fine Arts Commission Act	005
First War Powers Act of 1941	030
First War Powers Act of 1941	031
First War Powers Act of 1941, Amendment of 1946	031
Fish and Wildlife Act of 1956, Amendment of 1971	144
Fish and Wildlife Coordination Act	144
Fish and Wildlife Coordination Act, Amendment of 1946	144
Fish and Wildlife Coordination Act, Amendment of 1948	144

Popular Name	Record Number
For the Suppression of Lottery Traffic through National and Interstate Commerce and the Postal Service Subject to the Jurisdiction and Laws of the United States	003
Foreign Assistance Act of 1961	067
Foreign Assistance Act of 1961	144
Foreign Assistance Act of 1961, Amendment of 1966	067
Foreign Assistance Act of 1962	067
Foreign Assistance Act of 1963	067
Foreign Assistance Act of 1963	144
Foreign Assistance Act of 1965	067
Foreign Assistance Act of 1966	067
Foreign Assistance Act of 1967	067
Foreign Assistance Act of 1968	067
Foreign Assistance Act of 1969	067
Foreign Assistance Act of 1971	067
Foreign Assistance Act of 1973	067
Foreign Assistance Act of 1974	067
Foreign Investors Tax Act of 1966	117
Forest and Rangeland Renewable Resources Planning Act of 1974	162
Forest and Rangeland Renewable Resources Research Act of 1978	162
Forest Lieu Lands Act	001
Forest Reserve Homestead Act	001
Former Presidents Act of 1958	083
Former Prisoner of War Benefits Act of 1981	251

Popular Name	Record Number
Government in the Sunshine Act	190
Graduate Public Health Training Amendments of 1964	144
Grain Futures Act	226
Granting Half Pay to Widows or Orphans, Where their Husbands and Fathers have Died of Wounds Received in the Military Service of the United States, in Certain Cases	040
Granting Pensions and Increase of Pensions to Certain Soldiers, Sailors, and Nurses of the War with Spain, the Philippine Insurrection, or the China Relief Expedition	040
Granting Pensions to Certain Enlisted Men, Soldiers, and Officers who Served in the Civil War and the War with Mexico	040
Granting Pensions to Certain Soldiers and Sailors of the War of Eighteen Hundred and Twelve, and the Widows of Deceased Soldiers	040
Granting Pensions to the Soldiers and Sailors of the Mexican War	040
Granting Pensions to the Survivors of the Indian Wars of Eighteen Hundred and Thirty-Two to Eighteen Hundred and Forty-Two, Inclusive, known as the Black Hawk War, Creek War, Cherokee Disturbances, and the Seminole War	040
Granting Relief to Soldiers and Sailors of the War with Spain, Philippine Insurrection, and Chinese Boxer Rebellion Campaign; to Widows, Former Widows, and Dependent Parents of Such Soldiers and Sailors; and to Certain Army Nurses; and to Amend Section 2 of an Act Entitled "An Act to Pension the Survivors of Certain Indian Wars from January 1, 1859, to January, 1891, Inclusive, and for Other Purposes" Approved March 4, 1917	040
Granting the Right of Way to Ditch and Canal Owners over the Public Lands	004
Hatch Act (Political Activity)	055
Hatch Act (Political Activity), Amendment of 1940	055
Hawaii Omnibus Act	144
Hawaii's Water Pollution Control Act Amendments	144

Popular Name	Record Number
Housing Act of 1961	144
Housing Act of 1964	144
Housing and Community Development Act of 1974	163
Housing and Community Development Act of 1977	213
Housing and Community Development Amendments of 1979	242
Housing and Rent Act of 1947	040
Housing and Urban Development Act of 1965	144
Housing and Urban Development Act of 1968	144
Housing and Urban Development Act of 1969	144
Housing and Urban Development Act of 1970	144
Humphrey-Durham Act (Drug Prescriptions)	054
Humphrey-Durham Act (Drug Prescriptions)	072
Implementation of §25 of the Organic Act of Guam	144
Impoundment Control Act of 1974	158
Impoundment Control Act of 1974	159
Impoundment Control Act of 1974	160
In Addition to an Act, Entitled "An Act to Provide for Certain Persons Engaged in the Land and Naval Service of the United States in the Revolutionary War," Passed the Eighteenth Day of March, One Thousand Eight Hundred and Eighteen	040
In Reference to Writs of Error	144
Income Tax Act of 1894	079
Income Tax Act of 1913	079
Independent Offices Appropriation Act, 1955	040
Independent Maximum Rates Per Diem Allowance for Government Employees	144

Popular Name	Record Number
Indian General Allottment Act	001
Individual Income Tax Act of 1944	060
Insecticide Act	144
Interest Equalization Tax Act	100
Interest Equalization Tax Act	106
Interest Equalization Tax Act	121
Interest Equalization Tax Extension Act of 1965	106
Interest Equalization Tax Extension Act of 1965	121
Interest Equalization Tax Extension Act of 1967	121
Interior Department Appropriation Act, 1947	061
Interior Department Appropriation Act, 1948	061
Interior Department Appropriation Act, 1949	061
Interior Department Appropriation Act, 1950	061
Interior Department Appropriation Act, 1951	061
Interior Department Appropriation Act, 1952	061
Interior Department Appropriation Act, 1953	061
Internal Revenue Code of 1939	080
Internal Revenue Code of 1954	080
Internal Revenue Code of 1954, Amendment of 1966	116
Internal Revenue Code of 1954, Amendment of 1966	120
Internal Revenue Code of 1954, Amendment of 1967	120
Internal Revenue Code of 1954, Amendment of 1974	003
Internal Revenue Code of 1954, Amendment of 1978	217

Popular Name	Record Number
Kinkaid Act (Nebraska Homesteads)	001
Labor-Management Relations Act, 1947	037
Labor-Management Relations Act, 1947	064
Labor-Management Relations Act, 1947	065
Labor-Management Relations Act, 1947	087
Labor-Management Relations Act, 1947, Amendment of 1973	146
Labor-Management Relations Act, 1947, Amendment of 1974	161
Labor-Management Reporting and Disclosure Act of 1959	037
Labor-Management Reporting and Disclosure Act of 1959	087
Labor-Management Reporting and Disclosure Act of 1959	088
Land Act of 1796	001
Land Ordinance of 1785	001
Landrum-Griffin Act	037
Landrum-Griffin Act	087
Landrum-Griffin Act	088
Legislative Branch Appropriations Act, 1933	034
Lindbergh Act (Kidnapping)	045
Lindbergh Act (Kidnapping), Amendment of 1934	045
Lindbergh Act (Kidnapping), Amendment of 1936	045
Longshore and Harbor Workers' Compensation Act, Amendment of 1972	140
Longshoremen's and Harbor Workers' Compensation Act, Amendments of 1972	040

Popular Name	Record Number
Making a Repayable Advance to the Hazardous Substance Response Trust Fund	253
Making Appropriations for Sundry Civil Expenses of the Government for the Fiscal Year Ending June Thirtieth, Nineteen Hundred and Eleven	040
Making Appropriations for the Construction, Repair, and Preservation of Certain Public Works on Rivers and Harbors	004
Making Appropriations for the Construction, Repair, and Preservation of Certain Public Works on Rivers and Harbors	144
Making Appropriations for the Naval Service for the Fiscal Year Ending June Thirtieth, Nineteen Hundred and Sixteen	039
Making Further Provision for Military Services during the Late War	040
Marine Protection, Research, and Sanctuaries Act of 1972	144
Marine Protection, Research, and Sanctuaries Act of 1972, Amendment of 1974	156
Marine Resources and Engineering Development Act of 1966	144
Medical Facilities Construction and Modernization Amendments of 1970	144
Medicare-Medicaid Anti-Fraud and Abuse Amendments	142
Medicare-Medicaid Anti-Fraud and Abuse Amendments	214
Medicare-Medicaid Anti-Fraud and Abuse Amendments	217
Merchant Marine Act, 1936	051
Metric Conversion Act of 1975	183
Middle Income Student Assistance Act	236
Military Appropriation Act, 1943	057
Mineral Lands Leasing Act of 1920	001
Mineral Lands Leasing Act of 1920	033
Mines and Mining Act of 1872	001

Popular Name	Record Number
Penicillin Act	054
Pension Act (Civil War)	040
Pension Act (Civil War), Amendment of 1868	040
Pension Act (Civil War), Amendment of 1873	040
Pension Act (Civil War), Amendment of 1916	040
Pension Act (Civil War), Amendment of 1920	040
Pension Act (Revolutionary War), Amendment of 1818	040
Pension Act (Revolutionary War), Amendment of 1823	040
Pension Act (Revolutionary War), Amendment of 1832	040
Pension Act (Spanish-American War)	040
Pension Act (Spanish-American War), Amendment of 1920	040
Pension Act (World War I), Amendment of 1934	040
Pesticide Research Act	144
Phillipine Property Act of 1946	031
Pickett Act (Withdrawals of Public Lands)	001
Placer Mining Act of 1870	001
Poison Prevention Packaging Act of 1970	144
Port and Tanker Safety Act of 1978	208
Postal Reorganization Act	128
Postal Reorganization Act Amendments of 1976	193
Postal Revenue and Federal Salary Act of 1967	144
Postal Service and Federal Employees Salary Act of 1962	144
Powerplant and Industrial Fuel Use Act of 1978	208
Pregnancy Discrimination Act	235
Presidential Election Campaign Fund Act of 1966	117

Popular Name	Record Number
Presidential Election Campaign Fund Act of 1966	120
Presidential Libraries Act	083
Presidential Records Act of 1978	238
Presidential Transition Act of 1963	083
Printing and Binding Act of 1895	028
Privacy Act of 1974	173
Providing Additional Hospital Facilities for Patients of the Bureau of War Risk Insurance and of the Federal Board for Vocational Education, Division of Rehabilitation	040
Providing for the Construction of Demonstration Plants for the Production from Saline or Brackish Waters, of Water Suitable for Agricultural, Industrial, Municipal, and Other Beneficial Consumptive Uses	073
Public Health Service Act	144
Public Health Service Act, Amendment of 1948	144
Public Health Service Act, Amendment of 1958	144
Public Health Service Act, Amendment of 1959	144
Public Health Service Act, Amendment of 1960	144
Public Health Service Act, Amendment of 1962	144
Public Health Service Act, Amendment of 1970	144
Public Health Service Drug Abuse Research Act	144
Public Health Training Grants Act	144
Public Works and Economic Development Act Amendments of 1971	144
Public Works and Economic Development Act of 1965	144
Public Works and Economic Development Act of 1965, Amendment of 1967	144
Quiet Community Act of 1978	208
Radiation Control for Health and Safety Act of 1968	124

Popular Name	Record Number
Radio Act of 1927	038
Railroad Labor Dispute Arbitration Act, Amendment of 1963	037
Railroad Retirement Act	053
Railroad Retirement Act of 1935	053
Railroad Retirement Act of 1937	053
Railroad Retirement Act of 1937, Amendment of 1946	053
Railroad Retirement Act of 1937, Amendment of 1948	053
Railroad Retirement Act of 1937, Amendment of 1951	053
Railroad Retirement Act of 1937, Amendment of 1954	053
Railroad Retirement Act of 1937, Amendment of 1955	053
Railroad Retirement Act of 1937, Amendment of 1956	053
Railroad Retirement Act of 1937, Amendment of 1959	053
Railroad Retirement Act of 1937, Amendment of 1961	053
Railroad Retirement Act of 1937, Amendment of 1963	053
Railroad Retirement Act of 1937, Amendment of 1965	053
Railroad Retirement Act of 1937, Amendment of 1966	053
Railroad Retirement Act of 1937, Amendment of 1968	053
Railroad Retirement Act of 1937, Amendment of 1970	053
Railroad Retirement Act of 1937, Amendment of 1971	053
Railroad Retirement Act of 1937, Amendment of 1972	053
Railroad Retirement Act of 1937, Amendment of 1973	053
Railroad Retirement Act of 1974	053
Railroad Retirement Act of 1974, Amendment of 1975	053
Railroad Retirement Tax Act	053
Railroad Retirement Tax Act, Amendment of 1954	053

Popular Name	Record Number
Railroad Retirement Tax Act, Amendment of 1959	053
Railroad Retirement Tax Act, Amendment of 1963	053
Railroad Retirement Tax Act, Amendment of 1966	053
Railroad Retirement Tax Act, Amendment of 1970	053
Railroad Unemployment Insurance Act	053
Railroad Unemployment Insurance Act, Amendment of 1940	053
Railroad Unemployment Insurance Act, Amendment of 1946	053
Railroad Unemployment Insurance Act, Amendment of 1948	053
Railroad Unemployment Insurance Act, Amendment of 1951	053
Railroad Unemployment Insurance Act, Amendment of 1952	053
Railroad Unemployment Insurance Act, Amendment of 1954	053
Railroad Unemployment Insurance Act, Amendment of 1955	053
Railroad Unemployment Insurance Act, Amendment of 1959	053
Railroad Unemployment Insurance Act, Amendment of 1963	053
Railroad Unemployment Insurance Act, Amendment of 1966	053
Railroad Unemployment Insurance Act, Amendment of 1968	053
Railroad Unemployment Insurance Act, Amendment of 1975	053
Railway Labor Act	036
Railway Labor Act	037

Popular Name	Record Number
Reorganization Plan No. 3 of 1966	144
Reorganization Plan No. 3 of 1970	144
Reorganization Plan No. II of 1939	144
Reorganization Plan No. III of 1940	144
Reorganization Plan No. IV of 1940	144
Repealing Certain Obsolete Provisions of Law Relating to the Naval Service	144
Resource Conservation and Recovery Act of 1976	204
Resource Recovery Act of 1970	107
Resource Recovery Act of 1970	144
Revenue Act of 1918	040
Revenue Act of 1924	079
Revenue Act of 1934	079
Revenue Act of 1962	092
Revenue Act of 1964	094
Revenue Act of 1971	144
Revenue Act of 1978	217
Revenue and Expenditure Control Act of 1968	144
River and Harbor Act of 1886	144
River and Harbor Act of 1890	144
River and Harbor Act of 1910	144
River and Harbor Act of 1970	144
Rivers and Harbors Appropriation Act of 1894	144
Rivers and Harbors Appropriation Act of 1899	144
Rural Development Act of 1972	144
Safe Drinking Water Act	156

Popular Name	Record Number
Solid Waste Disposal Act, Amendment of 1975	156
Special Foreign Assistance Act of 1971	067
Speedy Trial Act Amendments Act of 1979	174
Speedy Trial Act of 1974	174
State and Local Fiscal Assistance Amendments of 1976	197
Sunshine Act	135
Sunshine Act	189
Sunshine Act	190
Superfund Act	249
Superfund Amendments and Reauthorization Act of 1986	253
Supplemental Appropriations Act, 1971	144
Supplemental Appropriations Act, 1974	144
Surface Mining Control and Reclamation Act of 1977	208
Surplus Property Act of 1944	040
Taft-Hartley Act	037
Taft-Hartley Act	064
Taft-Hartley Act	065
Taft-Hartley Act	087
Tahoe Regional Planning Compact Act, Amendment of 1980	250
Tariff Act of 1909	079
Tariff Classification Act of 1962	144
Tax Adjustment Act of 1966	109
Tax Reduction Act of 1975	175
Tax Reduction and Simplification Act of 1977	207
Tax Reduction and Simplification Act of 1977	217

Popular Name	Record Number
Tax Reform Act of 1969	144
Taylor Grazing Act	001
Temporary Extended Railroad Unemployment Insurance Benefits Act of 1961	053
Temporary Extended Railroad Unemployment Insurance Benefits Act of 1961, Amendment of 1963	053
Timber and Stone Act of 1878	001
Timber Culture Act of 1873	001
To Adjust Postal Rates	144
To Amend "An Act Granting the Right of Way to Ditch and Canal Owners over the Public Lands"	004
To Amend an Act Entitled "An Act Making Appropriations for Sundry Civil Expenses of the Government for the Fiscal Year Ending June Thirtieth, Eighteen Hundred and Eighty-Four"	039
To Amend an Act Entitled "An Act to Provide Aid to State or Territorial Homes for the Support of Disabled Soldiers and Sailors of the United States," Approved August 27, 1888, as Amended March 2, 1889	040
To Amend an Act of Congress Approved February 9, 1893 Entitled "An Act to Establish a Court of Appeals for the District of Columbia	144
To Amend an Act Regulating the Height of Buildings in the District of Columbia, Approved June 1, 1910	005
To Amend an Act Regulating the Height of Buildings in the District of Columbia, Approved June 1, 1910, as Amended	005
To Amend an Act Regulating the Height of Buildings in the District of Columbia, Approved June 1, 1910, as Amended by the Act of December 30, 1910	005
To Amend Certain Sections of the Revised Statutes Relating to Lotteries	003
To Amend Chapter 50 of Title 18, United States Code, with Respect to the Transmission of Bets, Wagers, and Related Information	003

Popular Name   **Record Number**

Popular Name   **Record Number**

Popular Name	Record Number

Popular Name	Record Number

Popular Name	Record Number
Veterans' Education and Training Amendments of 1950	040
Veterans' Emergency Housing Act of 1946	040
Veterans' Health Care Amendments of 1979	240
Veterans' Housing Benefits Act of 1978	228
Veterans' Preference Act of 1944	040
Veterans' Readjustment Assistance Act of 1952	040
Victims of Crime Act of 1984	252
Vocational Education Act of 1917	029
Vocational Education Act of 1934	029
Vocational Education Act of 1936	029
Vocational Education Act of 1946	029
Vocational Education Act of 1963	029
Vocational Education Act of 1963, Amendment of 1970	029
Vocational Education Act of 1963, Amendment of 1972	029
Vocational Education Amendments of 1968	029
Vocational Rehabilitation Act of 1918	040
Voting Rights Act Amendments of 1970	105
Voting Rights Act of 1965	105
WAAC Act (Women's Army Auxiliary Corps)	057
WAAC ACT (Women's Army Auxiliary Corps), Amendment of 1942	057
WAC Act (Women's Army Corps)	057
Wagering Tax Act	003
War Claims Act of 1948	031
War Labor Disputes Act	037
War Powers Resolution	148

Popular Name	Record Number
World War Veterans' Act, 1924	040
World War Veterans' Act, 1924, Amendment of 1937	040
World War Veterans' Act, 1928	040
World War Veterans' Paralysis Act	040
Writs of Error Abolished Amendments	144

Congressional Session Index

Public Law   **Record Number**

Public Law	Record Number
45th Cong., 2nd Sess., Ch. 028	040
45th Cong., 2nd Sess., Ch. 150	001
45th Cong., 2nd Sess., Ch. 151	001
45th Cong., 3rd Sess., Ch. 023	040
48th Cong., 1st Sess., Ch. 223	040
49th Cong., 1st Sess., Ch. 022	040
49th Cong., 1st Sess., Ch. 929	144
49th Cong., 2nd Sess., Ch. 070	040
49th Cong., 2nd Sess., Ch. 119	001
50th Cong., 1st Sess., Ch. 496	144
50th Cong., 1st Sess., Ch. 914	040
51st Cong., 1st Sess., Ch. 634	040
51st Cong., 1st Sess., Ch. 907	004
51st Cong., 1st Sess., Ch. 907	144
51st Cong., 1st Sess., Ch. 908	003
52nd Cong., 1st Sess., Ch. 277	040
53rd Cong., 2nd Sess., Ch. 299	144
53rd Cong., 2nd Sess., Ch. 349	079
53rd Cong., 3rd Sess., Ch. 023	028
53rd Cong., 3rd Sess., Ch. 191	003
55th Cong., 1st Sess., Ch. 002	001
55th Cong., 2nd Sess., Ch. 379	075
55th Cong., 3rd Sess., Ch. 322	005
55th Cong., 3rd Sess., Ch. 425	144
56th Cong., 2nd Sess., Ch. 184	040

Public Law Number Index

Public Law	Record Number	Public Law	Record Number
49-929	144	60-349	022
50-469	144	60-349	023
50-496	144	60-349	024
51-907	144	60-349	025
53-299	144	60-349	026
55-425	144	60-349	027
57-161	001	60-349	028
57-161	004	61-5	079
58-233	001	61-152	144
59-63	040	61-181	005
59-220	001	61-196	005
59-384	144	61-245	144
60-98	040	61-266	040
60-152	144	61-296	075
60-231	144	61-303	001
60-245	001	61-329	005
60-349	006	61-435	001
60-349	008	61-475	144
60-349	009	62-155	040
60-349	010	62-303	007
60-349	011	62-303	018
60-349	012	62-303	020
60-349	013	63-16	079
60-349	014	63-95	029
60-349	015	63-271	039
60-349	016	64-252	037
60-349	017	64-278	040
60-349	018	64-347	029
60-349	019	64-400	040
60-349	020	65-90	040
60-349	021	65-91	030

Public Law	Record Number	Public Law	Record Number
65-91	031	71-175	005
65-178	040	71-231	005
65-199	040	71-299	040
65-217	030	71-505	040
65-254	040	71-536	040
65-326	040	71-616	041
66-126	040	71-743	040
66-146	001	71-791	029
66-146	033	71-798	042
66-152	037	71-798	043
66-190	040	71-798	044
66-256	040	71-798	144
66-280	004	71-868	040
66-384	040	72-65	037
67-66	226	72-189	045
67-115	031	72-194	040
67-147	034	72-212	034
67-294	040	72-303	040
67-331	226	73-1	030
67-372	031	73-2	040
67-536	031	73-66	046
68-35	029	73-87	030
68-120	040	73-121	144
68-176	079	73-216	079
68-242	040	73-232	045
68-262	005	73-245	029
68-270	001	73-291	176
68-415	144	73-298	144
68-445	005	73-324	144
68-587	040	73-325	144
69-127	005	73-374	031
69-188	031	73-415	003
69-254	035	73-416	038
69-257	036	73-416	052
69-257	037	73-424	045
69-448	040	73-442	036
69-632	038	73-442	037
69-690	034	73-482	001
69-690	075	73-484	040
69-762	040	73-485	053
70-10	144	74-198	047
70-122	031	74-198	048
70-325	039	74-198	049
70-585	040	74-198	064
70-623	039	74-198	065
70-702	029	74-198	161
70-794	031	74-238	144
70-1031	040	74-399	053
71-6	031	74-400	053
71-112	034	74-401	050

Public Law	Record Number	Public Law	Record Number
74-403	042	77-554	057
74-403	043	77-649	057
74-403	044	77-690	040
74-403	144	77-761	057
74-425	040	78-10	040
74-460	029	78-16	040
74-487	036	78-68	058
74-487	037	78-89	037
74-673	029	78-110	057
74-675	226	78-149	059
74-738	004	78-202	040
74-835	051	78-225	040
75-97	052	78-244	054
75-127	040	78-315	060
75-304	040	78-346	040
75-347	031	78-359	040
75-541	040	78-410	144
75-626	029	78-457	040
75-656	144	78-483	040
75-706	085	78-534	061
75-717	054	79-22	005
75-717	144	79-139	054
75-718	047	79-182	040
75-722	053	79-268	040
76-1	080	79-292	040
76-151	054	79-322	031
76-196	040	79-336	040
76-198	040	79-377	062
76-248	005	79-388	040
76-252	055	79-404	063
76-287	075	79-404	144
76-288	075	79-478	061
76-341	075	79-485	031
76-358	075	79-487	144
76-434	026	79-572	053
76-633	042	79-577	040
76-633	043	79-585	144
76-633	044	79-586	029
76-633	144	79-600	144
76-753	055	79-671	031
76-783	056	79-732	144
76-833	053	80-16	054
77-22	042	80-101	037
77-22	043	80-101	064
77-241	042	80-101	065
77-241	043	80-101	087
77-354	030	80-101	161
77-354	031	80-104	144
77-366	054	80-104	224
77-539	040	80-129	040

Public Law	Record Number	Public Law	Record Number
80-247	061	82-23	040
80-253	066	82-69	068
80-281	008	82-96	068
80-370	031	82-108	040
80-377	040	82-136	061
80-392	226	82-181	031
80-655	144	82-183	003
80-697	144	82-212	144
80-744	053	82-215	054
80-749	054	82-215	072
80-755	144	82-215	144
80-772	045	82-234	053
80-772	144	82-343	053
80-773	144	82-356	040
80-781	144	82-357	040
80-841	061	82-378	031
80-845	004	82-400	067
80-845	144	82-427	040
80-868	040	82-429	068
80-874	031	82-437	039
80-876	040	82-448	073
80-896	031	82-470	061
81-72	144	82-526	144
81-110	066	82-550	040
81-144	144	82-554	038
81-164	054	82-557	144
81-329	067	82-575	014
81-339	040	82-575	018
81-350	061	82-575	020
81-351	144	82-577	144
81-360	054	82-579	144
81-452	034	82-582	039
81-452	075	82-593	074
81-459	054	82-593	075
81-507	039	83-88	112
81-598	039	83-95	068
81-610	040	83-118	067
81-744	144	83-121	040
81-754	144	83-149	040
81-759	061	83-163	232
81-774	068	83-201	054
81-774	247	83-212	144
81-791	040	83-217	054
81-808	005	83-241	040
81-823	040	83-280	076
81-857	031	83-335	054
81-859	031	83-335	144
81-865	069	83-398	053
81-906	003	83-428	040
81-914	036	83-480	077

Public Law	Record Number	Public Law	Record Number
83-518	054	85-250	054
83-518	144	85-256	144
83-560	144	85-287	144
83-566	078	85-307	231
83-584	052	85-471	068
83-585	001	85-479	144
83-591	079	85-507	144
83-591	080	85-544	144
83-613	040	85-568	039
83-629	112	85-582	144
83-665	067	85-602	144
83-695	040	85-624	144
83-698	040	85-681	144
83-703	081	85-699	232
83-703	082	85-726	085
83-703	144	85-726	144
83-740	144	85-726	231
83-743	006	85-744	144
83-746	053	85-745	083
83-768	144	85-752	069
84-111	073	85-791	144
84-119	068	85-800	144
84-138	067	85-802	144
84-159	144	85-836	086
84-189	144	85-864	029
84-295	068	85-883	073
84-330	037	85-929	054
84-373	083	85-929	144
84-383	053	86-2	054
84-511	046	86-28	053
84-632	068	86-70	144
84-646	054	86-105	144
84-652	144	86-108	067
84-660	004	86-139	144
84-660	144	86-257	037
84-672	054	86-257	087
84-722	144	86-257	088
84-726	067	86-274	038
84-896	144	86-279	144
84-905	144	86-300	144
84-911	029	86-341	077
84-983	045	86-365	144
84-1006	144	86-372	144
84-1013	053	86-373	144
84-1020	144	86-472	067
84-1027	029	86-493	144
84-1028	144	86-537	054
85-104	144	86-546	054
85-141	067	86-546	144
85-162	144	86-560	068

Public Law	Record Number	Public Law	Record Number
86-610	144	88-206	130
86-613	112	88-206	144
86-618	054	88-210	029
86-618	144	88-272	094
86-624	043	88-277	083
86-624	044	88-305	144
86-624	144	88-343	068
86-720	144	88-349	043
86-798	144	88-349	044
87-7	053	88-349	095
87-10	144	88-349	144
87-19	054	88-352	096
87-19	144	88-352	097
87-27	029	88-352	098
87-27	144	88-352	133
87-30	089	88-379	099
87-70	144	88-394	144
87-75	090	88-408	148
87-88	144	88-489	144
87-167	144	88-497	144
87-195	067	88-542	036
87-195	144	88-560	144
87-206	144	88-563	100
87-216	003	88-563	106
87-218	003	88-563	121
87-228	003	88-573	144
87-281	005	88-625	054
87-285	053	88-625	144
87-295	073	88-638	077
87-346	090	89-4	101
87-395	144	89-4	144
87-420	086	89-44	102
87-456	144	89-49	103
87-505	068	89-49	110
87-565	067	89-72	144
87-615	144	89-73	104
87-688	144	89-73	180
87-761	144	89-74	144
87-781	054	89-80	144
87-781	144	89-109	144
87-793	144	89-110	105
87-794	091	89-115	144
87-834	092	89-117	144
87-838	144	89-118	073
87-840	003	89-136	144
88-38	093	89-171	067
88-108	037	89-210	144
88-133	053	89-212	053
88-205	067	89-232	144
88-205	144	89-234	144

Public Law	Record Number	Public Law	Record Number
89-243	106	90-39	118
89-243	121	90-42	104
89-272	107	90-59	121
89-272	144	90-83	144
89-329	108	90-103	101
89-329	144	90-103	144
89-368	109	90-137	067
89-371	067	90-148	130
89-404	099	90-148	144
89-456	036	90-174	144
89-472	110	90-189	112
89-477	054	90-190	144
89-482	068	90-202	122
89-487	111	90-203	003
89-487	119	90-206	144
89-487	170	90-257	053
89-551	144	90-258	226
89-554	144	90-284	076
89-563	112	90-297	073
89-564	144	90-351	123
89-583	067	90-351	131
89-601	113	90-351	145
89-645	144	90-351	243
89-669	152	90-364	144
89-670	144	90-370	068
89-675	144	90-394	144
89-699	053	90-399	054
89-700	053	90-399	144
89-719	114	90-436	077
89-749	144	90-448	144
89-753	144	90-490	144
89-754	115	90-495	144
89-754	144	90-554	067
89-756	112	90-574	107
89-773	144	90-574	144
89-800	116	90-575	108
89-800	120	90-575	144
89-808	077	90-576	029
89-809	117	90-602	124
89-809	120	90-623	144
90-3	118	90-639	144
90-19	144	91-43	073
90-23	111	91-54	125
90-23	119	91-69	104
90-23	144	91-113	112
90-23	170	91-114	144
90-23	173	91-123	101
90-26	120	91-123	144
90-30	073	91-135	152
90-35	108	91-136	144

Public Law	Record Number	Public Law	Record Number
91-137	144	92-27	144
91-152	144	92-46	053
91-172	144	92-50	144
91-173	126	92-60	073
91-173	140	92-65	101
91-175	067	92-65	144
91-190	127	92-73	144
91-190	144	92-84	144
91-190	208	92-137	144
91-208	144	92-157	144
91-215	053	92-159	144
91-221	073	92-174	144
91-224	144	92-175	099
91-230	029	92-178	144
91-230	108	92-226	067
91-230	144	92-240	144
91-258	144	92-255	132
91-258	231	92-258	104
91-285	105	92-261	133
91-296	144	92-261	134
91-300	068	92-273	073
91-316	107	92-303	126
91-316	144	92-303	140
91-371	068	92-318	029
91-375	128	92-318	108
91-377	053	92-325	068
91-379	068	92-387	054
91-452	003	92-399	144
91-452	144	92-402	144
91-512	107	92-419	144
91-512	144	92-460	053
91-513	144	92-463	135
91-515	144	92-473	136
91-560	144	92-500	137
91-596	129	92-500	144
91-596	144	92-513	144
91-601	144	92-516	144
91-604	130	92-517	138
91-604	144	92-532	144
91-604	155	92-539	045
91-605	144	92-574	139
91-606	144	92-574	144
91-607	046	92-576	140
91-609	144	92-583	141
91-611	144	92-583	144
91-616	144	92-603	142
91-644	131	92-603	143
91-646	144	93-14	107
91-652	067	93-14	144
91-665	144	93-15	144

Public Law	Record Number	Public Law	Record Number
94-370	141	95-212	152
94-399	188	95-216	217
94-409	135	95-217	208
94-409	189	95-217	218
94-409	190	95-227	219
94-412	191	95-233	162
94-413	192	95-238	172
94-421	193	95-239	219
94-432	194	95-242	220
94-433	195	95-250	221
94-469	196	95-273	208
94-475	204	95-292	217
94-482	108	95-302	208
94-488	197	95-306	162
94-502	198	95-307	162
94-519	199	95-313	162
94-553	200	95-367	222
94-559	201	95-393	223
94-579	202	95-396	208
94-579	203	95-396	224
94-580	204	95-405	225
94-581	205	95-405	226
94-588	162	95-454	227
95-30	207	95-467	208
95-30	217	95-472	217
95-37	068	95-474	208
95-59	217	95-476	228
95-65	104	95-478	104
95-83	217	95-479	229
95-87	208	95-488	219
95-88	077	95-495	230
95-91	172	95-504	231
95-95	208	95-507	232
95-95	209	95-520	233
95-115	210	95-521	234
95-116	211	95-555	235
95-117	212	95-559	217
95-128	213	95-566	236
95-142	142	95-588	237
95-142	214	95-591	238
95-142	217	95-598	217
95-151	215	95-600	217
95-163	231	95-609	208
95-164	216	95-620	208
95-171	217	95-625	239
95-190	171	95-626	217
95-193	101	95-632	152
95-204	212	96-22	240
95-210	214	96-28	234
95-210	217	96-43	174

Bill Number Index

Bill No.	Congress	Year	Record Number
H.R. 1	100th	1987	254
H.R. 1	26th	1840	039
H.R. 1	62nd	1911-1912	040
H.R. 1	82nd	1951	040
H.R. 1	89th	1965	053
H.R. 1	92nd	1971-1972	142
H.R. 1	92nd	1971-1972	143
H.R. 1	95th	1977-1978	234
H.R. 2	66th	1919-1920	040
H.R. 2	89th	1965	144
H.R. 2	93rd	1973-1974	164
H.R. 2	95th	1977	208
H.R. 3	100th	1987-1988	255
H.R. 3	81st	1949	054
H.R. 3	95th	1977	142

Bill No.	Congress	Year	Record Number
H.R. 3	95th	1977	214
H.R. 3	95th	1977	217
H.R. 4	67th	1921-1922	040
H.R. 4	78th	1945	062
H.R. 4	93rd	1973	189
H.R. 5	29th	1845-1846	039
H.R. 5	42nd	1871-1872	002
H.R. 7	94th	1975	219
H.R. 8	94th	1975	219
H.R. 8	99th	1985	254
H.R. 10	89th	1965-1966	117
H.R. 12	72nd	1932	042
H.R. 12	81st	1949	039
H.R. 16	55th	1897	001
H.R. 17	95th	1977	220
H.R. 34	92nd	1971	185
H.R. 37	93rd	1973	152
H.R. 38	93rd	1973	156
H.R. 65	80th	1947	039
H.R. 69	93rd	1973-1974	029
H.R. 69	93rd	1973-1974	108
H.R. 77	93rd	1973	146
H.R. 85	39th	1866	001
H.R. 85	53rd	1893	075
H.R. 85	96th	1979-1980	249

Bill No.	Congress	Year	Record Number
H.R. 97	79th	1945	070
H.R. 98	93rd	1973	159
H.R. 109	78th	1943	070
H.R. 122	72nd	1932	042
H.R. 124	80th	1947	039
H.R. 125	37th	1862	001
H.R. 129	81st	1949	054
H.R. 134	81st	1949	054
H.R. 139	72nd	1931	006
H.R. 139	72nd	1931	008
H.R. 139	72nd	1931	010
H.R. 139	72nd	1931	012
H.R. 139	72nd	1931	014
H.R. 139	72nd	1931	026
H.R. 149	78th	1943	054
H.R. 160	81st	1949	054
H.R. 181	81st	1949	054
H.R. 184	79th	1945	063
H.R. 187	81st	1949	054
H.R. 200	94th	1975-1976	184
H.R. 207	90th	1967	073
H.R. 232	81st	1949	054
H.R. 243	60th	1907	006
H.R. 243	60th	1907	008
H.R. 243	60th	1907	021

Bill No.	Congress	Year	Record Number
H.R. 243	60th	1907	026
H.R. 254	94th	1975	183
H.R. 265	76th	1939	075
H.R. 271	54th	1895-1896	075
H.R. 279	81st	1949	054
H.R. 285	92nd	1971	144
H.R. 287	85th	1957	009
H.R. 300	75th	1937	054
H.R. 312	37th	1862	079
H.R. 315	82nd	1951	040
H.R. 323	82nd	1951	039
H.R. 336	81st	1949	054
H.R. 336	92nd	1971	144
H.R. 337	91st	1960	144
H.R. 337	92nd	1971	144
H.R. 339	79th	1945	063
H.R. 340	93rd	1973	176
H.R. 356	83rd	1953-1954	053
H.R. 357	81st	1949	054
H.R. 359	81st	1949	039
H.R. 359	81st	1949	071
H.R. 365	39th	1866	001
H.R. 365	39th	1866	004
H.R. 366	85th	1957	054
H.R. 386	27th	1842	039

Bill No.	Congress	Year	Record Number
H.R. 399	81st	1949	054
H.R. 404	88th	1963	095
H.R. 404	88th	1963	144
H.R. 405	88th	1963	096
H.R. 422	95th	1977	214
H.R. 438	37th	1862	040
H.R. 459	82nd	1952	076
H.R. 462	93rd	1973	164
H.R. 487	85th	1957	086
H.R. 492	94th	1975	183
H.R. 514	91st	1969-1970	029
H.R. 514	91st	1969-1970	108
H.R. 514	91st	1969-1970	144
H.R. 545	49th	1885-1886	040
H.R. 562	41st	1869-1870	001
H.R. 562	41st	1869-1870	004
H.R. 573	68th	1923	025
H.R. 585	73rd	1933	025
H.R. 627	94th	1975	183
H.R. 630	93rd	1973	159
H.R. 655	64th	1915-1917	040
H.R. 673	85th	1957	014
H.R. 706	89th	1965-1966	036
H.R. 706	89th	1965-1966	037
H.R. 741	84th	1955	004

Bill No.	Congress	Year	Record Number
H.R. 782	84th	1955	009
H.R. 783	95th	1977	222
H.R. 800	84th	1956	045
H.R. 805	92nd	1971	144
H.R. 807	49th	1886-1887	040
H.R. 831	51st	1889-1890	084
H.R. 842	81st	1949	075
H.R. 843	91st	1969-1970	129
H.R. 926	76th	1939	006
H.R. 926	76th	1939	008
H.R. 926	76th	1939	009
H.R. 926	76th	1939	021
H.R. 926	76th	1939	026
H.R. 942	80th	1947	039
H.R. 942	80th	1947	071
H.R. 983	92nd	1971	144
H.R. 997	83rd	1953	004
H.R. 1001	46th	1879	075
H.R. 1010	40th	1868	040
H.R. 1012	86th	1959	053
H.R. 1014	93rd	1973	156
H.R. 1016	42nd	1872	001
H.R. 1030	77th	1941-1942	040
H.R. 1059	93rd	1973	156
H.R. 1063	83rd	1953	076

Bill No.	Congress	Year	Record Number
H.R. 1095	92nd	1971	144
H.R. 1100	97th	1981	251
H.R. 1107	80th	1947	039
H.R. 1111	89th	1965	144
H.R. 1117	79th	1945	063
H.R. 1122	100th	1987	255
H.R. 1142	81st	1949	054
H.R. 1160	25th	1839	039
H.R. 1161	25th	1839	039
H.R. 1180	82nd	1951-1952	144
H.R. 1186	81st	1949	054
H.R. 1188	78th	1943	057
H.R. 1190	79th	1945	039
H.R. 1203	79th	1945	063
H.R. 1206	79th	1945	063
H.R. 1209	81st	1949	054
H.R. 1216	66th	1919-1920	040
H.R. 1228	83rd	1953	039
H.R. 1232	99th	1985	253
H.R. 1234	86th	1959	004
H.R. 1235	87th	1961-1962	054
H.R. 1236	93rd	1973	161
H.R. 1237	80th	1947	144
H.R. 1237	80th	1947	224
H.R. 1256	81st	1949	054

Bill No.	Congress	Year	Record Number
H.R. 1270	80th	1947	007
H.R. 1270	80th	1947	008
H.R. 1270	80th	1947	021
H.R. 1281	93rd	1973	173
H.R. 1297	86th	1959	144
H.R. 1301	83rd	1953	039
H.R. 1342	99th	1985	253
H.R. 1346	86th	1959	144
H.R. 1362	79th	1945-1946	053
H.R. 1371	78th	1943	070
H.R. 1383	92nd	1971	144
H.R. 1400	92nd	1971	099
H.R. 1404	95th	1977	217
H.R. 1427	42nd	1872	002
H.R. 1432	101st	1989	257
H.R. 1438	61st	1909	079
H.R. 1484	95th	1977	223
H.R. 1491	73rd	1933	030
H.R. 1532	95th	1977	219
H.R. 1535	95th	1977	223
H.R. 1536	95th	1977	223
H.R. 1537	81st	1949	076
H.R. 1547	94th	1975	205
H.R. 1570	78th	1943	021
H.R. 1571	78th	1943	008

Bill No.	Congress	Year	Record Number
H.R. 1612	45th	1877-1878	075
H.R. 1616	99th	1985	255
H.R. 1644	76th	1939	017
H.R. 1661	92nd	1971	144
H.R. 1700	63rd	1913	071
H.R. 1700	63rd	1913	075
H.R. 1703	81st	1949	054
H.R. 1723	81st	1949	054
H.R. 1744	78th	1943-1944	040
H.R. 1746	92nd	1971-1972	133
H.R. 1746	92nd	1971-1972	134
H.R. 1749	78th	1943	040
H.R. 1775	99th	1985	253
H.R. 1814	86th	1959	054
H.R. 1815	80th	1947	039
H.R. 1815	80th	1947	071
H.R. 1829	41st	1870-1871	040
H.R. 1830	80th	1947	039
H.R. 1830	80th	1947	071
H.R. 1834	80th	1947	039
H.R. 1834	80th	1947	071
H.R. 1845	81st	1949	039
H.R. 1862	95th	1977	212
H.R. 1897	88th	1963	037
H.R. 1900	78th	1943	059

Bill No.	Congress	Year	Record Number
H.R. 1932	71st	1929	071
H.R. 1940	99th	1985	253
H.R. 1984	80th	1947	039
H.R. 2004	88th	1963	037
H.R. 2005	99th	1985-1986	253
H.R. 2018	99th	1985	253
H.R. 2022	99th	1985	253
H.R. 2023	81st	1949-1950	054
H.R. 2027	80th	1947	039
H.R. 2027	80th	1947	071
H.R. 2032	81st	1949	037
H.R. 2042	78th	1943	058
H.R. 2045	80th	1947	054
H.R. 2054	96th	1979	246
H.R. 2060	95th	1977	216
H.R. 2061	96th	1979	243
H.R. 2063	81st	1949	054
H.R. 2083	80th	1947	008
H.R. 2100	78th	1943	071
H.R. 2126	84th	1955	073
H.R. 2128	84th	1955-1956	039
H.R. 2166	94th	1975	175
H.R. 2181	80th	1947	040
H.R. 2208	99th	1985	253
H.R. 2211	85th	1957	004

Bill No.	Congress	Year	Record Number
H.R. 2218	78th	1943	058
H.R. 2218	96th	1979	152
H.R. 2223	94th	1975	200
H.R. 2245	78th	1943	058
H.R. 2245	80th	1947-1948	054
H.R. 2245	83rd	1953	054
H.R. 2272	93rd	1973	185
H.R. 2273	101st	1989-1990	256
H.R. 2277	78th	1943	058
H.R. 2296	76th	1939	040
H.R. 2309	83rd	1953	039
H.R. 2312	42nd	1872-1873	040
H.R. 2331	88th	1963	037
H.R. 2336	86th	1959	054
H.R. 2347	86th	1959	144
H.R. 2363	86th	1959	004
H.R. 2380	78th	1943	059
H.R. 2380	95th	1977	209
H.R. 2400	78th	1943	054
H.R. 2437	85th	1957	086
H.R. 2443	93rd	1973	159
H.R. 2444	96th	1979	241
H.R. 2464	82nd	1951	021
H.R. 2492	92nd	1971	141
H.R. 2492	92nd	1971	144

Bill No.	Congress	Year	Record Number
H.R. 2493	92nd	1971	141
H.R. 2493	92nd	1971	144
H.R. 2499	92nd	1971	005
H.R. 2504	95th	1977	214
H.R. 2506	79th	1945	005
H.R. 2516	90th	1967-1968	076
H.R. 2520	80th	1947	034
H.R. 2559	94th	1975	178
H.R. 2570	78th	1943	058
H.R. 2575	44th	1876	003
H.R. 2577	78th	1943	058
H.R. 2602	79th	1945	063
H.R. 2612	79th	1945	070
H.R. 2630	79th	1945	071
H.R. 2631	79th	1945	075
H.R. 2632	79th	1945	070
H.R. 2633	94th	1975	181
H.R. 2633	94th	1975	204
H.R. 2633	94th	1975	209
H.R. 2650	53rd	1893-1895	028
H.R. 2650	81st	1949	054
H.R. 2650	94th	1975	209
H.R. 2660	80th	1947	075
H.R. 2663	68th	1923	025
H.R. 2663	81st	1949	066

Bill No.	Congress	Year	Record Number
H.R. 2683	88th	1963	099
H.R. 2689	88th	1963	099
H.R. 2695	75th	1937	006
H.R. 2695	75th	1937	008
H.R. 2695	75th	1937	010
H.R. 2695	75th	1937	026
H.R. 2701	95th	1977	223
H.R. 2702	95th	1977	223
H.R. 2703	95th	1977	223
H.R. 2704	68th	1923	025
H.R. 2721	80th	1947-1948	144
H.R. 2735	94th	1975-1976	205
H.R. 2762	76th	1939	080
H.R. 2769	83rd	1953	054
H.R. 2816	96th	1979-1980	245
H.R. 2817	99th	1985	253
H.R. 2820	73rd	1933	040
H.R. 2820	95th	1977	230
H.R. 2836	81st	1949	054
H.R. 2839	81st	1949	054
H.R. 2842	93rd	1973	159
H.R. 2854	96th	1979	246
H.R. 2857	42nd	1872	075
H.R. 2861	80th	1947	037
H.R. 2884	81st	1949	054

Bill No.	Congress	Year	Record Number
H.R. 2899	81st	1949	054
H.R. 2900	81st	1949	054
H.R. 2904	81st	1949	054
H.R. 2913	94th	1975	219
H.R. 2932	94th	1975	204
H.R. 2934	42nd	1872-1873	002
H.R. 2938	81st	1949	054
H.R. 2957	97th	1981	254
H.R. 2982	81st	1949	054
H.R. 2984	89th	1965	144
H.R. 2986	89th	1965	144
H.R. 2995	81st	1949	054
H.R. 3004	75th	1937	006
H.R. 3004	75th	1937	008
H.R. 3004	75th	1937	010
H.R. 3004	75th	1937	026
H.R. 3014	54th	1895-1897	075
H.R. 3020	80th	1947	037
H.R. 3020	80th	1947	064
H.R. 2836	81st	1949	054
H.R. 2839	81st	1949	054
H.R. 2842	93rd	1973	159
H.R. 3020	80th	1947	065
H.R. 3054	64th	1915	071
H.R. 3056	95th	1977	245

Bill No.	Congress	Year	Record Number
H.R. 3065	99th	1985	253
H.R. 3082	64th	1915	071
H.R. 3083	71st	1929	031
H.R. 3118	94th	1975	204
H.R. 3118	94th	1975	209
H.R. 3123	80th	1947	061
H.R. 3128	80th	1947	054
H.R. 3130	94th	1975	204
H.R. 3134	84th	1955	039
H.R. 3139	88th	1963	096
H.R. 3143	75th	1937	054
H.R. 3147	80th	1947	054
H.R. 3150	80th	1947	053
H.R. 3151	81st	1949	054
H.R. 3157	89th	1965	053
H.R. 3170	78th	1945	062
H.R. 3173	96th	1979	067
H.R. 3180	93rd	1973	149
H.R. 3183	86th	1959	144
H.R. 3184	66th	1919-1920	004
H.R. 3190	79th	1945	008
H.R. 3190	79th	1945	021
H.R. 3190	80th	1947-1948	045
H.R. 3190	80th	1947-1948	144
H.R. 3199	95th	1977	208

Bill No.	Congress	Year	Record Number
H.R. 3199	95th	1977	218
H.R. 3200	101st	1989-1990	257
H.R. 3203	80th	1947	040
H.R. 3209	95th	1977	208
H.R. 3211	77th	1941	075
H.R. 3214	80th	1947-1948	144
H.R. 3236	96th	1979	246
H.R. 3264	78th	1943	075
H.R. 3266	79th	1945	054
H.R. 3267	68th	1924	039
H.R. 3282	98th	1983-1984	254
H.R. 3298	81st	1951	054
H.R. 3298	82nd	1951	072
H.R. 3298	82nd	1951	144
H.R. 3302	86th	1959	088
H.R. 3310	88th	1963	053
H.R. 3321	63rd	1913	079
H.R. 3325	77th	1941	042
H.R. 3325	77th	1941	043
H.R. 3333	94th	1975	219
H.R. 3348	94th	1975-1976	205
H.R. 3378	85th	1957	135
H.R. 3387	95th	1977	217
H.R. 3399	95th	1977	222
H.R. 3404	84th	1955	004

Bill No.	Congress	Year	Record Number
H.R. 3409	95th	1977	223
H.R. 3453	99th	1985	253
H.R. 3456	77th	1941	008
H.R. 3462	79th	1945	070
H.R. 3464	96th	1979	246
H.R. 3476	93rd	1973	219
H.R. 3477	95th	1977	207
H.R. 3477	95th	1977	217
H.R. 3498	98th	1983-1984	252
H.R. 3505	92nd	1971	140
H.R. 3507	88th	1963	144
H.R. 3509	96th	1979	171
H.R. 3534	83rd	1953-1954	039
H.R. 3540	86th	1959	087
H.R. 3540	86th	1959	088
H.R. 3548	87th	1961	054
H.R. 3551	83rd	1953	054
H.R. 3558	96th	1979	248
H.R. 3589	82nd	1951-1952	014
H.R. 3589	82nd	1951-1952	018
H.R. 3589	82nd	1951-1952	020
H.R. 3604	83rd	1953	054
H.R. 3606	89th	1965-1966	099
H.R. 3615	78th	1945	062
H.R. 3615	92nd	1971	141

Bill No.	Congress	Year	Record Number
H.R. 3615	92nd	1971	144
H.R. 3639	90th	1967-1968	144
H.R. 3642	77th	1941	059
H.R. 3644	79th	1945	040
H.R. 3658	61st	1909	144
H.R. 3662	92nd	1971	144
H.R. 3669	82nd	1951	053
H.R. 3675	43rd	1874	075
H.R. 3694	79th	1945	074
H.R. 3699	75th	1937	017
H.R. 3700	80th	1947	034
H.R. 3708	89th	1965	104
H.R. 3708	89th	1965	180
H.R. 3730	86th	1959	144
H.R. 3744	95th	1977	215
H.R. 3748	80th	1947-1948	040
H.R. 3749	79th	1945	040
H.R. 3755	82nd	1951	053
H.R. 3756	79th	1945-1946	070
H.R. 3756	96th	1979-1980	244
H.R. 3757	79th	1945-1946	071
H.R. 3760	82nd	1951	074
H.R. 3760	82nd	1951	075
H.R. 3762	78th	1943	071
H.R. 3762	81st	1949	144

Bill No.	Congress	Year	Record Number
H.R. 3786	78th	1943	070
H.R. 3787	94th	1975	204
H.R. 3790	82nd	1951	061
H.R. 3809	91st	1969-1970	129
H.R. 3813	90th	1967	121
H.R. 3813	95th	1977-1978	221
H.R. 3835	92nd	1971	099
H.R. 3838	81st	1949	061
H.R. 3841	83rd	1953	054
H.R. 3841	95th	1977	223
H.R. 3852	99th	1985	253
H.R. 3861	88th	1963	093
H.R. 3874	78th	1943	070
H.R. 3875	96th	1979	242
H.R. 3884	94th	1975-1976	191
H.R. 3920	88th	1963	053
H.R. 3922	94th	1975	104
H.R. 3922	94th	1975	180
H.R. 3930	96th	1979	247
H.R. 3935	87th	1961	089
H.R. 3946	95th	1977-1978	236
H.R. 3961	78th	1944	061
H.R. 3972	74th	1935	054
H.R. 3975	82nd	1951-1952	039
H.R. 3980	87th	1961	054

Bill No.	Congress	Year	Record Number
H.R. 3980	87th	1961	144
H.R. 3981	94th	1975-1976	141
H.R. 3988	89th	1965	144
H.R. 3997	77th	1941	008
H.R. 3997	77th	1941	009
H.R. 3997	77th	1941	026
H.R. 4004	42nd	1873	075
H.R. 4014	85th	1957	054
H.R. 4018	91st	1969	144
H.R. 4022	88th	1963	093
H.R. 4023	96th	1979	254
H.R. 4036	87th	1961	144
H.R. 4044	80th	1947-1948	031
H.R. 4048	88th	1963	099
H.R. 4053	93rd	1973	159
H.R. 4054	82nd	1951	039
H.R. 4061	80th	1947	074
H.R. 4061	88th	1963	144
H.R. 4071	80th	1947-1948	054
H.R. 4073	94th	1975	101
H.R. 4099	84th	1955	054
H.R. 4100	84th	1955	054
H.R. 4102	80th	1947	039
H.R. 4111	94th	1975	176
H.R. 4114	80th	1947-1948	144

Bill No.	Congress	Year	Record Number
H.R. 4115	78th	1944	040
H.R. 4121	68th	1923-1924	029
H.R. 4148	91st	1969-1970	144
H.R. 4151	95th	1977	209
H.R. 4172	92nd	1971	053
H.R. 4191	93rd	1974	045
H.R. 4194	86th	1959	054
H.R. 4200	93rd	1973-1974	164
H.R. 4203	81st	1949	054
H.R. 4214	80th	1947	066
H.R. 4217	92nd	1971	144
H.R. 4222	87th	1961	053
H.R. 4234	45th	1878-1879	040
H.R. 4247	92nd	1971	144
H.R. 4249	91st	1969-1970	105
H.R. 4261	44th	1876-1877	001
H.R. 4261	44th	1876-1877	004
H.R. 4267	84th	1955	075
H.R. 4277	83rd	1953	054
H.R. 4279	90th	1967	144
H.R. 4287	95th	1977	216
H.R. 4292	93rd	1973	107
H.R. 4294	91st	1969-1970	129
H.R. 4299	87th	1961	090
H.R. 4304	80th	1947-1948	039

Bill No.	Congress	Year	Record Number
H.R. 4306	93rd	1973	107
H.R. 4341	95th	1977	228
H.R. 4353	85th	1957-1958	053
H.R. 4359	92nd	1971	144
H.R. 4369	94th	1975	209
H.R. 4383	92nd	1971-1972	135
H.R. 4384	79th	1945	029
H.R. 4387	82nd	1951-1952	040
H.R. 4388	96th	1979	152
H.R. 4389	95th	1977	219
H.R. 4394	82nd	1951-1952	040
H.R. 4409	95th	1977	220
H.R. 4415	88th	1963	144
H.R. 4432	85th	1957	054
H.R. 4433	76th	1939	015
H.R. 4433	76th	1939	017
H.R. 4461	94th	1975	185
H.R. 4466	86th	1959	144
H.R. 4468	95th	1977	222
H.R. 4470	80th	1947	054
H.R. 4473	82nd	1951	003
H.R. 4473	86th	1959	087
H.R. 4473	86th	1959	088
H.R. 4474	86th	1959	087
H.R. 4475	84th	1955	054

Bill No.	Congress	Year	Record Number
H.R. 4485	78th	1944	061
H.R. 4486	77th	1941	017
H.R. 4493	78th	1974	070
H.R. 4498	100th	1988	256
H.R. 4503	97th	1981	254
H.R. 4512	79th	1945-1946	144
H.R. 4523	74th	1935	070
H.R. 4544	95th	1977-1978	219
H.R. 4566	96th	1979	249
H.R. 4567	86th	1959	004
H.R. 4571	79th	1945-1946	031
H.R. 4571	96th	1979	249
H.R. 4572	85th	1957	014
H.R. 4573	90th	1967	118
H.R. 4584	92nd	1971	144
H.R. 4604	86th	1959	004
H.R. 4607	86th	1959	004
H.R. 4624	78th	1944	144
H.R. 4638	88th	1963-1964	083
H.R. 4646	78th	1944	060
H.R. 4653	85th	1957	086
H.R. 4662	87th	1961	144
H.R. 4672	45th	1878	075
H.R. 4674	93rd	1973	107
H.R. 4692	81st	1949-1950	039

Bill No.	Congress	Year	Record Number
H.R. 4696	48th	1884	040
H.R. 4700	84th	1955	039
H.R. 4700	86th	1959	053
H.R. 4716	94th	1975	053
H.R. 4723	92nd	1971	144
H.R. 4725	80th	1948	076
H.R. 4731	88th	1963-1964	054
H.R. 4744	84th	1955	053
H.R. 4749	92nd	1971	054
H.R. 4750	89th	1965	106
H.R. 4750	89th	1965	121
H.R. 4759	93rd	1973	156
H.R. 4761	79th	1945-1946	040
H.R. 4798	81st	1949	074
H.R. 4830	68th	1924	001
H.R. 4830	91st	1969	005
H.R. 4852	80th	1948	039
H.R. 4852	80th	1948	071
H.R. 4864	53rd	1894	079
H.R. 4871	76th	1939	006
H.R. 4871	76th	1939	008
H.R. 4871	76th	1939	009
H.R. 4871	76th	1939	021
H.R. 4871	76th	1939	026
H.R. 4873	93rd	1973	156

Bill No.	Congress	Year	Record Number
H.R. 4885	88th	1963	053
H.R. 4901	83rd	1953	054
H.R. 4906	77th	1941	057
H.R. 4908	79th	1945	037
H.R. 4918	84th	1955	144
H.R. 4929	87th	1961	086
H.R. 4937	80th	1948	054
H.R. 4944	83rd	1953	039
H.R. 4949	47th	1882	075
H.R. 4955	88th	1963	029
H.R. 4960	65th	1917	030
H.R. 4960	65th	1917	031
H.R. 4975	95th	1977	217
H.R. 4976	95th	1977	217
H.R. 4983	84th	1955	034
H.R. 4986	74th	1935	075
H.R. 4998	87th	1961	144
H.R. 5007	81st	1949	144
H.R. 5011	65th	1918	084
H.R. 5011	66th	1919	034
H.R. 5012	66th	1919	034
H.R. 5012	66th	1919	084
H.R. 5012	89th	1965	111
H.R. 5012	89th	1965	119
H.R. 5013	89th	1965	111

Bill No.	Congress	Year	Record Number
H.R. 5014	53rd	1894	075
H.R. 5014	89th	1965	111
H.R. 5015	89th	1965	111
H.R. 5016	83rd	1953	054
H.R. 5016	89th	1965	111
H.R. 5017	89th	1965	111
H.R. 5018	89th	1965	111
H.R. 5019	89th	1965	111
H.R. 5020	89th	1965	111
H.R. 5021	89th	1965	111
H.R. 5027	87th	1961	053
H.R. 5027	95th	1977	211
H.R. 5029	95th	1977-1978	233
H.R. 5030	75th	1937-1938	040
H.R. 5037	90th	1967-1968	123
H.R. 5037	90th	1967-1968	131
H.R. 5037	90th	1967-1968	145
H.R. 5037	90th	1967-1968	243
H.R. 5050	93rd	1973-1974	176
H.R. 5055	83rd	1953	054
H.R. 5055	95th	1977	235
H.R. 5060	92nd	1971	144
H.R. 5069	83rd	1953	112
H.R. 5075	87th	1961	053
H.R. 5075	94th	1975	189

Bill No.	Congress	Year	Record Number
H.R. 5087	93rd	1973	156
H.R. 5124	98th	1984	252
H.R. 5125	78th	1944	040
H.R. 5134	83rd	1953	144
H.R. 5146	95th	1977-1978	208
H.R. 5157	49th	1886	075
H.R. 5162	84th	1955	054
H.R. 5182	95th	1977	223
H.R. 5193	93rd	1973	160
H.R. 5237	89th	1965	111
H.R. 5248	80th	1948	074
H.R. 5257	84th	1955-1956	054
H.R. 5262	79th	1946	037
H.R. 5269	89th	1965	144
H.R. 5275	75th	1937	006
H.R. 5275	75th	1937	008
H.R. 5275	75th	1937	009
H.R. 5275	75th	1937	010
H.R. 5275	75th	1937	017
H.R. 5275	75th	1937	021
H.R. 5275	75th	1937	026
H.R. 5275	92nd	1971	139
H.R. 5284	80th	1948	054
H.R. 5286	75th	1937	054
H.R. 5292	80th	1948	054

Bill No.	Congress	Year	Record Number
H.R. 5294	56th	1900	084
H.R. 5312	77th	1941	042
H.R. 5312	77th	1941	043
H.R. 5315	72nd	1931-1932	037
H.R. 5319	76th	1939	015
H.R. 5319	76th	1939	017
H.R. 5322	95th	1977-1978	217
H.R. 5322	95th	1977-1978	219
H.R. 5333	92nd	1971	073
H.R. 5334	92nd	1971	073
H.R. 5356	93rd	1973	156
H.R. 5357	90th	1967	119
H.R. 5357	90th	1967	144
H.R. 5357	90th	1967	170
H.R. 5361	53rd	1894	075
H.R. 5368	93rd	1973	156
H.R. 5388	92nd	1971	139
H.R. 5388	93rd	1973	159
H.R. 5395	93rd	1973	156
H.R. 5406	89th	1965	111
H.R. 5414	75th	1937	054
H.R. 5445	93rd	1973	144
H.R. 5446	93rd	1973	107
H.R. 5446	93rd	1973	144
H.R. 5450	93rd	1973-1974	156

Bill No.	Congress	Year	Record Number
H.R. 5451	93rd	1973	144
H.R. 5452	76th	1939	040
H.R. 5458	75th	1937	054
H.R. 5470	94th	1975	192
H.R. 5478	75th	1937	040
H.R. 5487	94th	1975	204
H.R. 5506	79th	1946	071
H.R. 5520	89th	1965	111
H.R. 5528	91st	1969	005
H.R. 5554	73rd	1933	075
H.R. 5555	86th	1959	004
H.R. 5583	89th	1965	111
H.R. 5587	86th	1959	004
H.R. 5598	81st	1949	040
H.R. 5610	86th	1959	053
H.R. 5618	86th	1959	004
H.R. 5630	76th	1939	054
H.R. 5636	75th	1937	084
H.R. 5636	83rd	1953	040
H.R. 5640	98th	1985-1986	253
H.R. 5654	90th	1967	112
H.R. 5660	76th	1939	005
H.R. 5661	73rd	1933	046
H.R. 5667	48th	1884-1885	040
H.R. 5676	67th	1921	226

Bill No.	Congress	Year	Record Number
H.R. 5690	83rd	1953	040
H.R. 5690	98th	1984	252
H.R. 5710	83rd	1953	067
H.R. 5711	80th	1948	053
H.R. 5718	86th	1959	004
H.R. 5722	95th	1977	222
H.R. 5723	65th	1917	040
H.R. 5735	82nd	1951-1952	004
H.R. 5736	82nd	1951	004
H.R. 5740	83rd	1953	054
H.R. 5746	84th	1955	054
H.R. 5748	86th	1959	004
H.R. 5749	93rd	1973	183
H.R. 5759	101st	1990	257
H.R. 5762	76th	1939	054
H.R. 5791	76th	1939	021
H.R. 5813	86th	1959	144
H.R. 5841	69th	1925	006
H.R. 5841	69th	1925	008
H.R. 5841	69th	1925	010
H.R. 5841	69th	1925	020
H.R. 5841	69th	1925	021
H.R. 5853	73rd	1933	006
H.R. 5853	73rd	1933	009
H.R. 5853	73rd	1933	026

Bill No.	Congress	Year	Record Number
H.R. 5854	75th	1937	054
H.R. 5855	75th	1937	084
H.R. 5871	80th	1948	066
H.R. 5871	85th	1957	004
H.R. 5876	90th	1967	144
H.R. 5892	96th	1979-1980	248
H.R. 5895	81st	1949	067
H.R. 5900	87th	1961	089
H.R. 5916	89th	1965	117
H.R. 5930	89th	1965	099
H.R. 5940	79th	1946	071
H.R. 5974	54th	1896	075
H.R. 5994	85th	1957	086
H.R. 6007	80th	1948	039
H.R. 6009	77th	1941	040
H.R. 6010	95th	1977	231
H.R. 6012	73rd	1933	075
H.R. 6014	85th	1957	086
H.R. 6028	87th	1961	144
H.R. 6041	88th	1963-1964	043
H.R. 6041	88th	1963-1964	044
H.R. 6041	88th	1963-1964	095
H.R. 6041	88th	1963-1964	144
H.R. 6060	88th	1963	093
H.R. 6075	95th	1977-1978	235

Bill No.	Congress	Year	Record Number
H.R. 6097	79th	1946	144
H.R. 6098	53rd	1894	075
H.R. 6098	90th	1967	121
H.R. 6100	95th	1977	043
H.R. 6103	70th	1927-1928	039
H.R. 6105	70th	1927	076
H.R. 6110	73rd	1933	054
H.R. 6111	73rd	1933	054
H.R. 6111	95th	1977	210
H.R. 6116	80th	1948	031
H.R. 6118	73rd	1933	054
H.R. 6118	79th	1946	071
H.R. 6133	90th	1967	073
H.R. 6133	95th	1977	223
H.R. 6140	86th	1959	004
H.R. 6147	84th	1955	004
H.R. 6154	94th	1975	183
H.R. 6160	76th	1939	006
H.R. 6160	76th	1939	008
H.R. 6160	76th	1939	009
H.R. 6160	76th	1939	021
H.R. 6160	76th	1939	026
H.R. 6161	95th	1977	208
H.R. 6161	95th	1977	209
H.R. 6172	89th	1965	111

Bill No.	Congress	Year	Record Number
H.R. 6177	94th	1975	183
H.R. 6183	48th	1884	075
H.R. 6186	93rd	1973-1974	150
H.R. 6186	93rd	1973-1974	151
H.R. 6187	74th	1935	049
H.R. 6217	81st	1949-1950	040
H.R. 6218	94th	1975-1976	204
H.R. 6227	84th	1955-1956	046
H.R. 6228	91st	1970	134
H.R. 6233	77th	1941	030
H.R. 6233	77th	1941	031
H.R. 6238	80th	1948	039
H.R. 6243	76th	1939	008
H.R. 6245	87th	1961-1962	054
H.R. 6251	77th	1941	054
H.R. 6264	94th	1975	183
H.R. 6282	89th	1965	099
H.R. 6288	74th	1935	048
H.R. 6288	74th	1935	049
H.R. 6293	77th	1942	057
H.R. 6295	84th	1955	144
H.R. 6325	86th	1959	144
H.R. 6328	89th	1965	054
H.R. 6338	93rd	1973	144
H.R. 6346	79th	1946	039

Bill No.	Congress	Year	Record Number
H.R. 6350	55th	1898	075
H.R. 6355	79th	1946	061
H.R. 6359	74th	1935	079
H.R. 6359	92nd	1971	144
H.R. 6362	95th	1977-1978	162
H.R. 6376	73rd	1934	054
H.R. 6380	95th	1977	222
H.R. 6384	75th	1937	040
H.R. 6388	93rd	1973	144
H.R. 6400	89th	1965	105
H.R. 6403	92nd	1971	099
H.R. 6405	95th	1977	152
H.R. 6418	90th	1967	144
H.R. 6434	83rd	1953-1954	054
H.R. 6434	83rd	1953-1954	144
H.R. 6436	81st	1949	074
H.R. 6436	81st	1949	075
H.R. 6436	86th	1959	144
H.R. 6441	87th	1961	144
H.R. 6444	92nd	1971	053
H.R. 6447	75th	1937	075
H.R. 6448	79th	1946	039
H.R. 6448	79th	1946	071
H.R. 6452	93rd	1973	156
H.R. 6456	85th	1957	054

Bill No.	Congress	Year	Record Number
H.R. 6462	73rd	1934	001
H.R. 6501	95th	1977	212
H.R. 6501	95th	1977	229
H.R. 6501	95th	1977	233
H.R. 6502	95th	1977	211
H.R. 6512	77th	1942	040
H.R. 6513	85th	1957	086
H.R. 6518	53rd	1894	144
H.R. 6518	88th	1963	130
H.R. 6518	88th	1963	144
H.R. 6525	82nd	1952	053
H.R. 6533	79th	1946	144
H.R. 6539	63rd	1943-1944	028
H.R. 6558	94th	1975-1976	197
H.R. 6578	82nd	1952	073
H.R. 6590	84th	1955	037
H.R. 6597	53rd	1894	075
H.R. 6605	92nd	1971	144
H.R. 6608	83rd	1953	009
H.R. 6616	83rd	1953-1954	006
H.R. 6649	85th	1957	086
H.R. 6650	55th	1898	075
H.R. 6650	85th	1957	086
H.R. 6655	95th	1977	213
H.R. 6659	85th	1957	144

Bill No.	Congress	Year	Record Number
H.R. 6667	96th	1980	254
H.R. 6668	93rd	1973-1974	003
H.R. 6668	95th	1977	104
H.R. 6669	95th	1977-1978	222
H.R. 6670	83rd	1953	006
H.R. 6672	79th	1946	071
H.R. 6675	89th	1965	053
H.R. 6681	80th	1948	054
H.R. 6695	76th	1939	021
H.R. 6695	82nd	1952	076
H.R. 6705	80th	1948	061
H.R. 6714	95th	1977	077
H.R. 6715	68th	1924	079
H.R. 6716	91st	1969	073
H.R. 6726	80th	1948	144
H.R. 6729	80th	1948	144
H.R. 6736	81st	1950	003
H.R. 6739	89th	1965	111
H.R. 6747	85th	1957	054
H.R. 6750	91st	1969	144
H.R. 6760	92nd	1971	133
H.R. 6766	80th	1948	053
H.R. 6771	85th	1957	144
H.R. 6772	74th	1935-1936	226
H.R. 6775	87th	1961	090

Bill No.	Congress	Year	Record Number
H.R. 6778	91st	1969-1970	046
H.R. 6788	83rd	1953-1954	078
H.R. 6788	85th	1957-1958	144
H.R. 6827	95th	1977	171
H.R. 6828	88th	1963	144
H.R. 6839	96th	1980	152
H.R. 6852	77th	1942	071
H.R. 6852	86th	1959	054
H.R. 6856	82nd	1952	144
H.R. 6871	86th	1959-1960	144
H.R. 6873	76th	1939	075
H.R. 6874	76th	1939	075
H.R. 6875	76th	1939	075
H.R. 6878	76th	1939	075
H.R. 6890	79th	1946	031
H.R. 6900	71st	1929	010
H.R. 6900	95th	1977-1978	239
H.R. 6901	77th	1942	071
H.R. 6903	79th	1946	040
H.R. 6906	74th	1935	054
H.R. 6910	95th	1977	220
H.R. 6950	90th	1967	120
H.R. 6954	95th	1977	234
H.R. 6976	73rd	1934	030
H.R. 6987	71st	1929	010

Bill No.	Congress	Year	Record Number
H.R. 6989	71st	1929	008
H.R. 6990	71st	1929	006
H.R. 6990	71st	1929	007
H.R. 6990	71st	1929	009
H.R. 6990	71st	1929	014
H.R. 6990	71st	1929	016
H.R. 6990	71st	1929	018
H.R. 6990	71st	1929	020
H.R. 6990	71st	1929	021
H.R. 6990	71st	1929	025
H.R. 7002	77th	1942	054
H.R. 7005	72nd	1932	042
H.R. 7005	82nd	1952	067
H.R. 7010	66th	1919	034
H.R. 7010	89th	1965	111
H.R. 7014	94th	1975	181
H.R. 7020	96th	1980	249
H.R. 7040	87th	1961	086
H.R. 7042	89th	1965-1966	054
H.R. 7046	95th	1977	223
H.R. 7049	84th	1955-1956	144
H.R. 7059	73rd	1934	029
H.R. 7070	91st	1969	005
H.R. 7072	92nd	1971	144
H.R. 7073	95th	1977	208

Bill No.	Congress	Year	Record Number
H.R. 7077	67th	1921-1922	034
H.R. 7083	55th	1897	084
H.R. 7087	69th	1926	075
H.R. 7092	89th	1965	073
H.R. 7094	56th	1900-1901	040
H.R. 7107	92nd	1971	174
H.R. 7108	94th	1975-1976	204
H.R. 7120	86th	1959	144
H.R. 7125	83rd	1954	054
H.R. 7125	83rd	1954	144
H.R. 7130	93rd	1973-1974	157
H.R. 7130	93rd	1973-1974	158
H.R. 7130	93rd	1973-1974	159
H.R. 7130	93rd	1973-1974	160
H.R. 7151	85th	1957	034
H.R. 7152	88th	1963-1964	096
H.R. 7152	88th	1963-1964	097
H.R. 7152	88th	1963-1964	098
H.R. 7152	88th	1963-1964	133
H.R. 7159	97th	1982	254
H.R. 7161	89th	1965	111
H.R. 7173	77th	1942	008
H.R. 7173	77th	1942	021
H.R. 7175	95th	1977-1978	245
H.R. 7176	82nd	1952	061

Bill No.	Congress	Year	Record Number
H.R. 7187	76th	1939	084
H.R. 7192	76th	1939	071
H.R. 7200	75th	1937	047
H.R. 7200	93rd	1973	053
H.R. 7201	70th	1927-1928	031
H.R. 7211	92nd	1971-1972	202
H.R. 7211	92nd	1971-1972	203
H.R. 7234	87th	1961	086
H.R. 7234	88th	1963	099
H.R. 7235	87th	1961	086
H.R. 7239	88th	1963	099
H.R. 7248	92nd	1971	029
H.R. 7254	72nd	1932	042
H.R. 7258	88th	1963	099
H.R. 7265	86th	1959	087
H.R. 7265	86th	1959	088
H.R. 7273	68th	1924	071
H.R. 7280	77th	1942	057
H.R. 7293	92nd	1971	099
H.R. 7296	52nd	1892	040
H.R. 7304	77th	1942	059
H.R. 7306	96th	1980	250
H.R. 7309	95th	1977	223
H.R. 7345	95th	1977	212
H.R. 7353	94th	1975	183

Bill No.	Congress	Year	Record Number
H.R. 7366	92nd	1971	073
H.R. 7383	85th	1957	144
H.R. 7390	85th	1957	135
H.R. 7416	84th	1955-1956	034
H.R. 7426	73rd	1934	054
H.R. 7428	72nd	1932	075
H.R. 7430	86th	1959	054
H.R. 7476	86th	1959	144
H.R. 7480	49th	1886	144
H.R. 7480	86th	1959-1960	054
H.R. 7500	86th	1959	067
H.R. 7519	75th	1937	053
H.R. 7521	74th	1935	051
H.R. 7589	75th	1937	053
H.R. 7591	77th	1942	071
H.R. 7605	84th	1955	054
H.R. 7606	84th	1955	054
H.R. 7607	84th	1955	054
H.R. 7607	85th	1957	086
H.R. 7609	62nd	1911	075
H.R. 7624	86th	1959-1960	054
H.R. 7624	86th	1959-1960	144
H.R. 7655	89th	1965-1966	054
H.R. 7656	82nd	1952	040
H.R. 7670	81st	1950	005

Bill No.	Congress	Year	Record Number
H.R. 7672	73rd	1934	144
H.R. 7677	93rd	1973	173
H.R. 7679	95th	1977-1978	223
H.R. 7680	86th	1959	088
H.R. 7691	82nd	1952	004
H.R. 7700	85th	1957	054
H.R. 7704	94th	1975	209
H.R. 7705	91st	1969	005
H.R. 7710	62nd	1911	075
H.R. 7711	62nd	1911	075
H.R. 7713	77th	1942	070
H.R. 7716	72nd	1932-1933	038
H.R. 7732	84th	1955-1956	054
H.R. 7750	89th	1965	067
H.R. 7764	84th	1955	054
H.R. 7767	94th	1975	177
H.R. 7780	93rd	1973-1974	003
H.R. 7783	82nd	1952	040
H.R. 7786	81st	1950	061
H.R. 7794	82nd	1952	074
H.R. 7794	82nd	1952	075
H.R. 7797	89th	1965-1966	054
H.R. 7798	85th	1957	054
H.R. 7802	85th	1957	086
H.R. 7806	93rd	1973	144

Bill No.	Congress	Year	Record Number
H.R. 7815	89th	1965-1966	054
H.R. 7819	95th	1977-1978	223
H.R. 7820	89th	1965	054
H.R. 7830	94th	1975	185
H.R. 7835	73rd	1934	079
H.R. 7839	83rd	1954	144
H.R. 7840	83rd	1954	053
H.R. 7847	86th	1959-1960	054
H.R. 7847	86th	1959-1960	144
H.R. 7855	88th	1963	144
H.R. 7878	95th	1977	208
H.R. 7885	88th	1963	067
H.R. 7896	89th	1965	105
H.R. 7913	75th	1937	054
H.R. 7916	87th	1961	073
H.R. 7925	89th	1965	054
H.R. 7927	87th	1961-1962	144
H.R. 7935	93rd	1973	154
H.R. 7937	74th	1935	049
H.R. 7938	85th	1957	054
H.R. 7939	50th	1888	040
H.R. 7951	63rd	1913-1914	029
H.R. 7959	68th	1924	040
H.R. 7960	85th	1957	086
H.R. 7964	73rd	1934	054

Bill No.	Congress	Year	Record Number
H.R. 7977	90th	1967	144
H.R. 7978	74th	1935	047
H.R. 7978	74th	1935	048
H.R. 7978	74th	1935	049
H.R. 7980	74th	1935	144
H.R. 7981	74th	1935	051
H.R. 7984	89th	1965	144
H.R. 7985	86th	1959	038
H.R. 7995	71st	1930	042
H.R. 8000	88th	1963-1964	100
H.R. 8000	88th	1963-1964	106
H.R. 8000	88th	1963-1964	121
H.R. 8004	85th	1957	086
H.R. 8024	74th	1935-1936	029
H.R. 8065	92nd	1971	053
H.R. 8070	93rd	1973	147
H.R. 8073	56th	1900	075
H.R. 8076	95th	1977-1978	246
H.R. 8092	94th	1975-1976	152
H.R. 8100	88th	1963	053
H.R. 8112	85th	1957	054
H.R. 8117	96th	1980	171
H.R. 8152	87th	1961	144
H.R. 8152	93rd	1973	145
H.R. 8173	72nd	1932	040

Bill No.	Congress	Year	Record Number
H.R. 8177	68th	1924	006
H.R. 8177	68th	1924	010
H.R. 8177	68th	1924	011
H.R. 8177	68th	1924	012
H.R. 8177	68th	1924	016
H.R. 8177	68th	1924	020
H.R. 8177	68th	1924	025
H.R. 8177	68th	1924	027
H.R. 8180	83rd	1954	040
H.R. 8200	95th	1977-1978	217
H.R. 8206	68th	1924-1925	144
H.R. 8234	82nd	1952	144
H.R. 8235	96th	1980	250
H.R. 8238	86th	1959-1960	144
H.R. 8240	94th	1975	179
H.R. 8245	93rd	1973-1974	153
H.R. 8271	84th	1956	054
H.R. 8275	84th	1956	054
H.R. 8300	83rd	1954	079
H.R. 8300	83rd	1954	080
H.R. 8316	73rd	1934	054
H.R. 8323	89th	1965	054
H.R. 8325	84th	1956	004
H.R. 8342	86th	1959	087
H.R. 8342	86th	1959	088

Bill No.	Congress	Year	Record Number
H.R. 8344	88th	1963-1964	036
H.R. 8347	84th	1956	004
H.R. 8362	66th	1919	028
H.R. 8363	88th	1963-1964	094
H.R. 8364	95th	1977	223
H.R. 8368	56th	1900	075
H.R. 8371	89th	1965	102
H.R. 8377	89th	1965-1966	054
H.R. 8388	62nd	1911	075
H.R. 8390	85th	1957	054
H.R. 8400	86th	1959	087
H.R. 8400	86th	1959	088
H.R. 8400	87th	1961	144
H.R. 8418	83rd	1954	054
H.R. 8422	95th	1977	214
H.R. 8422	95th	1977	217
H.R. 8423	73rd	1934	049
H.R. 8423	95th	1977-1978	217
H.R. 8444	95th	1977	208
H.R. 8455	74th	1935-1936	004
H.R. 8458	59th	1905	084
H.R. 8464	89th	1965	103
H.R. 8465	81st	1950	040
H.R. 8480	93rd	1973	159
H.R. 8480	93rd	1973	160

Bill No.	Congress	Year	Record Number
H.R. 8490	86th	1959	087
H.R. 8496	89th	1965	144
H.R. 8533	53rd	1895	084
H.R. 8539	74th	1935	050
H.R. 8543	95th	1977	214
H.R. 8555	74th	1935-1936	051
H.R. 8557	74th	1935-1936	006
H.R. 8557	74th	1935-1936	010
H.R. 8560	84th	1956	004
H.R. 8578	72nd	1932	040
H.R. 8583	83rd	1954	040
H.R. 8597	87th	1961	053
H.R. 8599	87th	1961	144
H.R. 8603	94th	1975-1976	193
H.R. 8609	86th	1959	077
H.R. 8619	93rd	1973	144
H.R. 8624	83rd	1954	004
H.R. 8628	93rd	1973	166
H.R. 8629	85th	1957	054
H.R. 8629	92nd	1971	144
H.R. 8637	93rd	1973	156
H.R. 8638	95th	1977-1978	220
H.R. 8651	74th	1935	053
H.R. 8652	74th	1935	053
H.R. 8674	94th	1975	183

Bill No.	Congress	Year	Record Number
H.R. 8683	95th	1977	223
H.R. 8714	94th	1975	053
H.R. 8722	93rd	1974	045
H.R. 8722	95th	1977	230
H.R. 8723	87th	1961-1962	086
H.R. 8733	92nd	1971	053
H.R. 8748	84th	1956	054
H.R. 8754	86th	1959	144
H.R. 8755	86th	1959	144
H.R. 8760	89th	1965-1966	144
H.R. 8762	93rd	1973	159
H.R. 8773	94th	1975	182
H.R. 8776	62nd	1911	071
H.R. 8777	95th	1977	101
H.R. 8800	94th	1975-1976	192
H.R. 8805	74th	1935	054
H.R. 8811	95th	1977-1978	217
H.R. 8834	93rd	1973	219
H.R. 8835	93rd	1973	219
H.R. 8860	93rd	1973	156
H.R. 8862	83rd	1954	081
H.R. 8862	83rd	1954	082
H.R. 8870	74th	1935	050
H.R. 8873	85th	1957	015
H.R. 8873	85th	1957	022

Bill No.	Congress	Year	Record Number
H.R. 8876	93rd	1973	159
H.R. 8904	81st	1950	054
H.R. 8912	70th	1928	006
H.R. 8912	70th	1928	008
H.R. 8912	70th	1928	009
H.R. 8912	70th	1928	010
H.R. 8912	70th	1928	014
H.R. 8912	70th	1928	016
H.R. 8912	70th	1928	021
H.R. 8912	70th	1928	025
H.R. 8913	70th	1928-1929	010
H.R. 8916	89th	1965	099
H.R. 8923	85th	1958	069
H.R. 8941	74th	1935	054
H.R. 8945	85th	1957	054
H.R. 8963	92nd	1971	054
H.R. 8979	95th	1977	135
H.R. 8984	72nd	1932	071
H.R. 8994	85th	1957	144
H.R. 8996	85th	1957	144
H.R. 9005	94th	1975	067
H.R. 9005	94th	1975	077
H.R. 9009	87th	1961	005
H.R. 9020	83rd	1954	040
H.R. 9021	76th	1940	042

Bill No.	Congress	Year	Record Number
H.R. 9021	76th	1940	044
H.R. 9021	76th	1940	144
H.R. 9055	93rd	1973	144
H.R. 9056	93rd	1973	150
H.R. 9056	93rd	1973	151
H.R. 9058	94th	1975	185
H.R. 9065	84th	1956	053
H.R. 9084	50th	1888	084
H.R. 9093	92nd	1971	073
H.R. 9129	81st	1950	144
H.R. 9130	95th	1977	238
H.R. 9133	81st	1950	074
H.R. 9133	81st	1950	075
H.R. 9137	68th	1924	006
H.R. 9137	68th	1924	009
H.R. 9137	68th	1924	010
H.R. 9137	68th	1924	011
H.R. 9137	68th	1924	012
H.R. 9137	68th	1924	015
H.R. 9137	68th	1924	017
H.R. 9137	68th	1924	019
H.R. 9137	68th	1924	020
H.R. 9137	68th	1924	022
H.R. 9137	68th	1924	023
H.R. 9137	68th	1924	024

Bill No.	Congress	Year	Record Number
H.R. 9137	68th	1924	025
H.R. 9137	68th	1924	027
H.R. 9166	83rd	1954	054
H.R. 9176	81st	1950	068
H.R. 9176	81st	1950	247
H.R. 9212	92nd	1971-1972	126
H.R. 9212	92nd	1971-1972	140
H.R. 9215	93rd	1973	150
H.R. 9229	92nd	1971-1972	141
H.R. 9232	71st	1930	042
H.R. 9247	92nd	1971	133
H.R. 9247	92nd	1971	134
H.R. 9256	89th	1965-1966	115
H.R. 9259	75th	1938	071
H.R. 9264	92nd	1971	132
H.R. 9270	92nd	1971	144
H.R. 9294	94th	1975	204
H.R. 9296	58th	1904	084
H.R. 9304	81st	1950	071
H.R. 9323	73rd	1934	176
H.R. 9341	75th	1938	054
H.R. 9346	95th	1977	217
H.R. 9368	85th	1957	144
H.R. 9369	66th	1919-1920	040
H.R. 9388	92nd	1971	144

Bill No.	Congress	Year	Record Number
H.R. 9398	69th	1926	005
H.R. 9424	89th	1965-1966	152
H.R. 9437	73rd	1934	144
H.R. 9463	69th	1926	036
H.R. 9463	69th	1926	037
H.R. 9486	51st	1890	004
H.R. 9486	51st	1890	144
H.R. 9489	84th	1956	004
H.R. 9492	68th	1924	075
H.R. 9505	84th	1956	004
H.R. 9509	90th	1967	144
H.R. 9521	85th	1957-1958	054
H.R. 9542	89th	1965-1966	054
H.R. 9547	84th	1956	054
H.R. 9547	84th	1956	144
H.R. 9560	94th	1975-1976	204
H.R. 9567	89th	1965	108
H.R. 9567	89th	1965	144
H.R. 9576	94th	1975	198
H.R. 9590	88th	1964	144
H.R. 9596	73rd	1934	053
H.R. 9598	93rd	1973	150
H.R. 9601	95th	1977	239
H.R. 9611	75th	1938	029
H.R. 9617	93rd	1973	150

Bill No.	Congress	Year	Record Number
H.R. 9627	89th	1965	108
H.R. 9638	71st	1930	040
H.R. 9639	71st	1930	008
H.R. 9639	71st	1930	019
H.R. 9639	71st	1930	021
H.R. 9658	93rd	1973	166
H.R. 9678	83rd	1954	067
H.R. 9682	93rd	1973	150
H.R. 9682	93rd	1973	151
H.R. 9703	76th	1940	006
H.R. 9703	76th	1940	008
H.R. 9703	76th	1940	009
H.R. 9703	76th	1940	021
H.R. 9703	76th	1940	026
H.R. 9706	76th	1940	053
H.R. 9726	93rd	1973	156
H.R. 9727	92nd	1971-1972	144
H.R. 9729	83rd	1954	144
H.R. 9739	88th	1964	144
H.R. 9757	83rd	1954	081
H.R. 9757	83rd	1954	082
H.R. 9757	83rd	1954	144
H.R. 9766	75th	1938	054
H.R. 9794	83rd	1954	034
H.R. 9796	73rd	1934	054

Bill No.	Congress	Year	Record Number
H.R. 9815	55th	1898	075
H.R. 9815	75th	1938	071
H.R. 9824	93rd	1973	164
H.R. 9833	89th	1965	108
H.R. 9843	62nd	1911-1912	084
H.R. 9852	84th	1956	068
H.R. 9861	73rd	1934	036
H.R. 9861	73rd	1934	037
H.R. 9868	94th	1975	189
H.R. 9868	94th	1975	190
H.R. 9870	74th	1936	040
H.R. 9879	93rd	1973	159
H.R. 9892	90th	1967	003
H.R. 9900	87th	1962	091
H.R. 9911	73rd	1934	053
H.R. 9922	92nd	1971	144
H.R. 9928	89th	1965	108
H.R. 9932	66th	1919-1920	071
H.R. 9936	73rd	1934	040
H.R. 9936	92nd	1971-1972	054
H.R. 9953	51st	1890	075
H.R. 9962	83rd	1954	040
H.R. 9971	69th	1926-1927	038
H.R. 9981	71st	1930	075
H.R. 10000	88th	1964	068

Bill No.	Congress	Year	Record Number
H.R. 10000	93rd	1973	189
H.R. 10009	83rd	1954	144
H.R. 10013	94th	1975-1976	222
H.R. 10049	87th	1962	144
H.R. 10062	87th	1962	144
H.R. 10065	89th	1965-1966	134
H.R. 10068	75th	1938	071
H.R. 10076	71st	1930	034
H.R. 10082	76th	1940	053
H.R. 10085	76th	1940	053
H.R. 10104	89th	1965-1966	144
H.R. 10127	75th	1938	053
H.R. 10132	76th	1940	056
H.R. 10144	87th	1962	096
H.R. 10153	72nd	1932	075
H.R. 10155	72nd	1932	075
H.R. 10156	72nd	1932	075
H.R. 10157	72nd	1932	075
H.R. 10173	95th	1977-1978	237
H.R. 10203	92nd	1971	099
H.R. 10229	94th	1975-1976	152
H.R. 10230	94th	1975-1076	185
H.R. 10268	94th	1975-1976	205
H.R. 10268	95th	1977	228
H.R. 10269	95th	1977	228

Bill No.	Congress	Year	Record Number
H.R. 10284	94th	1975	142
H.R. 10285	95th	1977-1978	226
H.R. 10315	94th	1975	189
H.R. 10315	94th	1975	190
H.R. 10328	90th	1967	118
H.R. 10341	86th	1960	144
H.R. 10353	69th	1926	008
H.R. 10355	94th	1975	194
H.R. 10356	95th	1977	228
H.R. 10363	94th	1975	204
H.R. 10364	72nd	1932	006
H.R. 10364	72nd	1932	007
H.R. 10364	72nd	1932	009
H.R. 10364	72nd	1932	010
H.R. 10364	72nd	1932	011
H.R. 10364	72nd	1932	012
H.R. 10364	72nd	1932	014
H.R. 10364	72nd	1932	019
H.R. 10364	72nd	1932	020
H.R. 10364	72nd	1932	021
H.R. 10364	72nd	1932	024
H.R. 10364	72nd	1932	025
H.R. 10364	72nd	1932	026
H.R. 10394	94th	1975-1976	205
H.R. 10404	85th	1958	054

Bill No.	Congress	Year	Record Number
H.R. 10433	84th	1956	029
H.R. 10434	69th	1926	006
H.R. 10434	69th	1926	008
H.R. 10434	69th	1926	009
H.R. 10434	69th	1926	010
H.R. 10434	69th	1926	011
H.R. 10434	69th	1926	014
H.R. 10434	69th	1926	016
H.R. 10434	69th	1926	018
H.R. 10434	69th	1926	019
H.R. 10434	69th	1926	020
H.R. 10434	69th	1926	021
H.R. 10434	69th	1926	025
H.R. 10434	69th	1926	027
H.R. 10434	86th	1960	144
H.R. 10435	70th	1928	039
H.R. 10439	93rd	1973-1974	153
H.R. 10443	86th	1960	144
H.R. 10453	66th	1919-1920	037
H.R. 10456	86th	1960	144
H.R. 10463	86th	1960	144
H.R. 10475	86th	1960	144
H.R. 10498	94th	1975-1976	204
H.R. 10498	94th	1975-1976	209
H.R. 10503	75th	1938	026

Bill No.	Congress	Year	Record Number
H.R. 10518	89th	1965	113
H.R. 10519	84th	1956	054
H.R. 10519	87th	1962	144
H.R. 10528	71st	1930	005
H.R. 10578	84th	1956	053
H.R. 10595	90th	1967	003
H.R. 10597	93rd	1973	150
H.R. 10606	87th	1962	053
H.R. 10607	87th	1962	144
H.R. 10630	71st	1930	040
H.R. 10632	74th	1936	006
H.R. 10632	74th	1936	007
H.R. 10632	74th	1936	009
H.R. 10632	74th	1936	010
H.R. 10632	74th	1936	011
H.R. 10632	74th	1936	014
H.R. 10632	74th	1936	015
H.R. 10632	74th	1936	018
H.R. 10632	74th	1936	019
H.R. 10632	74th	1936	020
H.R. 10632	74th	1936	021
H.R. 10632	74th	1936	024
H.R. 10632	74th	1936	025
H.R. 10632	74th	1936	026
H.R. 10632	74th	1936	027

Bill No.	Congress	Year	Record Number
H.R. 10633	75th	1938	008
H.R. 10637	51st	1890	075
H.R. 10650	87th	1962	092
H.R. 10655	70th	1928	008
H.R. 10655	70th	1928	021
H.R. 10672	75th	1938	144
H.R. 10692	93rd	1973	150
H.R. 10692	93rd	1973	151
H.R. 10693	93rd	1973	150
H.R. 10693	93rd	1973	151
H.R. 10729	92nd	1971-1972	144
H.R. 10730	90th	1967	104
H.R. 10739	72nd	1932	042
H.R. 10740	72nd	1932	006
H.R. 10740	72nd	1932	007
H.R. 10740	72nd	1932	009
H.R. 10740	72nd	1932	010
H.R. 10740	72nd	1932	012
H.R. 10740	72nd	1932	014
H.R. 10740	72nd	1932	019
H.R. 10740	72nd	1932	020
H.R. 10740	72nd	1932	021
H.R. 10740	72nd	1932	025
H.R. 10740	72nd	1932	026
H.R. 10760	94th	1975-1976	219

Bill No.	Congress	Year	Record Number
H.R. 10769	58th	1904	084
H.R. 10790	90th	1967-1968	124
H.R. 10796	93rd	1973	156
H.R. 10854	95th	1977-1978	236
H.R. 10867	90th	1967	118
H.R. 10873	84th	1956	004
H.R. 10874	67th	1922	040
H.R. 10874	89th	1965	053
H.R. 10943	90th	1967	108
H.R. 10946	91st	1969	125
H.R. 10947	92nd	1971	144
H.R. 10952	93rd	1973	165
H.R. 10955	93rd	1973	156
H.R. 10969	85th	1958	068
H.R. 10976	72nd	1932	006
H.R. 10976	72nd	1932	007
H.R. 10976	72nd	1932	009
H.R. 10976	72nd	1932	010
H.R. 10976	72nd	1932	012
H.R. 10976	72nd	1932	014
H.R. 10976	72nd	1932	019
H.R. 10976	72nd	1932	020
H.R. 10976	72nd	1932	021
H.R. 10976	72nd	1932	022
H.R. 10976	72nd	1932	023

Bill No.	Congress	Year	Record Number
H.R. 10976	72nd	1932	025
H.R. 10976	72nd	1932	026
H.R. 10976	72nd	1932	027
H.R. 10987	69th	1926	008
H.R. 10998	95th	1978	238
H.R. 11001	95th	1978	238
H.R. 11007	94th	1975	189
H.R. 11009	94th	1975-1976	188
H.R. 11009	95th	1978	228
H.R. 11016	72nd	1932	075
H.R. 11019	72nd	1932	075
H.R. 11021	92nd	1971-1972	139
H.R. 11021	92nd	1971-1972	144
H.R. 11023	55th	1898-1899	005
H.R. 11035	93rd	1973-1974	183
H.R. 11071	92nd	1971	140
H.R. 11083	88th	1964	144
H.R. 11087	72nd	1932	075
H.R. 11099	87th	1962	144
H.R. 11101	90th	1967	124
H.R. 11102	91st	1969-1970	144
H.R. 11105	93rd	1974	104
H.R. 11107	90th	1967	124
H.R. 11124	92nd	1971	144
H.R. 11141	70th	1928	042

Bill No.	Congress	Year	Record Number
H.R. 11202	88th	1964	144
H.R. 11212	93rd	1973-1974	166
H.R. 11214	68th	1925	005
H.R. 11226	95th	1978	208
H.R. 11235	91st	1969	104
H.R. 11256	89th	1965-1966	114
H.R. 11258	68th	1924	006
H.R. 11258	68th	1924	008
H.R. 11258	68th	1924	009
H.R. 11258	68th	1924	010
H.R. 11258	68th	1924	011
H.R. 11258	68th	1924	014
H.R. 11258	68th	1924	015
H.R. 11258	68th	1924	016
H.R. 11258	68th	1924	017
H.R. 11258	68th	1924	020
H.R. 11258	68th	1924	021
H.R. 11258	68th	1924	022
H.R. 11258	68th	1924	023
H.R. 11258	68th	1924	024
H.R. 11258	68th	1924	025
H.R. 11258	68th	1924	027
H.R. 11266	93rd	1973	156
H.R. 11267	72nd	1932	034
H.R. 11274	95th	1977-1978	236

Bill No.	Congress	Year	Record Number
H.R. 11280	95th	1978	227
H.R. 11290	89th	1965-1966	114
H.R. 11297	89th	1965	117
H.R. 11318	95th	1978	232
H.R. 11356	84th	1956	067
H.R. 11363	91st	1969	152
H.R. 11365	90th	1967	124
H.R. 11374	74th	1936	021
H.R. 11401	90th	1967	124
H.R. 11403	68th	1925	039
H.R. 11414	85th	1958	144
H.R. 11420	74th	1936	006
H.R. 11420	74th	1936	007
H.R. 11420	74th	1936	009
H.R. 11420	74th	1936	010
H.R. 11420	74th	1936	011
H.R. 11420	74th	1936	012
H.R. 11420	74th	1936	014
H.R. 11420	74th	1936	017
H.R. 11420	74th	1936	018
H.R. 11420	74th	1936	019
H.R. 11420	74th	1936	020
H.R. 11420	74th	1936	021
H.R. 11420	74th	1936	023
H.R. 11420	74th	1936	024

Bill No.	Congress	Year	Record Number
H.R. 11420	74th	1936	025
H.R. 11420	74th	1936	026
H.R. 11420	74th	1936	027
H.R. 11450	93rd	1973	155
H.R. 11450	93rd	1973	156
H.R. 11476	67th	1920	025
H.R. 11501	94th	1976	209
H.R. 11510	86th	1960	067
H.R. 11510	94th	1976	204
H.R. 11522	84th	1956	144
H.R. 11569	51st	1890	003
H.R. 11576	93rd	1973-1974	144
H.R. 11581	87th	1962	054
H.R. 11581	87th	1962	144
H.R. 11582	87th	1962	054
H.R. 11602	86th	1960	043
H.R. 11602	86th	1960	044
H.R. 11602	86th	1960	144
H.R. 11607	91st	1969	053
H.R. 11633	68th	1924	040
H.R. 11656	94th	1976	189
H.R. 11656	94th	1976	190
H.R. 11697	85th	1958	144
H.R. 11707	64th	1916	040
H.R. 11742	84th	1956	144

Bill No.	Congress	Year	Record Number
H.R. 11764	84th	1956	053
H.R. 11765	89th	1965-1966	117
H.R. 11777	95th	1978	162
H.R. 11778	95th	1978	162
H.R. 11779	95th	1978	162
H.R. 11794	60th	1908	006
H.R. 11794	60th	1908	008
H.R. 11794	60th	1908	010
H.R. 11794	60th	1908	021
H.R. 11794	60th	1908	026
H.R. 11795	55th	1899	144
H.R. 11798	61st	1909-1911	001
H.R. 11814	85th	1958	054
H.R. 11832	88th	1964	144
H.R. 11833	91st	1969-1970	107
H.R. 11833	91st	1969-1970	144
H.R. 11843	67th	1922	226
H.R. 11864	93rd	1973-1974	165
H.R. 11865	72nd	1932	042
H.R. 11865	88th	1964	053
H.R. 11881	85th	1958	039
H.R. 11882	85th	1958	039
H.R. 11882	93rd	1973	155
H.R. 11886	95th	1978	229
H.R. 11887	85th	1958	039

Bill No.	Congress	Year	Record Number
H.R. 11888	85th	1958	039
H.R. 11888	95th	1978	229
H.R. 11888	95th	1978	233
H.R. 11896	92nd	1971-1972	137
H.R. 11896	92nd	1971-1972	144
H.R. 11926	84th	1956	144
H.R. 11928	93rd	1973	144
H.R. 11929	93rd	1973-1974	156
H.R. 11948	72nd	1932	006
H.R. 11948	72nd	1932	007
H.R. 11948	72nd	1932	009
H.R. 11948	72nd	1932	010
H.R. 11948	72nd	1932	012
H.R. 11948	72nd	1932	014
H.R. 11948	72nd	1932	019
H.R. 11948	72nd	1932	020
H.R. 11948	72nd	1932	021
H.R. 11948	72nd	1932	024
H.R. 11948	72nd	1932	025
H.R. 11948	72nd	1932	026
H.R. 11961	85th	1958	039
H.R. 11964	85th	1958	039
H.R. 11970	87th	1962	091
H.R. 11984	66th	1920-1921	034
H.R. 11984	66th	1920-1921	071

Bill No.	Congress	Year	Record Number
H.R. 12006	92nd	1971-1972	140
H.R. 12028	95th	1978	228
H.R. 12033	88th	1964	054
H.R. 12033	88th	1964	144
H.R. 12050	95th	1977-1978	236
H.R. 12052	86th	1960	068
H.R. 12085	91st	1969	144
H.R. 12089	92nd	1971-1972	132
H.R. 12092	90th	1967	124
H.R. 12094	72nd	1932	006
H.R. 12094	72nd	1932	009
H.R. 12094	72nd	1932	010
H.R. 12094	72nd	1932	012
H.R. 12094	72nd	1932	014
H.R. 12094	72nd	1932	015
H.R. 12094	72nd	1932	019
H.R. 12094	72nd	1932	020
H.R. 12094	72nd	1932	021
H.R. 12094	72nd	1932	025
H.R. 12094	72nd	1932	026
H.R. 12095	57th	1902	075
H.R. 12109	93rd	1973-1974	150
H.R. 12109	93rd	1973-1974	151
H.R. 12120	74th	1936	029
H.R. 12169	89th	1966	067

Bill No.	Congress	Year	Record Number
H.R. 12175	69th	1926	040
H.R. 12175	88th	1964	144
H.R. 12185	90th	1967	124
H.R. 12192	66th	1920	039
H.R. 12206	93rd	1974	173
H.R. 12215	84th	1956	144
H.R. 12216	51st	1890	075
H.R. 12228	88th	1964	144
H.R. 12250	95th	1978	230
H.R. 12255	95th	1977-1978	104
H.R. 12257	95th	1978	228
H.R. 12258	95th	1978	228
H.R. 12336	87th	1962	144
H.R. 12341	89th	1966	115
H.R. 12362	88th	1964	053
H.R. 12368	69th	1926	075
H.R. 12370	95th	1978	217
H.R. 12371	74th	1936	084
H.R. 12380	94th	1976	204
H.R. 12406	94th	1976	186
H.R. 12412	69th	1926	071
H.R. 12425	72nd	1932	006
H.R. 12425	72nd	1932	009
H.R. 12425	72nd	1932	010
H.R. 12425	72nd	1932	012

Bill No.	Congress	Year	Record Number
H.R. 12425	72nd	1932	014
H.R. 12425	72nd	1932	017
H.R. 12425	72nd	1932	019
H.R. 12425	72nd	1932	020
H.R. 12425	72nd	1932	021
H.R. 12425	72nd	1932	025
H.R. 12425	72nd	1932	026
H.R. 12425	72nd	1932	027
H.R. 12425	72nd	1932	028
H.R. 12435	93rd	1974	154
H.R. 12470	59th	1906	084
H.R. 12471	93rd	1974	170
H.R. 12481	93rd	1974	164
H.R. 12536	95th	1978	239
H.R. 12549	71st	1930-1931	006
H.R. 12549	71st	1930-1931	007
H.R. 12549	71st	1930-1931	008
H.R. 12549	71st	1930-1931	009
H.R. 12549	71st	1930-1931	010
H.R. 12549	71st	1930-1931	011
H.R. 12549	71st	1930-1931	014
H.R. 12549	71st	1930-1931	015
H.R. 12549	71st	1930-1931	016
H.R. 12549	71st	1930-1931	017
H.R. 12549	71st	1930-1931	018

Bill No.	Congress	Year	Record Number
H.R. 12549	71st	1930-1931	019
H.R. 12549	71st	1930-1931	020
H.R. 12549	71st	1930-1931	021
H.R. 12549	71st	1930-1931	022
H.R. 12549	71st	1930-1931	023
H.R. 12549	71st	1930-1931	024
H.R. 12549	71st	1930-1931	025
H.R. 12549	71st	1930-1931	027
H.R. 12549	71st	1930-1931	028
H.R. 12549	91st	1969	144
H.R. 12555	92nd	1972	183
H.R. 12575	85th	1958	039
H.R. 12580	86th	1960	053
H.R. 12611	95th	1978	231
H.R. 12616	85th	1958	085
H.R. 12647	95th	1978	208
H.R. 12677	86th	1960	089
H.R. 12695	70th	1928-1929	071
H.R. 12695	91st	1969	105
H.R. 12704	94th	1976	204
H.R. 12716	64th	1916-1917	075
H.R. 12716	85th	1958	144
H.R. 12741	92nd	1972	144
H.R. 12749	92nd	1972	073
H.R. 12752	89th	1966	109

Bill No.	Congress	Year	Record Number
H.R. 12784	85th	1958	054
H.R. 12815	87th	1962	054
H.R. 12831	86th	1960	054
H.R. 12833	87th	1962	144
H.R. 12853	86th	1960	089
H.R. 12855	93rd	1974	164
H.R. 12859	93rd	1974	156
H.R. 12863	65th	1918-1919	040
H.R. 12901	71st	1930-1931	029
H.R. 12906	93rd	1974	164
H.R. 12923	65th	1918	030
H.R. 12929	95th	1977-1978	236
H.R. 12931	92nd	1972	144
H.R. 12944	94th	1976	204
H.R. 12946	89th	1966	115
H.R. 12949	86th	1960	054
H.R. 12954	94th	1976	209
H.R. 12968	51st	1891	075
H.R. 12972	95th	1978	246
H.R. 13002	93rd	1974	171
H.R. 13026	65th	1918-1919	040
H.R. 13039	70th	1928	040
H.R. 13043	69th	1926	039
H.R. 13064	89th	1966	115
H.R. 13087	58th	1904	084

Bill No.	Congress	Year	Record Number
H.R. 13094	90th	1967-1968	226
H.R. 13103	89th	1966	117
H.R. 13103	89th	1966	120
H.R. 13104	89th	1966	144
H.R. 13113	93rd	1974	225
H.R. 13113	93rd	1974	226
H.R. 13138	85th	1958	144
H.R. 13141	69th	1926	075
H.R. 13167	95th	1978	219
H.R. 13176	93rd	1974	156
H.R. 13199	89th	1966	144
H.R. 13200	89th	1966	144
H.R. 13228	89th	1966	112
H.R. 13247	85th	1958	029
H.R. 13254	85th	1958	054
H.R. 13254	85th	1958	144
H.R. 13270	91st	1969	144
H.R. 13272	91st	1969	144
H.R. 13290	89th	1966	144
H.R. 13300	91st	1969-1970	053
H.R. 13311	95th	1978	208
H.R. 13324	92nd	1972	144
H.R. 13339	94th	1975-1976	204
H.R. 13343	95th	1978	241
H.R. 13364	95th	1978	238

Bill No.	Congress	Year	Record Number
H.R. 13367	93rd	1974	219
H.R. 13367	94th	1976	197
H.R. 13373	91st	1969-1970	129
H.R. 13450	65th	1918	039
H.R. 13452	70th	1928-1929	008
H.R. 13452	70th	1928-1929	021
H.R. 13455	85th	1958	144
H.R. 13456	85th	1958	144
H.R. 13482	85th	1958	144
H.R. 13487	69th	1926-1927	034
H.R. 13487	69th	1926-1927	075
H.R. 13500	95th	1978	238
H.R. 13511	95th	1978	217
H.R. 13511	95th	1978	236
H.R. 13517	91st	1970	134
H.R. 13565	93rd	1974	172
H.R. 13620	89th	1966	053
H.R. 13655	95th	1978	217
H.R. 13676	67th	1923	025
H.R. 13676	93rd	1974	161
H.R. 13678	93rd	1974	161
H.R. 13680	94th	1976	067
H.R. 13712	89th	1966	113
H.R. 13736	94th	1976	222
H.R. 13747	93rd	1974	156

Bill No.	Congress	Year	Record Number
H.R. 13777	94th	1976	202
H.R. 13777	94th	1976	203
H.R. 13778	95th	1978	241
H.R. 13826	91st	1969	144
H.R. 13827	91st	1969	144
H.R. 13834	93rd	1974	155
H.R. 13850	95th	1978	234
H.R. 13872	93rd	1974	173
H.R. 13906	93rd	1974	156
H.R. 13934	90th	1967	144
H.R. 13950	91st	1969	126
H.R. 14025	89th	1966	068
H.R. 14032	94th	1976	196
H.R. 14035	67th	1923	025
H.R. 14047	60th	1908	084
H.R. 14084	95th	1978	246
H.R. 14094	63rd	1914	033
H.R. 14096	90th	1967-1968	144
H.R. 14104	95th	1978	152
H.R. 14146	92nd	1972	141
H.R. 14146	92nd	1972	144
H.R. 14172	93rd	1974	166
H.R. 14173	91st	1969	143
H.R. 14222	67th	1923	031
H.R. 14249	95th	1978	238

Bill No.	Congress	Year	Record Number
H.R. 14298	94th	1976	194
H.R. 14299	94th	1976	195
H.R. 14355	89th	1966	053
H.R. 14368	93rd	1974	155
H.R. 14368	93rd	1974	156
H.R. 14451	94th	1976	199
H.R. 14465	91st	1969-1970	144
H.R. 14465	91st	1969-1970	231
H.R. 14493	93rd	1974	173
H.R. 14563	90th	1967-1968	053
H.R. 14580	91st	1969	067
H.R. 14622	61st	1909-1910	084
H.R. 14790	91st	1969	144
H.R. 14822	91st	1969	174
H.R. 14826	58th	1904	001
H.R. 14845	91st	1969	141
H.R. 14862	94th	1976	204
H.R. 14920	93rd	1974	166
H.R. 14929	89th	1966	077
H.R. 14944	65th	1919	071
H.R. 14965	94th	1976	204
H.R. 15023	92nd	1972	140
H.R. 15067	90th	1968	144
H.R. 15069	94th	1976	162
H.R. 15083	90th	1968	005

Bill No.	Congress	Year	Record Number
H.R. 15086	70th	1928	009
H.R. 15099	91st	1969	141
H.R. 15156	90th	1968	124
H.R. 15196	90th	1968	124
H.R. 15202	89th	1966	110
H.R. 15223	93rd	1974	156
H.R. 15263	90th	1968	067
H.R. 15276	93rd	1974	167
H.R. 15283	93rd	1974	162
H.R. 15288	64th	1916	075
H.R. 15301	93rd	1974	053
H.R. 15315	63rd	1914	075
H.R. 15361	93rd	1974	163
H.R. 15376	92nd	1972	136
H.R. 15382	93rd	1974	156
H.R. 15414	90th	1968	144
H.R. 15419	94th	1976	220
H.R. 15460	94th	1976	201
H.R. 15472	93rd	1974	156
H.R. 15479	91st	1970	144
H.R. 15537	69th	1926-1927	034
H.R. 15560	93rd	1974	156
H.R. 15612	93rd	1974	169
H.R. 15630	94th	1976	246
H.R. 15653	60th	1908	040

Bill No.	Congress	Year	Record Number
H.R. 15690	92nd	1972	144
H.R. 15700	91st	1970	073
H.R. 15733	91st	1970	053
H.R. 15750	89th	1966	067
H.R. 15757	90th	1968	144
H.R. 15758	90th	1968	144
H.R. 15785	90th	1968	107
H.R. 15791	93rd	1974	150
H.R. 15838	60th	1908	075
H.R. 15883	92nd	1972	045
H.R. 15890	89th	1966	115
H.R. 15894	66th	1921	040
H.R. 15927	92nd	1972	053
H.R. 15963	89th	1966	144
H.R. 15979	90th	1968	144
H.R. 15985	90th	1968	124
H.R. 15989	63rd	1914	071
H.R. 15989	63rd	1914	075
H.R. 16045	93rd	1974	156
H.R. 16076	89th	1966	144
H.R. 16090	93rd	1974	168
H.R. 16093	89th	1966	053
H.R. 16119	92nd	1972	138
H.R. 16136	63rd	1914-1915	033
H.R. 16155	91st	1970	141

Bill No.	Congress	Year	Record Number
H.R. 16215	93rd	1974	141
H.R. 16311	91st	1970	143
H.R. 16371	93rd	1974	169
H.R. 16373	93rd	1974	173
H.R. 16395	70th	1929	040
H.R. 16414	91st	1970	144
H.R. 16448	93rd	1974	219
H.R. 16562	92nd	1972	140
H.R. 16570	70th	1929	071
H.R. 16619	71st	1931	042
H.R. 16619	71st	1931	044
H.R. 16619	71st	1931	144
H.R. 16659	92nd	1972	138
H.R. 16668	93rd	1974	191
H.R. 16724	92nd	1972	138
H.R. 16725	92nd	1972	140
H.R. 16785	91st	1970	129
H.R. 16785	91st	1970	144
H.R. 16808	69th	1927	010
H.R. 16886	69th	1927	040
H.R. 16901	93rd	1974	156
H.R. 16982	71st	1931	040
H.R. 17054	71st	1931	040
H.R. 17069	69th	1927	042
H.R. 17070	91st	1970	128

Bill No.	Congress	Year	Record Number
H.R. 17085	57th	1903	075
H.R. 17090	92nd	1972	140
H.R. 17113	91st	1970	144
H.R. 17134	90th	1968	144
H.R. 17178	93rd	1974	219
H.R. 17255	91st	1970	130
H.R. 17255	91st	1970	144
H.R. 17268	90th	1968	068
H.R. 17276	69th	1927	008
H.R. 17285	89th	1966	053
H.R. 17409	93rd	1974	174
H.R. 17545	93rd	1974	156
H.R. 17550	91st	1970	143
H.R. 17555	91st	1970	134
H.R. 17570	91st	1970	144
H.R. 17576	59th	1906	001
H.R. 17577	93rd	1974	156
H.R. 17598	91st	1970	148
H.R. 17607	89th	1966	116
H.R. 17607	89th	1966	120
H.R. 17685	89th	1966	144
H.R. 17700	64th	1916	037
H.R. 17703	60th	1908	075
H.R. 17762	91st	1970	148
H.R. 17825	91st	1971	131

Bill No.	Congress	Year	Record Number
H.R. 17864	90th	1968	144
H.R. 17989	90th	1968	144
H.R. 18205	91st	1970	148
H.R. 18230	89th	1966	117
H.R. 18231	89th	1966	144
H.R. 18366	90th	1968	029
H.R. 18539	91st	1970	148
H.R. 18583	91st	1970	144
H.R. 18608	91st	1970	144
H.R. 18654	91st	1970	148
H.R. 18679	91st	1970	144
H.R. 18700	61st	1910	144
H.R. 18874	91st	1970	144
H.R. 18884	61st	1910	075
H.R. 18885	61st	1910	075
H.R. 18886	61st	1910	075
H.R. 18887	61st	1910	075
H.R. 19070	61st	1910	005
H.R. 19188	63rd	1914	071
H.R. 19195	91st	1970	144
H.R. 19200	91st	1970	129
H.R. 19389	61st	1910	075
H.R. 19436	91st	1970	144
H.R. 19466	60th	1908	084
H.R. 19504	91st	1970	144

Bill No.	Congress	Year	Record Number
H.R. 19853	59th	1906	006
H.R. 19853	59th	1906	008
H.R. 19853	59th	1906	009
H.R. 19853	59th	1906	010
H.R. 19853	59th	1906	014
H.R. 19853	59th	1906	015
H.R. 19853	59th	1906	017
H.R. 19853	59th	1906	020
H.R. 19853	59th	1906	021
H.R. 19853	59th	1906	024
H.R. 19853	59th	1906	026
H.R. 19853	59th	1906	028
H.R. 19877	91st	1970	144
H.R. 19911	91st	1970-1971	067
H.R. 19928	91st	1970-1971	144
H.R. 19962	61st	1910	005
H.R. 20386	60th	1908	084
H.R. 20388	60th	1908	008
H.R. 20585	61st	1910	075
H.R. 20975	63rd	1915	039
H.R. 20989	61st	1910	144
H.R. 21455	60th	1908-1909	084
H.R. 21481	61st	1910	075
H.R. 21592	60th	1908	006
H.R. 21592	60th	1908	008

Bill No.	Congress	Year	Record Number
H.R. 21592	60th	1908	010
H.R. 21592	60th	1908	021
H.R. 21592	60th	1908	026
H.R. 21776	62nd	1912	021
H.R. 21815	60th	1908	144
H.R. 21984	60th	1908	006
H.R. 21984	60th	1908	008
H.R. 21984	60th	1908	021
H.R. 21984	60th	1908	024
H.R. 21984	60th	1908	026
H.R. 22071	60th	1908	006
H.R. 22071	60th	1908	008
H.R. 22071	60th	1908	021
H.R. 22071	60th	1908	026
H.R. 22183	60th	1908	006
H.R. 22183	60th	1908	008
H.R. 22183	60th	1908	021
H.R. 22183	60th	1908	024
H.R. 22183	60th	1908	026
H.R. 22345	62nd	1912	075
H.R. 23193	62nd	1912	071
H.R. 23193	62nd	1912	075
H.R. 23377	61st	1910-1911	144
H.R. 23417	62nd	1912-1913	071
H.R. 23417	62nd	1912-1913	075

Bill No.	Congress	Year	Record Number
H.R. 23916	61st	1910	075
H.R. 24070	61st	1910	001
H.R. 24224	62nd	1912	007
H.R. 24224	62nd	1912	018
H.R. 24224	62nd	1912	020
H.R. 24782	60th	1908	006
H.R. 24782	60th	1908	008
H.R. 24782	60th	1908	010
H.R. 24782	60th	1908	021
H.R. 24782	60th	1908	024
H.R. 24782	60th	1908	026
H.R. 25133	59th	1907	006
H.R. 25133	59th	1907	008
H.R. 25133	59th	1907	015
H.R. 25133	59th	1907	026
H.R. 25162	60th	1909	008
H.R. 25162	60th	1909	021
H.R. 25162	60th	1909	024
H.R. 25162	60th	1909	026
H.R. 25552	61st	1910	040
H.R. 26277	62nd	1912	084
H.R. 27310	60th	1909	006
H.R. 27310	60th	1909	008
H.R. 27310	60th	1909	010
H.R. 27310	60th	1909	021

Bill No.	Congress	Year	Record Number
H.R. 27310	60th	1909	024
H.R. 27310	60th	1909	026
H.R. 27970	60th	1909	144
H.R. 28192	60th	1909	006
H.R. 28192	60th	1909	007
H.R. 28192	60th	1909	008
H.R. 28192	60th	1909	009
H.R. 28192	60th	1909	010
H.R. 28192	60th	1909	013
H.R. 28192	60th	1909	014
H.R. 28192	60th	1909	015
H.R. 28192	60th	1909	016
H.R. 28192	60th	1909	017
H.R. 28192	60th	1909	018
H.R. 28192	60th	1909	019
H.R. 28192	60th	1909	020
H.R. 28192	60th	1909	021
H.R. 28192	60th	1909	022
H.R. 28192	60th	1909	023
H.R. 28192	60th	1909	024
H.R. 28192	60th	1909	025
H.R. 28192	60th	1909	026
H.R. 28192	60th	1909	027
H.R. 28192	60th	1909	028
H.R. Con. Res. 24	100th	1987	254

Bill No.	Congress	Year	Record Number
H.R. Con. Res. 199	91st	1970	148
H.R. Con. Res. 559	95th	1977-1978	236
H.R. Con. Res. 611	91st	1970	148
H.R. Con. Res. 683	95th	1977-1978	236
H.R. Res. 47	82nd	1951	054
H.R. Res. 162	77th	1942	059
H.R. Res. 212	85th	1957	054
H.R. Res. 273	85th	1957	054
H.R. Res. 311	85th	1957	054
H.R. Res. 347	77th	1941	059
H.R. Res. 352	75th	1937	054
H.R. Res. 447	82nd	1951	054
H.R. Res. 1120	91st	1970	148
H.R. Res. 1964	91st	1970	148
H.R.J. Res. 1	92nd	1971-1972	148
H.R.J. Res. 2	93rd	1973	148
H.R.J. Res. 38	72nd	1932	042
H.R.J. Res. 277	65th	1918	029
H.R.J. Res. 278	82nd	1951	068
H.R.J. Res. 280	90th	1967	124
H.R.J. Res. 289	82nd	1951	031
H.R.J. Res. 330	84th	1955	083
H.R.J. Res. 331	84th	1955	083
H.R.J. Res. 332	84th	1955	083
H.R.J. Res. 375	73rd	1934	049

Bill No.	Congress	Year	Record Number
H.R.J. Res. 382	66th	1920-1921	030
H.R.J. Res. 406	96th	1979	068
H.R.J. Res. 413	63rd	1915	039
H.R.J. Res. 424	85th	1958	069
H.R.J. Res. 425	85th	1957-1958	069
H.R.J. Res. 478	96th	1980	068
H.R.J. Res. 516	81st	1950	031
H.R.J. Res. 520	96th	1980	068
H.R.J. Res. 542	93rd	1973	148
H.R.J. Res. 555	83rd	1954	082
H.R.J. Res. 573	99th	1986	253
H.R.J. Res. 615	85th	1958	069
H.R.J. Res. 648	98th	1984	252
H.R.J. Res. 649	86th	1960	144
H.R.J. Res. 669	92nd	1971	148
H.R.J. Res. 672	94th	1975	068
H.R.J. Res. 713	99th	1986	253
H.R.J. Res. 727	99th	1986	253
H.R.J. Res. 934	88th	1964	005
H.R.J. Res. 1056	93rd	1974	068
H.R.J. Res. 1151	91st	1970	148
H.R.J. Res. 1259	91st	1970	068
H.R.J. Res. 1302	91st	1970	148
H.R.J. Res. 1336	91st	1970	068
H.R.J. Res. 1355	91st	1970	148

Bill No.	Congress	Year	Record Number
S. 1	100th	1987	254
S. 1	87th	1961	029
S. 1	87th	1961	144
S. 1	91st	1969-1970	144
S. 2	79th	1945-1946	062
S. 2	88th	1963-1964	099
S. 3	89th	1965	101
S. 3	89th	1965	144
S. 4	65th	1917	084
S. 4	89th	1965	144
S. 4	93rd	1973	164
S. 5	74th	1935-1936	054
S. 5	75th	1937-1938	054
S. 5	75th	1937-1938	144
S. 5	82nd	1951-1952	073
S. 5	94th	1975-1976	135
S. 5	94th	1975-1976	189
S. 5	94th	1975-1976	190
S. 7	75th	1937	006
S. 7	75th	1937	008
S. 7	75th	1937	010
S. 7	75th	1937	026
S. 7	79th	1945-1946	063
S. 7	79th	1945-1946	144
S. 7	91st	1969	144

Bill No.	Congress	Year	Record Number
S. 7	95th	1977	208
S. 7	96th	1979	240
S. 10	78th	1943	070
S. 10	79th	1945	070
S. 10	80th	1947	070
S. 10	81st	1949	070
S. 10	92nd	1971	144
S. 11	79th	1945	070
S. 11	81st	1949	070
S. 13	95th	1977	212
S. 14	99th	1985	253
S. 17	45th	1877-1878	040
S. 18	28th	1844-1845	039
S. 20	45th	1877-1878	001
S. 21	89th	1965	144
S. 22	72nd	1931	071
S. 22	87th	1961	073
S. 22	89th	1965-1966	099
S. 22	94th	1975-1976	200
S. 24	89th	1965	073
S. 27	50th	1888	144
S. 30	91st	1969-1970	003
S. 30	91st	1969-1970	144
S. 32	92nd	1971-1972	185
S. 32	93rd	1973-1974	185

Bill No.	Congress	Year	Record Number
S. 32	94th	1975-1976	185
S. 34	79th	1945	062
S. 38	93rd	1973	144
S. 40	93rd	1973	159
S. 41	69th	1925-1926	035
S. 50	93rd	1973	104
S. 51	84th	1955	076
S. 51	99th	1985	253
S. 53	99th	1985	254
S. 54	101st	1989	257
S. 54	49th	1885-1887	001
S. 55	80th	1947	037
S. 65	98th	1984	101
S. 72	80th	1947	070
S. 74	68th	1923	025
S. 79	86th	1959	054
S. 88	59th	1905-1906	144
S. 100	93rd	1973	183
S. 100	94th	1975	183
S. 110	94th	1975	177
S. 117	81st	1949	054
S. 120	87th	1961	144
S. 121	92nd	1971	099
S. 143	95th	1977	142
S. 143	95th	1977	214

Bill No.	Congress	Year	Record Number
S. 143	95th	1977	217
S. 176	72nd	1931	006
S. 176	72nd	1931	008
S. 176	72nd	1931	010
S. 176	72nd	1931	012
S. 176	72nd	1931	014
S. 176	72nd	1931	019
S. 176	72nd	1931	025
S. 176	72nd	1931	026
S. 176	80th	1947	144
S. 188	28th	1844	039
S. 203	71st	1929	071
S. 210	96th	1979	241
S. 219	92nd	1971	099
S. 224	27th	1842	039
S. 226	86th	1959	053
S. 229	94th	1975-1976	152
S. 233	52nd	1891	075
S. 237	91st	1969	144
S. 241	96th	1979	243
S. 245	26th	1841	039
S. 247	81st	1949-1950	039
S. 249	94th	1975	176
S. 251	95th	1977	209
S. 251	97th	1981	251

Bill No.	Congress	Year	Record Number
S. 252	95th	1977	208
S. 252	95th	1977	209
S. 253	95th	1977	209
S. 257	39th	1866	001
S. 259	26th	1841	039
S. 260	93rd	1973-1974	189
S. 260	93rd	1973-1974	190
S. 275	92nd	1971	144
S. 276	86th	1959	054
S. 290	73rd	1933	071
S. 292	25th	1839	039
S. 293	25th	1839	039
S. 293	79th	1945	053
S. 297	35th	1858	040
S. 300	45th	1877-1878	075
S. 302	82nd	1951-1952	031
S. 306	89th	1965	107
S. 306	89th	1965	144
S. 342	73rd	1933	009
S. 342	73rd	1933	010
S. 342	73rd	1933	019
S. 342	73rd	1933	020
S. 342	73rd	1933	021
S. 342	73rd	1933	026
S. 355	91st	1969	126

Bill No.	Congress	Year	Record Number
S. 365	44th	1876	075
S. 370	89th	1965	108
S. 373	93rd	1973	159
S. 373	93rd	1973	160
S. 379	95th	1977	212
S. 379	95th	1977	229
S. 379	95th	1977	233
S. 383	74th	1935	071
S. 385	85th	1957-1958	144
S. 386	93rd	1973-1974	156
S. 389	51st	1889-1890	040
S. 415	71st	1929	071
S. 418	80th	1947-1948	004
S. 418	80th	1947-1948	144
S. 421	95th	1977	222
S. 424	93rd	1973-1974	202
S. 424	93rd	1973-1974	203
S. 426	93rd	1973	156
S. 431	98th	1983	254
S. 432	88th	1963	144
S. 433	93rd	1973-1974	156
S. 433	93rd	1973-1974	171
S. 440	93rd	1973	148
S. 441	86th	1959	144
S. 445	80th	1947	054

Bill No.	Congress	Year	Record Number
S. 455	87th	1961-1962	144
S. 467	91st	1969	126
S. 468	97th	1981	251
S. 475	75th	1937-1938	084
S. 476	71st	1929-1930	040
S. 476	95th	1977-1978	223
S. 477	95th	1977-1978	223
S. 478	95th	1977-1978	223
S. 489	93rd	1973	107
S. 491	95th	1977-1978	239
S. 494	99th	1985	253
S. 495	78th	1943	057
S. 502	93rd	1973	144
S. 502	93rd	1973	156
S. 505	86th	1959	087
S. 505	86th	1959	088
S. 506	67th	1921	040
S. 507	94th	1975-1976	202
S. 507	94th	1975-1976	203
S. 510	89th	1965	144
S. 510	96th	1979	241
S. 516	84th	1955	073
S. 521	94th	1975-1976	204
S. 525	80th	1947	039
S. 525	80th	1947	071

Bill No.	Congress	Year	Record Number
S. 525	92nd	1971-1972	140
S. 526	80th	1947	039
S. 526	80th	1947	071
S. 531	94th	1975	205
S. 538	100th	1987	255
S. 544	93rd	1973-1974	003
S. 547	76th	1939-1940	026
S. 555	95th	1977-1978	234
S. 565	93rd	1973	159
S. 579	66th	1919	028
S. 580	74th	1935	054
S. 582	92nd	1971-1972	141
S. 586	94th	1975-1976	141
S. 591	96th	1979	246
S. 595	75th	1937	052
S. 595	80th	1947-1948	040
S. 596	99th	1985	253
S. 600	89th	1965	108
S. 601	83rd	1953	054
S. 602	90th	1967	101
S. 602	90th	1967	144
S. 607	85th	1958	083
S. 609	85th	1958	083
S. 619	79th	1945-1946	029
S. 622	94th	1975	181

Bill No.	Congress	Year	Record Number
S. 637	67th	1921	028
S. 638	92nd	1971	141
S. 643	96th	1979-1980	245
S. 649	88th	1963-1964	144
S. 652	99th	1985	254
S. 658	82nd	1951-1952	038
S. 659	92nd	1971-1972	029
S. 659	92nd	1971-1972	108
S. 670	80th	1947	053
S. 670	97th	1981	251
S. 680	42nd	1873	001
S. 682	95th	1977-1978	208
S. 686	71st	1930	005
S. 686	79th	1945	005
S. 697	95th	1977	209
S. 702	78th	1943	071
S. 703	64th	1915-1917	029
S. 703	93rd	1973	159
S. 705	70th	1927	071
S. 714	95th	1977	209
S. 716	92nd	1971	073
S. 717	95th	1977	216
S. 719	95th	1977	209
S. 729	88th	1963	053
S. 731	86th	1959	144

Bill No.	Congress	Year	Record Number
S. 731	92nd	1971	148
S. 748	86th	1959	087
S. 748	86th	1959	088
S. 754	93rd	1973-1974	174
S. 758	80th	1947	066
S. 758	93rd	1973	159
S. 770	94th	1975	177
S. 777	97th	1981	254
S. 780	90th	1967	130
S. 780	90th	1967	144
S. 786	78th	1943	040
S. 788	90th	1967	122
S. 791	95th	1977-1978	239
S. 794	93rd	1973	161
S. 796	78th	1943	037
S. 817	94th	1975	198
S. 818	66th	1919	084
S. 818	91st	1969	105
S. 821	93rd	1973-1974	167
S. 821	93rd	1973-1974	210
S. 826	95th	1977	172
S. 830	90th	1967	122
S. 835	83rd	1953	054
S. 836	94th	1975	198
S. 846	93rd	1973	159

Bill No.	Congress	Year	Record Number
S. 851	86th	1959	004
S. 852	73rd	1933-1934	031
S. 853	95th	1977	068
S. 859	41st	1870-1871	002
S. 861	78th	1943	040
S. 863	84th	1955-1956	004
S. 869	96th	1979	234
S. 880	94th	1975	194
S. 882	88th	1963	093
S. 886	99th	1985	253
S. 887	93rd	1973	156
S. 888	93rd	1973	156
S. 890	84th	1955-1956	004
S. 890	84th	1955-1956	144
S. 892	77th	1941	075
S. 895	87th	1961	089
S. 895	92nd	1971	174
S. 897	95th	1977-1978	220
S. 901	96th	1979	254
S. 903	96th	1979	242
S. 905	93rd	1973	159
S. 910	88th	1963	093
S. 917	90th	1967-1968	123
S. 919	95th	1977	209
S. 921	92nd	1971	202

Bill No.	Congress	Year	Record Number
S. 921	92nd	1971	203
S. 921	93rd	1973-1974	155
S. 926	45th	1878	001
S. 928	77th	1941	084
S. 928	84th	1955	144
S. 932	96th	1979-1980	068
S. 932	96th	1979-1980	247
S. 933	101st	1989-1990	256
S. 946	94th	1975	204
S. 947	87th	1961	054
S. 955	99th	1985	253
S. 957	99th	1985	253
S. 961	89th	1965	076
S. 961	94th	1975-1976	184
S. 961	96th	1979	174
S. 962	89th	1965	076
S. 963	89th	1965	076
S. 964	89th	1965	076
S. 965	89th	1965	076
S. 966	89th	1965	076
S. 967	89th	1965	076
S. 968	89th	1965	076
S. 969	94th	1975-1976	198
S. 972	99th	1985	253
S. 974	91st	1969	003

Bill No.	Congress	Year	Record Number
S. 975	91st	1969	003
S. 976	59th	1905-1907	040
S. 976	91st	1969	003
S. 976	92nd	1971-1972	144
S. 977	94th	1975	191
S. 985	80th	1947	054
S. 987	86th	1959	053
S. 991	92nd	1971	073
S. 991	95th	1977-1978	241
S. 995	95th	1977-1978	235
S. 1002	86th	1959	087
S. 1002	86th	1959	088
S. 1003	90th	1967	112
S. 1011	91st	1969	073
S. 1013	89th	1965-1966	117
S. 1016	92nd	1971	139
S. 1021	95th	1977	210
S. 1028	87th	1961	144
S. 1028	96th	1979	174
S. 1030	93rd	1973	159
S. 1041	93rd	1973	202
S. 1042	79th	1945	054
S. 1051	91st	1969	099
S. 1053	95th	1977	209
S. 1064	96th	1979	242

Bill No.	Congress	Year	Record Number
S. 1067	93rd	1973	156
S. 1070	93rd	1973-1974	156
S. 1071	87th	1961	144
S. 1072	91st	1969	101
S. 1072	91st	1969	144
S. 1075	91st	1969	127
S. 1075	91st	1969	144
S. 1075	91st	1969	208
S. 1081	83rd	1953	068
S. 1086	93rd	1973	156
S. 1094	91st	1969	126
S. 1101	90th	1967	073
S. 1107	64th	1916-1917	028
S. 1111	88th	1963-1964	144
S. 1114	81st	1949	069
S. 1122	85th	1957	086
S. 1126	80th	1947	037
S. 1126	80th	1947	064
S. 1126	80th	1947	065
S. 1128	99th	1985-1986	254
S. 1136	93rd	1973	144
S. 1137	86th	1959	087
S. 1137	86th	1959	088
S. 1141	95th	1977	212
S. 1143	96th	1979	152

Bill No.	Congress	Year	Record Number
S. 1145	85th	1957	086
S. 1146	96th	1979	171
S. 1149	96th	1979	242
S. 1160	89th	1965-1966	111
S. 1160	89th	1965-1966	119
S. 1160	89th	1965-1966	170
S. 1163	92nd	1971-1972	104
S. 1172	89th	1965	108
S. 1178	91st	1969	126
S. 1179	93rd	1973	164
S. 1186	81st	1951	054
S. 1190	80th	1947-1948	054
S. 1196	87th	1961	053
S. 1206	79th	1945	008
S. 1206	79th	1945	021
S. 1213	93rd	1973	159
S. 1214	93rd	1973	159
S. 1215	93rd	1973	159
S. 1218	95th	1977	210
S. 1226	69th	1925-1926	031
S. 1229	89th	1965	144
S. 1238	92nd	1971	144
S. 1241	50th	1888	144
S. 1248	79th	1945-1946	071
S. 1256	95th	1977-1978	223

Bill No.	Congress	Year	Record Number
S. 1257	95th	1977-1978	223
S. 1261	92nd	1971	185
S. 1269	66th	1919	033
S. 1283	86th	1959-1960	112
S. 1283	93rd	1973-1974	172
S. 1285	79th	1945	039
S. 1285	79th	1945	071
S. 1292	81st	1949-1950	031
S. 1297	79th	1945	039
S. 1297	79th	1945	071
S. 1300	91st	1969	126
S. 1311	86th	1959	087
S. 1311	86th	1959	088
S. 1313	85th	1957-1958	053
S. 1316	95th	1977	152
S. 1325	96th	1979	249
S. 1329	95th	1977	135
S. 1340	95th	1977-1978	172
S. 1341	96th	1979	249
S. 1347	82nd	1951	053
S. 1351	93rd	1973	156
S. 1353	82nd	1951	053
S. 1356	88th	1963	053
S. 1360	95th	1977-1978	162
S. 1361	93rd	1973-1974	200

Bill No.	Congress	Year	Record Number
S. 1368	91st	1969	125
S. 1371	94th	1975	198
S. 1373	88th	1963	083
S. 1384	86th	1959	087
S. 1385	86th	1959	087
S. 1386	86th	1959	087
S. 1387	86th	1959	087
S. 1392	93rd	1973	159
S. 1404	48th	1884	040
S. 1406	94th	1975-1976	194
S. 1409	88th	1963	093
S. 1414	93rd	1973-1974	159
S. 1420	100th	1987	255
S. 1423	93rd	1973	146
S. 1425	94th	1975	180
S. 1428	81st	1949	054
S. 1432	94th	1975	177
S. 1432	95th	1977	220
S. 1435	93rd	1973	150
S. 1435	93rd	1973	151
S. 1439	94th	1975-1976	220
S. 1443	93rd	1973	067
S. 1457	87th	1961	089
S. 1466	46th	1880	075
S. 1474	94th	1975	204

Bill No.	Congress	Year	Record Number
S. 1476	78th	1943-1944	070
S. 1480	96th	1979-1980	249
S. 1501	93rd	1973	144
S. 1507	94th	1975	179
S. 1510	75th	1937	017
S. 1511	101st	1989-1990	257
S. 1516	93rd	1973	159
S. 1523	95th	1977	213
S. 1525	72nd	1932	045
S. 1528	95th	1977	171
S. 1529	87th	1961	005
S. 1537	82nd	1951-1952	039
S. 1537	94th	1975	068
S. 1538	95th	1977	219
S. 1540	95th	1977	043
S. 1541	86th	1959	144
S. 1541	93rd	1973-1974	157
S. 1541	93rd	1973-1974	158
S. 1541	93rd	1973-1974	159
S. 1541	93rd	1973-1974	160
S. 1542	83rd	1953	054
S. 1543	78th	1943-1944	040
S. 1547	92nd	1971-1972	140
S. 1552	87th	1961-1962	054
S. 1552	87th	1961-1962	144

Bill No.	Congress	Year	Record Number
S. 1555	86th	1959	037
S. 1555	86th	1959	087
S. 1555	86th	1959	088
S. 1556	95th	1977-1978	228
S. 1557	93rd	1973	164
S. 1563	82nd	1951-1952	003
S. 1564	82nd	1951-1952	003
S. 1564	89th	1965	105
S. 1575	86th	1959	144
S. 1576	86th	1959	073
S. 1588	51st	1889	084
S. 1589	84th	1955	053
S. 1597	94th	1975	177
S. 1604	57th	1901	075
S. 1605	88th	1963-1964	144
S. 1614	84th	1955-1956	054
S. 1617	95th	1977-1978	208
S. 1620	53rd	1894-1895	003
S. 1623	89th	1965	144
S. 1623	91st	1969	003
S. 1624	82nd	1951-1952	003
S. 1624	91st	1969-1970	003
S. 1625	94th	1975	197
S. 1631	93rd	1973	164
S. 1632	94th	1975-1976	192

Bill No.	Congress	Year	Record Number
S. 1637	92nd	1971	135
S. 1641	93rd	1973	159
S. 1642	95th	1977	212
S. 1643	95th	1977	228
S. 1644	92nd	1971	144
S. 1648	89th	1965	144
S. 1648	93rd	1973	159
S. 1652	95th	1977	222
S. 1653	87th	1961	003
S. 1654	87th	1961	003
S. 1655	87th	1961	003
S. 1656	87th	1961	003
S. 1656	95th	1977	219
S. 1657	87th	1961	003
S. 1658	87th	1961-1962	003
S. 1663	88th	1963-1964	111
S. 1663	88th	1963-1964	119
S. 1665	87th	1961	003
S. 1666	88th	1963-1964	111
S. 1666	88th	1963-1964	119
S. 1672	46th	1880	075
S. 1678	95th	1977-1978	208
S. 1678	95th	1977-1978	224
S. 1684	83rd	1953	040
S. 1686	93rd	1973	185

Bill No.	Congress	Year	Record Number
S. 1688	93rd	1973-1974	173
S. 1689	91st	1969	112
S. 1693	59th	1905	084
S. 1693	95th	1977	211
S. 1703	95th	1977	212
S. 1711	86th	1959	077
S. 1711	94th	1975	179
S. 1716	97th	1981	254
S. 1717	79th	1945-1946	144
S. 1717	82nd	1951	068
S. 1720	79th	1945	071
S. 1725	93rd	1973	154
S. 1731	70th	1927-1929	029
S. 1731	88th	1963	097
S. 1735	93rd	1973	156
S. 1744	94th	1975	204
S. 1752	91st	1969	144
S. 1753	95th	1977-1978	236
S. 1754	94th	1975	204
S. 1767	78th	1944	040
S. 1776	93rd	1973	144
S. 1794	81st	1949	144
S. 1795	84th	1955	144
S. 1801	70th	1927-1928	144
S. 1805	94th	1975	198

Bill No.	Congress	Year	Record Number
S. 1813	85th	1957-1958	086
S. 1821	79th	1946	040
S. 1838	67th	1921	071
S. 1838	95th	1977	135
S. 1839	89th	1965	054
S. 1843	90th	1967-1968	076
S. 1844	90th	1967	076
S. 1845	90th	1967	076
S. 1846	90th	1967	076
S. 1847	90th	1967	076
S. 1847	95th	1977	135
S. 1850	79th	1946	039
S. 1850	79th	1946	071
S. 1861	91st	1969	003
S. 1861	93rd	1973	154
S. 1866	83rd	1953	054
S. 1867	81st	1949	054
S. 1867	93rd	1973	053
S. 1871	76th	1939	055
S. 1871	95th	1977	215
S. 1872	90th	1967	067
S. 1880	92nd	1971	148
S. 1882	94th	1975	183
S. 1883	56th	1899	084
S. 1883	94th	1975	181

Bill No.	Congress	Year	Record Number
S. 1888	93rd	1973	156
S. 1895	85th	1957	054
S. 1901	83rd	1953	144
S. 1907	91st	1969	126
S. 1911	94th	1975-1976	187
S. 1922	87th	1961	144
S. 1928	73rd	1933	006
S. 1928	73rd	1933	009
S. 1928	73rd	1933	025
S. 1928	73rd	1933	026
S. 1929	95th	1977	229
S. 1929	95th	1977	233
S. 1937	88th	1963	096
S. 1944	73rd	1933	054
S. 1944	87th	1961	086
S. 1946	78th	1944	029
S. 1952	95th	1977	208
S. 1952	95th	1977	218
S. 1958	74th	1935	047
S. 1958	74th	1935	048
S. 1958	74th	1935	049
S. 1964	92nd	1971	135
S. 1976	95th	1977-1978	221
S. 1980	95th	1977	222
S. 1983	87th	1961	067

Bill No.	Congress	Year	Record Number
S. 1983	87th	1961	144
S. 1983	93rd	1973	152
S. 1991	94th	1975	187
S. 2000	73rd	1934	054
S. 2005	91st	1969-1970	107
S. 2005	91st	1969-1970	144
S. 2006	98th	1983	254
S. 2017	89th	1965	144
S. 2022	91st	1969	003
S. 2029	91st	1969	105
S. 2039	78th	1944	013
S. 2042	89th	1965	144
S. 2051	85th	1957	144
S. 2056	88th	1963	053
S. 2060	68th	1924-1925	144
S. 2062	93rd	1973	156
S. 2064	92nd	1971	135
S. 2067	90th	1967-1968	124
S. 2075	86th	1959	022
S. 2075	90th	1967	124
S. 2088	95th	1977	135
S. 2090	84th	1955	067
S. 2092	95th	1977	222
S. 2097	92nd	1971-1972	132
S. 2100	94th	1975	198

Bill No.	Congress	Year	Record Number
S. 2116	50th	1888	040
S. 2116	62nd	1911	071
S. 2116	82nd	1951-1952	003
S. 2117	95th	1977-1978	153
S. 2118	91st	1969	126
S. 2122	91st	1969	003
S. 2129	77th	1941	030
S. 2130	85th	1957	067
S. 2133	92nd	1971	144
S. 2137	85th	1957	086
S. 2141	50th	1888	084
S. 2141	77th	1941	054
S. 2150	94th	1975-1976	204
S. 2154	87th	1961	090
S. 2156	85th	1957	034
S. 2156	87th	1961	073
S. 2159	94th	1975	187
S. 2162	70th	1928	071
S. 2162	91st	1969-1970	144
S. 2162	94th	1975	204
S. 2167	92nd	1971	054
S. 2175	85th	1957	086
S. 2178	83rd	1953-1954	053
S. 2187	87th	1961	144
S. 2193	91st	1969-1970	129

Bill No.	Congress	Year	Record Number
S. 2193	91st	1969-1970	144
S. 2197	86th	1959-1960	054
S. 2197	86th	1959-1960	144
S. 2200	94th	1975	187
S. 2213	89th	1965	144
S. 2215	80th	1948	144
S. 2229	85th	1957	231
S. 2240	75th	1937	006
S. 2240	75th	1937	008
S. 2240	75th	1937	009
S. 2240	75th	1937	021
S. 2240	75th	1937	026
S. 2252	73rd	1934	045
S. 2257	68th	1924	040
S. 2266	95th	1977-1978	217
S. 2276	91st	1969	144
S. 2278	94th	1975-1976	201
S. 2282	89th	1965	144
S. 2284	91st	1969	126
S. 2289	92nd	1971	126
S. 2292	91st	1969	003
S. 2292	93rd	1973	161
S. 2296	93rd	1973-1974	162
S. 2302	89th	1965	108
S. 2303	77th	1942	071

Bill No.	Congress	Year	Record Number
S. 2317	92nd	1971	101
S. 2317	92nd	1971	144
S. 2318	92nd	1971-1972	140
S. 2328	69th	1926	008
S. 2328	81st	1949-1950	034
S. 2328	81st	1949-1950	075
S. 2331	94th	1975	195
S. 2345	100th	1988	256
S. 2345	79th	1946	031
S. 2355	73rd	1934	054
S. 2365	94th	1975-1976	198
S. 2379	84th	1955-1956	029
S. 2380	95th	1977-1978	208
S. 2384	95th	1977-1978	237
S. 2385	54th	1896	075
S. 2385	80th	1948	039
S. 2387	68th	1924	071
S. 2391	84th	1955	068
S. 2391	87th	1961	144
S. 2391	95th	1978	225
S. 2391	95th	1978	226
S. 2395	87th	1961	053
S. 2400	71st	1929-1930	005
S. 2401	92nd	1971-1972	202
S. 2401	92nd	1971-1972	203

Bill No.	Congress	Year	Record Number
S. 2405	91st	1969	126
S. 2421	73rd	1935-1936	045
S. 2423	98th	1984	252
S. 2424	86th	1959	038
S. 2428	92nd	1971	099
S. 2433	81st	1949	034
S. 2438	77th	1942	070
S. 2438	80th	1948	053
S. 2440	87th	1961	144
S. 2447	85th	1957-1958	144
S. 2453	83rd	1953-1954	052
S. 2453	91st	1969-1970	134
S. 2456	91st	1969	105
S. 2465	74th	1935	006
S. 2465	74th	1935	008
S. 2465	74th	1935	009
S. 2465	74th	1935	010
S. 2465	74th	1935	011
S. 2465	74th	1935	012
S. 2465	74th	1935	020
S. 2465	74th	1935	025
S. 2465	74th	1935	026
S. 2465	74th	1935	027
S. 2465	93rd	1973-1974	166
S. 2473	95th	1977-1978	236

Bill No.	Congress	Year	Record Number
S. 2474	95th	1978	217
S. 2475	75th	1937-1938	047
S. 2475	83rd	1953-1954	077
S. 2482	79th	1946	070
S. 2483	92nd	1971-1972	183
S. 2487	94th	1975	198
S. 2491	77th	1942	070
S. 2491	77th	1942	071
S. 2493	95th	1978	231
S. 2495	93rd	1973-1974	185
S. 2496	74th	1935-1936	036
S. 2496	74th	1935-1936	037
S. 2496	85th	1957	144
S. 2499	60th	1907	006
S. 2499	60th	1907	008
S. 2499	60th	1907	021
S. 2499	60th	1907	026
S. 2505	86th	1959	054
S. 2507	91st	1969	105
S. 2515	92nd	1971-1972	133
S. 2515	92nd	1971-1972	134
S. 2518	81st	1949	074
S. 2518	81st	1949	075
S. 2527	100th	1988	255
S. 2529	73rd	1934	144

Bill No.	Congress	Year	Record Number
S. 2529	94th	1975-1976	187
S. 2534	95th	1978	217
S. 2538	95th	1977-1978	236
S. 2539	95th	1977-1978	236
S. 2542	93rd	1973-1974	173
S. 2543	93rd	1973-1974	170
S. 2549	83rd	1953-1954	078
S. 2549	86th	1960	144
S. 2559	83rd	1953-1954	006
S. 2568	86th	1959	144
S. 2569	86th	1959	144
S. 2577	84th	1955-1956	046
S. 2578	94th	1975-1976	204
S. 2582	74th	1935	051
S. 2589	93rd	1973-1974	155
S. 2589	93rd	1973-1974	156
S. 2594	82nd	1952	068
S. 2596	81st	1949-1950	040
S. 2596	95th	1978	238
S. 2602	86th	1959	054
S. 2609	81st	1949-1950	069
S. 2613	53rd	1895	084
S. 2613	92nd	1971	144
S. 2617	92nd	1971	133
S. 2617	92nd	1971	134

Bill No.	Congress	Year	Record Number
S. 2632	58th	1903	084
S. 2635	94th	1975-1976	194
S. 2636	94th	1975	205
S. 2639	82nd	1952	053
S. 2640	95th	1978	227
S. 2644	90th	1967	144
S. 2650	93rd	1973-1974	165
S. 2652	97th	1982	254
S. 2654	86th	1959	144
S. 2657	94th	1976	108
S. 2658	93rd	1973-1974	165
S. 2674	85th	1957	144
S. 2675	92nd	1971	126
S. 2680	93rd	1973	155
S. 2687	76th	1939-1940	084
S. 2687	88th	1964	077
S. 2688	76th	1939-1940	075
S. 2688	80th	1948	066
S. 2704	95th	1978	208
S. 2710	94th	1975-1976	204
S. 2721	77th	1942	071
S. 2725	96th	1980	254
S. 2727	93rd	1973	154
S. 2730	77th	1942	070
S. 2747	93rd	1973-1974	154

Bill No.	Congress	Year	Record Number
S. 2751	77th	1942	057
S. 2758	95th	1978	225
S. 2770	92nd	1971-1972	137
S. 2770	92nd	1971-1972	144
S. 2771	94th	1975	205
S. 2772	93rd	1973	155
S. 2772	93rd	1973	156
S. 2775	66th	1919-1920	001
S. 2775	66th	1919-1920	033
S. 2776	94th	1975	187
S. 2780	67th	1921	031
S. 2782	88th	1964	101
S. 2788	91st	1969-1970	129
S. 2789	94th	1975-1976	198
S. 2800	73rd	1934	054
S. 2802	91st	1969-1970	141
S. 2805	90th	1968	144
S. 2806	91st	1969	134
S. 2809	91st	1969-1970	144
S. 2810	93rd	1973-1974	173
S. 2812	93rd	1973	144
S. 2816	86th	1960	073
S. 2819	92nd	1971-1972	067
S. 2825	80th	1948	040
S. 2828	95th	1978	229

Bill No.	Congress	Year	Record Number
S. 2828	95th	1978	233
S. 2839	90th	1968	053
S. 2846	93rd	1973-1974	156
S. 2856	94th	1976	205
S. 2858	73rd	1934	054
S. 2864	91st	1969	144
S. 2868	83rd	1954	054
S. 2868	94th	1976	205
S. 2870	95th	1978	228
S. 2876	95th	1978	239
S. 2880	85th	1957	054
S. 2883	74th	1935-1936	029
S. 2888	85th	1958	086
S. 2899	95th	1978	152
S. 2900	60th	1907	006
S. 2900	60th	1907	008
S. 2900	60th	1907	010
S. 2900	60th	1907	021
S. 2900	60th	1907	026
S. 2901	75th	1937	031
S. 2908	94th	1976	205
S. 2911	94th	1976	186
S. 2912	90th	1968	073
S. 2912	94th	1976	186
S. 2917	91st	1969	126

Bill No.	Congress	Year	Record Number
S. 2917	91st	1969	140
S. 2918	94th	1976	186
S. 2926	73rd	1934	047
S. 2926	73rd	1934	049
S. 2930	83rd	1954	053
S. 2947	89th	1966	144
S. 2953	94th	1976	186
S. 2956	92nd	1971-1972	148
S. 2963	88th	1964	144
S. 2963	93rd	1974	173
S. 2966	87th	1962	067
S. 2977	88th	1964	054
S. 2980	94th	1976	186
S. 2986	90th	1968	077
S. 2987	94th	1976	186
S. 2995	94th	1976	198
S. 2999	82nd	1952	037
S. 3005	89th	1966	112
S. 3008	89th	1966	144
S. 3010	89th	1966	144
S. 3022	56th	1900	075
S. 3033	95th	1978	162
S. 3034	93rd	1974	160
S. 3034	95th	1978	162
S. 3035	93rd	1974	156

Bill No.	Congress	Year	Record Number
S. 3035	95th	1978	162
S. 3037	94th	1976	204
S. 3038	94th	1976	204
S. 3040	73rd	1934	003
S. 3041	73rd	1934	144
S. 3043	76th	1940	008
S. 3043	76th	1940	009
S. 3043	76th	1940	010
S. 3043	76th	1940	011
S. 3043	76th	1940	012
S. 3043	76th	1940	013
S. 3043	76th	1940	014
S. 3043	76th	1940	015
S. 3043	76th	1940	016
S. 3043	76th	1940	017
S. 3043	76th	1940	018
S. 3043	76th	1940	019
S. 3043	76th	1940	020
S. 3043	76th	1940	021
S. 3043	76th	1940	022
S. 3043	76th	1940	023
S. 3043	76th	1940	024
S. 3043	76th	1940	025
S. 3043	76th	1940	026
S. 3043	76th	1940	027

Bill No.	Congress	Year	Record Number
S. 3043	76th	1940	028
S. 3044	93rd	1974	168
S. 3046	76th	1940	055
S. 3047	74th	1935-1936	006
S. 3047	74th	1935-1936	007
S. 3047	74th	1935-1936	008
S. 3047	74th	1935-1936	009
S. 3047	74th	1935-1936	010
S. 3047	74th	1935-1936	011
S. 3047	74th	1935-1936	012
S. 3047	74th	1935-1936	014
S. 3047	74th	1935-1936	015
S. 3047	74th	1935-1936	017
S. 3047	74th	1935-1936	018
S. 3047	74th	1935-1936	019
S. 3047	74th	1935-1936	020
S. 3047	74th	1935-1936	021
S. 3047	74th	1935-1936	022
S. 3047	74th	1935-1936	023
S. 3047	74th	1935-1936	024
S. 3047	74th	1935-1936	026
S. 3047	74th	1935-1936	027
S. 3049	88th	1964	144
S. 3052	89th	1966	144
S. 3057	57th	1901-1902	001

Bill No.	Congress	Year	Record Number
S. 3057	57th	1901-1902	004
S. 3057	93rd	1974	156
S. 3059	71st	1930	041
S. 3065	94th	1976	186
S. 3066	93rd	1974	163
S. 3067	91st	1969-1970	135
S. 3068	86th	1959	088
S. 3072	91st	1970	130
S. 3073	75th	1937-1938	054
S. 3075	88th	1964	144
S. 3076	84th	1956	144
S. 3083	95th	1978	208
S. 3088	93rd	1974	161
S. 3091	63rd	1913-1914	029
S. 3091	94th	1976	162
S. 3095	90th	1968	144
S. 3108	91st	1969-1970	144
S. 3112	89th	1966	144
S. 3116	93rd	1974	173
S. 3122	92nd	1972	144
S. 3122	94th	1976	152
S. 3149	94th	1976	196
S. 3150	74th	1935	053
S. 3151	74th	1935	053
S. 3160	70th	1928	008

Bill No.	Congress	Year	Record Number
S. 3161	60th	1908	084
S. 3183	91st	1970	141
S. 3183	94th	1976	219
S. 3187	95th	1978	229
S. 3187	95th	1978	233
S. 3201	90th	1968	107
S. 3203	87th	1962	068
S. 3203	93rd	1974	161
S. 3206	90th	1968	144
S. 3211	90th	1968	124
S. 3219	94th	1976	204
S. 3219	94th	1976	209
S. 3223	66th	1919-1920	071
S. 3224	85th	1958	144
S. 3225	94th	1976	198
S. 3229	91st	1969-1970	130
S. 3231	73rd	1934	053
S. 3231	93rd	1974	156
S. 3234	93rd	1974	169
S. 3242	95th	1978	230
S. 3246	91st	1969-1970	144
S. 3252	56th	1900-1901	040
S. 3254	89th	1966	144
S. 3266	73rd	1934	036
S. 3267	93rd	1974	155

Bill No.	Congress	Year	Record Number
S. 3269	68th	1924	005
S. 3270	93rd	1974	068
S. 3274	89th	1966	053
S. 3277	93rd	1974	156
S. 3285	73rd	1934	038
S. 3285	73rd	1934	052
S. 3287	93rd	1974	155
S. 3295	81st	1950-1951	036
S. 3298	89th	1966	112
S. 3302	91st	1969-1970	068
S. 3303	74th	1935	042
S. 3303	74th	1935	043
S. 3303	74th	1935	044
S. 3303	74th	1935	144
S. 3323	83rd	1954	081
S. 3323	83rd	1954	082
S. 3325	67th	1922	071
S. 3342	92nd	1972	139
S. 3342	92nd	1972	144
S. 3344	83rd	1954	001
S. 3355	91st	1970	144
S. 3357	81st	1950-1951	003
S. 3358	72nd	1932	075
S. 3370	85th	1958	073
S. 3376	74th	1935	051

Bill No.	Congress	Year	Record Number
S. 3379	83rd	1954	112
S. 3394	93rd	1974	067
S. 3400	89th	1966	144
S. 3410	67th	1922	071
S. 3418	90th	1968	144
S. 3418	93rd	1974	173
S. 3426	91st	1970	073
S. 3446	86th	1960	073
S. 3460	91st	1969-1970	141
S. 3462	92nd	1972	144
S. 3466	91st	1970	130
S. 3474	69th	1926	071
S. 3491	87th	1962	144
S. 3494	95th	1978	238
S. 3495	69th	1926	005
S. 3497	90th	1968	144
S. 3500	74th	1936	051
S. 3501	74th	1936	051
S. 3507	92nd	1972	141
S. 3507	92nd	1972	144
S. 3517	59th	1906	084
S. 3524	73rd	1934	144
S. 3529	92nd	1972	135
S. 3546	91st	1970	130
S. 3549	93rd	1974	156

Bill No.	Congress	Year	Record Number
S. 3553	91st	1970	099
S. 3557	86th	1960	073
S. 3560	93rd	1974	156
S. 3571	86th	1959	088
S. 3579	87th	1962	099
S. 3595	85th	1958	054
S. 3596	94th	1976	195
S. 3608	94th	1976	188
S. 3609	85th	1958	039
S. 3612	93rd	1974	053
S. 3614	91st	1970	144
S. 3616	84th	1956	053
S. 3619	91st	1970	144
S. 3622	94th	1976	204
S. 3633	93rd	1974	173
S. 3650	76th	1940	042
S. 3650	76th	1940	043
S. 3650	76th	1940	044
S. 3650	76th	1940	144
S. 3677	86th	1960	054
S. 3679	93rd	1974	156
S. 3690	83rd	1954	082
S. 3690	83rd	1954	144
S. 3708	89th	1966	115
S. 3708	89th	1966	144

Bill No.	Congress	Year	Record Number
S. 3711	89th	1966	115
S. 3715	92nd	1972	068
S. 3725	85th	1958	144
S. 3738	83rd	1954	034
S. 3744	84th	1956	084
S. 3745	84th	1956	075
S. 3745	91st	1970	144
S. 3758	86th	1960	089
S. 3769	90th	1968	108
S. 3769	90th	1968	144
S. 3770	94th	1976	220
S. 3777	89th	1966	053
S. 3815	86th	1960	054
S. 3823	74th	1936	084
S. 3823	89th	1966	073
S. 3827	92nd	1972	136
S. 3830	89th	1966	144
S. 3835	91st	1970	144
S. 3842	81st	1950	144
S. 3842	91st	1970	128
S. 3847	72nd	1932	042
S. 3852	81st	1950	054
S. 3855	84th	1956	144
S. 3880	85th	1958	085
S. 3880	85th	1958	144

Bill No.	Congress	Year	Record Number
S. 3880	85th	1958	231
S. 3881	92nd	1972	189
S. 3881	92nd	1972	190
S. 3889	81st	1950	040
S. 3912	85th	1958	144
S. 3920	76th	1940	053
S. 3922	93rd	1974	141
S. 3925	76th	1940	053
S. 3934	93rd	1974	156
S. 3936	81st	1950	068
S. 3936	91st	1970	174
S. 3940	92nd	1972	126
S. 3952	93rd	1974	219
S. 3957	93rd	1974	191
S. 3958	84th	1956	029
S. 3959	81st	1950	144
S. 3964	91st	1970	148
S. 3966	92nd	1972	138
S. 3969	75th	1938	026
S. 3970	60th	1908	075
S. 3972	60th	1908	075
S. 3974	86th	1959	088
S. 3983	65th	1918	028
S. 3985	72nd	1932	009
S. 3985	72nd	1932	010

Bill No.	Congress	Year	Record Number
S. 3985	72nd	1932	012
S. 3985	72nd	1932	014
S. 3985	72nd	1932	019
S. 3985	72nd	1932	020
S. 3985	72nd	1932	024
S. 3985	72nd	1932	025
S. 3985	72nd	1932	026
S. 4012	91st	1970	107
S. 4012	91st	1970	144
S. 4062	92nd	1972	138
S. 4100	67th	1922	031
S. 4101	67th	1922	025
S. 4110	74th	1936	051
S. 4141	91st	1970	144
S. 4164	76th	1940	056
S. 4164	85th	1958	144
S. 4165	85th	1958	144
S. 4166	85th	1958	144
S. 4193	85th	1958	054
S. 4203	84th	1956	144
S. 4220	57th	1902	075
S. 4220	84th	1956	054
S. 4231	84th	1956	054
S. 4237	85th	1958	029
S. 4256	55th	1898	084

Bill No.	Congress	Year	Record Number
S. 4332	74th	1936	051
S. 4355	68th	1925	008
S. 4355	68th	1925	010
S. 4355	68th	1925	014
S. 4355	68th	1925	020
S. 4355	68th	1925	021
S. 4358	91st	1970	130
S. 4358	91st	1970	144
S. 4360	69th	1926	076
S. 4368	91st	1970	144
S. 4404	91st	1970	129
S. 4418	91st	1970	144
S. 4444	65th	1918	040
S. 4557	65th	1918	040
S. 4569	72nd	1932	040
S. 4572	91st	1970	144
S. 4656	58th	1904	084
S. 4812	69th	1926-1927	034
S. 4812	69th	1926-1927	075
S. 4956	69th	1926	034
S. 4982	61st	1910	084
S. 5066	65th	1919	039
S. 5139	71st	1930-1931	029
S. 5265	65th	1919	071
S. 5452	70th	1929	031

Bill No.	Congress	Year	Record Number
S. 5635	61st	1910	075
S. 5636	61st	1910	075
S. 5687	71st	1931	019
S. 5687	71st	1931	025
S. 5714	61st	1910	005
S. 5776	71st	1931	041
S. 5904	71st	1931	042
S. 5904	71st	1931	043
S. 5904	71st	1931	044
S. 5904	71st	1931	144
S. 6131	61st	1910	144
S. 6155	60th	1908-1909	001
S. 6273	62nd	1912	071
S. 6273	62nd	1912	075
S. 6330	59th	1906	006
S. 6330	59th	1906	008
S. 6330	59th	1906	010
S. 6330	59th	1906	014
S. 6330	59th	1906	015
S. 6330	59th	1906	017
S. 6330	59th	1906	020
S. 6330	59th	1906	021
S. 6330	59th	1906	024
S. 6330	59th	1906	026
S. 6330	59th	1906	028

Bill No.	Congress	Year	Record Number
S. 7031	61st	1910-1911	144
S. 7795	64th	1917	028
S. 8190	59th	1907	006
S. 8190	59th	1907	008
S. 8190	59th	1907	010
S. 8190	59th	1907	015
S. 8190	59th	1907	021
S. 8190	59th	1907	026
S. 9439	61st	1910	005
S. 9440	60th	1909	006
S. 9440	60th	1909	010
S. 9440	60th	1909	021
S. 9440	60th	1909	024
S. 9440	60th	1909	026
S. Con. Res. 11	90th	1968	076
S. Con. Res. 51	82nd	1951	053
S. Con. Res. 80	95th	1977-1978	236
S. Con. Res. 104	95th	1977-1978	236
S. Res. 4	94th	1975	032
S. Res. 5	65th	1917	032
S. Res. 5	86th	1959	032
S. Res. 7	74th	1935	052
S. Res. 15	81st	1949	032
S. Res. 25	80th	1947	032
S. Res. 30	85th	1957	032

Bill No.	Congress	Year	Record Number
S. Res. 42	87th	1961	054
S. Res. 52	87th	1961	054
S. Res. 92	84th	1955	075
S. Res. 135	93rd	1973	156
S. Res. 194	75th	1937	054
S. Res. 195	64th	1916-1917	032
S. Res. 202	81st	1950	003
S. Res. 239	94th	1975	178
S. Res. 268	94th	1975-1976	032
S. Res. 400	94th	1976	206
S. Res. 524	95th	1977-1978	236
S.J. Res. 18	92nd	1971	148
S.J. Res. 40	89th	1965	076
S.J. Res. 41	86th	1959-1960	144
S.J. Res. 42	90th	1967	144
S.J. Res. 59	92nd	1971	148
S.J. Res. 85	84th	1955	068
S.J. Res. 87	90th	1967	076
S.J. Res. 94	94th	1975	068
S.J. Res. 102	88th	1963	037
S.J. Res. 109	71st	1929-1930	031
S.J. Res. 122	79th	1945	040
S.J. Res. 135	85th	1958	073
S.J. Res. 138	80th	1947	031
S.J. Res. 143	73rd	1934	049

Bill No.	Congress	Year	Record Number
S.J. Res. 170	80th	1947	226
S.J. Res. 172	83rd	1954	082
S.J. Res. 175	96th	1980	068
S.J. Res. 181	89th	1966	037
S.J. Res. 186	89th	1966	037
S.J. Res. 228	93rd	1974	068
S.J. Res. 229	63rd	1915	039
S.J. Res. 235	63rd	1915	039
S.J. Res. 252	76th	1940	030
S.J. Res. 252	76th	1940	031
H.R. 1122	100th	1987	255
H.R. 1142	81st	1949	054
H.R. 1160	25th	1839	039
H.R. 1161	25th	1839	039
H.R. 1180	82nd	1951-1952	144
H.R. 1186	81st	1949	054
H.R. 1188	78th	1943	057
H.R. 1190	79th	1945	039
H.R. 1203	79th	1945	063
H.R. 1206	79th	1945	063
H.R. 1209	81st	1949	054
H.R. 1216	66th	1919-1920	040
H.R. 1228	83rd	1953	039
H.R. 1232	99th	1985	253
H.R. 1234	86th	1959	004

Bill No.	Congress	Year	Record Number
H.R. 1235	87th	1961-1962	054
H.R. 1236	93rd	1973	161
H.R. 1237	80th	1947	144
H.R. 1237	80th	1947	224
H.R. 1256	81st	1949	054
H.R. 1270	80th	1947	007
H.R. 1270	80th	1947	008
H.R. 1270	80th	1947	021
H.R. 1281	93rd	1973	173
H.R. 1297	86th	1959	144
H.R. 1301	83rd	1953	039
H.R. 1342	99th	1985	253
H.R. 1346	86th	1959	144
H.R. 1362	79th	1945-1946	053
H.R. 1371	78th	1943	070
H.R. 1383	92nd	1971	144
H.R. 1400	92nd	1971	099
H.R. 1404	95th	1977	217
H.R. 1427	42nd	1872	002
H.R. 1432	101st	1989	257
H.R. 1438	61st	1909	079
H.R. 1484	95th	1977	223
H.R. 1491	73rd	1933	030
H.R. 1532	95th	1977	219
H.R. 1535	95th	1977	223

Bill No.	Congress	Year	Record Number
H.R. 1536	95th	1977	223
H.R. 1537	81st	1949	076
H.R. 1547	94th	1975	205
H.R. 1570	78th	1943	021
H.R. 1571	78th	1943	008
H.R. 1612	45th	1877-1878	075
H.R. 1616	99th	1985	255
H.R. 1644	76th	1939	017
H.R. 1661	92nd	1971	144
H.R. 1700	63rd	1913	071
H.R. 1700	63rd	1913	075
H.R. 1703	81st	1949	054
H.R. 1723	81st	1949	054
H.R. 1744	78th	1943-1944	040
H.R. 1746	92nd	1971-1972	133
H.R. 1746	92nd	1971-1972	134
H.R. 1749	78th	1943	040
H.R. 1775	99th	1985	253
H.R. 1814	86th	1959	054
H.R. 1815	80th	1947	039
H.R. 1815	80th	1947	071
H.R. 1829	41st	1870-1871	040
H.R. 1830	80th	1947	039
H.R. 1830	80th	1947	071
H.R. 1834	80th	1947	039

Bill No.	Congress	Year	Record Number
H.R. 1834	80th	1947	071
H.R. 1845	81st	1949	039
H.R. 1862	95th	1977	212
H.R. 1897	88th	1963	037
H.R. 1900	78th	1943	059
H.R. 1932	71st	1929	071
H.R. 1940	99th	1985	253
H.R. 1984	80th	1947	039
H.R. 2004	88th	1963	037
H.R. 2005	99th	1985-1986	253
H.R. 2018	99th	1985	253
H.R. 2022	99th	1985	253
H.R. 2023	81st	1949-1950	054
H.R. 2027	80th	1947	039
H.R. 2027	80th	1947	071
H.R. 2032	81st	1949	037
H.R. 2042	78th	1943	058
H.R. 2045	80th	1947	054
H.R. 2054	96th	1979	246
H.R. 2060	95th	1977	216
H.R. 2061	96th	1979	243
H.R. 2063	81st	1949	054
H.R. 2083	80th	1947	008
H.R. 2100	78th	1943	071
H.R. 2126	84th	1955	073

Bill No.	Congress	Year	Record Number
H.R. 2128	84th	1955-1956	039
H.R. 2166	94th	1975	175
H.R. 2181	80th	1947	040
H.R. 2208	99th	1985	253
H.R. 2211	85th	1957	004
H.R. 2218	78th	1943	058
H.R. 2218	96th	1979	152
H.R. 2223	94th	1975	200
H.R. 2245	78th	1943	058
H.R. 2245	80th	1947-1948	054
H.R. 2245	83rd	1953	054
H.R. 2272	93rd	1973	185
H.R. 2273	101st	1989-1990	256
H.R. 2277	78th	1943	058
H.R. 2296	76th	1939	040
H.R. 2309	83rd	1953	039
H.R. 2312	42nd	1872-1873	040
H.R. 2331	88th	1963	037
H.R. 2336	86th	1959	054
H.R. 2347	86th	1959	144
H.R. 2363	86th	1959	004
H.R. 2380	78th	1943	059
H.R. 2380	95th	1977	209
H.R. 2400	78th	1943	054
H.R. 2437	85th	1957	086

Bill No.	Congress	Year	Record Number
H.R. 2443	93rd	1973	159
H.R. 2444	96th	1979	241
H.R. 2464	82nd	1951	021
H.R. 2492	92nd	1971	141
H.R. 2492	92nd	1971	144
H.R. 2493	92nd	1971	141
H.R. 2493	92nd	1971	144
H.R. 2499	92nd	1971	005
H.R. 2504	95th	1977	214
H.R. 2506	79th	1945	005
H.R. 2516	90th	1967-1968	076
H.R. 2520	80th	1947	034
H.R. 2559	94th	1975	178
H.R. 2570	78th	1943	058
H.R. 2575	44th	1876	003
H.R. 2577	78th	1943	058
H.R. 2602	79th	1945	063
H.R. 2612	79th	1945	070
H.R. 2630	79th	1945	071
H.R. 2631	79th	1945	075
H.R. 2632	79th	1945	070
H.R. 2633	94th	1975	181
H.R. 2633	94th	1975	204
H.R. 2633	94th	1975	209
H.R. 2650	53rd	1893-1895	028

Bill No.	Congress	Year	Record Number
H.R. 2650	81st	1949	054
H.R. 2650	94th	1975	209
H.R. 2660	80th	1947	075
H.R. 2663	68th	1923	025
H.R. 2663	81st	1949	066
H.R. 2683	88th	1963	099
H.R. 2689	88th	1963	099
H.R. 2695	75th	1937	006
H.R. 2695	75th	1937	008
H.R. 2695	75th	1937	010
H.R. 2695	75th	1937	026
H.R. 2701	95th	1977	223
H.R. 2702	95th	1977	223
H.R. 2703	95th	1977	223
H.R. 2704	68th	1923	025
H.R. 2721	80th	1947-1948	144
H.R. 2735	94th	1975-1976	205
H.R. 2762	76th	1939	080
H.R. 2769	83rd	1953	054
H.R. 2816	96th	1979-1980	245
H.R. 2817	99th	1985	253
H.R. 2820	73rd	1933	040
H.R. 2820	95th	1977	230
H.R. 2836	81st	1949	054
H.R. 2839	81st	1949	054

Bill No.	Congress	Year	Record Number
H.R. 2842	93rd	1973	159
H.R. 2854	96th	1979	246
H.R. 2857	42nd	1872	075
H.R. 2861	80th	1947	037
H.R. 2884	81st	1949	054
H.R. 2899	81st	1949	054
H.R. 2900	81st	1949	054
H.R. 2904	81st	1949	054
H.R. 2913	94th	1975	219
H.R. 2932	94th	1975	204
H.R. 2934	42nd	1872-1873	002
H.R. 2938	81st	1949	054
H.R. 2957	97th	1981	254
H.R. 2982	81st	1949	054
H.R. 2984	89th	1965	144
H.R. 2986	89th	1965	144
H.R. 2995	81st	1949	054
H.R. 3004	75th	1937	006
H.R. 3004	75th	1937	008
H.R. 3004	75th	1937	010
H.R. 3004	75th	1937	026
H.R. 3014	54th	1895-1897	075
H.R. 3020	80th	1947	037
H.R. 3020	80th	1947	064
H.R. 3020	80th	1947	065

Bill No.	Congress	Year	Record Number
H.R. 3054	64th	1915	071
H.R. 3056	95th	1977	245
H.R. 3065	99th	1985	253
H.R. 3082	64th	1915	071
H.R. 3083	71st	1929	031
H.R. 3118	94th	1975	204
H.R. 3118	94th	1975	209
H.R. 3123	80th	1947	061
H.R. 3128	80th	1947	054
H.R. 3130	94th	1975	204
H.R. 3134	84th	1955	039
H.R. 3139	88th	1963	096
H.R. 3143	75th	1937	054
H.R. 3147	80th	1947	054
H.R. 3150	80th	1947	053
H.R. 3151	81st	1949	054
H.R. 3157	89th	1965	053
H.R. 3170	78th	1945	062
H.R. 3173	96th	1979	067
H.R. 3180	93rd	1973	149
H.R. 3183	86th	1959	144
H.R. 3184	66th	1919-1920	004
H.R. 3190	79th	1945	008
H.R. 3190	79th	1945	021
H.R. 3190	80th	1947-1948	045

Bill No.	Congress	Year	Record Number
H.R. 3190	80th	1947-1948	144
H.R. 3199	95th	1977	208
H.R. 3199	95th	1977	218
H.R. 3200	101st	1989-1990	257
H.R. 3203	80th	1947	040
H.R. 3209	95th	1977	208
H.R. 3211	77th	1941	075
H.R. 3214	80th	1947-1948	144
H.R. 3236	96th	1979	246
H.R. 3264	78th	1943	075
H.R. 3266	79th	1945	054
H.R. 3267	68th	1924	039
H.R. 3282	98th	1983-1984	254
H.R. 3298	81st	1951	054
H.R. 3298	82nd	1951	072
H.R. 3298	82nd	1951	144
H.R. 3302	86th	1959	088
H.R. 3310	88th	1963	053
H.R. 3321	63rd	1913	079
H.R. 3325	77th	1941	042
H.R. 3325	77th	1941	043
H.R. 3333	94th	1975	219
H.R. 3348	94th	1975-1976	205
H.R. 3378	85th	1957	135
H.R. 3387	95th	1977	217

Bill No.	Congress	Year	Record Number
H.R. 3399	95th	1977	222
H.R. 3404	84th	1955	004
H.R. 3409	95th	1977	223
H.R. 3453	99th	1985	253
H.R. 3456	77th	1941	008
H.R. 3462	79th	1945	070
H.R. 3464	96th	1979	246
H.R. 3476	93rd	1973	219
H.R. 3477	95th	1977	207
H.R. 3477	95th	1977	217
H.R. 3498	98th	1983-1984	252
H.R. 3505	92nd	1971	140
H.R. 3507	88th	1963	144
H.R. 3509	96th	1979	171
H.R. 3534	83rd	1953-1954	039
H.R. 3540	86th	1959	087
H.R. 3540	86th	1959	088
H.R. 3548	87th	1961	054
H.R. 3551	83rd	1953	054
H.R. 3558	96th	1979	248
H.R. 3589	82nd	1951-1952	014
H.R. 3589	82nd	1951-1952	018
H.R. 3589	82nd	1951-1952	020
H.R. 3604	83rd	1953	054
H.R. 3606	89th	1965-1966	099

Bill No.	Congress	Year	Record Number
H.R. 3615	78th	1945	062
H.R. 3615	92nd	1971	141
H.R. 3615	92nd	1971	144
H.R. 3639	90th	1967-1968	144
H.R. 3642	77th	1941	059
H.R. 3644	79th	1945	040
H.R. 3658	61st	1909	144
H.R. 3662	92nd	1971	144
H.R. 3669	82nd	1951	053
H.R. 3675	43rd	1874	075
H.R. 3694	79th	1945	074
H.R. 3699	75th	1937	017
H.R. 3700	80th	1947	034
H.R. 3708	89th	1965	104
H.R. 3708	89th	1965	180
H.R. 3730	86th	1959	144
H.R. 3744	95th	1977	215
H.R. 3748	80th	1947-1948	040
H.R. 3749	79th	1945	040
H.R. 3755	82nd	1951	053
H.R. 3756	79th	1945-1946	070
H.R. 3756	96th	1979-1980	244
H.R. 3757	79th	1945-1946	071
H.R. 3760	82nd	1951	074
H.R. 3760	82nd	1951	075

Bill No.	Congress	Year	Record Number
H.R. 3762	78th	1943	071
H.R. 3762	81st	1949	144
H.R. 3786	78th	1943	070
H.R. 3787	94th	1975	204
H.R. 3790	82nd	1951	061
H.R. 3809	91st	1969-1970	129
H.R. 3813	90th	1967	121
H.R. 3813	95th	1977-1978	221
H.R. 3835	92nd	1971	099
H.R. 3838	81st	1949	061
H.R. 3841	83rd	1953	054
H.R. 3841	95th	1977	223
H.R. 3852	99th	1985	253
H.R. 3861	88th	1963	093
H.R. 3874	78th	1943	070
H.R. 3875	96th	1979	242
H.R. 3884	94th	1975-1976	191
H.R. 3920	88th	1963	053
H.R. 3922	94th	1975	104
H.R. 3922	94th	1975	180
H.R. 3930	96th	1979	247
H.R. 3935	87th	1961	089
H.R. 3946	95th	1977-1978	236
H.R. 3961	78th	1944	061
H.R. 3972	74th	1935	054

Bill No.	Congress	Year	Record Number
H.R. 3975	82nd	1951-1952	039
H.R. 3980	87th	1961	054
H.R. 3980	87th	1961	144
H.R. 3981	94th	1975-1976	141
H.R. 3988	89th	1965	144
H.R. 3997	77th	1941	008
H.R. 3997	77th	1941	009
H.R. 3997	77th	1941	026
H.R. 4004	42nd	1873	075
H.R. 4014	85th	1957	054
H.R. 4018	91st	1969	144
H.R. 4022	88th	1963	093
H.R. 4023	96th	1979	254
H.R. 4036	87th	1961	144
H.R. 4044	80th	1947-1948	031
H.R. 4048	88th	1963	099
H.R. 4053	93rd	1973	159
H.R. 4054	82nd	1951	039
H.R. 4061	80th	1947	074
H.R. 4061	88th	1963	144
H.R. 4071	80th	1947-1948	054
H.R. 4073	94th	1975	101
H.R. 4099	84th	1955	054
H.R. 4100	84th	1955	054
H.R. 4102	80th	1947	039

Bill No.	Congress	Year	Record Number
H.R. 4111	94th	1975	176
H.R. 4114	80th	1947-1948	144
H.R. 4115	78th	1944	040
H.R. 4121	68th	1923-1924	029
H.R. 4148	91st	1969-1970	144
H.R. 4151	95th	1977	209
H.R. 4172	92nd	1971	053
H.R. 4191	93rd	1974	045
H.R. 4194	86th	1959	054
H.R. 4200	93rd	1973-1974	164
H.R. 4203	81st	1949	054
H.R. 4214	80th	1947	066
H.R. 4217	92nd	1971	144
H.R. 4222	87th	1961	053
H.R. 4234	45th	1878-1879	040
H.R. 4247	92nd	1971	144
H.R. 4249	91st	1969-1970	105
H.R. 4261	44th	1876-1877	001
H.R. 4261	44th	1876-1877	004
H.R. 4267	84th	1955	075
H.R. 4277	83rd	1953	054
H.R. 4279	90th	1967	144
H.R. 4287	95th	1977	216
H.R. 4292	93rd	1973	107
H.R. 4294	91st	1969-1970	129

Bill No.	Congress	Year	Record Number
H.R. 4299	87th	1961	090
H.R. 4304	80th	1947-1948	039
H.R. 4306	93rd	1973	107
H.R. 4341	95th	1977	228
H.R. 4353	85th	1957-1958	053
H.R. 4359	92nd	1971	144
H.R. 4369	94th	1975	209
H.R. 4383	92nd	1971-1972	135
H.R. 4384	79th	1945	029
H.R. 4387	82nd	1951-1952	040
H.R. 4388	96th	1979	152
H.R. 4389	95th	1977	219
H.R. 4394	82nd	1951-1952	040
H.R. 4409	95th	1977	220
H.R. 4415	88th	1963	144
H.R. 4432	85th	1957	054
H.R. 4433	76th	1939	015
H.R. 4433	76th	1939	017
H.R. 4461	94th	1975	185
H.R. 4466	86th	1959	144
H.R. 4468	95th	1977	222
H.R. 4470	80th	1947	054
H.R. 4473	82nd	1951	003
H.R. 4473	86th	1959	087
H.R. 4473	86th	1959	088

Bill No.	Congress	Year	Record Number
H.R. 4474	86th	1959	087
H.R. 4475	84th	1955	054
H.R. 4485	78th	1944	061
H.R. 4486	77th	1941	017
H.R. 4493	78th	1974	070
H.R. 4498	100th	1988	256
H.R. 4503	97th	1981	254
H.R. 4512	79th	1945-1946	144
H.R. 4523	74th	1935	070
H.R. 4544	95th	1977-1978	219
H.R. 4566	96th	1979	249
H.R. 4567	86th	1959	004
H.R. 4571	79th	1945-1946	031
H.R. 4571	96th	1979	249
H.R. 4572	85th	1957	014
H.R. 4573	90th	1967	118
H.R. 4584	92nd	1971	144
H.R. 4604	86th	1959	004
H.R. 4607	86th	1959	004
H.R. 4624	78th	1944	144
H.R. 4638	88th	1963-1964	083
H.R. 4646	78th	1944	060
H.R. 4653	85th	1957	086
H.R. 4662	87th	1961	144
H.R. 4672	45th	1878	075

Bill No.	Congress	Year	Record Number
H.R. 4674	93rd	1973	107
H.R. 4692	81st	1949-1950	039
H.R. 4696	48th	1884	040
H.R. 4700	84th	1955	039
H.R. 4700	86th	1959	053
H.R. 4716	94th	1975	053
H.R. 4723	92nd	1971	144
H.R. 4725	80th	1948	076
H.R. 4731	88th	1963-1964	054
H.R. 4744	84th	1955	053
H.R. 4749	92nd	1971	054
H.R. 4750	89th	1965	106
H.R. 4750	89th	1965	121
H.R. 4759	93rd	1973	156
H.R. 4761	79th	1945-1946	040
H.R. 4798	81st	1949	074
H.R. 4830	68th	1924	001
H.R. 4830	91st	1969	005
H.R. 4852	80th	1948	039
H.R. 4852	80th	1948	071
H.R. 4864	53rd	1894	079
H.R. 4871	76th	1939	006
H.R. 4871	76th	1939	008
H.R. 4871	76th	1939	009
H.R. 4871	76th	1939	021

Bill No.	Congress	Year	Record Number
H.R. 4871	76th	1939	026
H.R. 4873	93rd	1973	156
H.R. 4885	88th	1963	053
H.R. 4901	83rd	1953	054
H.R. 4906	77th	1941	057
H.R. 4908	79th	1945	037
H.R. 4918	84th	1955	144
H.R. 4929	87th	1961	086
H.R. 4937	80th	1948	054
H.R. 4944	83rd	1953	039
H.R. 4949	47th	1882	075
H.R. 4955	88th	1963	029
H.R. 4960	65th	1917	030
H.R. 4960	65th	1917	031
H.R. 4975	95th	1977	217
H.R. 4976	95th	1977	217
H.R. 4983	84th	1955	034
H.R. 4986	74th	1935	075
H.R. 4998	87th	1961	144
H.R. 5007	81st	1949	144
H.R. 5011	65th	1918	084
H.R. 5011	66th	1919	034
H.R. 5012	66th	1919	034
H.R. 5012	66th	1919	084
H.R. 5012	89th	1965	111

Bill No.	Congress	Year	Record Number
H.R. 5012	89th	1965	119
H.R. 5013	89th	1965	111
H.R. 5014	53rd	1894	075
H.R. 5014	89th	1965	111
H.R. 5015	89th	1965	111
H.R. 5016	83rd	1953	054
H.R. 5016	89th	1965	111
H.R. 5017	89th	1965	111
H.R. 5018	89th	1965	111
H.R. 5019	89th	1965	111
H.R. 5020	89th	1965	111
H.R. 5021	89th	1965	111
H.R. 5027	87th	1961	053
H.R. 5027	95th	1977	211
H.R. 5029	95th	1977-1978	233
H.R. 5030	75th	1937-1938	040
H.R. 5037	90th	1967-1968	123
H.R. 5037	90th	1967-1968	131
H.R. 5037	90th	1967-1968	145
H.R. 5037	90th	1967-1968	243
H.R. 5050	93rd	1973-1974	176
H.R. 5055	83rd	1953	054
H.R. 5055	95th	1977	235
H.R. 5060	92nd	1971	144
H.R. 5069	83rd	1953	112

Bill No.	Congress	Year	Record Number
H.R. 5075	87th	1961	053
H.R. 5075	94th	1975	189
H.R. 5087	93rd	1973	156
H.R. 5124	98th	1984	252
H.R. 5125	78th	1944	040
H.R. 5134	83rd	1953	144
H.R. 5146	95th	1977-1978	208
H.R. 5157	49th	1886	075
H.R. 5162	84th	1955	054
H.R. 5182	95th	1977	223
H.R. 5193	93rd	1973	160
H.R. 5237	89th	1965	111
H.R. 5248	80th	1948	074
H.R. 5257	84th	1955-1956	054
H.R. 5262	79th	1946	037
H.R. 5269	89th	1965	144
H.R. 5275	75th	1937	006
H.R. 5275	75th	1937	008
H.R. 5275	75th	1937	009
H.R. 5275	75th	1937	010
H.R. 5275	75th	1937	017
H.R. 5275	75th	1937	021
H.R. 5275	75th	1937	026
H.R. 5275	92nd	1971	139
H.R. 5284	80th	1948	054

Bill No.	Congress	Year	Record Number
H.R. 5286	75th	1937	054
H.R. 5292	80th	1948	054
H.R. 5294	56th	1900	084
H.R. 5312	77th	1941	042
H.R. 5312	77th	1941	043
H.R. 5315	72nd	1931-1932	037
H.R. 5319	76th	1939	015
H.R. 5319	76th	1939	017
H.R. 5322	95th	1977-1978	217
H.R. 5322	95th	1977-1978	219
H.R. 5333	92nd	1971	073
H.R. 5334	92nd	1971	073
H.R. 5356	93rd	1973	156
H.R. 5357	90th	1967	119
H.R. 5357	90th	1967	144
H.R. 5357	90th	1967	170
H.R. 5361	53rd	1894	075
H.R. 5368	93rd	1973	156
H.R. 5388	92nd	1971	139
H.R. 5388	93rd	1973	159
H.R. 5395	93rd	1973	156
H.R. 5406	89th	1965	111
H.R. 5414	75th	1937	054
H.R. 5445	93rd	1973	144
H.R. 5446	93rd	1973	107

Bill No.	Congress	Year	Record Number
H.R. 5446	93rd	1973	144
H.R. 5450	93rd	1973-1974	156
H.R. 5451	93rd	1973	144
H.R. 5452	76th	1939	040
H.R. 5458	75th	1937	054
H.R. 5470	94th	1975	192
H.R. 5478	75th	1937	040
H.R. 5487	94th	1975	204
H.R. 5506	79th	1946	071
H.R. 5520	89th	1965	111
H.R. 5528	91st	1969	005
H.R. 5554	73rd	1933	075
H.R. 5555	86th	1959	004
H.R. 5583	89th	1965	111
H.R. 5587	86th	1959	004
H.R. 5598	81st	1949	040
H.R. 5610	86th	1959	053
H.R. 5618	86th	1959	004
H.R. 5630	76th	1939	054
H.R. 5636	75th	1937	084
H.R. 5636	83rd	1953	040
H.R. 5640	98th	1985-1986	253
H.R. 5654	90th	1967	112
H.R. 5660	76th	1939	005
H.R. 5661	73rd	1933	046

Bill No.	Congress	Year	Record Number
H.R. 5667	48th	1884-1885	040
H.R. 5676	67th	1921	226
H.R. 5690	83rd	1953	040
H.R. 5690	98th	1984	252
H.R. 5710	83rd	1953	067
H.R. 5711	80th	1948	053
H.R. 5718	86th	1959	004
H.R. 5722	95th	1977	222
H.R. 5723	65th	1917	040
H.R. 5735	82nd	1951-1952	004
H.R. 5736	82nd	1951	004
H.R. 5740	83rd	1953	054
H.R. 5746	84th	1955	054
H.R. 5748	86th	1959	004
H.R. 5749	93rd	1973	183
H.R. 5759	101st	1990	257
H.R. 5762	76th	1939	054
H.R. 5791	76th	1939	021
H.R. 5813	86th	1959	144
H.R. 5841	69th	1925	006
H.R. 5841	69th	1925	008
H.R. 5841	69th	1925	010
H.R. 5841	69th	1925	020
H.R. 5841	69th	1925	021
H.R. 5853	73rd	1933	006

Bill No.	Congress	Year	Record Number
H.R. 5853	73rd	1933	009
H.R. 5853	73rd	1933	026
H.R. 5854	75th	1937	054
H.R. 5855	75th	1937	084
H.R. 5871	80th	1948	066
H.R. 5871	85th	1957	004
H.R. 5876	90th	1967	144
H.R. 5892	96th	1979-1980	248
H.R. 5895	81st	1949	067
H.R. 5900	87th	1961	089
H.R. 5916	89th	1965	117
H.R. 5930	89th	1965	099
H.R. 5940	79th	1946	071
H.R. 5974	54th	1896	075
H.R. 5994	85th	1957	086
H.R. 6007	80th	1948	039
H.R. 6009	77th	1941	040
H.R. 6010	95th	1977	231
H.R. 6012	73rd	1933	075
H.R. 6014	85th	1957	086
H.R. 6028	87th	1961	144
H.R. 6041	88th	1963-1964	043
H.R. 6041	88th	1963-1964	044
H.R. 6041	88th	1963-1964	095
H.R. 6041	88th	1963-1964	144

Bill No.	Congress	Year	Record Number
H.R. 6060	88th	1963	093
H.R. 6075	95th	1977-1978	235
H.R. 6097	79th	1946	144
H.R. 6098	53rd	1894	075
H.R. 6098	90th	1967	121
H.R. 6100	95th	1977	043
H.R. 6103	70th	1927-1928	039
H.R. 6105	70th	1927	076
H.R. 6110	73rd	1933	054
H.R. 6111	73rd	1933	054
H.R. 6111	95th	1977	210
H.R. 6116	80th	1948	031
H.R. 6118	73rd	1933	054
H.R. 6118	79th	1946	071
H.R. 6133	90th	1967	073
H.R. 6133	95th	1977	223
H.R. 6140	86th	1959	004
H.R. 6147	84th	1955	004
H.R. 6154	94th	1975	183
H.R. 6160	76th	1939	006
H.R. 6160	76th	1939	008
H.R. 6160	76th	1939	009
H.R. 6160	76th	1939	021
H.R. 6160	76th	1939	026
H.R. 6161	95th	1977	208

Bill No.	Congress	Year	Record Number
H.R. 6161	95th	1977	209
H.R. 6172	89th	1965	111
H.R. 6177	94th	1975	183
H.R. 6183	48th	1884	075
H.R. 6186	93rd	1973-1974	150
H.R. 6186	93rd	1973-1974	151
H.R. 6187	74th	1935	049
H.R. 6217	81st	1949-1950	040
H.R. 6218	94th	1975-1976	204
H.R. 6227	84th	1955-1956	046
H.R. 6228	91st	1970	134
H.R. 6233	77th	1941	030
H.R. 6233	77th	1941	031
H.R. 6238	80th	1948	039
H.R. 6243	76th	1939	008
H.R. 6245	87th	1961-1962	054
H.R. 6251	77th	1941	054
H.R. 6264	94th	1975	183
H.R. 6282	89th	1965	099
H.R. 6288	74th	1935	048
H.R. 6288	74th	1935	049
H.R. 6293	77th	1942	057
H.R. 6295	84th	1955	144
H.R. 6325	86th	1959	144
H.R. 6328	89th	1965	054

Bill No.	Congress	Year	Record Number
H.R. 6338	93rd	1973	144
H.R. 6346	79th	1946	039
H.R. 6350	55th	1898	075
H.R. 6355	79th	1946	061
H.R. 6359	74th	1935	079
H.R. 6359	92nd	1971	144
H.R. 6362	95th	1977-1978	162
H.R. 6376	73rd	1934	054
H.R. 6380	95th	1977	222
H.R. 6384	75th	1937	040
H.R. 6388	93rd	1973	144
H.R. 6400	89th	1965	105
H.R. 6403	92nd	1971	099
H.R. 6405	95th	1977	152
H.R. 6418	90th	1967	144
H.R. 6434	83rd	1953-1954	054
H.R. 6434	83rd	1953-1954	144
H.R. 6436	81st	1949	074
H.R. 6436	81st	1949	075
H.R. 6436	86th	1959	144
H.R. 6441	87th	1961	144
H.R. 6444	92nd	1971	053
H.R. 6447	75th	1937	075
H.R. 6448	79th	1946	039
H.R. 6448	79th	1946	071

Bill No.	Congress	Year	Record Number
H.R. 6452	93rd	1973	156
H.R. 6456	85th	1957	054
H.R. 6462	73rd	1934	001
H.R. 6501	95th	1977	212
H.R. 6501	95th	1977	229
H.R. 6501	95th	1977	233
H.R. 6502	95th	1977	211
H.R. 6512	77th	1942	040
H.R. 6513	85th	1957	086
H.R. 6518	53rd	1894	144
H.R. 6518	88th	1963	130
H.R. 6518	88th	1963	144
H.R. 6525	82nd	1952	053
H.R. 6533	79th	1946	144
H.R. 6539	63rd	1943-1944	028
H.R. 6558	94th	1975-1976	197
H.R. 6578	82nd	1952	073
H.R. 6590	84th	1955	037
H.R. 6597	53rd	1894	075
H.R. 6605	92nd	1971	144
H.R. 6608	83rd	1953	009
H.R. 6616	83rd	1953-1954	006
H.R. 6649	85th	1957	086
H.R. 6650	55th	1898	075
H.R. 6650	85th	1957	086

Bill No.	Congress	Year	Record Number
H.R. 6655	95th	1977	213
H.R. 6659	85th	1957	144
H.R. 6667	96th	1980	254
H.R. 6668	93rd	1973-1974	003
H.R. 6668	95th	1977	104
H.R. 6669	95th	1977-1978	222
H.R. 6670	83rd	1953	006
H.R. 6672	79th	1946	071
H.R. 6675	89th	1965	053
H.R. 6681	80th	1948	054
H.R. 6695	76th	1939	021
H.R. 6695	82nd	1952	076
H.R. 6705	80th	1948	061
H.R. 6714	95th	1977	077
H.R. 6715	68th	1924	079
H.R. 6716	91st	1969	073
H.R. 6726	80th	1948	144
H.R. 6729	80th	1948	144
H.R. 6736	81st	1950	003
H.R. 6739	89th	1965	111
H.R. 6747	85th	1957	054
H.R. 6750	91st	1969	144
H.R. 6760	92nd	1971	133
H.R. 6766	80th	1948	053
H.R. 6771	85th	1957	144

Bill No.	Congress	Year	Record Number
H.R. 6772	74th	1935-1936	226
H.R. 6775	87th	1961	090
H.R. 6778	91st	1969-1970	046
H.R. 6788	83rd	1953-1954	078
H.R. 6788	85th	1957-1958	144
H.R. 6827	95th	1977	171
H.R. 6828	88th	1963	144
H.R. 6839	96th	1980	152
H.R. 6852	77th	1942	071
H.R. 6852	86th	1959	054
H.R. 6856	82nd	1952	144
H.R. 6871	86th	1959-1960	144
H.R. 6873	76th	1939	075
H.R. 6874	76th	1939	075
H.R. 6875	76th	1939	075
H.R. 6878	76th	1939	075
H.R. 6890	79th	1946	031
H.R. 6900	71st	1929	010
H.R. 6900	95th	1977-1978	239
H.R. 6901	77th	1942	071
H.R. 6903	79th	1946	040
H.R. 6906	74th	1935	054
H.R. 6910	95th	1977	220
H.R. 6950	90th	1967	120
H.R. 6954	95th	1977	234

Bill No.	Congress	Year	Record Number
H.R. 6976	73rd	1934	030
H.R. 6987	71st	1929	010
H.R. 6989	71st	1929	008
H.R. 6990	71st	1929	006
H.R. 6990	71st	1929	007
H.R. 6990	71st	1929	009
H.R. 6990	71st	1929	014
H.R. 6990	71st	1929	016
H.R. 6990	71st	1929	018
H.R. 6990	71st	1929	020
H.R. 6990	71st	1929	021
H.R. 6990	71st	1929	025
H.R. 7002	77th	1942	054
H.R. 7005	72nd	1932	042
H.R. 7005	82nd	1952	067
H.R. 7010	66th	1919	034
H.R. 7010	89th	1965	111
H.R. 7014	94th	1975	181
H.R. 7020	96th	1980	249
H.R. 7040	87th	1961	086
H.R. 7042	89th	1965-1966	054
H.R. 7046	95th	1977	223
H.R. 7049	84th	1955-1956	144
H.R. 7059	73rd	1934	029
H.R. 7070	91st	1969	005

Bill No.	Congress	Year	Record Number
H.R. 7072	92nd	1971	144
H.R. 7073	95th	1977	208
H.R. 7077	67th	1921-1922	034
H.R. 7083	55th	1897	084
H.R. 7087	69th	1926	075
H.R. 7092	89th	1965	073
H.R. 7094	56th	1900-1901	040
H.R. 7107	92nd	1971	174
H.R. 7108	94th	1975-1976	204
H.R. 7120	86th	1959	144
H.R. 7125	83rd	1954	054
H.R. 7125	83rd	1954	144
H.R. 7130	93rd	1973-1974	157
H.R. 7130	93rd	1973-1974	158
H.R. 7130	93rd	1973-1974	159
H.R. 7130	93rd	1973-1974	160
H.R. 7151	85th	1957	034
H.R. 7152	88th	1963-1964	096
H.R. 7152	88th	1963-1964	097
H.R. 7152	88th	1963-1964	098
H.R. 7152	88th	1963-1964	133
H.R. 7159	97th	1982	254
H.R. 7161	89th	1965	111
H.R. 7173	77th	1942	008
H.R. 7173	77th	1942	021

Bill No.	Congress	Year	Record Number
H.R. 7175	95th	1977-1978	245
H.R. 7176	82nd	1952	061
H.R. 7187	76th	1939	084
H.R. 7192	76th	1939	071
H.R. 7200	75th	1937	047
H.R. 7200	93rd	1973	053
H.R. 7201	70th	1927-1928	031
H.R. 7211	92nd	1971-1972	202
H.R. 7211	92nd	1971-1972	203
H.R. 7234	87th	1961	086
H.R. 7234	88th	1963	099
H.R. 7235	87th	1961	086
H.R. 7239	88th	1963	099
H.R. 7248	92nd	1971	029
H.R. 7254	72nd	1932	042
H.R. 7258	88th	1963	099
H.R. 7265	86th	1959	087
H.R. 7265	86th	1959	088
H.R. 7273	68th	1924	071
H.R. 7280	77th	1942	057
H.R. 7293	92nd	1971	099
H.R. 7296	52nd	1892	040
H.R. 7304	77th	1942	059
H.R. 7306	96th	1980	250
H.R. 7309	95th	1977	223

Bill No.	Congress	Year	Record Number
H.R. 7345	95th	1977	212
H.R. 7353	94th	1975	183
H.R. 7366	92nd	1971	073
H.R. 7383	85th	1957	144
H.R. 7390	85th	1957	135
H.R. 7416	84th	1955-1956	034
H.R. 7426	73rd	1934	054
H.R. 7428	72nd	1932	075
H.R. 7430	86th	1959	054
H.R. 7476	86th	1959	144
H.R. 7480	49th	1886	144
H.R. 7480	86th	1959-1960	054
H.R. 7500	86th	1959	067
H.R. 7519	75th	1937	053
H.R. 7521	74th	1935	051
H.R. 7589	75th	1937	053
H.R. 7591	77th	1942	071
H.R. 7605	84th	1955	054
H.R. 7606	84th	1955	054
H.R. 7607	84th	1955	054
H.R. 7607	85th	1957	086
H.R. 7609	62nd	1911	075
H.R. 7624	86th	1959-1960	054
H.R. 7624	86th	1959-1960	144
H.R. 7655	89th	1965-1966	054

Bill No.	Congress	Year	Record Number
H.R. 7656	82nd	1952	040
H.R. 7670	81st	1950	005
H.R. 7672	73rd	1934	144
H.R. 7677	93rd	1973	173
H.R. 7679	95th	1977-1978	223
H.R. 7680	86th	1959	088
H.R. 7691	82nd	1952	004
H.R. 7700	85th	1957	054
H.R. 7704	94th	1975	209
H.R. 7705	91st	1969	005
H.R. 7710	62nd	1911	075
H.R. 7711	62nd	1911	075
H.R. 7713	77th	1942	070
H.R. 7716	72nd	1932-1933	038
H.R. 7732	84th	1955-1956	054
H.R. 7750	89th	1965	067
H.R. 7764	84th	1955	054
H.R. 7767	94th	1975	177
H.R. 7780	93rd	1973-1974	003
H.R. 7783	82nd	1952	040
H.R. 7786	81st	1950	061
H.R. 7794	82nd	1952	074
H.R. 7794	82nd	1952	075
H.R. 7797	89th	1965-1966	054
H.R. 7798	85th	1957	054

Bill No.	Congress	Year	Record Number
H.R. 7802	85th	1957	086
H.R. 7806	93rd	1973	144
H.R. 7815	89th	1965-1966	054
H.R. 7819	95th	1977-1978	223
H.R. 7820	89th	1965	054
H.R. 7830	94th	1975	185
H.R. 7835	73rd	1934	079
H.R. 7839	83rd	1954	144
H.R. 7840	83rd	1954	053
H.R. 7847	86th	1959-1960	054
H.R. 7847	86th	1959-1960	144
H.R. 7855	88th	1963	144
H.R. 7878	95th	1977	208
H.R. 7885	88th	1963	067
H.R. 7896	89th	1965	105
H.R. 7913	75th	1937	054
H.R. 7916	87th	1961	073
H.R. 7925	89th	1965	054
H.R. 7927	87th	1961-1962	144
H.R. 7935	93rd	1973	154
H.R. 7937	74th	1935	049
H.R. 7938	85th	1957	054
H.R. 7939	50th	1888	040
H.R. 7951	63rd	1913-1914	029
H.R. 7959	68th	1924	040

Bill No.	Congress	Year	Record Number
H.R. 7960	85th	1957	086
H.R. 7964	73rd	1934	054
H.R. 7977	90th	1967	144
H.R. 7978	74th	1935	047
H.R. 7978	74th	1935	048
H.R. 7978	74th	1935	049
H.R. 7980	74th	1935	144
H.R. 7981	74th	1935	051
H.R. 7984	89th	1965	144
H.R. 7985	86th	1959	038
H.R. 7995	71st	1930	042
H.R. 8000	88th	1963-1964	100
H.R. 8000	88th	1963-1964	106
H.R. 8000	88th	1963-1964	121
H.R. 8004	85th	1957	086
H.R. 8024	74th	1935-1936	029
H.R. 8065	92nd	1971	053
H.R. 8070	93rd	1973	147
H.R. 8073	56th	1900	075
H.R. 8076	95th	1977-1978	246
H.R. 8092	94th	1975-1976	152
H.R. 8100	88th	1963	053
H.R. 8112	85th	1957	054
H.R. 8117	96th	1980	171
H.R. 8152	87th	1961	144

Bill No.	Congress	Year	Record Number
H.R. 8152	93rd	1973	145
H.R. 8173	72nd	1932	040
H.R. 8177	68th	1924	006
H.R. 8177	68th	1924	010
H.R. 8177	68th	1924	011
H.R. 8177	68th	1924	012
H.R. 8177	68th	1924	016
H.R. 8177	68th	1924	020
H.R. 8177	68th	1924	025
H.R. 8177	68th	1924	027
H.R. 8180	83rd	1954	040
H.R. 8200	95th	1977-1978	217
H.R. 8206	68th	1924-1925	144
H.R. 8234	82nd	1952	144
H.R. 8235	96th	1980	250
H.R. 8238	86th	1959-1960	144
H.R. 8240	94th	1975	179
H.R. 8245	93rd	1973-1974	153
H.R. 8271	84th	1956	054
H.R. 8275	84th	1956	054
H.R. 8300	83rd	1954	079
H.R. 8300	83rd	1954	080
H.R. 8316	73rd	1934	054
H.R. 8323	89th	1965	054
H.R. 8325	84th	1956	004

Bill No.	Congress	Year	Record Number
H.R. 8342	86th	1959	087
H.R. 8342	86th	1959	088
H.R. 8344	88th	1963-1964	036
H.R. 8347	84th	1956	004
H.R. 8362	66th	1919	028
H.R. 8363	88th	1963-1964	094
H.R. 8364	95th	1977	223
H.R. 8368	56th	1900	075
H.R. 8371	89th	1965	102
H.R. 8377	89th	1965-1966	054
H.R. 8388	62nd	1911	075
H.R. 8390	85th	1957	054
H.R. 8400	86th	1959	087
H.R. 8400	86th	1959	088
H.R. 8400	87th	1961	144
H.R. 8418	83rd	1954	054
H.R. 8422	95th	1977	214
H.R. 8422	95th	1977	217
H.R. 8423	73rd	1934	049
H.R. 8423	95th	1977-1978	217
H.R. 8444	95th	1977	208
H.R. 8455	74th	1935-1936	004
H.R. 8458	59th	1905	084
H.R. 8464	89th	1965	103
H.R. 8465	81st	1950	040

Bill No.	Congress	Year	Record Number
H.R. 8480	93rd	1973	159
H.R. 8480	93rd	1973	160
H.R. 8490	86th	1959	087
H.R. 8496	89th	1965	144
H.R. 8533	53rd	1895	084
H.R. 8539	74th	1935	050
H.R. 8543	95th	1977	214
H.R. 8555	74th	1935-1936	051
H.R. 8557	74th	1935-1936	006
H.R. 8557	74th	1935-1936	010
H.R. 8560	84th	1956	004
H.R. 8578	72nd	1932	040
H.R. 8583	83rd	1954	040
H.R. 8597	87th	1961	053
H.R. 8599	87th	1961	144
H.R. 8603	94th	1975-1976	193
H.R. 8609	86th	1959	077
H.R. 8619	93rd	1973	144
H.R. 8624	83rd	1954	004
H.R. 8628	93rd	1973	166
H.R. 8629	85th	1957	054
H.R. 8629	92nd	1971	144
H.R. 8637	93rd	1973	156
H.R. 8638	95th	1977-1978	220
H.R. 8651	74th	1935	053

Bill No.	Congress	Year	Record Number
H.R. 8652	74th	1935	053
H.R. 8674	94th	1975	183
H.R. 8683	95th	1977	223
H.R. 8714	94th	1975	053
H.R. 8722	93rd	1974	045
H.R. 8722	95th	1977	230
H.R. 8723	87th	1961-1962	086
H.R. 8733	92nd	1971	053
H.R. 8748	84th	1956	054
H.R. 8754	86th	1959	144
H.R. 8755	86th	1959	144
H.R. 8760	89th	1965-1966	144
H.R. 8762	93rd	1973	159
H.R. 8773	94th	1975	182
H.R. 8776	62nd	1911	071
H.R. 8777	95th	1977	101
H.R. 8800	94th	1975-1976	192
H.R. 8805	74th	1935	054
H.R. 8811	95th	1977-1978	217
H.R. 8834	93rd	1973	219
H.R. 8835	93rd	1973	219
H.R. 8860	93rd	1973	156
H.R. 8862	83rd	1954	081
H.R. 8862	83rd	1954	082
H.R. 8870	74th	1935	050

Bill No.	Congress	Year	Record Number
H.R. 8873	85th	1957	015
H.R. 8873	85th	1957	022
H.R. 8876	93rd	1973	159
H.R. 8904	81st	1950	054
H.R. 8912	70th	1928	006
H.R. 8912	70th	1928	008
H.R. 8912	70th	1928	009
H.R. 8912	70th	1928	010
H.R. 8912	70th	1928	014
H.R. 8912	70th	1928	016
H.R. 8912	70th	1928	021
H.R. 8912	70th	1928	025
H.R. 8913	70th	1928-1929	010
H.R. 8916	89th	1965	099
H.R. 8923	85th	1958	069
H.R. 8941	74th	1935	054
H.R. 8945	85th	1957	054
H.R. 8963	92nd	1971	054
H.R. 8979	95th	1977	135
H.R. 8984	72nd	1932	071
H.R. 8994	85th	1957	144
H.R. 8996	85th	1957	144
H.R. 9005	94th	1975	067
H.R. 9005	94th	1975	077
H.R. 9009	87th	1961	005

Bill No.	Congress	Year	Record Number
H.R. 9020	83rd	1954	040
H.R. 9021	76th	1940	042
H.R. 9021	76th	1940	044
H.R. 9021	76th	1940	144
H.R. 9055	93rd	1973	144
H.R. 9056	93rd	1973	150
H.R. 9056	93rd	1973	151
H.R. 9058	94th	1975	185
H.R. 9065	84th	1956	053
H.R. 9084	50th	1888	084
H.R. 9093	92nd	1971	073
H.R. 9129	81st	1950	144
H.R. 9130	95th	1977	238
H.R. 9133	81st	1950	074
H.R. 9133	81st	1950	075
H.R. 9137	68th	1924	006
H.R. 9137	68th	1924	009
H.R. 9137	68th	1924	010
H.R. 9137	68th	1924	011
H.R. 9137	68th	1924	012
H.R. 9137	68th	1924	015
H.R. 9137	68th	1924	017
H.R. 9137	68th	1924	019
H.R. 9137	68th	1924	020
H.R. 9137	68th	1924	022

Bill No.	Congress	Year	Record Number
H.R. 9137	68th	1924	023
H.R. 9137	68th	1924	024
H.R. 9137	68th	1924	025
H.R. 9137	68th	1924	027
H.R. 9166	83rd	1954	054
H.R. 9176	81st	1950	068
H.R. 9176	81st	1950	247
H.R. 9212	92nd	1971-1972	126
H.R. 9212	92nd	1971-1972	40
H.R. 9215	93rd	1973	150
H.R. 9229	92nd	1971-1972	141
H.R. 9232	71st	1930	042
H.R. 9247	92nd	1971	133
H.R. 9247	92nd	1971	134
H.R. 9256	89th	1965-1966	115
H.R. 9259	75th	1938	071
H.R. 9264	92nd	1971	132
H.R. 9270	92nd	1971	144
H.R. 9294	94th	1975	204
H.R. 9296	58th	1904	084
H.R. 9304	81st	1950	071
H.R. 9323	73rd	1934	176
H.R. 9341	75th	1938	054
H.R. 9346	95th	1977	217
H.R. 9368	85th	1957	144

Bill No.	Congress	Year	Record Number
H.R. 9369	66th	1919-1920	040
H.R. 9388	92nd	1971	144
H.R. 9398	69th	1926	005
H.R. 9424	89th	1965-1966	152
H.R. 9437	73rd	1934	144
H.R. 9463	69th	1926	036
H.R. 9463	69th	1926	037
H.R. 9486	51st	1890	004
H.R. 9486	51st	1890	144
H.R. 9489	84th	1956	004
H.R. 9492	68th	1924	075
H.R. 9505	84th	1956	004
H.R. 9509	90th	1967	144
H.R. 9521	85th	1957-1958	054
H.R. 9542	89th	1965-1966	054
H.R. 9547	84th	1956	054
H.R. 9547	84th	1956	144
H.R. 9560	94th	1975-1976	204
H.R. 9567	89th	1965	108
H.R. 9567	89th	1965	144
H.R. 9576	94th	1975	198
H.R. 9590	88th	1964	144
H.R. 9596	73rd	1934	053
H.R. 9598	93rd	1973	150
H.R. 9601	95th	1977	239

Bill No.	Congress	Year	Record Number
H.R. 9611	75th	1938	029
H.R. 9617	93rd	1973	150
H.R. 9627	89th	1965	108
H.R. 9638	71st	1930	040
H.R. 9639	71st	1930	008
H.R. 9639	71st	1930	019
H.R. 9639	71st	1930	021
H.R. 9658	93rd	1973	166
H.R. 9678	83rd	1954	067
H.R. 9682	93rd	1973	150
H.R. 9682	93rd	1973	151
H.R. 9703	76th	1940	006
H.R. 9703	76th	1940	008
H.R. 9703	76th	1940	009
H.R. 9703	76th	1940	021
H.R. 9703	76th	1940	026
H.R. 9706	76th	1940	053
H.R. 9726	93rd	1973	156
H.R. 9727	92nd	1971-1972	144
H.R. 9729	83rd	1954	144
H.R. 9739	88th	1964	144
H.R. 9757	83rd	1954	081
H.R. 9757	83rd	1954	082
H.R. 9757	83rd	1954	144
H.R. 9766	75th	1938	054

Bill No.	Congress	Year	Record Number
H.R. 9794	83rd	1954	034
H.R. 9796	73rd	1934	054
H.R. 9815	55th	1898	075
H.R. 9815	75th	1938	071
H.R. 9824	93rd	1973	164
H.R. 9833	89th	1965	108
H.R. 9843	62nd	1911-1912	084
H.R. 9852	84th	1956	068
H.R. 9861	73rd	1934	036
H.R. 9861	73rd	1934	037
H.R. 9868	94th	1975	189
H.R. 9868	94th	1975	190
H.R. 9870	74th	1936	040
H.R. 9879	93rd	1973	159
H.R. 9892	90th	1967	003
H.R. 9900	87th	1962	091
H.R. 9911	73rd	1934	053
H.R. 9922	92nd	1971	144
H.R. 9928	89th	1965	108
H.R. 9932	66th	1919-1920	071
H.R. 9936	73rd	1934	040
H.R. 9936	92nd	1971-1972	054
H.R. 9953	51st	1890	075
H.R. 9962	83rd	1954	040
H.R. 9971	69th	1926-1927	038

Bill No.	Congress	Year	Record Number
H.R. 9981	71st	1930	075
H.R. 10000	88th	1964	068
H.R. 10000	93rd	1973	189
H.R. 10009	83rd	1954	144
H.R. 10013	94th	1975-1976	222
H.R. 10049	87th	1962	144
H.R. 10062	87th	1962	144
H.R. 10065	89th	1965-1966	134
H.R. 10068	75th	1938	071
H.R. 10076	71st	1930	034
H.R. 10082	76th	1940	053
H.R. 10085	76th	1940	053
H.R. 10104	89th	1965-1966	144
H.R. 10127	75th	1938	053
H.R. 10132	76th	1940	056
H.R. 10144	87th	1962	096
H.R. 10153	72nd	1932	075
H.R. 10155	72nd	1932	075
H.R. 10156	72nd	1932	075
H.R. 10157	72nd	1932	075
H.R. 10173	95th	1977-1978	237
H.R. 10203	92nd	1971	099
H.R. 10229	94th	1975-1976	152
H.R. 10230	94th	1975-1076	185
H.R. 10268	94th	1975-1976	205

Bill No.	Congress	Year	Record Number
H.R. 10268	95th	1977	228
H.R. 10269	95th	1977	228
H.R. 10284	94th	1975	142
H.R. 10285	95th	1977-1978	226
H.R. 10315	94th	1975	189
H.R. 10315	94th	1975	190
H.R. 10328	90th	1967	118
H.R. 10341	86th	1960	144
H.R. 10353	69th	1926	008
H.R. 10355	94th	1975	194
H.R. 10356	95th	1977	228
H.R. 10363	94th	1975	204
H.R. 10364	72nd	1932	006
H.R. 10364	72nd	1932	007
H.R. 10364	72nd	1932	009
H.R. 10364	72nd	1932	010
H.R. 10364	72nd	1932	011
H.R. 10364	72nd	1932	012
H.R. 10364	72nd	1932	014
H.R. 10364	72nd	1932	019
H.R. 10364	72nd	1932	020
H.R. 10364	72nd	1932	021
H.R. 10364	72nd	1932	024
H.R. 10364	72nd	1932	025
H.R. 10364	72nd	1932	026

Bill No.	Congress	Year	Record Number
H.R. 10394	94th	1975-1976	205
H.R. 10404	85th	1958	054
H.R. 10433	84th	1956	029
H.R. 10434	69th	1926	006
H.R. 10434	69th	1926	008
H.R. 10434	69th	1926	009
H.R. 10434	69th	1926	010
H.R. 10434	69th	1926	011
H.R. 10434	69th	1926	014
H.R. 10434	69th	1926	016
H.R. 10434	69th	1926	018
H.R. 10434	69th	1926	019
H.R. 10434	69th	1926	020
H.R. 10434	69th	1926	021
H.R. 10434	69th	1926	025
H.R. 10434	69th	1926	027
H.R. 10434	86th	1960	144
H.R. 10435	70th	1928	039
H.R. 10439	93rd	1973-1974	153
H.R. 10443	86th	1960	144
H.R. 10453	66th	1919-1920	037
H.R. 10456	86th	1960	144
H.R. 10463	86th	1960	144
H.R. 10475	86th	1960	144
H.R. 10498	94th	1975-1976	204

Bill No.	Congress	Year	Record Number
H.R. 10498	94th	1975-1976	209
H.R. 10503	75th	1938	026
H.R. 10518	89th	1965	113
H.R. 10519	84th	1956	054
H.R. 10519	87th	1962	144
H.R. 10528	71st	1930	005
H.R. 10578	84th	1956	053
H.R. 10595	90th	1967	003
H.R. 10597	93rd	1973	150
H.R. 10606	87th	1962	053
H.R. 10607	87th	1962	144
H.R. 10630	71st	1930	040
H.R. 10632	74th	1936	006
H.R. 10632	74th	1936	007
H.R. 10632	74th	1936	009
H.R. 10632	74th	1936	010
H.R. 10632	74th	1936	011
H.R. 10632	74th	1936	014
H.R. 10632	74th	1936	015
H.R. 10632	74th	1936	018
H.R. 10632	74th	1936	019
H.R. 10632	74th	1936	020
H.R. 10632	74th	1936	021
H.R. 10632	74th	1936	024
H.R. 10632	74th	1936	025

Bill No.	Congress	Year	Record Number
H.R. 10632	74th	1936	026
H.R. 10632	74th	1936	027
H.R. 10633	75th	1938	008
H.R. 10637	51st	1890	075
H.R. 10650	87th	1962	092
H.R. 10655	70th	1928	008
H.R. 10655	70th	1928	021
H.R. 10672	75th	1938	144
H.R. 10692	93rd	1973	150
H.R. 10692	93rd	1973	151
H.R. 10693	93rd	1973	150
H.R. 10693	93rd	1973	151
H.R. 10729	92nd	1971-1972	144
H.R. 10730	90th	1967	104
H.R. 10739	72nd	1932	042
H.R. 10740	72nd	1932	006
H.R. 10740	72nd	1932	007
H.R. 10740	72nd	1932	009
H.R. 10740	72nd	1932	010
H.R. 10740	72nd	1932	012
H.R. 10740	72nd	1932	014
H.R. 10740	72nd	1932	019
H.R. 10740	72nd	1932	020
H.R. 10740	72nd	1932	021
H.R. 10740	72nd	1932	025

Bill No.	Congress	Year	Record Number
H.R. 10740	72nd	1932	026
H.R. 10760	94th	1975-1976	219
H.R. 10769	58th	1904	084
H.R. 10790	90th	1967-1968	124
H.R. 10796	93rd	1973	156
H.R. 10854	95th	1977-1978	236
H.R. 10867	90th	1967	118
H.R. 10873	84th	1956	004
H.R. 10874	67th	1922	040
H.R. 10874	89th	1965	053
H.R. 10943	90th	1967	108
H.R. 10946	91st	1969	125
H.R. 10947	92nd	1971	144
H.R. 10952	93rd	1973	165
H.R. 10955	93rd	1973	156
H.R. 10969	85th	1958	068
H.R. 10976	72nd	1932	006
H.R. 10976	72nd	1932	007
H.R. 10976	72nd	1932	009
H.R. 10976	72nd	1932	010
H.R. 10976	72nd	1932	012
H.R. 10976	72nd	1932	014
H.R. 10976	72nd	1932	019
H.R. 10976	72nd	1932	020
H.R. 10976	72nd	1932	021

Bill No.	Congress	Year	Record Number
H.R. 10976	72nd	1932	022
H.R. 10976	72nd	1932	023
H.R. 10976	72nd	1932	025
H.R. 10976	72nd	1932	026
H.R. 10976	72nd	1932	027
H.R. 10987	69th	1926	008
H.R. 10998	95th	1978	238
H.R. 11001	95th	1978	238
H.R. 11007	94th	1975	189
H.R. 11009	94th	1975-1976	188
H.R. 11009	95th	1978	228
H.R. 11016	72nd	1932	075
H.R. 11019	72nd	1932	075
H.R. 11021	92nd	1971-1972	139
H.R. 11021	92nd	1971-1972	144
H.R. 11023	55th	1898-1899	005
H.R. 11035	93rd	1973-1974	183
H.R. 11071	92nd	1971	140
H.R. 11083	88th	1964	144
H.R. 11087	72nd	1932	075
H.R. 11099	87th	1962	144
H.R. 11101	90th	1967	124
H.R. 11102	91st	1969-1970	144
H.R. 11105	93rd	1974	104
H.R. 11107	90th	1967	124

Bill No.	Congress	Year	Record Number
H.R. 11124	92nd	1971	144
H.R. 11141	70th	1928	042
H.R. 11202	88th	1964	144
H.R. 11212	93rd	1973-1974	166
H.R. 11214	68th	1925	005
H.R. 11226	95th	1978	208
H.R. 11235	91st	1969	104
H.R. 11256	89th	1965-1966	114
H.R. 11258	68th	1924	006
H.R. 11258	68th	1924	008
H.R. 11258	68th	1924	009
H.R. 11258	68th	1924	010
H.R. 11258	68th	1924	011
H.R. 11258	68th	1924	014
H.R. 11258	68th	1924	015
H.R. 11258	68th	1924	016
H.R. 11258	68th	1924	017
H.R. 11258	68th	1924	020
H.R. 11258	68th	1924	021
H.R. 11258	68th	1924	022
H.R. 11258	68th	1924	023
H.R. 11258	68th	1924	024
H.R. 11258	68th	1924	025
H.R. 11258	68th	1924	027
H.R. 11266	93rd	1973	156

Bill No.	Congress	Year	Record Number
H.R. 11267	72nd	1932	034
H.R. 11274	95th	1977-1978	236
H.R. 11280	95th	1978	227
H.R. 11290	89th	1965-1966	114
H.R. 11297	89th	1965	117
H.R. 11318	95th	1978	232
H.R. 11356	84th	1956	067
H.R. 11363	91st	1969	152
H.R. 11365	90th	1967	124
H.R. 11374	74th	1936	021
H.R. 11401	90th	1967	124
H.R. 11403	68th	1925	039
H.R. 11414	85th	1958	144
H.R. 11420	74th	1936	006
H.R. 11420	74th	1936	007
H.R. 11420	74th	1936	009
H.R. 11420	74th	1936	010
H.R. 11420	74th	1936	011
H.R. 11420	74th	1936	012
H.R. 11420	74th	1936	014
H.R. 11420	74th	1936	017
H.R. 11420	74th	1936	018
H.R. 11420	74th	1936	019
H.R. 11420	74th	1936	020
H.R. 11420	74th	1936	021

Bill No.	Congress	Year	Record Number
H.R. 11420	74th	1936	023
H.R. 11420	74th	1936	024
H.R. 11420	74th	1936	025
H.R. 11420	74th	1936	026
H.R. 11420	74th	1936	027
H.R. 11450	93rd	1973	155
H.R. 11450	93rd	1973	156
H.R. 11476	67th	1920	025
H.R. 11501	94th	1976	209
H.R. 11510	86th	1960	067
H.R. 11510	94th	1976	204
H.R. 11522	84th	1956	144
H.R. 11569	51st	1890	003
H.R. 11576	93rd	1973-1974	144
H.R. 11581	87th	1962	054
H.R. 11581	87th	1962	144
H.R. 11582	87th	1962	054
H.R. 11602	86th	1960	043
H.R. 11602	86th	1960	044
H.R. 11602	86th	1960	144
H.R. 11607	91st	1969	053
H.R. 11633	68th	1924	040
H.R. 11656	94th	1976	189
H.R. 11656	94th	1976	190
H.R. 11697	85th	1958	144

Bill No.	Congress	Year	Record Number
H.R. 11707	64th	1916	040
H.R. 11742	84th	1956	144
H.R. 11764	84th	1956	053
H.R. 11765	89th	1965-1966	117
H.R. 11777	95th	1978	162
H.R. 11778	95th	1978	162
H.R. 11779	95th	1978	162
H.R. 11794	60th	1908	006
H.R. 11794	60th	1908	008
H.R. 11794	60th	1908	010
H.R. 11794	60th	1908	021
H.R. 11794	60th	1908	026
H.R. 11795	55th	1899	144
H.R. 11798	61st	1909-1911	001
H.R. 11814	85th	1958	054
H.R. 11832	88th	1964	144
H.R. 11833	91st	1969-1970	107
H.R. 11833	91st	1969-1970	144
H.R. 11843	67th	1922	226
H.R. 11864	93rd	1973-1974	165
H.R. 11865	72nd	1932	042
H.R. 11865	88th	1964	053
H.R. 11881	85th	1958	039
H.R. 11882	85th	1958	039
H.R. 11882	93rd	1973	155

Bill No.	Congress	Year	Record Number
H.R. 11886	95th	1978	229
H.R. 11887	85th	1958	039
H.R. 11888	85th	1958	039
H.R. 11888	95th	1978	229
H.R. 11888	95th	1978	233
H.R. 11896	92nd	1971-1972	137
H.R. 11896	92nd	1971-1972	144
H.R. 11926	84th	1956	144
H.R. 11928	93rd	1973	144
H.R. 11929	93rd	1973-1974	156
H.R. 11948	72nd	1932	006
H.R. 11948	72nd	1932	007
H.R. 11948	72nd	1932	009
H.R. 11948	72nd	1932	010
H.R. 11948	72nd	1932	012
H.R. 11948	72nd	1932	014
H.R. 11948	72nd	1932	019
H.R. 11948	72nd	1932	020
H.R. 11948	72nd	1932	021
H.R. 11948	72nd	1932	024
H.R. 11948	72nd	1932	025
H.R. 11948	72nd	1932	026
H.R. 11961	85th	1958	039
H.R. 11964	85th	1958	039
H.R. 11970	87th	1962	091

Bill No.	Congress	Year	Record Number
H.R. 11984	66th	1920-1921	034
H.R. 11984	66th	1920-1921	071
H.R. 12006	92nd	1971-1972	140
H.R. 12028	95th	1978	228
H.R. 12033	88th	1964	054
H.R. 12033	88th	1964	144
H.R. 12050	95th	1977-1978	236
H.R. 12052	86th	1960	068
H.R. 12085	91st	1969	144
H.R. 12089	92nd	1971-1972	132
H.R. 12092	90th	1967	124
H.R. 12094	72nd	1932	006
H.R. 12094	72nd	1932	009
H.R. 12094	72nd	1932	010
H.R. 12094	72nd	1932	012
H.R. 12094	72nd	1932	014
H.R. 12094	72nd	1932	015
H.R. 12094	72nd	1932	019
H.R. 12094	72nd	1932	020
H.R. 12094	72nd	1932	021
H.R. 12094	72nd	1932	025
H.R. 12094	72nd	1932	026
H.R. 12095	57th	1902	075
H.R. 12109	93rd	1973-1974	150
H.R. 12109	93rd	1973-1974	151

Bill No.	Congress	Year	Record Number
H.R. 12120	74th	1936	029
H.R. 12169	89th	1966	067
H.R. 12175	69th	1926	040
H.R. 12175	88th	1964	144
H.R. 12185	90th	1967	124
H.R. 12192	66th	1920	039
H.R. 12206	93rd	1974	173
H.R. 12215	84th	1956	144
H.R. 12216	51st	1890	075
H.R. 12228	88th	1964	144
H.R. 12250	95th	1978	230
H.R. 12255	95th	1977-1978	104
H.R. 12257	95th	1978	228
H.R. 12258	95th	1978	228
H.R. 12336	87th	1962	144
H.R. 12341	89th	1966	115
H.R. 12362	88th	1964	053
H.R. 12368	69th	1926	075
H.R. 12370	95th	1978	217
H.R. 12371	74th	1936	084
H.R. 12380	94th	1976	204
H.R. 12406	94th	1976	186
H.R. 12412	69th	1926	071
H.R. 12425	72nd	1932	006
H.R. 12425	72nd	1932	009

Bill No.	Congress	Year	Record Number
H.R. 12425	72nd	1932	010
H.R. 12425	72nd	1932	012
H.R. 12425	72nd	1932	014
H.R. 12425	72nd	1932	017
H.R. 12425	72nd	1932	019
H.R. 12425	72nd	1932	020
H.R. 12425	72nd	1932	021
H.R. 12425	72nd	1932	025
H.R. 12425	72nd	1932	026
H.R. 12425	72nd	1932	027
H.R. 12425	72nd	1932	028
H.R. 12435	93rd	1974	154
H.R. 12470	59th	1906	084
H.R. 12471	93rd	1974	170
H.R. 12481	93rd	1974	164
H.R. 12536	95th	1978	239
H.R. 12549	71st	1930-1931	006
H.R. 12549	71st	1930-1931	007
H.R. 12549	71st	1930-1931	008
H.R. 12549	71st	1930-1931	009
H.R. 12549	71st	1930-1931	010
H.R. 12549	71st	1930-1931	011
H.R. 12549	71st	1930-1931	014
H.R. 12549	71st	1930-1931	015
H.R. 12549	71st	1930-1931	016

Bill No.	Congress	Year	Record Number
H.R. 12549	71st	1930-1931	017
H.R. 12549	71st	1930-1931	018
H.R. 12549	71st	1930-1931	019
H.R. 12549	71st	1930-1931	020
H.R. 12549	71st	1930-1931	021
H.R. 12549	71st	1930-1931	022
H.R. 12549	71st	1930-1931	023
H.R. 12549	71st	1930-1931	024
H.R. 12549	71st	1930-1931	025
H.R. 12549	71st	1930-1931	027
H.R. 12549	71st	1930-1931	028
H.R. 12549	91st	1969	144
H.R. 12555	92nd	1972	183
H.R. 12575	85th	1958	039
H.R. 12580	86th	1960	053
H.R. 12611	95th	1978	231
H.R. 12616	85th	1958	085
H.R. 12647	95th	1978	208
H.R. 12677	86th	1960	089
H.R. 12695	70th	1928-1929	071
H.R. 12695	91st	1969	105
H.R. 12704	94th	1976	204
H.R. 12716	64th	1916-1917	075
H.R. 12716	85th	1958	144
H.R. 12741	92nd	1972	144

Bill No.	Congress	Year	Record Number
H.R. 12749	92nd	1972	073
H.R. 12752	89th	1966	109
H.R. 12784	85th	1958	054
H.R. 12815	87th	1962	054
H.R. 12831	86th	1960	054
H.R. 12833	87th	1962	144
H.R. 12853	86th	1960	089
H.R. 12855	93rd	1974	164
H.R. 12859	93rd	1974	156
H.R. 12863	65th	1918-1919	040
H.R. 12901	71st	1930-1931	029
H.R. 12906	93rd	1974	164
H.R. 12923	65th	1918	030
H.R. 12929	95th	1977-1978	236
H.R. 12931	92nd	1972	144
H.R. 12944	94th	1976	204
H.R. 12946	89th	1966	115
H.R. 12949	86th	1960	054
H.R. 12954	94th	1976	209
H.R. 12968	51st	1891	075
H.R. 12972	95th	1978	246
H.R. 13002	93rd	1974	171
H.R. 13026	65th	1918-1919	040
H.R. 13039	70th	1928	040
H.R. 13043	69th	1926	039

Bill No.	Congress	Year	Record Number
H.R. 13064	89th	1966	115
H.R. 13087	58th	1904	084
H.R. 13094	90th	1967-1968	226
H.R. 13103	89th	1966	117
H.R. 13103	89th	1966	120
H.R. 13104	89th	1966	144
H.R. 13113	93rd	1974	225
H.R. 13113	93rd	1974	226
H.R. 13138	85th	1958	144
H.R. 13141	69th	1926	075
H.R. 13167	95th	1978	219
H.R. 13176	93rd	1974	156
H.R. 13199	89th	1966	144
H.R. 13200	89th	1966	144
H.R. 13228	89th	1966	112
H.R. 13247	85th	1958	029
H.R. 13254	85th	1958	054
H.R. 13254	85th	1958	144
H.R. 13270	91st	1969	144
H.R. 13272	91st	1969	144
H.R. 13290	89th	1966	144
H.R. 13300	91st	1969-1970	053
H.R. 13311	95th	1978	208
H.R. 13324	92nd	1972	144
H.R. 13339	94th	1975-1976	204

Bill No.	Congress	Year	Record Number
H.R. 13343	95th	1978	241
H.R. 13364	95th	1978	238
H.R. 13367	93rd	1974	219
H.R. 13367	94th	1976	197
H.R. 13373	91st	1969-1970	129
H.R. 13450	65th	1918	039
H.R. 13452	70th	1928-1929	008
H.R. 13452	70th	1928-1929	021
H.R. 13455	85th	1958	144
H.R. 13456	85th	1958	144
H.R. 13482	85th	1958	144
H.R. 13487	69th	1926-1927	034
H.R. 13487	69th	1926-1927	075
H.R. 13500	95th	1978	238
H.R. 13511	95th	1978	217
H.R. 13511	95th	1978	236
H.R. 13517	91st	1970	134
H.R. 13565	93rd	1974	172
H.R. 13620	89th	1966	053
H.R. 13655	95th	1978	217
H.R. 13676	67th	1923	025
H.R. 13676	93rd	1974	161
H.R. 13678	93rd	1974	161
H.R. 13680	94th	1976	067
H.R. 13712	89th	1966	113

Bill No.	Congress	Year	Record Number
H.R. 13736	94th	1976	222
H.R. 13747	93rd	1974	156
H.R. 13777	94th	1976	202
H.R. 13777	94th	1976	203
H.R. 13778	95th	1978	241
H.R. 13826	91st	1969	144
H.R. 13827	91st	1969	144
H.R. 13834	93rd	1974	155
H.R. 13850	95th	1978	234
H.R. 13872	93rd	1974	173
H.R. 13906	93rd	1974	156
H.R. 13934	90th	1967	144
H.R. 13950	91st	1969	126
H.R. 14025	89th	1966	068
H.R. 14032	94th	1976	196
H.R. 14035	67th	1923	025
H.R. 14047	60th	1908	084
H.R. 14084	95th	1978	246
H.R. 14094	63rd	1914	033
H.R. 14096	90th	1967-1968	144
H.R. 14104	95th	1978	152
H.R. 14146	92nd	1972	141
H.R. 14146	92nd	1972	144
H.R. 14172	93rd	1974	166
H.R. 14173	91st	1969	143

Bill No.	Congress	Year	Record Number
H.R. 14222	67th	1923	031
H.R. 14249	95th	1978	238
H.R. 14298	94th	1976	194
H.R. 14299	94th	1976	195
H.R. 14355	89th	1966	053
H.R. 14368	93rd	1974	155
H.R. 14368	93rd	1974	156
H.R. 14451	94th	1976	199
H.R. 14465	91st	1969-1970	144
H.R. 14465	91st	1969-1970	231
H.R. 14493	93rd	1974	173
H.R. 14563	90th	1967-1968	053
H.R. 14580	91st	1969	067
H.R. 14622	61st	1909-1910	084
H.R. 14790	91st	1969	144
H.R. 14822	91st	1969	174
H.R. 1482	58th	1904	001
H.R. 1484	91st	1969	141
H.R. 14862	94th	1976	204
H.R. 14920	93rd	1974	166
H.R. 14929	89th	1966	077
H.R. 14944	65th	1919	071
H.R. 14965	94th	1976	204
H.R. 15023	92nd	1972	140
H.R. 15067	90th	1968	144

Bill No.	Congress	Year	Record Number
H.R. 15069	94th	1976	162
H.R. 15083	90th	1968	005
H.R. 15086	70th	1928	009
H.R. 15099	91st	1969	141
H.R. 15156	90th	1968	124
H.R. 15196	90th	1968	124
H.R. 15202	89th	1966	110
H.R. 15223	93rd	1974	156
H.R. 15263	90th	1968	067
H.R. 15276	93rd	1974	167
H.R. 15283	93rd	1974	162
H.R. 15288	64th	1916	075
H.R. 15301	93rd	1974	053
H.R. 15315	63rd	1914	075
H.R. 15361	93rd	1974	163
H.R. 15376	92nd	1972	136
H.R. 15382	93rd	1974	156
H.R. 15414	90th	1968	144
H.R. 15419	94th	1976	220
H.R. 15460	94th	1976	201
H.R. 15472	93rd	1974	156
H.R. 15479	91st	1970	144
H.R. 15537	69th	1926-1927	034
H.R. 15560	93rd	1974	156
H.R. 15612	93rd	1974	169

Bill No.	Congress	Year	Record Number
H.R. 15630	94th	1976	246
H.R. 15653	60th	1908	040
H.R. 15690	92nd	1972	144
H.R. 15700	91st	1970	073
H.R. 15733	91st	1970	053
H.R. 15750	89th	1966	067
H.R. 15757	90th	1968	144
H.R. 15758	90th	1968	144
H.R. 15785	90th	1968	107
H.R. 15791	93rd	1974	150
H.R. 15838	60th	1908	075
H.R. 15883	92nd	1972	045
H.R. 15890	89th	1966	115
H.R. 15894	66th	1921	040
H.R. 15927	92nd	1972	053
H.R. 15963	89th	1966	144
H.R. 15979	90th	1968	144
H.R. 15985	90th	1968	124
H.R. 15989	63rd	1914	071
H.R. 15989	63rd	1914	075
H.R. 16045	93rd	1974	156
H.R. 16076	89th	1966	144
H.R. 16090	93rd	1974	168
H.R. 16093	89th	1966	053
H.R. 16119	92nd	1972	138

Bill No.	Congress	Year	Record Number
H.R. 16136	63rd	1914-1915	033
H.R. 16155	91st	1970	141
H.R. 16215	93rd	1974	141
H.R. 16311	91st	1970	143
H.R. 16371	93rd	1974	169
H.R. 16373	93rd	1974	173
H.R. 16395	70th	1929	040
H.R. 16414	91st	1970	144
H.R. 16448	93rd	1974	219
H.R. 16562	92nd	1972	140
H.R. 16570	70th	1929	071
H.R. 16619	71st	1931	042
H.R. 16619	71st	1931	044
H.R. 16619	71st	1931	144
H.R. 16659	92nd	1972	138
H.R. 16668	93rd	1974	191
H.R. 16724	92nd	1972	138
H.R. 16725	92nd	1972	140
H.R. 16785	91st	1970	129
H.R. 16785	91st	1970	144
H.R. 16808	69th	1927	010
H.R. 16886	69th	1927	040
H.R. 16901	93rd	1974	156
H.R. 16982	71st	1931	040
H.R. 17054	71st	1931	040

Bill No.	Congress	Year	Record Number
H.R. 17069	69th	1927	042
H.R. 17070	91st	1970	128
H.R. 17085	57th	1903	075
H.R. 17090	92nd	1972	140
H.R. 17113	91st	1970	144
H.R. 17134	90th	1968	144
H.R. 17178	93rd	1974	219
H.R. 17255	91st	1970	130
H.R. 17255	91st	1970	144
H.R. 17268	90th	1968	068
H.R. 17276	69th	1927	008
H.R. 17285	89th	1966	053
H.R. 17409	93rd	1974	174
H.R. 17545	93rd	1974	156
H.R. 17550	91st	1970	143
H.R. 17555	91st	1970	134
H.R. 17570	91st	1970	144
H.R. 17576	59th	1906	001
H.R. 17577	93rd	1974	156
H.R. 17598	91st	1970	148
H.R. 17607	89th	1966	116
H.R. 17607	89th	1966	120
H.R. 17685	89th	1966	144
H.R. 17700	64th	1916	037
H.R. 17703	60th	1908	075

Bill No.	Congress	Year	Record Number
H.R. 17762	91st	1970	148
H.R. 17825	91st	1971	131
H.R. 17864	90th	1968	144
H.R. 17989	90th	1968	144
H.R. 18205	91st	1970	148
H.R. 18230	89th	1966	117
H.R. 18231	89th	1966	144
H.R. 18366	90th	1968	029
H.R. 18539	91st	1970	148
H.R. 18583	91st	1970	144
H.R. 18608	91st	1970	144
H.R. 18654	91st	1970	148
H.R. 18679	91st	1970	144
H.R. 18700	61st	1910	144
H.R. 18874	91st	1970	144
H.R. 18884	61st	1910	075
H.R. 18885	61st	1910	075
H.R. 18886	61st	1910	075
H.R. 18887	61st	1910	075
H.R. 19070	61st	1910	005
H.R. 19188	63rd	1914	071
H.R. 19195	91st	1970	144
H.R. 19200	91st	1970	129
H.R. 19389	61st	1910	075
H.R. 19436	91st	1970	144

Bill No.	Congress	Year	Record Number
H.R. 19466	60th	1908	084
H.R. 19504	91st	1970	144
H.R. 19853	59th	1906	006
H.R. 19853	59th	1906	008
H.R. 19853	59th	1906	009
H.R. 19853	59th	1906	010
H.R. 19853	59th	1906	014
H.R. 19853	59th	1906	015
H.R. 19853	59th	1906	017
H.R. 19853	59th	1906	020
H.R. 19853	59th	1906	021
H.R. 19853	59th	1906	024
H.R. 19853	59th	1906	026
H.R. 19853	59th	1906	028
H.R. 19877	91st	1970	144
H.R. 19911	91st	1970-1971	067
H.R. 19928	91st	1970-1971	144
H.R. 19962	61st	1910	005
H.R. 20386	60th	1908	084
H.R. 20388	60th	1908	008
H.R. 20585	61st	1910	075
H.R. 20975	63rd	1915	039
H.R. 20989	61st	1910	144
H.R. 21455	60th	1908-1909	084
H.R. 21481	61st	1910	075

Bill No.	Congress	Year	Record Number
H.R. 21592	60th	1908	006
H.R. 21592	60th	1908	008
H.R. 21592	60th	1908	010
H.R. 21592	60th	1908	021
H.R. 21592	60th	1908	026
H.R. 21776	62nd	1912	021
H.R. 21815	60th	1908	144
H.R. 21984	60th	1908	006
H.R. 21984	60th	1908	008
H.R. 21984	60th	1908	021
H.R. 21984	60th	1908	024
H.R. 21984	60th	1908	026
H.R. 22071	60th	1908	006
H.R. 22071	60th	1908	008
H.R. 22071	60th	1908	021
H.R. 22071	60th	1908	026
H.R. 22183	60th	1908	006
H.R. 22183	60th	1908	008
H.R. 22183	60th	1908	021
H.R. 22183	60th	1908	024
H.R. 22183	60th	1908	026
H.R. 22345	62nd	1912	075
H.R. 23193	62nd	1912	071
H.R. 23193	62nd	1912	075
H.R. 23377	61st	1910-1911	144

Bill No.	Congress	Year	Record Number
H.R. 23417	62nd	1912-1913	071
H.R. 23417	62nd	1912-1913	075
H.R. 23916	61st	1910	075
H.R. 24070	61st	1910	001
H.R. 24224	62nd	1912	007
H.R. 24224	62nd	1912	018
H.R. 24224	62nd	1912	020
H.R. 24782	60th	1908	006
H.R. 24782	60th	1908	008
H.R. 24782	60th	1908	010
H.R. 24782	60th	1908	021
H.R. 24782	60th	1908	024
H.R. 24782	60th	1908	026
H.R. 25133	59th	1907	006
H.R. 25133	59th	1907	008
H.R. 25133	59th	1907	015
H.R. 25133	59th	1907	026
H.R. 25162	60th	1909	008
H.R. 25162	60th	1909	021
H.R. 25162	60th	1909	024
H.R. 25162	60th	1909	026
H.R. 25552	61st	1910	040
H.R. 26277	62nd	1912	084
H.R. 27310	60th	1909	006
H.R. 27310	60th	1909	008

Bill No.	Congress	Year	Record Number
H.R. 27310	60th	1909	010
H.R. 27310	60th	1909	021
H.R. 27310	60th	1909	024
H.R. 27310	60th	1909	026
H.R. 27970	60th	1909	144
H.R. 28192	60th	1909	006
H.R. 28192	60th	1909	007
H.R. 28192	60th	1909	008
H.R. 28192	60th	1909	009
H.R. 28192	60th	1909	010
H.R. 28192	60th	1909	013
H.R. 28192	60th	1909	014
H.R. 28192	60th	1909	015
H.R. 28192	60th	1909	016
H.R. 28192	60th	1909	017
H.R. 28192	60th	1909	018
H.R. 28192	60th	1909	019
H.R. 28192	60th	1909	020
H.R. 28192	60th	1909	021
H.R. 28192	60th	1909	022
H.R. 28192	60th	1909	023
H.R. 28192	60th	1909	024
H.R. 28192	60th	1909	025
H.R. 28192	60th	1909	026
H.R. 28192	60th	1909	027

Bill No.	Congress	Year	Record Number
H.R. 28192	60th	1909	028
H.R. Con. Res. 24	100th	1987	254
H.R. Con. Res. 199	91st	1970	148
H.R. Con. Res. 559	95th	1977-1978	236
H.R. Con. Res. 611	91st	1970	148
H.R. Con. Res. 683	95th	1977-1978	236
H.R. Res. 47	82nd	1951	054
H.R. Res. 162	77th	1942	059
H.R. Res. 212	85th	1957	054
H.R. Res. 273	85th	1957	054
H.R. Res. 311	85th	1957	054
H.R. Res. 347	77th	1941	059
H.R. Res. 352	75th	1937	054
H.R. Res. 447	82nd	1951	054
H.R. Res. 1120	91st	1970	148
H.R. Res. 1964	91st	1970	148
H.R.J. Res. 1	92nd	1971-1972	148
H.R.J. Res. 2	93rd	1973	148
H.R.J. Res. 38	72nd	1932	042
H.R.J. Res. 277	65th	1918	029
H.R.J. Res. 278	82nd	1951	068
H.R.J. Res. 280	90th	1967	124
H.R.J. Res. 289	82nd	1951	031
H.R.J. Res. 330	84th	1955	083
H.R.J. Res. 331	84th	1955	083

Bill No.	Congress	Year	Record Number
H.R.J. Res. 332	84th	1955	083
H.R.J. Res. 375	73rd	1934	049
H.R.J. Res. 382	66th	1920-1921	030
H.R.J. Res. 406	96th	1979	068
H.R.J. Res. 413	63rd	1915	039
H.R.J. Res. 424	85th	1958	069
H.R.J. Res. 425	85th	1957-1958	069
H.R.J. Res. 478	96th	1980	068
H.R.J. Res. 516	81st	1950	031
H.R.J. Res. 520	96th	1980	068
H.R.J. Res. 542	93rd	1973	148
H.R.J. Res. 555	83rd	1954	082
H.R.J. Res. 573	99th	1986	253
H.R.J. Res. 615	85th	1958	069
H.R.J. Res. 648	98th	1984	252
H.R.J. Res. 649	86th	1960	144
H.R.J. Res. 669	92nd	1971	148
H.R.J. Res. 672	94th	1975	068
H.R.J. Res. 713	99th	1986	253
H.R.J. Res. 727	99th	1986	253
H.R.J. Res. 934	88th	1964	005
H.R.J. Res. 1056	93rd	1974	068
H.R.J. Res. 1151	91st	1970	148
H.R.J. Res. 1259	91st	1970	068
H.R.J. Res. 1302	91st	1970	148

Bill No.	Congress	Year	Record Number
H.R.J. Res. 1336	91st	1970	068
H.R.J. Res. 1355	91st	1970	148
S. 1	100th	1987	254
S. 1	87th	1961	029
S. 1	87th	1961	144
S. 1	91st	1969-1970	144
S. 2	79th	1945-1946	062
S. 2	88th	1963-1964	099
S. 3	89th	1965	101
S. 3	89th	1965	144
S. 4	65th	1917	084
S. 4	89th	1965	144
S. 4	93rd	1973	164
S. 5	74th	1935-1936	054
S. 5	75th	1937-1938	054
S. 5	75th	1937-1938	144
S. 5	82nd	1951-1952	073
S. 5	94th	1975-1976	135
S. 5	94th	1975-1976	189
S. 5	94th	1975-1976	190
S. 7	75th	1937	006
S. 7	75th	1937	008
S. 7	75th	1937	010
S. 7	75th	1937	026
S. 7	79th	1945-1946	063

Bill No.	Congress	Year	Record Number
S. 7	79th	1945-1946	144
S. 7	91st	1969	144
S. 7	95th	1977	208
S. 7	96th	1979	240
S. 10	78th	1943	070
S. 10	79th	1945	070
S. 10	80th	1947	070
S. 10	81st	1949	070
S. 10	92nd	1971	144
S. 11	79th	1945	070
S. 11	81st	1949	070
S. 13	95th	1977	212
S. 14	99th	1985	253
S. 17	45th	1877-1878	040
S. 18	28th	1844-1845	039
S. 20	45th	1877-1878	001
S. 21	89th	1965	144
S. 22	72nd	1931	071
S. 22	87th	1961	073
S. 22	89th	1965-1966	099
S. 22	94th	1975-1976	200
S. 24	89th	1965	073
S. 27	50th	1888	144
S. 30	91st	1969-1970	003
S. 30	91st	1969-1970	144

Bill No.	Congress	Year	Record Number
S. 32	92nd	1971-1972	185
S. 32	93rd	1973-1974	185
S. 32	94th	1975-1976	185
S. 34	79th	1945	062
S. 38	93rd	1973	144
S. 40	93rd	1973	159
S. 41	69th	1925-1926	035
S. 50	93rd	1973	104
S. 51	84th	1955	076
S. 51	99th	1985	253
S. 53	99th	1985	254
S. 54	101st	1989	257
S. 54	49th	1885-1887	001
S. 55	80th	1947	037
S. 65	98th	1984	101
S. 72	80th	1947	070
S. 74	68th	1923	025
S. 79	86th	1959	054
S. 88	59th	1905-1906	144
S. 100	93rd	1973	183
S. 100	94th	1975	183
S. 110	94th	1975	177
S. 117	81st	1949	054
S. 120	87th	1961	144
S. 121	92nd	1971	099

Bill No.	Congress	Year	Record Number
S. 143	95th	1977	142
S. 143	95th	1977	214
S. 143	95th	1977	217
S. 176	72nd	1931	006
S. 176	72nd	1931	008
S. 176	72nd	1931	010
S. 176	72nd	1931	012
S. 176	72nd	1931	014
S. 176	72nd	1931	019
S. 176	72nd	1931	025
S. 176	72nd	1931	026
S. 176	80th	1947	144
S. 188	28th	1844	039
S. 203	71st	1929	071
S. 210	96th	1979	241
S. 219	92nd	1971	099
S. 224	27th	1842	039
S. 226	86th	1959	053
S. 229	94th	1975-1976	152
S. 233	52nd	1891	075
S. 237	91st	1969	144
S. 241	96th	1979	243
S. 245	26th	1841	039
S. 247	81st	1949-1950	039
S. 249	94th	1975	176

Bill No.	Congress	Year	Record Number
S. 251	95th	1977	209
S. 251	97th	1981	251
S. 252	95th	1977	208
S. 252	95th	1977	209
S. 253	95th	1977	209
S. 257	39th	1866	001
S. 259	26th	1841	039
S. 260	93rd	1973-1974	189
S. 260	93rd	1973-1974	190
S. 275	92nd	1971	144
S. 276	86th	1959	054
S. 290	73rd	1933	071
S. 292	25th	1839	039
S. 293	25th	1839	039
S. 293	79th	1945	053
S. 297	35th	1858	040
S. 300	45th	1877-1878	075
S. 302	82nd	1951-1952	031
S. 306	89th	1965	107
S. 306	89th	1965	144
S. 342	73rd	1933	009
S. 342	73rd	1933	010
S. 342	73rd	1933	019
S. 342	73rd	1933	020
S. 342	73rd	1933	021

Bill No.	Congress	Year	Record Number
S. 342	73rd	1933	026
S. 355	91st	1969	126
S. 365	44th	1876	075
S. 370	89th	1965	108
S. 373	93rd	1973	159
S. 373	93rd	1973	160
S. 379	95th	1977	212
S. 379	95th	1977	229
S. 379	95th	1977	233
S. 383	74th	1935	071
S. 385	85th	1957-1958	144
S. 386	93rd	1973-1974	156
S. 389	51st	1889-1890	040
S. 415	71st	1929	071
S. 418	80th	1947-1948	004
S. 418	80th	1947-1948	144
S. 421	95th	1977	222
S. 424	93rd	1973-1974	202
S. 424	93rd	1973-1974	203
S. 426	93rd	1973	156
S. 431	98th	1983	254
S. 432	88th	1963	144
S. 433	93rd	1973-1974	156
S. 433	93rd	1973-1974	171
S. 440	93rd	1973	148

Bill No.	Congress	Year	Record Number
S. 441	86th	1959	144
S. 445	80th	1947	054
S. 455	87th	1961-1962	144
S. 467	91st	1969	126
S. 468	97th	1981	251
S. 475	75th	1937-1938	084
S. 476	71st	1929-1930	040
S. 476	95th	1977-1978	223
S. 477	95th	1977-1978	223
S. 478	95th	1977-1978	223
S. 489	93rd	1973	107
S. 491	95th	1977-1978	239
S. 494	99th	1985	253
S. 495	78th	1943	057
S. 502	93rd	1973	144
S. 502	93rd	1973	156
S. 505	86th	1959	087
S. 505	86th	1959	088
S. 506	67th	1921	040
S. 507	94th	1975-1976	202
S. 507	94th	1975-1976	203
S. 510	89th	1965	144
S. 510	96th	1979	241
S. 516	84th	1955	073
S. 521	94th	1975-1976	204

Bill No.	Congress	Year	Record Number
S. 525	80th	1947	039
S. 525	80th	1947	071
S. 525	92nd	1971-1972	140
S. 526	80th	1947	039
S. 526	80th	1947	071
S. 531	94th	1975	205
S. 538	100th	1987	255
S. 544	93rd	1973-1974	003
S. 547	76th	1939-1940	026
S. 555	95th	1977-1978	234
S. 565	93rd	1973	159
S. 579	66th	1919	028
S. 580	74th	1935	054
S. 582	92nd	1971-1972	141
S. 586	94th	1975-1976	141
S. 591	96th	1979	246
S. 595	75th	1937	052
S. 595	80th	1947-1948	040
S. 596	99th	1985	253
S. 600	89th	1965	108
S. 601	83rd	1953	054
S. 602	90th	1967	101
S. 602	90th	1967	144
S. 607	85th	1958	083
S. 609	85th	1958	083

Bill No.	Congress	Year	Record Number
S. 619	79th	1945-1946	029
S. 622	94th	1975	181
S. 637	67th	1921	028
S. 638	92nd	1971	141
S. 643	96th	1979-1980	245
S. 649	88th	1963-1964	144
S. 652	99th	1985	254
S. 658	82nd	1951-1952	038
S. 659	92nd	1971-1972	029
S. 659	92nd	1971-1972	108
S. 670	80th	1947	053
S. 670	97th	1981	251
S. 680	42nd	1873	001
S. 682	95th	1977-1978	208
S. 686	71st	1930	005
S. 686	79th	1945	005
S. 697	95th	1977	209
S. 702	78th	1943	071
S. 703	64th	1915-1917	029
S. 703	93rd	1973	159
S. 705	70th	1927	071
S. 714	95th	1977	209
S. 716	92nd	1971	073
S. 717	95th	1977	216
S. 719	95th	1977	209

Bill No.	Congress	Year	Record Number
S. 729	88th	1963	053
S. 731	86th	1959	144
S. 731	92nd	1971	148
S. 748	86th	1959	087
S. 748	86th	1959	088
S. 754	93rd	1973-1974	174
S. 758	80th	1947	066
S. 758	93rd	1973	159
S. 770	94th	1975	177
S. 777	97th	1981	254
S. 780	90th	1967	130
S. 780	90th	1967	144
S. 786	78th	1943	040
S. 788	90th	1967	122
S. 791	95th	1977-1978	239
S. 794	93rd	1973	161
S. 796	78th	1943	037
S. 817	94th	1975	198
S. 818	66th	1919	084
S. 818	91st	1969	105
S. 821	93rd	1973-1974	167
S. 821	93rd	1973-1974	210
S. 826	95th	1977	172
S. 830	90th	1967	122
S. 835	83rd	1953	054

Bill No.	Congress	Year	Record Number
S. 836	94th	1975	198
S. 846	93rd	1973	159
S. 851	86th	1959	004
S. 852	73rd	1933-1934	031
S. 853	95th	1977	068
S. 859	41st	1870-1871	002
S. 861	78th	1943	040
S. 863	84th	1955-1956	004
S. 869	96th	1979	234
S. 880	94th	1975	194
S. 882	88th	1963	093
S. 886	99th	1985	253
S. 887	93rd	1973	156
S. 888	93rd	1973	156
S. 890	84th	1955-1956	004
S. 890	84th	1955-1956	144
S. 892	77th	1941	075
S. 895	87th	1961	089
S. 895	92nd	1971	174
S. 897	95th	1977-1978	220
S. 901	96th	1979	254
S. 903	96th	1979	242
S. 905	93rd	1973	159
S. 910	88th	1963	093
S. 917	90th	1967-1968	123

Bill No.	Congress	Year	Record Number
S. 919	95th	1977	209
S. 921	92nd	1971	202
S. 921	92nd	1971	203
S. 921	93rd	1973-1974	155
S. 926	45th	1878	001
S. 928	77th	1941	084
S. 928	84th	1955	144
S. 932	96th	1979-1980	068
S. 932	96th	1979-1980	247
S. 933	101st	1989-1990	256
S. 946	94th	1975	204
S. 947	87th	1961	054
S. 955	99th	1985	253
S. 957	99th	1985	253
S. 961	89th	1965	076
S. 961	94th	1975-1976	184
S. 961	96th	1979	174
S. 962	89th	1965	076
S. 963	89th	1965	076
S. 964	89th	1965	076
S. 965	89th	1965	076
S. 966	89th	1965	076
S. 967	89th	1965	076
S. 968	89th	1965	076
S. 969	94th	1975-1976	198

Bill No.	Congress	Year	Record Number
S. 972	99th	1985	253
S. 974	91st	1969	003
S. 975	91st	1969	003
S. 976	59th	1905-1907	040
S. 976	91st	1969	003
S. 976	92nd	1971-1972	144
S. 977	94th	1975	191
S. 985	80th	1947	054
S. 987	86th	1959	053
S. 991	92nd	1971	073
S. 991	95th	1977-1978	241
S. 995	95th	1977-1978	235
S. 1002	86th	1959	087
S. 1002	86th	1959	088
S. 1003	90th	1967	112
S. 1011	91st	1969	073
S. 1013	89th	1965-1966	117
S. 1016	92nd	1971	139
S. 1021	95th	1977	210
S. 1028	87th	1961	144
S. 1028	96th	1979	174
S. 1030	93rd	1973	159
S. 1041	93rd	1973	202
S. 1042	79th	1945	054
S. 1051	91st	1969	099

Bill No.	Congress	Year	Record Number
S. 1053	95th	1977	209
S. 1064	96th	1979	242
S. 1067	93rd	1973	156
S. 1070	93rd	1973-1974	156
S. 1071	87th	1961	144
S. 1072	91st	1969	101
S. 1072	91st	1969	144
S. 1075	91st	1969	127
S. 1075	91st	1969	144
S. 1075	91st	1969	208
S. 1081	83rd	1953	068
S. 1086	93rd	1973	156
S. 1094	91st	1969	126
S. 1101	90th	1967	073
S. 1107	64th	1916-1917	028
S. 1111	88th	1963-1964	144
S. 1114	81st	1949	069
S. 1122	85th	1957	086
S. 1126	80th	1947	037
S. 1126	80th	1947	064
S. 1126	80th	1947	065
S. 1128	99th	1985-1986	254
S. 1136	93rd	1973	144
S. 1137	86th	1959	087
S. 1137	86th	1959	088

Bill No.	Congress	Year	Record Number
S. 1141	95th	1977	212
S. 1143	96th	1979	152
S. 1145	85th	1957	086
S. 1146	96th	1979	171
S. 1149	96th	1979	242
S. 1160	89th	1965-1966	111
S. 1160	89th	1965-1966	119
S. 1160	89th	1965-1966	170
S. 1163	92nd	1971-1972	104
S. 1172	89th	1965	108
S. 1178	91st	1969	126
S. 1179	93rd	1973	164
S. 1186	81st	1951	054
S. 1190	80th	1947-1948	054
S. 1196	87th	1961	053
S. 1206	79th	1945	008
S. 1206	79th	1945	021
S. 1213	93rd	1973	159
S. 1214	93rd	1973	159
S. 1215	93rd	1973	159
S. 1218	95th	1977	210
S. 1226	69th	1925-1926	031
S. 1229	89th	1965	144
S. 1238	92nd	1971	144
S. 1241	50th	1888	144

Bill No.	Congress	Year	Record Number
S. 1248	79th	1945-1946	071
S. 1256	95th	1977-1978	223
S. 1257	95th	1977-1978	223
S. 1261	92nd	1971	185
S. 1269	66th	1919	033
S. 1283	86th	1959-1960	112
S. 1283	93rd	1973-1974	172
S. 1285	79th	1945	039
S. 1285	79th	1945	071
S. 1292	81st	1949-1950	031
S. 1297	79th	1945	039
S. 1297	79th	1945	071
S. 1300	91st	1969	126
S. 1311	86th	1959	087
S. 1311	86th	1959	088
S. 1313	85th	1957-1958	053
S. 1316	95th	1977	152
S. 1325	96th	1979	249
S. 1329	95th	1977	135
S. 1340	95th	1977-1978	172
S. 1341	96th	1979	249
S. 1347	82nd	1951	053
S. 1351	93rd	1973	156
S. 1353	82nd	1951	053
S. 1356	88th	1963	053

Bill No.	Congress	Year	Record Number
S. 1360	95th	1977-1978	162
S. 1361	93rd	1973-1974	200
S. 1368	91st	1969	125
S. 1371	94th	1975	198
S. 1373	88th	1963	083
S. 1384	86th	1959	087
S. 1385	86th	1959	087
S. 1386	86th	1959	087
S. 1387	86th	1959	087
S. 1392	93rd	1973	159
S. 1404	48th	1884	040
S. 1406	94th	1975-1976	194
S. 1409	88th	1963	093
S. 1414	93rd	1973-1974	159
S. 1420	100th	1987	255
S. 1423	93rd	1973	146
S. 1425	94th	1975	180
S. 1428	81st	1949	054
S. 1432	94th	1975	177
S. 1432	95th	1977	220
S. 1435	93rd	1973	150
S. 1435	93rd	1973	151
S. 1439	94th	1975-1976	220
S. 1443	93rd	1973	067
S. 1457	87th	1961	089

Bill No.	Congress	Year	Record Number
S. 1466	46th	1880	075
S. 1474	94th	1975	204
S. 1476	78th	1943-1944	070
S. 1480	96th	1979-1980	249
S. 1501	93rd	1973	144
S. 1507	94th	1975	179
S. 1510	75th	1937	017
S. 1511	101st	1989-1990	257
S. 1516	93rd	1973	159
S. 1523	95th	1977	213
S. 1525	72nd	1932	045
S. 1528	95th	1977	171
S. 1529	87th	1961	005
S. 1537	82nd	1951-1952	039
S. 1537	94th	1975	068
S. 1538	95th	1977	219
S. 1540	95th	1977	043
S. 1541	86th	1959	144
S. 1541	93rd	1973-1974	157
S. 1541	93rd	1973-1974	158
S. 1541	93rd	1973-1974	159
S. 1541	93rd	1973-1974	160
S. 1542	83rd	1953	054
S. 1543	78th	1943-1944	040
S. 1547	92nd	1971-1972	140

Bill No.	Congress	Year	Record Number
S. 1552	87th	1961-1962	054
S. 1552	87th	1961-1962	144
S. 1555	86th	1959	037
S. 1555	86th	1959	087
S. 1555	86th	1959	088
S. 1556	95th	1977-1978	228
S. 1557	93rd	1973	164
S. 1563	82nd	1951-1952	003
S. 1564	82nd	1951-1952	003
S. 1564	89th	1965	105
S. 1575	86th	1959	144
S. 1576	86th	1959	073
S. 1588	51st	1889	084
S. 1589	84th	1955	053
S. 1597	94th	1975	177
S. 1604	57th	1901	075
S. 1605	88th	1963-1964	144
S. 1614	84th	1955-1956	054
S. 1617	95th	1977-1978	208
S. 1620	53rd	1894-1895	003
S. 1623	89th	1965	144
S. 1623	91st	1969	003
S. 1624	82nd	1951-1952	003
S. 1624	91st	1969-1970	003
S. 1625	94th	1975	197

Bill No.	Congress	Year	Record Number
S. 1631	93rd	1973	164
S. 1632	94th	1975-1976	192
S. 1637	92nd	1971	135
S. 1641	93rd	1973	159
S. 1642	95th	1977	212
S. 1643	95th	1977	228
S. 1644	92nd	1971	144
S. 1648	89th	1965	144
S. 1648	93rd	1973	159
S. 1652	95th	1977	222
S. 1653	87th	1961	003
S. 1654	87th	1961	003
S. 1655	87th	1961	003
S. 1656	87th	1961	003
S. 1656	95th	1977	219
S. 1657	87th	1961	003
S. 1658	87th	1961-1962	003
S. 1663	88th	1963-1964	111
S. 1663	88th	1963-1964	119
S. 1665	87th	1961	003
S. 1666	88th	1963-1964	111
S. 1666	88th	1963-1964	119
S. 1672	46th	1880	075
S. 1678	95th	1977-1978	208
S. 1678	95th	1977-1978	224

Bill No.	Congress	Year	Record Number
S. 1684	83rd	1953	040
S. 1686	93rd	1973	185
S. 1688	93rd	1973-1974	173
S. 1689	91st	1969	112
S. 1693	59th	1905	084
S. 1693	95th	1977	211
S. 1703	95th	1977	212
S. 1711	86th	1959	077
S. 1711	94th	1975	179
S. 1716	97th	1981	254
S. 1717	79th	1945-1946	144
S. 1717	82nd	1951	068
S. 1720	79th	1945	071
S. 1725	93rd	1973	154
S. 1731	70th	1927-1929	029
S. 1731	88th	1963	097
S. 1735	93rd	1973	156
S. 1744	94th	1975	204
S. 1752	91st	1969	144
S. 1753	95th	1977-1978	236
S. 1754	94th	1975	204
S. 1767	78th	1944	040
S. 1776	93rd	1973	144
S. 1794	81st	1949	144
S. 1795	84th	1955	144

Bill No.	Congress	Year	Record Number
S. 1801	70th	1927-1928	144
S. 1805	94th	1975	198
S. 1813	85th	1957-1958	086
S. 1821	79th	1946	040
S. 1838	67th	1921	071
S. 1838	95th	1977	135
S. 1839	89th	1965	054
S. 1843	90th	1967-1968	076
S. 1844	90th	1967	076
S. 1845	90th	1967	076
S. 1846	90th	1967	076
S. 1847	90th	1967	076
S. 1847	95th	1977	135
S. 1850	79th	1946	039
S. 1850	79th	1946	071
S. 1861	91st	1969	003
S. 1861	93rd	1973	154
S. 1866	83rd	1953	054
S. 1867	81st	1949	054
S. 1867	93rd	1973	053
S. 1871	76th	1939	055
S. 1871	95th	1977	215
S. 1872	90th	1967	067
S. 1880	92nd	1971	148
S. 1882	94th	1975	183

Bill No.	Congress	Year	Record Number
S. 1883	56th	1899	084
S. 1883	94th	1975	181
S. 1888	93rd	1973	156
S. 1895	85th	1957	054
S. 1901	83rd	1953	144
S. 1907	91st	1969	126
S. 1911	94th	1975-1976	187
S. 1922	87th	1961	144
S. 1928	73rd	1933	006
S. 1928	73rd	1933	009
S. 1928	73rd	1933	025
S. 1928	73rd	1933	026
S. 1929	95th	1977	229
S. 1929	95th	1977	233
S. 1937	88th	1963	096
S. 1944	73rd	1933	054
S. 1944	87th	1961	086
S. 1946	78th	1944	029
S. 1952	95th	1977	208
S. 1952	95th	1977	218
S. 1958	74th	1935	047
S. 1958	74th	1935	048
S. 1958	74th	1935	049
S. 1964	92nd	1971	135
S. 1976	95th	1977-1978	221

Bill No.	Congress	Year	Record Number
S. 1980	95th	1977	222
S. 1983	87th	1961	067
S. 1983	87th	1961	144
S. 1983	93rd	1973	152
S. 1991	94th	1975	187
S. 2000	73rd	1934	054
S. 2005	91st	1969-1970	107
S. 2005	91st	1969-1970	144
S. 2006	98th	1983	254
S. 2017	89th	1965	144
S. 2022	91st	1969	003
S. 2029	91st	1969	105
S. 2039	78th	1944	013
S. 2042	89th	1965	144
S. 2051	85th	1957	144
S. 2056	88th	1963	053
S. 2060	68th	1924-1925	144
S. 2062	93rd	1973	156
S. 2064	92nd	1971	135
S. 2067	90th	1967-1968	124
S. 2075	86th	1959	022
S. 2075	90th	1967	124
S. 2088	95th	1977	135
S. 2090	84th	1955	067
S. 2092	95th	1977	222

Bill No.	Congress	Year	Record Number
S. 2097	92nd	1971-1972	132
S. 2100	94th	1975	198
S. 2116	50th	1888	040
S. 2116	62nd	1911	071
S. 2116	82nd	1951-1952	003
S. 2117	95th	1977-1978	153
S. 2118	91st	1969	126
S. 2122	91st	1969	003
S. 2129	77th	1941	030
S. 2130	85th	1957	067
S. 2133	92nd	1971	144
S. 2137	85th	1957	086
S. 2141	50th	1888	084
S. 2141	77th	1941	054
S. 2150	94th	1975-1976	204
S. 2154	87th	1961	090
S. 2156	85th	1957	034
S. 2156	87th	1961	073
S. 2159	94th	1975	187
S. 2162	70th	1928	071
S. 2162	91st	1969-1970	144
S. 2162	94th	1975	204
S. 2167	92nd	1971	054
S. 2175	85th	1957	086
S. 2178	83rd	1953-1954	053

Bill No.	Congress	Year	Record Number
S. 2187	87th	1961	144
S. 2193	91st	1969-1970	129
S. 2193	91st	1969-1970	144
S. 2197	86th	1959-1960	054
S. 2197	86th	1959-1960	144
S. 2200	94th	1975	187
S. 2213	89th	1965	144
S. 2215	80th	1948	144
S. 2229	85th	1957	231
S. 2240	75th	1937	006
S. 2240	75th	1937	008
S. 2240	75th	1937	009
S. 2240	75th	1937	021
S. 2240	75th	1937	026
S. 2252	73rd	1934	045
S. 2257	68th	1924	040
S. 2266	95th	1977-1978	217
S. 2276	91st	1969	144
S. 2278	94th	1975-1976	201
S. 2282	89th	1965	144
S. 2284	91st	1969	126
S. 2289	92nd	1971	126
S. 2292	91st	1969	003
S. 2292	93rd	1973	161
S. 2296	93rd	1973-1974	162

Bill No.	Congress	Year	Record Number
S. 2302	89th	1965	108
S. 2303	77th	1942	071
S. 2317	92nd	1971	101
S. 2317	92nd	1971	144
S. 2318	92nd	1971-1972	140
S. 2328	69th	1926	008
S. 2328	81st	1949-1950	034
S. 2328	81st	1949-1950	075
S. 2331	94th	1975	195
S. 2345	100th	1988	256
S. 2345	79th	1946	031
S. 2355	73rd	1934	054
S. 2365	94th	1975-1976	198
S. 2379	84th	1955-1956	029
S. 2380	95th	1977-1978	208
S. 2384	95th	1977-1978	237
S. 2385	54th	1896	075
S. 2385	80th	1948	039
S. 2387	68th	1924	071
S. 2391	84th	1955	068
S. 2391	87th	1961	144
S. 2391	95th	1978	225
S. 2391	95th	1978	226
S. 2395	87th	1961	053
S. 2400	71st	1929-1930	005

Bill No.	Congress	Year	Record Number
S. 2401	92nd	1971-1972	202
S. 2401	92nd	1971-1972	203
S. 2405	91st	1969	126
S. 2421	73rd	1935-1936	045
S. 2423	98th	1984	252
S. 2424	86th	1959	038
S. 2428	92nd	1971	099
S. 2433	81st	1949	034
S. 2438	77th	1942	070
S. 2438	80th	1948	053
S. 2440	87th	1961	144
S. 2447	85th	1957-1958	144
S. 2453	83rd	1953-1954	052
S. 2453	91st	1969-1970	134
S. 2456	91st	1969	105
S. 2465	74th	1935	006
S. 2465	74th	1935	008
S. 2465	74th	1935	009
S. 2465	74th	1935	010
S. 2465	74th	1935	011
S. 2465	74th	1935	012
S. 2465	74th	1935	020
S. 2465	74th	1935	025
S. 2465	74th	1935	026
S. 2465	74th	1935	027

Bill No.	Congress	Year	Record Number
S. 2465	93rd	1973-1974	166
S. 2473	95th	1977-1978	236
S. 2474	95th	1978	217
S. 2475	75th	1937-1938	047
S. 2475	83rd	1953-1954	077
S. 2482	79th	1946	070
S. 2483	92nd	1971-1972	183
S. 2487	94th	1975	198
S. 2491	77th	1942	070
S. 2491	77th	1942	071
S. 2493	95th	1978	231
S. 2495	93rd	1973-1974	185
S. 2496	74th	1935-1936	036
S. 2496	74th	1935-1936	037
S. 2496	85th	1957	144
S. 2499	60th	1907	006
S. 2499	60th	1907	008
S. 2499	60th	1907	021
S. 2499	60th	1907	026
S. 2505	86th	1959	054
S. 2507	91st	1969	105
S. 2515	92nd	1971-1972	133
S. 2515	92nd	1971-1972	134
S. 2518	81st	1949	074
S. 2518	81st	1949	075

Bill No.	Congress	Year	Record Number
S. 2527	100th	1988	255
S. 2529	73rd	1934	144
S. 2529	94th	1975-1976	187
S. 2534	95th	1978	217
S. 2538	95th	1977-1978	236
S. 2539	95th	1977-1978	236
S. 2542	93rd	1973-1974	173
S. 2543	93rd	1973-1974	170
S. 2549	83rd	1953-1954	078
S. 2549	86th	1960	144
S. 2559	83rd	1953-1954	006
S. 2568	86th	1959	144
S. 2569	86th	1959	144
S. 2577	84th	1955-1956	046
S. 2578	94th	1975-1976	204
S. 2582	74th	1935	051
S. 2589	93rd	1973-1974	155
S. 2589	93rd	1973-1974	156
S. 2594	82nd	1952	068
S. 2596	81st	1949-1950	040
S. 2596	95th	1978	238
S. 2602	86th	1959	054
S. 2609	81st	1949-1950	069
S. 2613	53rd	1895	084
S. 2613	92nd	1971	144

Bill No.	Congress	Year	Record Number
S. 2617	92nd	1971	133
S. 2617	92nd	1971	134
S. 2632	58th	1903	084
S. 2635	94th	1975-1976	194
S. 2636	94th	1975	205
S. 2639	82nd	1952	053
S. 2640	95th	1978	227
S. 2644	90th	1967	144
S. 2650	93rd	1973-1974	165
S. 2652	97th	1982	254
S. 2654	86th	1959	144
S. 2657	94th	1976	108
S. 2658	93rd	1973-1974	165
S. 2674	85th	1957	144
S. 2675	92nd	1971	126
S. 2680	93rd	1973	155
S. 2687	76th	1939-1940	084
S. 2687	88th	1964	077
S. 2688	76th	1939-1940	075
S. 2688	80th	1948	066
S. 2704	95th	1978	208
S. 2710	94th	1975-1976	204
S. 2721	77th	1942	071
S. 2725	96th	1980	254
S. 2727	93rd	1973	154

Bill No.	Congress	Year	Record Number
S. 2730	77th	1942	070
S. 2747	93rd	1973-1974	154
S. 2751	77th	1942	057
S. 2758	95th	1978	225
S. 2770	92nd	1971-1972	137
S. 2770	92nd	1971-1972	144
S. 2771	94th	1975	205
S. 2772	93rd	1973	155
S. 2772	93rd	1973	156
S. 2775	66th	1919-1920	001
S. 2775	66th	1919-1920	033
S. 2776	94th	1975	187
S. 2780	67th	1921	031
S. 2782	88th	1964	101
S. 2788	91st	1969-1970	129
S. 2789	94th	1975-1976	198
S. 2800	73rd	1934	054
S. 2802	91st	1969-1970	141
S. 2805	90th	1968	144
S. 2806	91st	1969	134
S. 2809	91st	1969-1970	144
S. 2810	93rd	1973-1974	173
S. 2812	93rd	1973	144
S. 2816	86th	1960	073
S. 2819	92nd	1971-1972	067

Bill No.	Congress	Year	Record Number
S. 2825	80th	1948	040
S. 2828	95th	1978	229
S. 2828	95th	1978	233
S. 2839	90th	1968	053
S. 2846	93rd	1973-1974	156
S. 2856	94th	1976	205
S. 2858	73rd	1934	054
S. 2864	91st	1969	144
S. 2868	83rd	1954	054
S. 2868	94th	1976	205
S. 2870	95th	1978	228
S. 2876	95th	1978	239
S. 2880	85th	1957	054
S. 2883	74th	1935-1936	029
S. 2888	85th	1958	086
S. 2899	95th	1978	152
S. 2900	60th	1907	006
S. 2900	60th	1907	008
S. 2900	60th	1907	010
S. 2900	60th	1907	021
S. 2900	60th	1907	026
S. 2901	75th	1937	031
S. 2908	94th	1976	205
S. 2911	94th	1976	186
S. 2912	90th	1968	073

Bill No.	Congress	Year	Record Number
S. 2912	94th	1976	186
S. 2917	91st	1969	126
S. 2917	91st	1969	140
S. 2918	94th	1976	186
S. 2926	73rd	1934	047
S. 2926	73rd	1934	049
S. 2930	83rd	1954	053
S. 2947	89th	1966	144
S. 2953	94th	1976	186
S. 2956	92nd	1971-1972	148
S. 2963	88th	1964	144
S. 2963	93rd	1974	173
S. 2966	87th	1962	067
S. 2977	88th	1964	054
S. 2980	94th	1976	186
S. 2986	90th	1968	077
S. 2987	94th	1976	186
S. 2995	94th	1976	198
S. 2999	82nd	1952	037
S. 3005	89th	1966	112
S. 3008	89th	1966	144
S. 3010	89th	1966	144
S. 3022	56th	1900	075
S. 3033	95th	1978	162
S. 3034	93rd	1974	160

Bill No.	Congress	Year	Record Number
S. 3034	95th	1978	162
S. 3035	93rd	1974	156
S. 3035	95th	1978	162
S. 3037	94th	1976	204
S. 3038	94th	1976	204
S. 3040	73rd	1934	003
S. 3041	73rd	1934	144
S. 3043	76th	1940	008
S. 3043	76th	1940	009
S. 3043	76th	1940	010
S. 3043	76th	1940	011
S. 3043	76th	1940	012
S. 3043	76th	1940	013
S. 3043	76th	1940	014
S. 3043	76th	1940	015
S. 3043	76th	1940	016
S. 3043	76th	1940	017
S. 3043	76th	1940	018
S. 3043	76th	1940	019
S. 3043	76th	1940	020
S. 3043	76th	1940	021
S. 3043	76th	1940	022
S. 3043	76th	1940	023
S. 3043	76th	1940	024
S. 3043	76th	1940	025

Bill No.	Congress	Year	Record Number
S. 3043	76th	1940	026
S. 3043	76th	1940	027
S. 3043	76th	1940	028
S. 3044	93rd	1974	168
S. 3046	76th	1940	055
S. 3047	74th	1935-1936	006
S. 3047	74th	1935-1936	007
S. 3047	74th	1935-1936	008
S. 3047	74th	1935-1936	009
S. 3047	74th	1935-1936	010
S. 3047	74th	1935-1936	011
S. 3047	74th	1935-1936	012
S. 3047	74th	1935-1936	014
S. 3047	74th	1935-1936	015
S. 3047	74th	1935-1936	017
S. 3047	74th	1935-1936	018
S. 3047	74th	1935-1936	019
S. 3047	74th	1935-1936	020
S. 3047	74th	1935-1936	021
S. 3047	74th	1935-1936	022
S. 3047	74th	1935-1936	023
S. 3047	74th	1935-1936	024
S. 3047	74th	1935-1936	026
S. 3047	74th	1935-1936	027
S. 3049	88th	1964	144

Bill No.	Congress	Year	Record Number
S. 3052	89th	1966	144
S. 3057	57th	1901-1902	001
S. 3057	57th	1901-1902	004
S. 3057	93rd	1974	156
S. 3059	71st	1930	041
S. 3065	94th	1976	186
S. 3066	93rd	1974	163
S. 3067	91st	1969-1970	135
S. 3068	86th	1959	088
S. 3072	91st	1970	130
S. 3073	75th	1937-1938	054
S. 3075	88th	1964	144
S. 3076	84th	1956	144
S. 3083	95th	1978	208
S. 3088	93rd	1974	161
S. 3091	63rd	1913-1914	029
S. 3091	94th	1976	162
S. 3095	90th	1968	144
S. 3108	91st	1969-1970	144
S. 3112	89th	1966	144
S. 3116	93rd	1974	173
S. 3122	92nd	1972	144
S. 3122	94th	1976	152
S. 3149	94th	1976	196
S. 3150	74th	1935	053

Bill No.	Congress	Year	Record Number
S. 3151	74th	1935	053
S. 3160	70th	1928	008
S. 3161	60th	1908	084
S. 3183	91st	1970	141
S. 3183	94th	1976	219
S. 3187	95th	1978	229
S. 3187	95th	1978	233
S. 3201	90th	1968	107
S. 3203	87th	1962	068
S. 3203	93rd	1974	161
S. 3206	90th	1968	144
S. 3211	90th	1968	124
S. 3219	94th	1976	204
S. 3219	94th	1976	209
S. 3223	66th	1919-1920	071
S. 3224	85th	1958	144
S. 3225	94th	1976	198
S. 3229	91st	1969-1970	130
S. 3231	73rd	1934	053
S. 3231	93rd	1974	156
S. 3234	93rd	1974	169
S. 3242	95th	1978	230
S. 3246	91st	1969-1970	144
S. 3252	56th	1900-1901	040
S. 3254	89th	1966	144

Bill No.	Congress	Year	Record Number
S. 3266	73rd	1934	036
S. 3267	93rd	1974	155
S. 3269	68th	1924	005
S. 3270	93rd	1974	068
S. 3274	89th	1966	053
S. 3277	93rd	1974	156
S. 3285	73rd	1934	038
S. 3285	73rd	1934	052
S. 3287	93rd	1974	155
S. 3295	81st	1950-1951	036
S. 3298	89th	1966	112
S. 3302	91st	1969-1970	068
S. 3303	74th	1935	042
S. 3303	74th	1935	043
S. 3303	74th	1935	044
S. 3303	74th	1935	144
S. 3323	83rd	1954	081
S. 3323	83rd	1954	082
S. 3325	67th	1922	071
S. 3342	92nd	1972	139
S. 3342	92nd	1972	144
S. 3344	83rd	1954	001
S. 3355	91st	1970	144
S. 3357	81st	1950-1951	003
S. 3358	72nd	1932	075

Bill No.	Congress	Year	Record Number
S. 3370	85th	1958	073
S. 3376	74th	1935	051
S. 3379	83rd	1954	112
S. 3394	93rd	1974	067
S. 3400	89th	1966	144
S. 3410	67th	1922	071
S. 3418	90th	1968	144
S. 3418	93rd	1974	173
S. 3426	91st	1970	073
S. 3446	86th	1960	073
S. 3460	91st	1969-1970	141
S. 3462	92nd	1972	144
S. 3466	91st	1970	130
S. 3474	69th	1926	071
S. 3491	87th	1962	144
S. 3494	95th	1978	238
S. 3495	69th	1926	005
S. 3497	90th	1968	144
S. 3500	74th	1936	051
S. 3501	74th	1936	051
S. 3507	92nd	1972	141
S. 3507	92nd	1972	144
S. 3517	59th	1906	084
S. 3524	73rd	1934	144
S. 3529	92nd	1972	135

Bill No.	Congress	Year	Record Number
S. 3546	91st	1970	130
S. 3549	93rd	1974	156
S. 3553	91st	1970	099
S. 3557	86th	1960	073
S. 3560	93rd	1974	156
S. 3571	86th	1959	088
S. 3579	87th	1962	099
S. 3595	85th	1958	054
S. 3596	94th	1976	195
S. 3608	94th	1976	188
S. 3609	85th	1958	039
S. 3612	93rd	1974	053
S. 3614	91st	1970	144
S. 3616	84th	1956	053
S. 3619	91st	1970	144
S. 3622	94th	1976	204
S. 3633	93rd	1974	173
S. 3650	76th	1940	042
S. 3650	76th	1940	043
S. 3650	76th	1940	044
S. 3650	76th	1940	144
S. 3677	86th	1960	054
S. 3679	93rd	1974	156
S. 3690	83rd	1954	082
S. 3690	83rd	1954	144

Bill No.	Congress	Year	Record Number
S. 3708	89th	1966	115
S. 3708	89th	1966	144
S. 3711	89th	1966	115
S. 3715	92nd	1972	068
S. 3725	85th	1958	144
S. 3738	83rd	1954	034
S. 3744	84th	1956	084
S. 3745	84th	1956	075
S. 3745	91st	1970	144
S. 3758	86th	1960	089
S. 3769	90th	1968	108
S. 3769	90th	1968	144
S. 3770	94th	1976	220
S. 3777	89th	1966	053
S. 3815	86th	1960	054
S. 3823	74th	1936	084
S. 3823	89th	1966	073
S. 3827	92nd	1972	136
S. 3830	89th	1966	144
S. 3835	91st	1970	144
S. 3842	81st	1950	144
S. 3842	91st	1970	128
S. 3847	72nd	1932	042
S. 3852	81st	1950	054
S. 3855	84th	1956	144

Bill No.	Congress	Year	Record Number
S. 3880	85th	1958	085
S. 3880	85th	1958	144
S. 3880	85th	1958	231
S. 3881	92nd	1972	189
S. 3881	92nd	1972	190
S. 3889	81st	1950	040
S. 3912	85th	1958	144
S. 3920	76th	1940	053
S. 3922	93rd	1974	141
S. 3925	76th	1940	053
S. 3934	93rd	1974	156
S. 3936	81st	1950	068
S. 3936	91st	1970	174
S. 3940	92nd	1972	126
S. 3952	93rd	1974	219
S. 3957	93rd	1974	191
S. 3958	84th	1956	029
S. 3959	81st	1950	144
S. 3964	91st	1970	148
S. 3966	92nd	1972	138
S. 3969	75th	1938	026
S. 3970	60th	1908	075
S. 3972	60th	1908	075
S. 3974	86th	1959	088
S. 3983	65th	1918	028

Bill No.	Congress	Year	Record Number
S. 3985	72nd	1932	009
S. 3985	72nd	1932	010
S. 3985	72nd	1932	012
S. 3985	72nd	1932	014
S. 3985	72nd	1932	019
S. 3985	72nd	1932	020
S. 3985	72nd	1932	024
S. 3985	72nd	1932	025
S. 3985	72nd	1932	026
S. 4012	91st	1970	107
S. 4012	91st	1970	144
S. 4062	92nd	1972	138
S. 4100	67th	1922	031
S. 4101	67th	1922	025
S. 4110	74th	1936	051
S. 4141	91st	1970	144
S. 4164	76th	1940	056
S. 4164	85th	1958	144
S. 4165	85th	1958	144
S. 4166	85th	1958	144
S. 4193	85th	1958	054
S. 4203	84th	1956	144
S. 4220	57th	1902	075
S. 4220	84th	1956	054
S. 4231	84th	1956	054

Bill No.	Congress	Year	Record Number
S. 4237	85th	1958	029
S. 4256	55th	1898	084
S. 4332	74th	1936	051
S. 4355	68th	1925	008
S. 4355	68th	1925	010
S. 4355	68th	1925	014
S. 4355	68th	1925	020
S. 4355	68th	1925	021
S. 4358	91st	1970	130
S. 4358	91st	1970	144
S. 4360	69th	1926	076
S. 4368	91st	1970	144
S. 4404	91st	1970	129
S. 4418	91st	1970	144
S. 4444	65th	1918	040
S. 4557	65th	1918	040
S. 4569	72nd	1932	040
S. 4572	91st	1970	144
S. 4656	58th	1904	084
S. 4812	69th	1926-1927	034
S. 4812	69th	1926-1927	075
S. 4956	69th	1926	034
S. 4982	61st	1910	084
S. 5066	65th	1919	039
S. 5139	71st	1930-1931	029

Bill No.	Congress	Year	Record Number
S. 5265	65th	1919	071
S. 5452	70th	1929	031
S. 5635	61st	1910	075
S. 5636	61st	1910	075
S. 5687	71st	1931	019
S. 5687	71st	1931	025
S. 5714	61st	1910	005
S. 5776	71st	1931	041
S. 5904	71st	1931	042
S. 5904	71st	1931	043
S. 5904	71st	1931	044
S. 5904	71st	1931	144
S. 6131	61st	1910	144
S. 6155	60th	1908-1909	001
S. 6273	62nd	1912	071
S. 6273	62nd	1912	075
S. 6330	59th	1906	006
S. 6330	59th	1906	008
S. 6330	59th	1906	010
S. 6330	59th	1906	014
S. 6330	59th	1906	015
S. 6330	59th	1906	017
S. 6330	59th	1906	020
S. 6330	59th	1906	021
S. 6330	59th	1906	024

Bill No.	Congress	Year	Record Number
S. 6330	59th	1906	026
S. 6330	59th	1906	028
S. 7031	61st	1910-1911	144
S. 7795	64th	1917	028
S. 8190	59th	1907	006
S. 8190	59th	1907	008
S. 8190	59th	1907	010
S. 8190	59th	1907	015
S. 8190	59th	1907	021
S. 8190	59th	1907	026
S. 9439	61st	1910	005
S. 9440	60th	1909	006
S. 9440	60th	1909	010
S. 9440	60th	1909	021
S. 9440	60th	1909	024
S. 9440	60th	1909	026
S. Con. Res. 11	90th	1968	076
S. Con. Res. 51	82nd	1951	053
S. Con. Res. 80	95th	1977-1978	236
S. Con. Res. 104	95th	1977-1978	236
S. Res. 4	94th	1975	032
S. Res. 5	65th	1917	032
S. Res. 5	86th	1959	032
S. Res. 7	74th	1935	052
S. Res. 15	81st	1949	032

Bill No.	Congress	Year	Record Number
S. Res. 25	80th	1947	032
S. Res. 30	85th	1957	032
S. Res. 42	87th	1961	054
S. Res. 52	87th	1961	054
S. Res. 92	84th	1955	075
S. Res. 135	93rd	1973	156
S. Res. 194	75th	1937	054
S. Res. 195	64th	1916-1917	032
S. Res. 202	81st	1950	003
S. Res. 239	94th	1975	178
S. Res. 268	94th	1975-1976	032
S. Res. 400	94th	1976	206
S. Res. 524	95th	1977-1978	236
S.J. Res. 18	92nd	1971	148
S.J. Res. 40	89th	1965	076
S.J. Res. 41	86th	1959-1960	144
S.J. Res. 42	90th	1967	144
S.J. Res. 59	92nd	1971	148
S.J. Res. 85	84th	1955	068
S.J. Res. 87	90th	1967	076
S.J. Res. 94	94th	1975	068
S.J. Res. 102	88th	1963	037
S.J. Res. 109	71st	1929-1930	031
S.J. Res. 122	79th	1945	040
S.J. Res. 135	85th	1958	073

Statutes at Large/ Record Number Table

Statutes at Large		Record Number	Statutes at Large		Record Number
12 Stat. 392	(1862)	001	40 Stat. 411 (1917)		030
17 Stat. 424	(1873)	002	40 Stat. 411 (1917)		031
19 Stat. 90	(1876)	003	N/A		032
19 Stat. 3777	(1877)	004	41 Stat. 437 (1920)		033
30 Stat. 922	(1899)	005	42 Stat. 389 (1922)		034
35 Stat. 1075	(1909)	006	44 Stat. 568	(1926)	035
35 Stat. 1075	(1909)	007	44 Stat. 577	(1926)	036
35 Stat. 1075	(1909)	008	44 Stat. 577	(1926)	037
35 Stat. 1075	(1909)	009	44 Stat. 1162	(1927)	038
35 Stat. 1075	(1909)	010	45 Stat. 467	(1928)	039
35 Stat. 1075	(1909)	011	46 Stat. 1016	(1930)	040
35 Stat. 1075	(1909)	012	46 Stat. 1084	(1931)	041
35 Stat. 1075	(1909)	013	46 Stat. 1494	(1931)	042
35 Stat. 1075	(1909)	014	46 Stat. 1494	(1931)	043
35 Stat. 1075	(1909)	015	46 Stat. 1494	(1931)	044
35 Stat. 1075	(1909)	016	47 Stat. 326	(1932)	045
35 Stat. 1075	(1909)	017	48 Stat. 162	(1933)	046
35 Stat. 1075	(1909)	018	49 Stat. 449	(1935)	047
35 Stat. 1075	(1909)	019	49 Stat. 449	(1935)	048
35 Stat. 1075	(1909)	020	49 Stat. 449	(1935)	049
35 Stat. 1075	(1909)	021	49 Stat. 977	(1935)	050
35 Stat. 1075	(1909)	022	49 Stat. 1985	(1936)	051
35 Stat. 1075	(1909)	023	50 Stat. 189	(1937)	052
35 Stat. 1075	(1909)	024	50 Stat. 307	(1937)	053
35 Stat. 1075	(1909)	025	52 Stat. 1040	(1938)	054
35 Stat. 1075	(1909)	026	53 Stat. 1147	(1939)	055
35 Stat. 1075	(1909)	027	54 Stat. 885	(1940)	056
35 Stat. 1075	(1909)	028	56 Stat. 278	(1942)	058
39 Stat. 929	(1917)	029	57 Stat. 126	(1943)	058

Statutes at Large		Record Number	Statutes at Large		Record Number
57 Stat. 564	(1943)	059	80 Stat. 38	(1966)	109
58 Stat. 231	(1944)	060	80 Stat. 221	(1966)	110
58 Stat. 887	(1944)	061	80 Stat. 250	(1966)	111
60 Stat. 170	(1946)	062	80 Stat. 718	(1966)	112
60 Stat. 237	(1946)	063	80 Stat. 830	(1966)	113
61 Stat. 136	(1947)	064	80 Stat. 1125	(1966)	114
61 Stat. 136	(1947)	065	80 Stat. 1255	(1966)	115
63 Stat. 208	(1949)	066	80 Stat. 1508	(1966)	116
63 Stat. 714	(1949)	067	80 Stat. 1539	(1966)	117
64 Stat. 798	(1950)	068	81 Stat. 4	(1967)	118
64 Stat. 1085	(1950)	069	81 Stat. 54	(1967)	119
N/A		070	81 Stat. 57	(1967)	120
N/A		071	81 Stat. 145	(1967)	121
65 Stat. 648	(1951)	072	81 Stat. 602	(1967)	122
66 Stat. 328	(1952)	073	82 Stat. 197	(1968)	123
66 Stat. 792	(1952)	074	82 Stat. 1173	(1968)	124
66 Stat. 792	(1952)	075	83 Stat. 96	(1969)	125
67 Stat. 588	(1953)	076	83 Stat. 742	(1969)	126
68 Stat. 454	(1954)	077	83 Stat. 852	(1970)	127
68 Stat. 666	(1954)	078	84 Stat. 719	(1970)	128
68A Stat. 3	(1954)	079	84 Stat. 1590	(1970)	129
68A Stat. 3	(1954)	080	84 Stat. 1676	(1970)	130
68 Stat. 919	(1954)	081	84 Stat. 1880	(1971)	131
68 Stat. 919	(1954)	082	86 Stat. 65	(1972)	132
69 Stat. 695	(1955)	083	86 Stat. 103	(1972)	133
N/A		084	86 Stat. 103	(1972)	134
72 Stat. 731	(1958)	085	86 Stat. 770	(1972)	135
72 Stat. 997	(1958)	086	86 Stat. 789	(1972)	136
73 Stat. 519	(1959)	087	86 Stat. 816	(1972)	137
73 Stat. 519	(1959)	088	86 Stat. 999	(1972)	138
75 Stat. 65	(1961)	089	86 Stat. 1234	1972)	139
75 Stat. 762	(1961)	090	86 Stat. 1251	(1972)	140
76 Stat. 872	(1962)	091	86 Stat. 1280	(1972)	141
76 Stat. 960	(1962)	092	86 Stat. 1329	(1972)	142
77 Stat. 56	(1963)	093	86 Stat. 1329	(1972	143
78 Stat. 19	(1964)	094	84 Stat. 2086	(1970)	144
78 Stat. 238	(1964)	095	87 Stat. 197	(1973)	145
78 Stat. 241	(1964)	096	87 Stat. 314	(1973)	146
78 Stat. 241	(1964)	097	87 Stat. 355	(1973)	147
78 Stat. 241	(1964)	098	87 Stat. 555	(1973)	148
78 Stat. 329	(1964)	099	87 Stat. 737	(1973)	150
78 Stat. 809	(1964)	100	87 Stat. 774	(1973)	151
79 Stat. 5	(1965)	101	87 Stat. 774	(1973)	152
79 Stat. 136	(1965)	102	87 Stat. 884	(1973)	153
79 Stat. 172	(1965)	103	88 Stat. 55	(1974)	154
79 Stat. 218	(1965)	104	88 Stat. 246	(1974)	155
79 Stat. 437	(1965)	105	88 Stat. 297	(1974)	156
79 Stat. 954	(1965)	106	88 Stat. 297	(1974)	157
79 Stat. 992	(1965)	107	88 Stat. 297	(1974)	158
79 Stat. 1219	(1965)	108	88 Stat. 297	(1974)	159

Statutes at Large		Record Number	Statutes at Large		Record Number
88 Stat. 297	(1974)	160	91 Stat. 1048	(1977)	210
88 Stat. 395	(1974)	161	91 Stat. 1062	(1977)	211
88 Stat. 476	(1974)	162	91 Stat. 1063	(1977)	212
88 Stat. 633	(1974)	163	91 Stat. 1111	(1977)	213
88 Stat. 829	(1974)	164	91 Stat. 1175	(1977)	214
88 Stat. 1069	(1974)	165	91 Stat. 1245	(1977)	215
88 Stat. 1079	(1974)	166	91 Stat. 1290	(1977)	216
88 Stat. 1109	(1974)	167	91 Stat. 1509	(1977)	217
88 Stat. 1263	(1974)	168	91 Stat. 1566	(1977)	218
88 Stat. 1431	(1974)	169	92 Stat. 95	(1978)	219
88 Stat. 1561	(1974)	170	92 Stat. 120	(1978)	220
88 Stat. 1660	(1974)	171	92 Stat. 163	(1978)	221
88 Stat. 1878	(1974)	172	92 Stat. 601	(1978)	222
88 Stat. 1896	(1974)	173	92 Stat. 808	(1978)	223
88 Stat. 2076	(1975)	174	92 Stat. 819	(1978)	224
89 Stat. 26	(1975)	175	92 Stat. 865	(1978)	225
89 Stat. 97	(1975)	176	92 Stat. 865	(1978)	226
89 Stat. 395	(1975)	177	92 Stat. 1111	(1978)	227
89 Stat. 419	(1975)	178	92 Stat. 1497	(1978)	228
89 Stat. 669	(1975)	179	92 Stat. 1560	(1978)	229
89 Stat. 713	(1975)	180	92 Stat. 1649	(1978)	230
89 Stat. 871	(1975)	181	92 Stat. 1075	(1978)	231
89 Stat. 977	(1975)	182	92 Stat. 1757	(1978)	232
89 Stat. 1007	(1975)	183	92 Stat. 1820	(1978)	233
90 Stat. 331	(1975)	184	92 Stat. 1824	(1978)	234
90 Stat. 459	(1976)	185	92 Stat. 2076	(1978)	235
90 Stat. 475	(1976)	186	92 Stat. 2402	(1978)	236
90 Stat. 720	(1976)	187	92 Stat. 2497	(1978)	237
90 Stat. 1205	(1976)	188	92 Stat. 2523	(1978)	238
90 Stat. 1241	(1976)	189	92 Stat. 3467	(1978)	239
90 Stat. 1241	(1976)	190	93 Stat. 47	(1979)	240
90 Stat. 1255	(1976)	191	93 Stat. 668	(1979)	241
90 Stat. 1260	(1976)	192	93 Stat. 1101	(1979)	242
90 Stat. 1303	(1976)	193	93 Stat. 1167	(1979)	243
90 Stat. 1369	(1976)	194	94 Stat. 84	(1980)	244
90 Stat. 1374	(1976)	195	94 Stat. 102	(1980)	245
90 Stat. 2003	(1976)	196	94 Stat. 441	(1980)	246
90 Stat. 2341	(1976)	197	94 Stat. 611	(1980)	247
90 Stat. 2383	(1976)	198	94 Stat. 1139	(1980)	248
90 Stat. 2451	(1976)	199	94 Stat. 2767	(1980)	249
90 Stat. 2541	(1976)	200	94 Stat. 3381	(1980)	250
90 Stat. 2641	(1976)	201	95 Stat. 935	(1981)	251
90 Stat. 2743	(1976)	202	98 Stat. 1837	(1984)	252
90 Stat. 2743	(1976)	203	100 Stat. 1613	(1986)	253
90 Stat. 2795	(1976)	204	101 Stat. 7	(1987)	254
90 Stat. 2842	(1976)	205	102 Stat. 890	(1988)	255
N/A		206	104 Stat. 327	(1990)	256
91 Stat. 126	(1977)	207	104 Stat. 978	(1990)	257
91 Stat. 685	(1977)	208			
91 Stat. 685	(1977)	209			

About the Author

BERNARD D. REAMS, JR., J.D., Ph.D., is a professor of law, a professor of technology management, and the director of the law library at Washington University School of Law in St. Louis, Missouri. Dr. Reams is a member of the Kansas, Missouri, and federal bars. He is also the author of numerous books, including *University-Industry Research Partnerships, The Health Care Quality Improvement Act of 1986: A Legislative History of Pub. L. No. 99-660,* and *Disability Law in the United States: A Legislative History of the Americans with Disabilities Act of 1990, Public Law 101-336.*

ISBN 0-313-23092-7

90000>

EAN

9 780313 230929

HARDCOVER BAR CODE